Windows Server 2003 Networking Recipes

Robbie Allen, Laura E. Hunter, and Bradley J. Dinerman

Windows Server 2003 Networking Recipes

Copyright © 2006 by Robbie Allen, Laura E. Hunter, and Bradley J. Dinerman

ISBN-13 (pbk): 978-1-59059-713-2

ISBN-10 (pbk): 1-59059-713-3

Printed and bound in the United States of America 9 8 7 6 5 4 3 2 1

Lead Editors: Jim Sumser, Jonathan Gennick
Technical Reviewers: Ed Crowley, Jonathan Hassell, William Lefkovics
Editorial Board: Steve Anglin, Ewan Buckingham, Gary Cornell, Jason Gilmore, Jonathan Gennick,
    Jonathan Hassell, James Huddleston, Chris Mills, Matthew Moodie, Dominic Shakeshaft, Jim Sumser,
    Keir Thomas, Matt Wade
Project Manager: Richard Dal Porto
Copy Edit Manager: Nicole LeClerc
Copy Editor: Andy Carroll
Assistant Production Director: Kari Brooks-Copony
Production Editor: Ellie Fountain
Compositor: Susan Glinert
Proofreader: Elizabeth Berry
Indexer: Julie Grady
Cover Designer: Kurt Krames
Manufacturing Director: Tom Debolski

Distributed to the book trade worldwide by Springer-Verlag New York, Inc., 233 Spring Street, 6th Floor, New York, NY 10013. Phone 1-800-SPRINGER, fax 201-348-4505, e-mail orders-ny@springer-sbm.com, or visit http://www.springeronline.com.

For information on translations, please contact Apress directly at 2560 Ninth Street, Suite 219, Berkeley, CA 94710. Phone 510-549-5930, fax 510-549-5939, e-mail info@apress.com, or visit http://www.apress.com.

The source code for this book is available to readers at http://www.apress.com in the Source Code section.

Contents at a Glance

Contents

■CHAPTER 7   Internet Protocol Security (IPSec) 285

■CHAPTER 8   Network Printing 325

About the Authors

ROBBIE ALLEN is a technical leader at Cisco Systems, where he's worked since 1997. He has been a Microsoft MVP for Windows Server (Directory Services) since 2004. Robbie has authored or coauthored ten books on Windows Server and Desktop technologies.

LAURA HUNTER is currently a senior information technology specialist at the University of Pennsylvania. She is the author of *Active Directory Field Guide* (Apress 2005, ISBN 1-59059-492-4) and has coauthored or technically reviewed ten books on Microsoft technologies. She has also written numerous articles for TechTarget.com and *Microsoft Certified Professional Magazine*. For a complete list of her work experience and publications, see http://www.laurahcomputing.com.

BRAD DINERMAN is a Microsoft MVP in Windows Server Systems (Networking), one of only fifty worldwide to possess the award in this category. He also possesses an MCSE and MCP+I in Windows NT 4 and 2000, and is a Certified SonicWALL Security Administrator. He earned a Ph.D. in physics from Boston College.

Brad is a frequent contributor to various online tech tips sites and gives user group/conference presentations on topics ranging from spam and security solutions to Internet development techniques. He also published numerous articles in international physics journals in his earlier, scientific career.

Brad is the founder and president of the New England Information Security Group, the former chair of the Boston Area Exchange Server User Group, and a member of the FBI's InfraGard Boston Members Alliance.

Acknowledgments

The authors would like to collectively thank all the individuals and organizations that helped to pull this book together. These include the following:

The Microsoft MVP Program: The three authors are all Microsoft Most Valuable Professionals (MVPs) and met through this program. Microsoft defines MVPs as "recognized, credible, and accessible individuals with expertise in one or more Microsoft products who actively participate in online and offline communities to share their knowledge and expertise with other Microsoft customers" (http://mvp.support.microsoft.com/mvpexecsum). The authors would like to acknowledge the large number of other MVPs and Microsoft MVP Technical Leads that helped them to research the material for this book, whether explicitly for that purpose or just through day-to-day interactions.

Technical Reviewers: We would like to thank Ed Crowley, Jonathan Hassell, and William Lefkovics for the time that they spent reviewing and critiquing our work so that we could produce this fantastic content.

On a more personal note, we would each like to express our acknowledgment and thanks.

I don't think that any of the material that I wrote for this book would have been possible without the unending support of my wife, Davida. Through countless hours of research and typing, she was always there with words of encouragement for me to continue. I love her and thank her from the bottom of my heart. And, of course,
I can't forget to thank the other two cuties in my life, Abby and Ari, who always give the unsolicited hug.

Bradley Dinerman

I would like to thank my wonderful family for standing by me and believing in everything I set out to achieve, as well as some of the numerous members of my Microsoft and MVP extended family who have supported me throughout this and all of my endeavors: Suzanna Moran, Emily Freet, Sean O'Driscoll, Mark Arnold, and Dean Wells for his considerable assistance with the early stages of my involvement in this project.

Laura Hunter

I'd like to thank the most important person in my life, my wife, Janet.
I look forward to the next chapter of our life together.

Robbie Allen

Introduction

This book contains more than 200 recipes that address many of the "How do I . . .?" questions that you could pose about Windows networking. It is a straightforward reference for a variety of tasks, ranging from handling everyday chores to solving more specialized problems. *Windows Server 2003 Networking Recipes* will be a great addition to your technical library.

Who Should Read This Book

Windows Server 2003 Networking Recipes can be useful to anyone who needs to deploy, administer, or automate Windows Server 2003 or even Windows 2000 networks. This book can serve as a great reference for those who work with Windows servers on a day-to-day basis. And because of all the scripting samples, this book can be extremely beneficial to programmers who want to accomplish various tasks in an application. For those without much programming background, the VBScript solutions are straightforward, and they should be easy to follow and use as a basis for more involved scripts.

What's in This Book

This book consists of nine chapters. Here is a brief overview of each chapter:

Chapter 1, "Basic TCP/IP Configuration," covers the most widely used networking protocols in modern operating systems. This chapter provides recipes to configure and manage the protocols, including Domain Name Service (DNS), Windows Internet Name Service (WINS), and gateway settings. It also covers basic management of the Windows firewall and network interfaces.

Chapter 2, "Windows Internet Name Service (WINS)," covers managing WINS, a service that is still alive and well in Windows Server 2003. The recipes include management of the WINS database, backup and restore techniques, and push and pull replication strategies.

Chapter 3, "Windows Firewall," covers enabling and managing the Windows Firewall. It describes techniques to create and manage service and port exceptions, including deployment through Group Policy as well as logging and auditing for security review.

Chapter 4, "Routing and Remote Access Service (Remote Access)," provides recipes to configure a remote access server, both with and without virtual private network (VPN) support. It also covers techniques to manage auditing and logging levels, authentication providers, remote access policies, and site-to-site VPNs.

Chapter 5, "Routing and Remote Access Service (Routing)," provides recipes to configure your Windows Server 2003 as a full-featured network router, including management of your IP routing table, packet filters, network address translation (NAT) interfaces, Dynamic Host Configuration Protocol (DHCP) relay agents, and DNS proxies.

Chapter 6, "Internet Authentication Service (IAS)," provides recipes to register and configure an IAS server on your network, configure Remote Authentication Dial-In User Service (RADIUS) server groups and clients, manage lockout policies, and handle authentication and accounting.

Chapter 7, "Internet Protocol Security (IPSec)," provides recipes to create and manage IPSec policies and filters, including security and authentication methods.

Chapter 8, "Network Printing," provides recipes to create and manage your network printers, including how to share and publish them, remotely manage printer drivers, and deploy printers to workstations through Group Policy.

Chapter 9, "Network Troubleshooting," covers troubleshooting problems that may occur (on very rare occasions, of course) on your network. The recipes include techniques to troubleshoot the TCP/IP stack, repair network connections, correct name resolution issues, verify services, troubleshoot remote administration, and restore proper Active Directory replication.

This book covers hundreds of tasks you'll need to do at one point or another with Windows Server 2003 or its clients. If you feel something important has been omitted, let us know; we'll work to get it in a future edition.

Conventions in This Book

The following typographical conventions are used in this book:

`Monospace font`: Indicates command-line elements, computer output, code examples, paths, and URIs.

`Monospace font italic`: Indicates placeholders (for which you substitute actual values in examples and in Registry keys).

Bold: Indicates user input.

■**Note** Indicates a tip, suggestion, or general note. For example, we'll tell you if you need to use a particular version or if an operation requires certain privileges.

■**Caution** Indicates a warning or caution. For example, we'll tell you if Active Directory does not behave as you would expect or if a particular operation has a negative impact on performance.

Approach to the Book

This book is composed of nine chapters, each containing from ten to thirty recipes that describe how to perform a particular task. Within each recipe are four sections:

Problem: The Problem section briefly describes the task the recipe addresses and when you might need to use it.

Solution: The Solution section contains step-by-step instructions on how to accomplish the task. Depending on the task, up to five different sets of solutions might be covered.

How It Works: The How It Works section goes into detail about the solution(s).

See Also: The See Also section contains references to additional sources of information that can be useful if you still need more information after reading the discussion. The See Also section may reference other recipes, Microsoft Knowledge Base (http://support. microsoft.com) articles, documentation from the Microsoft Developers Network (http:// msdn.microsoft.com), Microsoft TechNet material (http://technet.microsoft.com), and other sources.

Solution Alternatives

People like to work in different ways. Some prefer a graphical user interface (GUI); others like to work from the command-line interface (CLI). Many experienced network administrators like to automate tasks using scripts. Since people prefer different methods, and no one method is necessarily better than another, we decided to write solutions to recipes using as many techniques as we know to be available. That means instead of just a single solution per recipe, we include up to five solutions using the GUI, the CLI, the Registry, Group Policy, and scripting examples. However, some recipes cannot be accomplished with all of those methods, so they will have fewer alternatives.

In the GUI and CLI solutions, we use standard tools that are readily accessible. There are other freeware, shareware, or commercial tools that we could have used that would have made some of the tasks easier to accomplish, but we wanted to make this book as useful as possible without requiring you to hunt down the tools or purchase an expensive software package.

We took a similar approach with the scripting solutions. We use VBScript due to its widespread use among Windows administrators. It is also the most straightforward from a coding perspective when using Windows Management Instrumentation (WMI) and Windows Scripting Host (WSH). For those familiar with other languages—such as Visual Basic, Perl, and JScript—it is very easy to convert code from VBScript.

Windows 2000 vs. Windows Server 2003

Another challenge with writing this book was determining which operating system version to cover. Many organizations still run Windows 2000, but Windows Server 2003 has been a big seller (at least according to Microsoft). Since Windows Server 2003 is the latest and greatest version and includes a lot of new tools that aren't present in Windows 2000, our approach is to make everything work under Windows Server 2003. If we know of a compatibility issue with Windows 2000, we'll mention it.

In practice, the majority of the solutions will work with Windows 2000. Most GUI and scripting solutions work with either version. Microsoft introduced several new command-line tools with Windows Server 2003, so many of these tools cannot run on Windows 2000. Typically, you can still use these newer tools on a Windows XP or Windows Server 2003 computer to manage Windows 2000.

Where to Find the Tools

For the GUI and CLI solutions to mean much to you, you need access to the tools that are used in the examples. For this reason, in the majority of cases and unless otherwise noted, the recipes use tools that are part of the default operating system or available in the Resource Kit or Support Tools.

The Windows 2000 Server Resource Kit and Windows Server 2003 Resource Kit are invaluable sources of information, and they provide numerous tools that aid administrators in their daily tasks. You can find more information about the Resource Kits at http://www.microsoft.com/windows/reskits/. Some of the Resource Kit tools are freely available; others are available only if you buy the Resource Kit.

The Windows 2000 Support Tools, which are called the Windows Support Tools in Windows Server 2003, contain many "must-have" tools for people that work with Windows Server. The installation MSI for the Windows Support Tools can be found on a Windows 2000 Server or Windows Server 2003 CD, in the \support\tools directory.

In some cases, we use non-Microsoft utilities from the Sysinternals website (http://www.sysinternals.com/). Mark Russinovich and Bryce Cogswell have developed a suite of extremely useful tools that every Windows Server network administrator should have. These tools are free, and they often come with complete source code for the tool.

Where to Find More Information

While this book provides you with enough information to perform the majority of Windows network administration tasks you are likely to do, it is not realistic to think every possible task can be covered. You can find a wealth of additional resources and information on the Internet or in a bookstore. In this section, we cover some of the resources we use most frequently.

Help and Support Center

Windows Server 2003 comes with a new feature called the Help and Support Center, which is available directly from the Start menu. It is a great resource of information, and it serves as the central location to obtain help information about the operating system, applications, and installed utilities.

Command-Line Tools

If you have any questions about the complete syntax or usage of a command-line tool we use in the book, you should first take a look at the help information available with the tool. The vast majority of CLI tools provide syntax information by simply passing /? as a parameter. For example, to get information about the netsh utility, enter the following:

```
> netsh /?
```

Microsoft Knowledge Base

The Microsoft Help and Support website is a great source of information and is home to the Microsoft Knowledge Base (KB) articles. Throughout this book, we include references to pertinent Microsoft KB articles. You can find the complete text for a KB article by searching on the KB number at `http://support.microsoft.com/default.aspx`. You can also append the KB article number to the end of this URL to go directly to the article: `http://support.microsoft.com/?kbid=article_number`.

Microsoft Developers Network

Microsoft Developers Network (MSDN) contains a ton of information on Windows Server and programmatic interfaces such as WMI. Throughout this book, we'll reference MSDN pages where applicable. Unfortunately, there is no easy way to reference the exact page we are referring to unless we provided the URL or navigation to the page, which would more than likely change by the time the book was printed. Instead, we provide the title of the page, which you can use to search via `http://msdn.microsoft.com/library/`.

Websites

The following websites are great starting points for information that helps you perform the tasks covered in this book:

Microsoft Windows Server 2003 Home Page (`http://www.microsoft.com/windowsserver2003/default.mspx`): This site is the starting point for Windows Server information provided by Microsoft. It contains links to whitepapers, case studies, and tools.

Microsoft Support WebCasts (`http://support.microsoft.com/default.aspx?scid=fh;EN-US;pwebcst`): Webcasts are on-demand audio/video technical presentations that cover a wide range of Microsoft products. There are numerous webcasts related to Windows Server technologies that cover topics such as disaster recovery, upgrading to Windows Server 2003, and deploying Terminal Services.

Google (`http://www.google.com`): Google is our primary starting point for locating information. Google is often quicker and easier to use to search the Microsoft websites (such as MSDN) than the search engines provided on those sites.

myITforum (`http://www.myitforum.com`): The myITforum site has very active online forums for various Microsoft technologies. It also has a large repository of scripts.

LabMice (`http://www.labmice.net`): The LabMice website contains a large collection of links to information on Windows Server, including Microsoft KB articles, whitepapers, and other useful websites.

Robbie Allen's Home Page (`http://www.rallenhome.com`): This is Robbie's personal website, which has information about the books he has written and links to download the code contained in each (including this book).

Microsoft TechNet Script Center (`http://www.microsoft.com/technet/community/scriptcenter/default.mspx`): This site contains a large collection of WSH, WMI, and Active Directory Service Interfaces (ADSI) scripts.

■ ■ ■

CHAPTER 1

Basic TCP/IP Configuration

Before you can enable Windows Server 2003 services such as DHCP, DNS, or Active Directory, or even communicate on most modern computer networks *at all*, you first need to configure the TCP/IP stack. Each TCP/IP-enabled device on your network requires at minimum an IP address and a subnet mask to communicate with other computers on the same local network. To communicate across multiple networks or subnets, each device also requires a default gateway to route traffic to remote destinations. A Windows Server 2003 computer can have its IP address information assigned statically, or it can receive an IP address automatically from a Dynamic Host Configuration Protocol (DHCP) server.

In addition to this mandatory information, you can also configure Windows Server 2003 computers with the IP addresses of Windows Internet Name Service (WINS) and/or Domain Name Service (DNS) servers to provide name resolution services. These services allow you to locate another computer on the network using a friendly name like COMPUTER1 or www.mycompany.com rather than needing to remember unwieldy (for human beings, at least) numeric IP addresses. Windows Server 2003 is capable of using both DNS and NetBIOS name resolution to locate another host, and you can customize the behavior of each of these to improve the performance and security of a Windows Server 2003 server.

Using a Graphical User Interface

You'll configure basic TCP/IP information in the graphical user interface (GUI) using the Network Connections Control Panel applet in the properties of the individual network interface—this applet is built into all editions of Windows Server 2003. You can configure most basic TCP/IP information from this applet, including whether an IP address is statically or dynamically assigned, WINS and DNS information, and what alternate IP configuration a machine should use if it cannot locate a DHCP server.

Using a Command-Line Interface

One of the advantages of Windows Server 2003 is that you can perform a great deal of TCP/IP configuration from the command line using the netsh utility. This utility is a veritable goldmine, allowing you to configure settings relating to basic IP configuration, the Windows Firewall, routing and remote access, and more. We'll return to netsh again and again throughout this cookbook, as well as ipconfig, which provides additional configuration options and informational output.

Using the Registry

The majority of the Registry settings that control TCP/IP configuration are found in the following subkey:

```
[HKEY_LOCAL_MACHINE\SYSTEM\Current Control Set\Services\Tcpip\Parameters\]
```

When configuring a setting that is specific to a particular network interface card (NIC) installed in a server, you'll use the subkey that corresponds to the globally unique identifier (GUID) of the interface. It might look something like this:

```
HKEY_LOCAL_MACHINE\SYSTEM\Current Control Set\
Services\Tcpip\Parameters\Interfaces\
{01B3816C-AB47-3E53-CB7C-88345293465}
```

To find the GUID that corresponds to a particular IP address in your computer, use the WMI command-line tool (wmic) with the following syntax:

```
> wmic nicconfig get ipaddress,settingid
```

Using VBScript

Basic TCP/IP information is exposed through WMI through the Win32_NetworkAdapterConfiguration WMI class. This class exposes a number of variables and methods that you can use to configure TCP/IP on a local or remote computer. These are some of the methods that you'll see used in the recipes in this chapter:

- EnableDHCP()
- EnableWINS()
- SetDNSDomain()
- SetDNSServerSearchOrder()
- SetDNSServerSuffixOrder()

1-1. Configuring the Computer Host Name

Problem

You want to change the name of your Windows Server 2003 computer.

Solution

Using a Graphical User Interface

1. Right-click on My Computer and select Properties.

2. From the Computer Name tab, select Change.

3. Enter the new computer name in the Computer Name text box.

4. Click OK twice, and reboot when prompted to do so.

Using a Command-Line Interface

The following command renames the local computer to the name Computer2 (change this as appropriate for your environment):

```
> wmic COMPUTERSYSTEM SET Name = Computer2
```

Note You need to reboot the local computer for the new name to take effect.

Using the Registry

To configure an individual computer name, set the following Registry values and reboot the server:

```
[HKEY_LOCAL_MACHINE\SYSTEM\Current Control Set\Control\Computername\]
"ComputerName"=REG_SZ:"<ComputerName>"
[HKEY_LOCAL_MACHINE\SYSTEM\Current Control Set\Services\Tcpip\Parameters\]
"HostName"=REG_SZ:"<ComputerName>"
[HKEY_LOCAL_MACHINE\SYSTEM\Current Control Set\Services\Tcpip\Parameters\]
"NV HostName"=REG_SZ:"<ComputerName>"
```

Using VBScript

This code renames the local computer to the name Computer2.

```
' ------ SCRIPT CONFIGURATION ------
  strComputer = "."
  strNewName = "Computer2" ' Change this to fit your environment
' ------ END CONFIGURATION ---------

Set objWMIService = GetObject("winmgmts:{impersonationLevel=impersonate}!\\" _
    & strComputer & "\root\cimv2")
Set colComputers = objWMIService.ExecQuery ("Select * from Win32_ComputerSystem")
For Each objComputer in colComputers
    errReturn = ObjComputer.Rename(strNewName)
    WScript.Echo "Computer successfully renamed"
Next
```

How It Works

The reasons for changing a computer's name are many and obvious—in most cases this will be because the computer's role is changing on the network or you're moving it to another physical location. It's usually helpful to develop a standardized naming scheme for the computers on your network to help you better organize and identify your systems, especially in a large enterprise network, though from a security standpoint it would probably be advisable to avoid naming your web servers using a scheme like "WEBSERVER1," "WEBSERVER2," and the like.

The instructions we've listed here are based on the assumption that the Windows Server 2003 computer is a member server, not a domain controller. Windows Server 2003 *does* permit you to rename a domain controller using the netdom utility, but the procedure is not quite as simple as renaming it from My Computer, and even that method should be used with caution if the domain controller is running other software applications such as Microsoft Exchange.

Of the methods we've included here, the most foolproof is making the change using the GUI, since a server's computer name is embedded into the Registry in numerous locations. Renaming a server using the GUI ensures that you haven't missed anything, since the operating system makes the necessary changes in the background.

See Also

- Rename method of the `Win32_ComputerSystem` class

- Microsoft TechNet: "Rename a Domain Controller" (`http://www.microsoft.com/technet/prodtechnol/windowsserver2003/library/ServerHelp/aad1169a-f0d2-47d5-b0ea-989081ce62be.mspx`)

- Microsoft KB 325354: "How to Use the Netdom.exe Utility to Rename a Computer in Windows Server 2003"

1-2. Configuring a Static IP Address

Problem

You want to configure a Windows Server 2003 computer with a statically assigned IP address.

Solution

Using a Graphical User Interface

1. Open the Network Connections applet.

2. Double-click on the Local Area Connection icon.

3. Click on Internet Protocol (TCP/IP), and select Properties.

4. Select the radio button next to Use the Following IP Address.

5. Fill in the appropriate configuration information in the IP Address, Subnet Mask, and Default Gateway text boxes.

6. Click Close when you're finished.

Using a Command-Line Interface

The following command configures a static IP, subnet mask, default gateway, and gateway metric for the local area connection (change "Local Area Connection" to fit the name of a particular connection):

```
> netsh interface ip set address "Local Area Connection"
static addr = <IP Address> mask = <Subnet Mask>
gateway = <Gateway IP> gwmetric = <Metric>
```

As an example, plugging actual numeric values into this syntax would produce something like this:

```
> netsh interface ip set address "Local Area Connection"
static addr = 10.0.0.100 mask = 255.0.0.0 gateway = 10.0.0.1 gwmetric = 1
```

Using the Registry

To configure a static IP address for the interface represented by <Interface GUID>, set the following Registry values:

```
[HKEY_LOCAL_MACHINE\SYSTEM\Current Control Set\
Services\Tcpip\Parameters\Interfaces\{<Interface GUID>}]
"IPAddress"=REG_MULTI_SZ:"<IP Address>"

[HKEY_LOCAL_MACHINE\SYSTEM\Current Control Set\Services\
Tcpip\Parameters\ Interfaces\{<Interface GUID>}]
"SubnetMask"=REG_MULTI_SZ:"<Subnet Mask>"

[HKEY_LOCAL_MACHINE\SYSTEM\Current Control Set\Services\
Tcpip\Parameters\ Interfaces\{<Interface GUID>}]
"DefaultGateway"=REG_MULTI_SZ:"<Default Gateway>"
```

Using VBScript

This code sets the local IP address to a static IP of 10.0.0.100 with a subnet mask of 255.0.0.0, a default gateway of 10.0.0.1, and a metric of 1. Change these values as needed to fit your environment.

```
' ------ SCRIPT CONFIGURATION ------
strComputer = "."
strIPAddress = Array("10.0.0.100")
strSubnetMask = Array("255.0.0.0")
strGateway = Array("10.0.0.1")
strGatewayMetric = Array(1)
' --------- END CONFIGURATION ------

Set objWMIService = GetObject("winmgmts:" _
    & "{impersonationLevel=impersonate}!\\" & strComputer & "\root\cimv2")
```

```
Set adapters = objWMIService.ExecQuery _
    ("Select * from Win32_NetworkAdapterConfiguration where IPEnabled=TRUE")

For Each a in adapters
    errIP = a.EnableStatic(strIPAddress, strSubnetMask)
    errGateways = a.SetGateways(strGateway, strGatewaymetric)
    If errIP = 0 Then
        WScript.Echo "Success! The IP address has been changed."
    Else
        WScript.Echo "Error! The IP address could not be changed."
    End If
Next
```

How It Works

While you can use the Dynamic Host Configuration Protocol (DHCP) to automatically assign IP address information to multiple computers, many administrators choose to use static IP configurations for the servers on their networks. Using a static IP ensures that the server will always maintain the same IP address even if a DHCP server cannot be contacted, so other computers will be able to locate it using one consistent address.

When using a statically assigned IP address, keep in mind that you need to manually configure all IP configuration options, particularly the subnet mask and default gateway, as well as the IP addresses of DNS and WINS servers on your network. If any of these addresses change, you'll need to manually update the configuration of any computer with a static IP address. (Refer to Recipe 1-9 for information on statically configuring DNS servers and Recipe 1-13 to configure WINS server information.)

■**Note** Because of this need to manually configure and update statically configured computers, the increasingly preferred approach is instead to configure DHCP *reservations* for those computers that require a consistent IP address.

If a computer is multi-homed, that is, it has more than one NIC installed that needs to be configured for TCP/IP, you can use any of these solutions to configure IP information for each adapter.

See Also

Recipe 1-3 for more on configuring the gateway metric

1-3. Configuring Dead-Gateway Detection

Problem

You want to configure dead-gateway detection on a Windows Server 2003 computer so that the computer can continue to route traffic even if its default gateway becomes unavailable.

Solution

Using the Registry

To enable dead-gateway detection for a Windows Server 2003 computer, set the following Registry value:

```
[HKEY_LOCAL_MACHINE\SYSTEM\Current Control Set\Services\Tcpip\Parameters\]
"EnableDeadGWDetect"=dword:1
```

To disable dead-gateway detection, set the previous DWORD value to 0 (false).

Using VBScript

This code enables dead-gateway detection for all configured network adapters.

```
' ------ SCRIPT CONFIGURATION ------
strComputer = "."
boolEnable  = TRUE   ' set to FALSE to disable
' ------ END CONFIGURATION ---------
Set objWMIService = GetObject("winmgmts:" _
    & "{impersonationLevel=impersonate}!\\" & strComputer & "\root\cimv2")

Set objSettings = objWMIService.Get("Win32_NetworkAdapterConfiguration")
objSettings.SetDeadGWDetect(boolEnable)

WScript.Echo "Dead-gateway detection set to " & boolEnable
```

How It Works

Dead-gateway detection is a feature of Windows Server 2003 that allows a local machine to detect the failure of its default gateway, and to route traffic to another configured gateway to ensure uninterrupted connectivity. This setting is useful for computers that have multiple network interface cards (NICs) attached to the same subnet, where more than one NIC could be configured as the default gateway for a particular connection. In this instance, default gateway detection allows you to create fault tolerance for traffic being routed from the local Windows Server 2003 computer.

When transmitting a TCP packet to a particular destination, TCP/IP in Windows Server 2003 will keep track of whether it receives a response or not; if it does not receive responses when using a particular gateway within a configurable amount of time (one half of the value of the TcpMaxDataRetransmissions DWORD value in the Tcpip\Parameters Registry section), it will then move to the next available gateway and begin to use that address to route outgoing traffic. In effect, this new IP address will become the Windows Server 2003 computer's default gateway until the computer is restarted or the new default gateway also fails.

■**Note** When Windows Server 2003 reaches the end of its list of available default gateways, it will return to the beginning of the list when transmitting subsequent packets in an attempt to locate a functioning default gateway.

See Also

- Recipe 4-7 for more on displaying and working with the Windows IP routing table

- Recipe 4-11 for more on working with static Windows routes

- Microsoft TechNet: The Cable Guy, September 2003, "Default Gateway Behavior for Windows TCP/IP" (http://www.microsoft.com/technet/community/columns/cableguy/cg0903.mspx#EDAA)

1-4. Configuring a Gateway Metric

Problem

You want to specify the gateway metric for the default gateway on a Windows Server 2003 computer.

Solution

Using a Graphical User Interface

1. Open the Network Connections applet.

2. Double-click on the Local Area Connection icon.

3. Click on Internet Protocol (TCP/IP), and select Properties and then Advanced.

4. In the Default Gateways section, highlight the gateway whose metric you want to modify, and click on Edit. Clear the check mark next to Automatic Metric, and enter a numerical value in the Interface Metric text box.

5. Click OK when you're finished.

Using a Command-Line Interface

The following command adds a default gateway of 10.0.0.1 with a metric of 1 to the network connection called Local Area Connection. You can modify the IP address of the gateway, its metric, and the name of the network connection to fit your environment as needed:

```
> netsh interface ip add address name = "Local Area Connection"
gateway = 10.0.0.1 gwmetric = 1
```

Continuing the example, to change the metric of a gateway that you've already configured, you need to first delete the gateway using the following command:

```
> netsh interface ip delete address name = "Local Area Connection" gateway = 10.0.0.1
```

After that, you can add the gateway again using the new metric.

Note If you've renamed the network connection from the default of `Local Area Connection`, you'll need to adjust the previous syntax accordingly.

Using the Registry

To configure the gateway metric, configure the following Registry value:

```
[HKEY_LOCAL_MACHINE\SYSTEM\Current Control Set\Services\
Tcpip\Parameters\ Interfaces\{<Interface GUID>}]
"DefaultGatewayMetric"=REG_MULTI_SZ:"<Metric>"
```

Caution If you are configuring metrics for multiple interfaces, you need to list the gateway metrics in the same order that the gateways are listed in the `DefaultGateway` key.

Using VBScript

This code configures the local interface with a default gateway of 10.0.0.1 and a metric of 1.

```
' ------ SCRIPT CONFIGURATION ------
strComputer = "."
strGateway = Array("10.0.0.1") ' Modify this value as needed
strGatewayMetric = Array(1) ' Modify this value as needed
' --------- END CONFIGURATION ------

Set objWMIService = GetObject("winmgmts:" _
    & "{impersonationLevel=impersonate}!\\" & strComputer & "\root\cimv2")

Set adapters = objWMIService.ExecQuery _
    ("Select * from Win32_NetworkAdapterConfiguration where IPEnabled=TRUE")

For Each a in adapters
    errGateways = a.SetGateways(strGateway, strGatewaymetric)
    If errGateways = 0 Then
        WScript.Echo "Success! The default gateway has been set."
    Else
        WScript.Echo "Error! The default gateway could not be set."
    End If
Next
```

How It Works

In TCP/IP, the default gateway associated with an IP address indicates the path through which all non-local traffic should be routed. On a device with only one configured gateway, all traffic will be directed to that one gateway address. If you have a multi-homed computer or a device that has more than one gateway configured, the gateway metric allows the OS to determine which gateway will be used first—a gateway with a metric of 1 will be used before a gateway with a metric of 2, and so forth. To optimize network performance, you should configure the gateway attached to the highest-speed link with the lower gateway metric. This also allows you to create fault tolerance by configuring a secondary gateway attached to a lower-speed link. For example, if the gateway attached to a T-1 line is unavailable, the device can transmit network packets over a gateway attached to a lower-speed ISDN line.

In Windows Server 2003, the gateway metric is configured automatically; the NIC attached to the higher-speed link receives the lower (and therefore preferred) metric. To manually control which gateway receives traffic first, you can configure a gateway metric using any of the methods described in this section.

See Also

- Recipe 1-3 for more on configuring dead-gateway detection

- Microsoft KB 258487: "Configuring Multiple Adapters on the Same Physical Network"

1-5. Assigning Multiple IP Addresses

Problem

You want to assign multiple IP addresses to a single NIC on a Windows Server 2003 computer.

Solution

Using a Graphical User Interface

1. Open the Network Connections applet.

2. Double-click on the Local Area Connection icon.

3. Click on Internet Protocol (TCP/IP), and select Properties and then Advanced.

4. In the IP Addresses section, click on Add. Specify the IP address and subnet mask of the additional IP address, and then click OK.

5. Click Close when you're finished.

Note To remove an additional static IP address that you've already specified, highlight the IP address on the screen in step 4, and then click on Remove.

Using a Command-Line Interface

To add an additional IP address using netsh, see the syntax used in the following example:

```
> netsh interface ip add address "Local Area Connection" 10.1.1.150 255.255.255.0
```

Using the Registry

The Registry entries controlling IP configuration are stored in a subkey of Tcpip\Parameters\ Interfaces that corresponds to the GUID of the NIC. If you have more than one NIC installed in your server, you can find the one that corresponds to a particular IP by using the following commands:

```
> wmic nicconfig get ipaddress,settingid > \foo.txt
> for /f "tokens=2" %a in ('type foo.txt ^| findstr "<IP Address>"') do echo %a
```

> **Note** You can enumerate the GUID for all installed NICs in your server by eliminating the ^| findstr "<IP Address>" portion of that command.

When assigning an IP address to a NIC using the Registry, you may have also noticed that the IPAddress, SubnetMask, and DefaultGateway Registry values listed in this section are all REG_MULTI_SZ values, which means that they can hold more than one value. To add multiple IP addresses to a single NIC, simply add more than one IP address to these three Registry keys— you can separate them using the Enter key or the space bar. Populating both the IPAddress and SubnetMask Registry keys is mandatory when adding an additional IP to a NIC—the additional IP address will not be recognized unless you add an entry to both keys. The DefaultGateway key is optional when specifying additional IP addresses—if you do not specify a new default gateway, it will use the gateway that is already in place for that NIC.

> **Note** To remove an additional static IP address from the Registry, simply delete the IP address and corresponding subnet mask from the IPAddress and SubnetMask keys.

How It Works

When configuring a NIC in Windows Server 2003, you'll typically only configure a single IP address, subnet mask, and default gateway for each installed NIC. But in some cases, particularly when you're dealing with a web server and SSL certificates, you can assign more than one IP address on one physical NIC. This will allow you to assign a unique IP address to multiple websites without needing to install additional hardware in your server.

At a minimum, you need to configure a subnet mask associated with each additional IP address; unless you specify otherwise, all configured IP addresses will use the default gateway assigned to the physical NIC. Keep in mind, however, that this process will increase the performance demands on the NIC for each additional IP address that it needs to route and manage traffic for.

See Also

Windows IT Pro, "Run Multiple Sites on Your IIS Server" (`http://www.windowsitpro.com/Windows/Article/ArticleID/21871/21871.html`)

1-6. Configuring Dynamic IP Address Assignment

Problem

You want to configure a Windows Server 2003 computer to receive IP addressing information from a Dynamic Host Configuration Protocol (DHCP) server.

Solution

Using a Graphical User Interface

1. Open the Network Connections applet.

2. Double-click on the Local Area Connection icon.

3. Click on Internet Protocol (TCP/IP), and select Properties.

4. Select the radio button next to Obtain an IP Address Automatically.

5. Click Close when you're finished.

Using a Command-Line Interface

The following command configures the NIC associated with the connection called `Local Area Connection` to receive its IP address automatically. You can change the name of the connection being configured to meet the needs of your environment:

```
> netsh interface ip set address "Local Area Connection" dhcp
```

Using the Registry

To configure an individual NIC to receive its IP address automatically from DHCP, set the following Registry value:

```
[HKEY_LOCAL_MACHINE\SYSTEM\CurrentControlSet\Services\
Tcpip\Parameters\Interfaces\{<Interface GUID>}\]
"EnableDHCP"=dword:1
```

Using VBScript

This code will configure the local computer to receive its IP configuration from a DHCP server.

```
' ------ SCRIPT CONFIGURATION ------
strComputer = "."
' --------- END CONFIGURATION ------
```

```
Set objWMIService = GetObject("winmgmts:" _
    & "{impersonationLevel=impersonate}!\\" & strComputer & "\root\cimv2")

Set adapters = objWMIService.ExecQuery _
    ("Select * from Win32_NetworkAdapterConfiguration where IPEnabled=TRUE")

For Each adapter In adapters
    errEnable = adapter.EnableDHCP()
    WScript.Echo "Successfully enabled DHCP on interface"
Next
```

How It Works

For ease of administration, you can use DHCP to provide IP address configuration information to a Windows Server 2003 computer. A computer that is relying on DHCP will request an IP address when it first boots, using a four-step process:

1. The computer broadcasts a DHCPDiscover packet, requesting an IP address from any DHCP server on the network.

2. A DHCP server broadcasts a DHCPOffer packet containing a valid IP address from its scope of addresses, as well as any configuration information that the administrator has configured to go along with the IP address. (This packet is still sent using broadcasts because the requesting computer doesn't actually have an IP address yet.)

3. The computer that requested the IP address will send a DHCPRequest packet in response to the *first* DHCPOffer packet it receives, requesting use of that particular IP address. This is a unicast packet, sent to the IP address of the DHCP server whose DHCPOffer packet was accepted.

4. The DHCP server that received the DHCPRequest packet will respond with a DHCPAcknowledge packet, certifying that it will be using this particular IP address and configuration. This is also a unicast packet sent directly to the client computer.

Note It may seem odd to refer to a Windows Server 2003 computer as a "client computer." In this case, "client" refers to the fact that the Windows Server 2003 computer is requesting resources (an IP address) from another computer that is "serving" those resources. So a computer can function as both a client *and* a server, regardless of what operating system it is running.

A DHCP server sends an IP address and subnet mask to a requesting computer in the form of a DHCP *lease*. This lease specifies for how long the IP address is valid before the requesting computer will be required to contact the DHCP server again to *renew* its lease. In addition to an IP address and subnet mask, a DHCP lease can contain several DHCP *options* to further customize the client computer's TCP/IP configuration. These options can include configuration information such as the following:

- Default gateway

- DNS servers

- WINS servers

- NetBIOS node type

Caution If you are switching a computer from a statically assigned IP address to a dynamically assigned one, it's recommended that you remove any statically assigned configuration information, such as manually configured DNS or WINS servers. If you've specified a DNS server address on the DNS tab of the local computer's network configuration, for example, this will override anything that was configured through DHCP options; if this is not the effect that you had in mind, you should remove the manually configured information.

See Also

- Recipe 1-9 for modifying the DNS search order

- Microsoft TechNet: "DHCP Options" (http://www.microsoft.com/ technet/prodtechnol/windowsserver2003/library/ServerHelp/ fe1d3ba8-e400-4ab3-be4f-684c9cb9b301.mspx)

1-7. Configuring Automatic Private IP Addressing (APIPA)

Problem

You want to enable or disable Automatic Private IP Addressing (APIPA) on a Windows Server 2003 computer.

Solution

To disable APIPA for a particular adapter, create the following Registry value:

```
[HKEY_LOCAL_MACHINE\SYSTEM\CurrentControlSet\Services\
Tcpip\Parameters\Interfaces\{<Interface GUID>}\]
"IPAutoConfigurationEnabled"=dword:0
```

To disable APIPA for all adapters installed in a particular computer, create the following Registry value—no reboot is necessary:

```
[HKEY_LOCAL_MACHINE\SYSTEM\CurrentControlSet\Services\Tcpip\Parameters]
"IPAutoConfigurationEnabled"=dword:0
```

Note If either of these Registry entries is not present, the operating system assumes a default value of 1. This means that APIPA is turned on and enabled on all Windows Server 2003 adapters by default.

How It Works

Similar to Windows 2000, Windows Server 2003 offers you the ability to configure an alternate IP configuration for a DHCP-enabled computer that is unable to contact a DHCP server. When your Windows Server 2003 computer is unable to obtain or renew a DHCP lease, it will configure itself with an IP address in the 169.254.0.0 Class B network. This can be used to enable temporary (albeit restricted) network access if your DHCP server becomes unavailable, or to provide a primary access solution for a small office with limited connectivity needs that does not have a DHCP server available.

By default, a computer that has received its IP address through APIPA will attempt to contact a DHCP server every five minutes in an attempt to obtain a valid IP address. (To prevent address collision on a network where multiple computers might be using APIPA, each workstation will perform its own collision detection to ensure that the IP address it is assigning itself is not already active on the APIPA subnet.)

APIPA addresses have a few limitations, including the following:

- 169.254.0.0 is a private network, which means that any traffic from an APIPA-enabled computer will not be transmitted by a router—this limits APIPA traffic to a single subnet.

- APIPA address information does not include a default gateway, further restricting traffic to the local subnet only.

- APIPA addresses do not allow for DHCP configuration options such as DNS and WINS server information.

To prevent APIPA from creating unnecessary confusion for the users of a Windows Server 2003 computer or network, you can choose to disable APIPA addressing. You can disable APIPA for a single installed NIC, or globally for all NICs installed in a computer.

See Also

- Recipe 1-7 for more on configuring an alternate IP configuration

- Microsoft KB 220874: "How to Use Automatic TCP/IP Addressing Without a DHCP Server"

1-8. Configuring an Alternate IP Configuration

Problem

You want to manually configure an alternate TCP/IP configuration for a Windows Server 2003 computer that has a dynamically assigned address. This creates a static IP address that a machine can use if it is unable to obtain an IP address automatically.

Solution

Using a Graphical User Interface

1. Open the Network Connections applet.

2. Double-click on the Local Area Connection icon.

3. Click on Internet Protocol (TCP/IP), and select Properties.

4. Select the Alternate Configuration tab. Select the radio button next to User Configured.

5. Enter the static address information in the following text boxes:

   - IP Address (required)

   - Subnet Mask (required)

   - Default Gateway

   - Primary DNS Server (for the alternate configuration)

   - Alternate DNS Server (for the alternate configuration)

   - Preferred WINS Server

   - Alternate WINS Server

6. Click OK when you're finished.

Using VBScript

This code configures the Registry blob that enables alternate IP configuration on a particular NIC. Before you run this script, you need to obtain the GUID for the appropriate NIC at the command line using the following syntax:

```
> wmic nicconfig get ipaddress,settingid > \foo.txt
> for /f "tokens=2" %a in ('type foo.txt ^| findstr
    "<IP Address>"') do echo %a
```

Here is the VBScript code:

```
' ------ SCRIPT CONFIGURATION ------
  Const CONNECTED = 2
  Const HKEY_LOCAL_MACHINE  = &H80000002
  Const strComputer = "."

  ' Modify the following six variables
  ' to meet the needs of your environment
  strTargetGUID = "{01B3816C-AB47-3E53-CB7C-88345293465}"
  strAlternateIP = "192.168.1.151"
  strAlternateMask = "255.255.255.0"
  strAlternateGW = "192.168.1.1"
  strAlternateDNS1 = "192.168.1.120"
  strAlternateDNS2 = "192.168.1.121"
  ' ------ END CONFIGURATION ---------

Set objWMIService = GetObject("winmgmts:\\" & strComputer & "\root\cimv2")
```

```
Set nics = objWMIService.ExecQuery _
 ("SELECT * FROM Win32_NetworkAdapterConfiguration WHERE IPEnabled = True")

For Each nic in nics
  strGUID = nic.SettingID

  ' only populate the alternate IP information for the correct NIC
  If strGUID = strTargetGUID Then

    ' make sure that DHCP is enabled
    If nic.DHCPEnabled = False Then
      Wscript.Echo("Error! DHCP must be enabled for " _
        & "alternate IP configurations to function.")

    ' now you can get to work
    Else
      ' first enable alternate IP configuration for this NIC
      strPath = "SYSTEM\CurrentControlSet\Services\" _
        & "Tcpip\Parameters\Interfaces\" & strGUID
      strValue = "ActiveConfigurations"
      strRegValue = "Alternate_" & strGUID
      arrValues = Array(strRegValue)

      Set Registry = GetObject _
        ("winmgmts:{impersonationLevel=impersonate}!\\" & _
        strComputer & "\root\default:StdRegProv")
      Registry.SetMultiStringValue HKEY_LOCAL_MACHINE, strPath, _
        strValue, arrValues

      ' now populate the alternate config with the appropriate values
      ' the first 20 values of the blob are fixed
      arrBlobValues(0)  = &H32
      arrBlobValues(1)  = &H00
      arrBlobValues(2)  = &H00
      arrBlobValues(3)  = &H00
      arrBlobValues(4)  = &H00
      arrBlobValues(5)  = &H00
      arrBlobValues(6)  = &H00
      arrBlobValues(7)  = &H00
      arrBlobValues(8)  = &H04
      arrBlobValues(9)  = &H00
      arrBlobValues(10) = &H00
      arrBlobValues(11) = &H00
      arrBlobValues(12) = &H00
      arrBlobValues(13) = &H00
      arrBlobValues(14) = &H00
      arrBlobValues(15) = &H00
```

```
arrBlobValues(16) = &HFF
arrBlobValues(17) = &HFF
arrBlobValues(18) = &HFF
arrBlobValues(19) = &H7F

' next insert the 4 octets of the IP address into
' array index 20 - 23
arrIP = Split(strAlternateIP, ".")
index = 20
For Each octet in arrIP
  arrBlobValues(index) = CInt(octet)
  index = index + 1
Next

' the next 20 values of the blob are fixed
arrBlobValues(24) = &H01
arrBlobValues(25) = &H00
arrBlobValues(26) = &H00
arrBlobValues(27) = &H00
arrBlobValues(28) = &H00
arrBlobValues(29) = &H00
arrBlobValues(30) = &H00
arrBlobValues(31) = &H00
arrBlobValues(32) = &H04
arrBlobValues(33) = &H00
arrBlobValues(34) = &H00
arrBlobValues(35) = &H00
arrBlobValues(36) = &H00
arrBlobValues(37) = &H00
arrBlobValues(38) = &H00
arrBlobValues(39) = &H00
arrBlobValues(40) = &HFF
arrBlobValues(41) = &HFF
arrBlobValues(42) = &HFF
arrBlobValues(43) = &H7F

' now insert the 4 octets of the subnet mask
' into array index 44 - 47
arrIP = Split(strAlternateMask, ".")
index = 44
For Each octet in arrIP
  arrBlobValues(index) = CInt(octet)
  index = index + 1
Next
```

```
' now insert another 20 fixed values
arrBlobValues(48) = &H03
arrBlobValues(49) = &H00
arrBlobValues(50) = &H00
arrBlobValues(51) = &H00
arrBlobValues(52) = &H00
arrBlobValues(53) = &H00
arrBlobValues(54) = &H00
arrBlobValues(55) = &H00
arrBlobValues(56) = &H04
arrBlobValues(57) = &H00
arrBlobValues(58) = &H00
arrBlobValues(59) = &H00
arrBlobValues(60) = &H00
arrBlobValues(61) = &H00
arrBlobValues(62) = &H00
arrBlobValues(63) = &H00
arrBlobValues(64) = &HFF
arrBlobValues(65) = &HFF
arrBlobValues(66) = &HFF
arrBlobValues(67) = &H7F

' now insert the 4 octets of the default gateway
' into array index 68 - 71
arrIP = Split(strAlternateGW, ".")
index = 68
For Each octet in arrIP
  arrBlobValues(index) = CInt(octet)
  index = index + 1
Next

' 20 more fixed values
arrBlobValues(72) = &H06
arrBlobValues(73) = &H00
arrBlobValues(74) = &H00
arrBlobValues(75) = &H00
arrBlobValues(76) = &H00
arrBlobValues(77) = &H00
arrBlobValues(78) = &H00
arrBlobValues(79) = &H00
arrBlobValues(80) = &H08
arrBlobValues(81) = &H00
arrBlobValues(82) = &H00
arrBlobValues(83) = &H00
arrBlobValues(84) = &H00
arrBlobValues(85) = &H00
arrBlobValues(86) = &H00
```

```
            arrBlobValues(87) = &H00
            arrBlobValues(88) = &HFF
            arrBlobValues(89) = &HFF
            arrBlobValues(90) = &HFF
            arrBlobValues(91) = &H7F

            ' now insert the 4 octets of the primary DNS server
            ' into array index 92 - 95
            arrIP = Split(strAlternateDNS1, ".")
            index = 92
            For Each octet in arrIP
              arrBlobValues(index) = CInt(octet)
              index = index + 1
            Next

            ' now insert the 4 octets of the secondary DNS server
            ' into array index 96 - 99
            arrIP = Split(strAlternateDNS2, ".")
            index = 96
            For Each octet in arrIP
              arrBlobValues(index) = CInt(octet)
              index = index + 1
            Next

            ' finally, save this information to the Registry
            strPath = "SYSTEM\ControlSet001\Services\Dhcp\Configurations\Alternate_" _
              & strGUID
            strValue = "Options"

            Set Registry = GetObject _
              ("winmgmts:{impersonationLevel=impersonate}!\\" & _
              strComputer & "\root\default:StdRegProv")

            Return = Registry.CreateKey(HKEY_LOCAL_MACHINE,strPath)

            Return = Registry.SetBinaryValue(HKEY_LOCAL_MACHINE,strKeyPath,_
              strValue,arrBlobValues)
          End If
       End If
Next
WScript.Echo "Script completed successfully. "
```

How It Works

As you saw in the previous recipe, you can allow a DHCP-enabled computer to receive an IP address from Automatic Private IP Addressing (APIPA) if it cannot contact a DHCP server. Alternatively, you can specify a static IP configuration that should be used. This is often useful for a laptop whose owner travels from a DHCP-enabled network to a non-DHCP network, or for a DHCP-enabled computer that should fall back to a particular IP configuration to ensure continued client access in the event of a DHCP failure.

Caution You can only enable an alternate IP configuration for a NIC that is configured to obtain its IP address automatically; if you've configured a NIC with a static IP address, the Alternate Configuration tab will not be available.

The simplest way to enable an alternate IP configuration is through the GUI, but you can also configure it using VBScript. Unlike the configuration information used for a primary IP configuration, you unfortunately cannot use netsh to configure a static alternate address. Further complicating matters is the fact that the Registry entry that stores alternate IP information is a binary large object, or blob, rather than the simple strings that you used to configure a primary static IP address. To edit this blob, you need to enter information into an array, one hexadecimal number at a time, using a specific format. As you saw, much of the information in the blob doesn't change from one computer to the next—these are standard entries that need to be present whenever you configure an alternate IP configuration. So you'll have twenty standard array entries such as these:

```
' now insert another 20 fixed values
arrBlobValues(48) = &H03
arrBlobValues(49) = &H00
arrBlobValues(50) = &H00
arrBlobValues(51) = &H00
arrBlobValues(52) = &H00
arrBlobValues(53) = &H00
arrBlobValues(54) = &H00
arrBlobValues(55) = &H00
arrBlobValues(56) = &H04
arrBlobValues(57) = &H00
arrBlobValues(58) = &H00
arrBlobValues(59) = &H00
arrBlobValues(60) = &H00
arrBlobValues(61) = &H00
arrBlobValues(62) = &H00
arrBlobValues(63) = &H00
arrBlobValues(64) = &HFF
arrBlobValues(65) = &HFF
arrBlobValues(66) = &HFF
arrBlobValues(67) = &H7F
```

These fixed entries will then be followed by computer-specific entries that encode the actual IP address, subnet mask, default gateway, and DNS servers into the Registry blob, like this:

```
' now insert the 4 octets of the default gateway
' into array index 68 - 71
arrIP = Split(strAlternateGW, ".")
index = 68
For Each octet in arrIP
  arrBlobValues(index) = CInt(octet)
  index = index + 1
Next
```

Once the array has been populated with the appropriate values, you'll then use the SetBinaryValue() method to insert the array values into the blob, as follows:

```
Registry.SetBinaryValue(HKEY_LOCAL_MACHINE,strKeyPath,_
        strValue,arrBlobValues)
```

See Also

Recipe 1-7 for configuring Automatic Private IP Addressing (APIPA)

1-9. Configuring DNS Servers Used for Name Resolution

Problem

You want to configure the DNS servers that will be used for name resolution on a Windows Server 2003 computer.

Solution

Using a Graphical User Interface

1. Open the Network Connections applet.

2. Double-click on the Local Area Connection icon.

3. Click on Internet Protocol (TCP/IP), and select Properties.

4. Verify that the radio button next to Use the Following IP Address is selected, and that the IP address, subnet mask, and default gateway are configured.

5. Fill in the IP address of the primary DNS server in the Preferred DNS Server text box, and the IP address of an alternate server in the Alternate DNS Server text box.

6. To add more than two DNS servers, click on Advanced. From the DNS tab, select Add and enter the IP address of one or more additional DNS servers.

7. Click OK when you're finished.

Using a Command-Line Interface

The following command configures two DNS servers for the NIC associated with your local area connection. In the first command, you'll specify that you're configuring static DNS server information and supply the primary DNS server's IP address. In the second command, you're simply adding an additional DNS server for redundancy. Modify the name of the connection (Local Area Connection in our example) and the IP addresses of the DNS servers to fit your environment.

```
> netsh interface ip set dns name = "Local Area Connection"
source = static addr = 192.168.1.151
> netsh interface ip add dns name = "Local Area Connection"
addr = 192.168.1.152
```

Note Using add dns here will append the second DNS server to the end of the DNS search order. The next recipe will discuss changing the search order.

Using the Registry

To configure the DNS servers used for name resolution, set the following Registry value:

```
[HKey_Local_Machine\System\CurrentControlSet\Services\Tcpip\Parameters\]
"NameServer" = REG_SZ:"<IP Address>"
```

Note You can enter multiple IP addresses in this key, separating the addresses with spaces.

Using VBScript

This code example will configure the local computer with two DNS servers: 192.168.1.151 and 192.168.1.152. To adjust this script for your environment, simply enter the appropriate values in the arrDNSServers array.

```
' ------ SCRIPT CONFIGURATION ------
strComputer = "."
arrDNSServers = Array("192.168.1.151", "192.168.1.152")
' --------- END CONFIGURATION ------

Set objWMIService = GetObject("winmgmts:" _
  & "{impersonationLevel=impersonate}!\\" & strComputer & "\root\cimv2")
Set Nics = objWMIService.ExecQuery _
  ("SELECT * FROM Win32_NetworkAdapterConfiguration WHERE IPEnabled = True")
```

```
For Each Nic In Nics
  intSetDNSServers = Nic.SetDNSServerSearchOrder(arrDNSServers)
  If intSetDNSServers = 0 Then
    WScript.Echo " DNS Servers set!"
  Else
    WScript.Echo " Error setting DNS server info."
  End If
Next
```

How It Works

Windows Server 2003 relies on the DNS to translate human-readable resource names like www.microsoft.com into the numeric IP addresses that are used by computers and routers on TCP/IP-based networks. When you enter a computer name into a web browser or Windows Explorer, the operating system will submit a name resolution query to the DNS servers listed on the DNS tab in the order that they appear. If the first DNS server does not respond to the query within a set amount of time (5 seconds by default), the client computer will submit the query to the second and subsequent DNS servers in the list before giving up.

DNS has been the default name resolution protocol for Windows operating systems since Windows 2000 was released. It is crucial for the functionality of Active Directory because it allows client computers to locate servers that are operating as domain controllers, global catalogs, and the Primary Domain Controller (PDC) Emulator for each domain. You should specify a minimum of two DNS servers for fault tolerance purposes, using any of the methods listed in this recipe.

See Also

- Recipe 1-10 for modifying the DNS search order

- Microsoft KB 825036: "Best Practices for DNS Client Settings in Windows 2000 Server and in Windows Server 2003"

1-10. Modifying the DNS Search Order

Problem

You want to change the order of the DNS servers that a Windows Server 2003 computer consults for DNS name resolution.

Solution

Using a Graphical User Interface

1. Open the Network Connections applet.

2. Double-click on the Local Area Connection icon.

3. Click on Internet Protocol (TCP/IP), and select Properties.

4. Verify that the radio button next to Use the Following IP Address is selected, and that the IP address, subnet mask, and default gateway are configured.

5. Click on Advanced and select the DNS tab. Use the Add button to add a server to the DNS search order. To remove a server from the list, select the IP address of the server and click on Remove. To change the order of the DNS servers that are listed, select the IP address of a server and click on the Up or Down arrows—DNS servers are queried from top to bottom in the order that they are listed. You can also use the Edit button to modify the IP address of an existing DNS server.

6. Click OK when you're finished.

Using a Command-Line Interface

The following example adds a new DNS server, 10.0.0.100, as the second server in the DNS search order for the Local Area Connection interface:

```
> netsh interface ip add dns "Local Area Connection" 10.0.0.100 index=2
```

Using the Registry

To configure the DNS servers for a network interface card, configure the following Registry value. Add the IP addresses of the DNS servers in the order that they should appear in the search list:

```
[HKey_Local_Machine\System\CurrentControlSet\Services\Tcpip\Parameters\]
"NameServer" = REG_SZ:"<IP Address1>" "<IP Address2>" "<IP Address3>"
```

Using VBScript

This code example will add a DNS server with the IP address of 192.168.1.151 to the beginning of the DNS search order.

```
' ------ SCRIPT CONFIGURATION ------
strComputer = "."
strNewDNSServer = "192.168.1.151"
' --------- END CONFIGURATION ------

Set objWMIService = GetObject("winmgmts:" _
 & "{impersonationLevel=impersonate}!\\" & strComputer & "\root\cimv2")
Set nics = objWMIService.ExecQuery _
 ("SELECT * FROM Win32_NetworkAdapterConfiguration WHERE IPEnabled = True")

For Each nic  In nics
  ' grab the current DNS search order
  arrDNSServerOrder = nic.DNSServerSearchOrder

  ' create a new array to hold the current DNS servers, plus one new one
  intNewArraySize = UBound(arrDNSServerOrder) + 1
  ReDim Preserve arrDNSServerOrder(intNewArraySize)
```

```
' Count backwards from the end of the array back to the first
' element, which is at index (0)
For i = (intNewArraySize - 1) To 0 Step -1
  ' Move each element one index "higher" in the array
  arrDNSServerOrder(i + 1) = arrDNSServerOrder(i)
Next

' Add the new server to index (0) of the array
arrDNSServerOrder(0) = strNewDNSServer
intNewDNS = nic.SetDNSServerSearchOrder(arrDNSServerOrder)
If intNewDNS = 0 Then
  WScript.Echo "Success!! Added " & strNewDNSServer & _
    " to the top of the DNS search order."
Else
  WScript.Echo "Error!! Unable to change DNS server search order."
End If
Next
```

How It Works

Since DNS queries are sent to each server in the order that they're listed, configuring the DNS search order correctly can optimize name resolution performance. When requesting a DNS lookup, the client computer (in this case, a Windows Server 2003 computer) will send a query to the first server listed in the DNS search order. If the first server does not respond after a specific amount of time (5 seconds by default), the 2003 computer will send the query to the second server in the search order, and so on. The name resolution query will only fail if none of the DNS servers in the search order have responded, or if any server in the search order has provided a negative response to the query. Depending on the configuration of your network, you can configure your Windows Server 2003 clients to query a DNS server on your internal network, or (as is often the case in a small or home office environment), you can configure them to query your ISP's DNS servers directly.

Because of the importance of the DNS search order, optimizing your computer's name resolution performance involves a few important factors:

1. Which DNS server(s) will be most likely to successfully answer client queries?

2. Which DNS server(s) will be able to accommodate the processing and memory requirements of numerous client queries?

3. Which DNS server(s) are located physically close to the DNS clients, thus ensuring a rapid response?

Clearly, creating the optimal search order will occasionally become a balancing act, where you need to decide whether to point your clients to a high-powered DNS server located across a slower WAN link in a central office, or to direct your clients to a lower-powered server in the same site. There is no hard and fast "right" answer to this question; you'll need to monitor performance and throughput on your network to determine which option will provide the best performance for your clients.

Using a Command-Line Interface

The index = x syntax in the netsh interface ip add dns command will add a new DNS server at the location specified by x. In this case, the numbering sequence starts at 1, so adding a DNS server with index = 2 will place the new server second in the DNS search order. Any existing DNS servers, including those specified by DHCP or Group Policy, will be moved down to make room for the one you just added.

Using VBScript

DNS server information is stored in WMI as an *array* of IP addresses. A typical array consists of a number of similar items (usually called *elements*), each with an associated *index* that's used to reference the item contained at that location. In most programming languages, array indexes start at zero, not one, and VBScript is no exception. So an array of IP addresses called myArray might be visualized like this:

```
myArray[0] = 10.0.0.1
myArray[1] = 10.0.0.2
myArray[2] = 10.0.0.154
```

In the case of the DNS search order, these array elements are read in order from index 0 through index $(n-1)$, where n is the number of elements in the array. This can sometimes be confusing to people who are new to scripting or programming, so look at it this way: if there are five elements in the array, they are located at 0, 1, 2, 3, and 4. In this case, n is equal to 5, and the final element of the array is located at array index $(n-1)$, or 4.

One restriction of arrays is that you need to tell VBScript how large the array is before you start using it. In this case, we do so by setting the array equal to the current array of DNS servers configured in the DNS search order, like this:

```
arrDNSServerOrder = nic.DNSServerSearchOrder
```

In order to add a new server to this array, we need to first make the array one element larger in order to hold the new value. We do this by using the command ReDim Preserve arrDNSServerOrder(intNewArraySize). Here, ReDim sets a new size for the array, and Preserve ensures that the elements already present in the array will not be erased. (If we hadn't used Preserve here, all existing entries in the arrDNSServerOrder array would have been erased.) As you saw in the code comments, we then moved each element in the array to a position that was one higher in the array, so that arrDNSServerOrder[4] was moved to arrDNSServerOrder[5], and so forth. To add the new DNS server to the beginning of the search order, we finally added the new server to arrDNSServerOrder[0], which is the first element of the array.

See Also

- MSDN: "VBScript Variables"

- Microsoft KB 200525: "Using NSLookup.exe"

1-11. Managing DNS Suffixes

Problem

You want to add, modify, or delete the DNS domain name suffixes that are used by a Windows Server 2003 computer, also referred to as the *domain suffix search order*. The domain name suffix order helps Windows resolve an "unqualified" name; that is, a computer name that does not have a domain name appended to it.

Solution

Using a Graphical User Interface

1. Open the Network Connections applet.

2. Double-click on the Local Area Connection icon.

3. Click on Internet Protocol (TCP/IP), and select Properties.

4. Verify that the radio button next to Use the Following IP Address is selected, and that the IP address, subnet mask, and default gateway are configured.

5. Click on Advanced and select the DNS tab. By default, the Append Primary and Connection Specific DNS Suffixes radio box will be selected, and there will be a check mark next to Append Parent Suffixes of the Primary DNS Suffix. To change this default behavior, select the radio button next to Append These DNS Suffixes (in Order).

6. To add a new DNS suffix, click the Add button. Use the Edit button to modify an existing DNS suffix, or the Remove button to delete a DNS suffix from the manually created suffix list.

7. To specify the DNS suffix for this network connection, enter the appropriate DNS suffix in the DNS Suffix for This Connection text box.

8. Click OK when you've made your changes.

Using Group Policy

Tables 1-1, 1-2, and 1-3 contain the Group Policy settings that control the behavior of the DNS server search order.

Table 1-1. *Setting the Primary DNS Suffix*

Path	Computer Configuration\Administrative Templates\Network\DNS Client
Policy name	Primary DNS Suffix
Value	DNS domain name

Table 1-2. *Creating the DNS Suffix Search Order*

Path	Computer Configuration\Administrative Templates\Network\DNS Client
Policy Name	DNS Suffix Search List
Value	One or more DNS domain names

Table 1-3. *Controlling DNS Suffix Devolution*

Path	Computer Configuration\Administrative Templates\Network\DNS Client
Policy Name	Primary DNS Suffix Devolution
Value	Enabled or Disabled

Using the Registry

To manually configure the DNS suffix search order, configure the following Registry value. Add the DNS domain names in the order that they should appear in the search list:

```
[HKey_Local_Machine\System\CurrentControlSet\Services\Tcpip\Parameters\]
"SearchList" = REG_SZ:"<DomainName>","<DomainName>","<DomainName>"
```

Note In this case, multiple entries are separated by commas instead of spaces.

To configure the DNS suffix search order to use the Windows default, set the previous Registry entry to a blank value.

To configure the connection-specific DNS suffix, configure the following Registry value:

```
[HKEY_LOCAL_MACHINE\System\CurrentControlSet\Services\
Tcpip\Parameters\Interfaces\{<Interface GUID>}\]
"Domain" = REG_SZ: "<DNS suffix>"
```

To prevent the computer from performing primary DNS suffix devolution in a name resolution process, configure the following Registry value:

```
HKEY_LOCAL_MACHINE\System\CurentControlSet\Services\Tcpip\Parameters\
"UseDomainNameDevolution" = REG_DWORD: 0
```

Using VBScript

This code will change the DNS suffix search order to mycompany.com followed by east. mycompany.com. Simply modify the arrNewDNSSuffixOrder array with the appropriate DNS domain name values for your environment.

```
' ------ SCRIPT CONFIGURATION ------
strComputer = "."
arrNewDNSSuffixOrder = Array("mycompany.com", "east.mycompany.com")
' --------- END CONFIGURATION ------

Set objWMIService = GetObject("winmgmts:" _
 & "{impersonationLevel=impersonate}!\\" & strComputer & "\root\cimv2")
Set nics = objWMIService.ExecQuery _
 ("SELECT * FROM Win32_NetworkAdapterConfiguration WHERE IPEnabled = True")

Set Network = objWMIService.Get("Win32_NetworkAdapterConfiguration")

' now set the new DNS suffix search order
SetSuffixes = _
  Network.SetDNSSuffixSearchOrder(arrNewDNSSuffixOrder)

If SetSuffixes = 0 Then
  WScript.Echo "Success! Replaced DNS domain suffix search order."
ElseIf SetSuffixes = 1 Then
  WScript.Echo "Success! Replaced DNS domain suffix search order - pls. reboot."
Else
  WScript.Echo "Error! Unable to replace DNS domain suffix search order list."
End If
```

How It Works

A *fully qualified domain name* (FQDN) consists of a host name, followed by domain names up to and including the top-level domain name (TLD). For example, a computer with the hostname of computer1 located in the east.mycompany.com domain would have a FQDN of computer1. east.mycompany.com. The *domain name suffix* refers to the domain name that is appended to the hostname in order to create the FQDN. A Windows computer can have two possible domain name suffixes appended to it:

- The *primary DNS suffix*, which applies to all NICs configured on the computer.

- The *connection-specific suffix,* which only applies to one particular NIC. For example, a computer might have two NICs attached to two separate LANs and have a different connection-specific DNS suffix for each.

By contrast, an *unqualified* host name consists only of the hostname without any domain names appended to it. (This would be computer1 in the previous example.) When presented with an unqualified hostname, Windows Server 2003 will append any configured DNS suffixes to the unqualified name in an attempt to resolve the name. If a Windows Server 2003 computer is presented with an unqualified hostname to resolve, by default it will append the following DNS suffixes in this order in an attempt to resolve the name:

1. The primary DNS suffix.

2. Any connection-specific DNS suffix that is present.

3. The *parent suffixes* of the primary DNS suffix. This means that if the primary domain suffix is east.mycompany.com, DNS will try to append both east.mycompany.com as well as mycompany.com in an attempt to resolve the name.

You can modify this default behavior so that Windows will only append the DNS suffixes that you specify when attempting to resolve an unqualified name, using any of the methods specified in this section.

Using a Command-Line Interface

Unfortunately, there is no netsh option available for specifying the DNS suffix search order.

See Also

- Microsoft TechNet: "DNS Tools and Settings" (http://www.microsoft.com/technet/prodtechnol/windowsserver2003/library/TechRef/099d4168-4ac1-441d-81b7-0f3f4909fbd4.mspx)

- Windows IT Pro, "Using VBScript Arrays in Scripts" (http://www.windowsitpro.com/Article/ArticleID/5628/5628.html)

1-12. Configuring Dynamic DNS Registration

Problem

You want to enable or disable dynamic DNS registration for a Windows Server 2003 computer.

Solution

Using a Graphical User Interface

1. Open the Network Connections applet.

2. Double-click on the Local Area Connection icon.

3. Click on Internet Protocol (TCP/IP), and select Properties.

4. Click on Advanced and select the DNS tab. To enable dynamic DNS registration, place a check mark next to Register This Connection's Address in DNS. To disable dynamic DNS registration, remove the check mark next to this item.

5. To use the connection-specific DNS suffix for DNS registration, place a check mark next to Use This Connection's DNS Suffix in DNS Registration.

6. Click OK when you've made your changes.

Using a Command-Line Interface

To configure this setting via the command line, you first need to create a .reg file containing the Registry key in the following "Using the Registry" section, then use Regedit to import the file into your local Registry. A shell script to automate this process is as follows. This script takes the IP address of the interface you're trying to change as a command-line argument. It then grabs the GUID of the appropriate interface and sets the RegistrationEnabled Registry key programmatically:

```
set IPADDRESS=%1
set TFILE=%TEMP%\HWIDfile.tmp
set ON=00000001
set OFF=00000000

wmic nicconfig get ipaddress,settingid > %TFILE%

for /f "tokens=2" %%h in ('type %TFILE% ^| findstr "%IPADDRESS%"') do set HWID=%%h

echo Windows Registry Editor Version 5.00 >%TFILE%
echo >> %TFILE%
echo [HKEY_LOCAL_MACHINE\SYSTEM\CurrentControlSet\Services\
    Tcpip\Parameters\Interfaces\%HWID%] >>%TFILE%
echo "RegistrationEnabled"=dword:%OFF% >>%TFILE%

:: regedit /s %TFILE%

del %TFILE% >null
```

Note Save these commands to a .bat or a .cmd file before running the script.

Using Group Policy

Table 1-4 contains the Group Policy setting that enables or disables dynamic DNS updates for a Windows Server 2003 computer.

Table 1-4. *Dynamic Update Setting*

Path	Computer Configuration\Administrative Templates\Network\DNS Client
Policy name	Dynamic Update
Value	Enabled or Disabled
Location	If enabled, dynamic update can be enabled on a per-connection basis on the client computer. If disabled, dynamic update cannot be enabled on any connection.

Using the Registry

To disable dynamic DNS registration for all NICs installed in a computer, configure the following Registry value:

```
[HKEY_LOCAL_MACHINE\SYSTEM\CurrentControlSet\Services\Tcpip\Parameters\]
"DisableDynamicUpdate"=dword:1
```

To disable dynamic DNS registration for a particular interface, configure the following Registry value:

```
[HKEY_LOCAL_MACHINE\SYSTEM\CurrentControlSet\Services\
Tcpip\Parameters\Interfaces\{<Interface GUID>}\]
"RegistrationEnabled"=dword:0
```

Using VBScript

This code enables dynamic DNS registration on each NIC installed in the local computer.

```
' ------ SCRIPT CONFIGURATION ------
  strComputer = "."
  boolEnabled = True
' ------ END CONFIGURATION ---------

Set objWMIService = GetObject("winmgmts:" _
 & "{impersonationLevel=impersonate}!\\" & strComputer & "\root\cimv2")
Set nics = objWMIService.ExecQuery _
 ("SELECT * FROM Win32_NetworkAdapterConfiguration WHERE IPEnabled = True")

For Each nic In nics
  intDynamicRegistration = nic.SetDynamicDNSRegistration _
  (boolEnabled, boolEnabled)
  If intDynamicRegistration = 0 Then
    WScript.Echo VbCrLf & "Success! Dynamic Registration enabled!"
  ElseIf intDynamicRegistration = 1 Then
    WScript.Echo "Success! Dynamic Registration enabled! Please reboot."
  Else
    WScript.Echo "Error! Unable to enable Dynamic Registration."
  End If
Next
```

How It Works

Beginning with Windows 2000, you have had the ability to enable dynamic DNS registration for your clients and servers. This allows your clients to automatically update their forward lookup (A) and reverse lookup (PTR) resource records on the DNS server. This makes your life easier as an administrator since it reduces the amount of time you need to spend manually updating DNS records, though the process needs to be secured to prevent rogue machines or attackers from compromising the integrity of your DNS servers. You can also combine the dynamic DNS functionality with the DHCP service so that client resource records are automatically updated whenever a computer leases a new IP address.

In Active Directory–integrated DNS zones, you can enable secure dynamic updates so that only authorized users can make changes to DNS zones and individual records. Dynamic DNS registration is enabled by default in Windows 2000, Windows XP, and Windows Server 2003. However, you should take care to ensure that your production DNS servers have this feature enabled, as computers attempting to perform dynamic DNS registrations against servers that do not permit them can create unnecessary network traffic.

See Also

- Microsoft TechNet: "Dynamic Update" (`http://www.microsoft.com/ technet/prodtechnol/windowsserver2003/library/ServerHelp/ e760737e-9e55-458d-b5ed-a1ae9e04819e.mspx`)

- Microsoft KB 816592: "How to Configure DNS Dynamic Updates in Windows Server 2003"

1-13. Managing WINS Server Lookups

Problem

You want to add or remove a WINS server address that's used by a Windows Server 2003 computer for NetBIOS name lookups.

Solution

Using a Graphical User Interface

1. Open the Network Connections applet.

2. Double-click on the Local Area Connection icon.

3. Click on Internet Protocol (TCP/IP), and select Properties.

4. Verify that the radio button next to Use the Following IP Address is selected, and that the IP address, subnet mask, and default gateway are configured.

5. Click on Advanced. From the WINS tab, click Add and enter the IP address of one or more additional WINS servers.

6. To remove an existing WINS server, select the IP address of the server and click Remove. You can also use the Up or Down arrows to change the order in which WINS servers are queried, or use the Edit button to modify the IP address of an existing WINS server.

7. Click OK when you're finished.

Using a Command-Line Interface

The following command configures two WINS servers for the NIC associated with a connection named Local Area Connection. Change the name of the connection and the IP addresses of the WINS servers as necessary for your environment.

```
> netsh interface ip set wins name = "Local Area Connection"
source = static addr = 192.168.1.151
> netsh interface ip add wins name = "Local Area Connection"
addr = 192.168.1.152
```

■ **Note** Using add wins here will append the second WINS server to the end of the WINS search order. Just like with add dns, you can use index = x to insert a new server at a specific location in the search order (see Recipe 1-10).

Using the Registry

To configure one or more WINS servers for a particular NIC, set the following Registry value. You can enter multiple IP addresses separated by pressing the Enter key:

```
[HKEY_LOCAL_MACHINE\SYSTEM\CurrentControlSet\Services\
NetBT\Parameters\Interfaces\Tcp_{<Interface GUID>}\]
"NameServerList"=reg_multi_sz:"<IP Address>"
```

To remove an existing WINS server, delete the corresponding IP address from this key. WINS servers are queried in the order in which they're listed in this key, so you can move them around within the key as necessary to change the search order.

Using VBScript

This code configures two WINS servers for the local computer. To customize this code for your environment, simply change the values in strWins1 and strWins2.

```
' ------ SCRIPT CONFIGURATION ------
strComputer = "."
strWins1 = "192.168.1.151"
strWins2 = "192.168.1.152"
' --------- END CONFIGURATION ------

Set objWMIService = GetObject("winmgmts:" _
 & "{impersonationLevel=impersonate}!\\" & strComputer & "\root\cimv2")
Set nics = objWMIService.ExecQuery _
 ("SELECT * FROM Win32_NetworkAdapterConfiguration WHERE IPEnabled = True")

For Each nic In nics
  intSetWINS = nic.SetWINSServer(strWINS1, strWINS2)
  If intSetWINSServer = 0 Then
    WScript.Echo "Success! WINS servers configured."
```

```
    ElseIf intSetWINSServer = 1 Then
      WScript.Echo "WINS servers configured, please reboot."
    Else
      WScript.Echo "Error!! Unable to configure WINS servers."
    End If
Next
```

How It Works

In order to translate human-readable NetBIOS names like \\COMPUTER1 into the numeric IP addresses that are used by computers and routers on TCP/IP-based networks, Windows Server 2003 will use a combination of NetBIOS broadcasts and the Windows Internet Name Service (WINS). WINS servers significantly reduce network traffic associated with NetBIOS name resolution, since they allow clients to locate NetBIOS resources without relying on broadcast traffic.

When you enter a computer name using the \\COMPUTERNAME Universal Naming Convention (UNC) notation, the operating system will submit a name resolution query to the WINS servers listed on the WINS tab in the order that they appear. If the first WINS server is unable to answer the query within a certain amount of time, the client computer will submit the query to the second WINS server in the list before giving up.

WINS has largely been replaced by DNS as the default name resolution protocol for Windows operating systems, but certain applications and legacy operating systems still require it for name resolution. If you require NetBIOS name resolution on your network, you should specify a minimum of two WINS servers for fault tolerance purposes using any of the methods listed in this recipe.

See Also

- Microsoft TechNet: "Windows Server 2003 Windows Internet Name Service (WINS)" (http://www.microsoft.com/technet/prodtechnol/windowsserver2003/technologies/wins.mspx)

- Chapter 2 for more on WINS

1-14. Configuring NetBIOS over TCP/IP

Problem

You want to configure the NetBIOS over TCP/IP settings for a Windows Server 2003 computer.

Solution

Using a Graphical User Interface

1. Open the Network Connections applet.

2. Double-click on the Local Area Connection icon.

3. Click on Internet Protocol (TCP/IP), and select Properties.

4. Click on Advanced. From the WINS tab, select the radio button next to one of the following settings for NetBIOS over TCP/IP:

  • Use NetBIOS settings from the DHCP server. (This is the default. If a static IP address is used or the DHCP server does not provide NetBIOS settings, enable NetBIOS over TCP/IP.)

  • Enable NetBIOS over TCP/IP.

  • Disable NetBIOS over TCP/IP.

5. Click OK when you're finished.

Using a Command-Line Interface

To configure this setting via the command line, you first need to create a .reg file containing the Registry key described in the "Using the Registry" section, and then use Regedit to import the file into your local Registry.

The following shell script will automate the process of importing the .reg file; it takes the IP address of the interface you are trying to change as a command-line argument, and it disables TCP/IP over NetBIOS for that interface.

```
set IPADDRESS=%1
set TFILE=%TEMP%\HWIDfile.tmp
set DEFAULT=00000000
set ON=00000001
set OFF=00000002

wmic nicconfig get ipaddress,settingid >%TFILE%

for /f "tokens=2" %%h in ('type %TFILE% ^| findstr "%IPADDRESS%"') do set HWID=%%h

echo Windows Registry Editor Version 5.00 >%TFILE%
echo >> %TFILE%
echo [HKEY_LOCAL_MACHINE\SYSTEM\CurrentControlSet\Services\
    NetBT\Parameters\Interfaces\Tcpip_%HWID%] >>%TFILE%
echo "RegistrationEnabled"=dword:%OFF% >>%TFILE%

:: regedit /s %TFILE%

del %TFILE% >null
```

Using the Registry

To configure the NetBIOS over TCP/IP settings for a Windows Server 2003 computer, set the following Registry value:

```
[HKEY_LOCAL_MACHINE\SYSTEM\CurrentControlSet\Services\
NetBT\Parameters\Interfaces\Tcp_{<Interface GUID>}\]
"NetbiosOptions"=dword:0 (to use DHCP settings)
"NetbiosOptions"=dword:1 (to enable NetBIOS over TCP/IP)
"NetbiosOptions"=dword:2 (to disable NetBIOS over TCP/IP)
```

Using VBScript

This code enables NetBIOS over TCP/IP.

```
' ------ SCRIPT CONFIGURATION ------
strComputer = "."

Const DEFAULT = 0
Const ENABLED = 1
Const DISABLED = 2
' ------ END CONFIGURATION ---------

Set objWMIService = GetObject("winmgmts:" _
 & "{impersonationLevel=impersonate}!\\" & strComputer & "\root\cimv2")

Set nics = objWMIService.ExecQuery _
 ("SELECT * FROM Win32_NetworkAdapterConfiguration WHERE IPEnabled = True")

For Each nic in nics
  intNetBT = nic.SetTCPIPNetBIOS(ENABLED)
  If intNetBT = 0 Then
    WScript.Echo "Success! NetBIOS over TCP/IP enabled!"
  ElseIf intNetBT = 1 Then
    WScript.Echo "Success! NetBIOS over TCP/IP enabled, please reboot."
  Else
    WScript.Echo "Error! Unable to enable NetBIOS over TCP/IP."
  End If
Next
```

How It Works

While Microsoft has gone to great lengths to increase the security of Windows Server 2003 compared to previous versions of the operating system, the NetBIOS ports (TCP 135, 137, and 139) remain well-known attack vectors that are often used by malicious users to exploit Windows systems. Because of this, disabling NetBIOS traffic wherever possible will increase the overall security of your Windows Server 2003 network.

Windows Server 2003 has largely rendered NetBIOS obsolete by replacing it with *direct hosting,* which operates on TCP port 445 and uses DNS for name resolution instead of relying on WINS or NetBIOS broadcasts. If you are not supporting any clients or applications that require NetBIOS name resolution, you can increase the security of your Windows Server 2003 computers by disabling NetBIOS over TCP/IP and forcing your client and server computers to utilize direct hosting.

■**Caution** Be sure to test all of your mission-critical applications and production Windows services before disabling NetBIOS over TCP/IP on a Windows Server 2003 computer. Even modern applications like Microsoft Exchange Server (up to Exchange 2003) can still require NetBIOS name resolution in certain situations.

Using the Registry

Like some of the DNS recipes we've seen in this chapter, configuring interface-specific NetBIOS settings requires you to find the GUID of the NIC that you want to configure. In this case, the path has Tcpip_ prepended to the GUID, so a sample Registry path might look like this:

```
[HKEY_LOCAL_MACHINE\SYSTEM\CurrentControlSet\Services\NetBT\
Parameters\Interfaces\Tcpip_{91271921-ECEA-4185-A19C-A6343E941BDA}\]
```

Using VBScript

The SetTCPIPNetBIOS() method in the Win32_NetworkAdapterConfiguration WMI class is new to the Windows Server 2003 and Windows XP operating systems. The three numeric values that you can input into this method correspond to the three radio buttons in the GUI:

- 0: Use the DHCP value or the default settings

- 1: Enable NetBIOS over TCP/IP

- 2: Disable NetBIOS over TCP/IP

See Also

- Microsoft TechNet: "Microsoft Windows Server 2003 TCP/IP Implementation Details" (http://www.microsoft.com/technet/prodtechnol/windowsserver2003/technologies/networking/tcpip03.mspx)

- Chapter 2 for more on Windows Internet Name Service (WINS)

- Recipe 1-13 for configuring WINS for DNS name resolution

- Recipe 1-15 for configuring a NetBIOS scope ID and enabling Lmhosts lookups

- Microsoft KB 323357: "How To Configure TCP/IP Networking While NetBIOS Is Turned Off on a Server Running Windows Server 2003"

1-15. Configuring NetBIOS Options

Problem

You want to configure NetBIOS options on your Windows Server 2003 computer. These options include using DNS as a secondary method of NetBIOS name resolution, configuring a NetBIOS scope ID, and configuring the use of an Lmhosts file.

Solution

Using a Graphical User Interface

To enable Lmhosts lookups via the GUI, follow these steps:

1. Open the Network Connections applet.

2. Double-click on the Local Area Connection icon.

3. Click on Internet Protocol (TCP/IP), and select Properties.

4. Click on Advanced. From the WINS tab, place a check mark next to Enable LMHOSTS Lookup. (This is selected by default.)

5. To import the Lmhosts file from a central or alternate location, click on Import LMHOSTS. Browse to the location of the Lmhosts file and click on Open.

6. Click OK when you're finished.

Note If any entries in the Lmhosts file contain the #PRE tag, designating them as preloaded entries, you should issue the following command to load these entries into memory: nbtstat -R

Using the Registry

To disable the use of Lmhosts for NetBIOS name resolution, configure the following Registry value:

```
[HKEY_LOCAL_MACHINE\SYSTEM\CurrentControlSet\Services\NetBT\Parameters\]
"EnableLMHOSTS"=dword:0
```

To configure a NetBIOS scope ID for a Windows Server 2003 computer, create and configure the following Registry value:

```
HKEY_LOCAL_MACHINE\SYSTEM\CurrentControlSet\Services\NetBT\Parameters\
"ScopeID"=REG_SZ: "<Scope ID>"
```

Using VBScript

This code enables the following three optional WINS parameters:

- Enables DNS as a backup for WINS name resolution

- Enables lookup from a central Lmhosts file

- Configures the local computer with a NetBIOS scope ID of FINANCE

```
' ------ SCRIPT CONFIGURATION ------
strComputer = "."
EnableDNS = True
EnableLMHosts = True
```

```
LMHOSTSFile = "\\server1\admin\lmhosts"
ScopeID = "FINANCE" ' set this to the name of your NetBIOS
                               ' scope
' ------ END CONFIGURATION ---------

Set objWMIService = GetObject("winmgmts:" _
 & "{impersonationLevel=impersonate}!\\" & strComputer & "\root\cimv2")

Set nicConfig = objWMIService.Get("Win32_NetworkAdapterConfiguration")

EnableWINS = nicConfig.EnableWINS(EnableDNS, EnableLMHosts, _
  LMHOSTSFile, ScopeID)
If EnableWINS = 0 Then
  WScript.Echo "Set WINS options successfully!"
ElseIf intEnableWINS = 1 Then
  WScript.Echo "Set WINS options successfully! Please reboot."
Else
  WScript.Echo "Error! Unable to set WINS options."
End If
```

How It Works

Even though WINS and NetBIOS name resolution is waning in popularity, there are still a number of advanced options that you can configure to customize the behavior of NetBIOS on your Windows Server 2003 computers. The advanced options that you can configure include the following:

- **Enabling DNS as a backup for WINS name resolution:** If you enter a NetBIOS name (such as \\COMPUTER1) that cannot be resolved from WINS servers or a NetBIOS broadcast, this setting will instruct your computer to use DNS as a last-resort attempt to resolve the NetBIOS name.

- **Enabling lookups from an Lmhosts file:** Before WINS was developed, administrators would maintain a text file on the local hard drive that contained NetBIOS name mappings. This file, called Lmhosts, can still be used as part of the NetBIOS name resolution process; in this way, you can prepopulate the Lmhosts file with NetBIOS name mappings such as domain controllers or other critical servers whose IP addresses don't change very often. By default, the Lmhosts file resides in the %systemroot%\system32\drivers\ etc directory, but you can configure your computer to look up entries from an Lmhosts file in another location. You can use this capability to point your client computers to an Lmhosts file located on a centralized file server that can be easily kept up to date.

- **Configuring one or more NetBIOS scope IDs:** Scope IDs are text strings such as FINANCE or WORKGROUP. If you configure a computer with a specific scope ID, that computer will only be able to communicate with other computers that have the same scope ID. This was used extensively in earlier versions of Windows to restrict NetBIOS traffic to particular groups of computers that needed to communicate only with each other.

Note The NetBIOS scope ID can no longer be configured via the GUI; it can only be configured via the Registry or VBScript.

See Also

Microsoft TechNet: "Advanced Configuration" (http://www.microsoft.com/ technet/prodtechnol/windowsserver2003/library/ServerHelp/ edf66ed4-a258-4d09-8d6f-60b0d95cfbcf.mspx)

1-16. Displaying TCP/IP Information

Problem

You want to display the current TCP/IP configuration of a Windows Server 2003 computer.

Solution

Using a Command-Line Interface

The following command displays configuration information for the local computer:

```
> netsh interface ip show config
```

As an alternative, you can also issue the following command:

```
> ipconfig /all
```

Note To view all of the output switches available for `ipconfig`, issue the following at the command line: `ipconfig /?`.

Using VBScript

This code displays the TCP/IP configuration for the local computer.

```
' ------ SCRIPT CONFIGURATION ------
  strComputer = "."
' ------ END CONFIGURATION ---------

Set objWMIService = GetObject("winmgmts:" _
    & "{impersonationLevel=impersonate}!\\" & strComputer & "\root\cimv2")

Set nics = objWMIService.ExecQuery _
    ("SELECT * FROM Win32_NetworkAdapterConfiguration WHERE IPEnabled = True")
```

```
' set a counter to number the NICs, in case you need to display info
' for more than one.
n = 1
WScript.Echo

For Each nic in nics
    WScript.Echo "Network Interface Card: " & n
    WScript.Echo "=================="
    WScript.Echo "  Description: " & nic.Description

    WScript.Echo "  Physical (MAC) address: " & nic.MACAddress
    WScript.Echo "  Host name:              " & nic.DNSHostName

  ' display all IP addresses configured for this adapter
  If Not IsNull(nic.IPAddress) Then
     For x = 0 To UBound(nic.IPAddress)
        WScript.Echo "  IP address:           " & nic.IPAddress(x)
     Next
  End If

  If Not IsNull(nic.IPSubnet) Then
     For x = 0 To UBound(nic.IPSubnet)
        WScript.Echo "  Subnet:               " & nic.IPSubnet(x)
     Next
  End If

  If Not IsNull(nic.DefaultIPGateway) Then
     For x = 0 To UBound(nic.DefaultIPGateway)
        WScript.Echo "  Default gateway:      " & _
           nic.DefaultIPGateway(x)
     Next
  End If

  ' now display DNS configuration information

  WScript.Echo
  WScript.Echo "  DNS Settings"
  WScript.Echo "  ------------"
  WScript.Echo "     DNS search order:"

  If Not IsNull(nic.DNSServerSearchOrder) Then
     For x = 0 To UBound(nic.DNSServerSearchOrder)
        WScript.Echo "         " & nic.DNSServerSearchOrder(x)
     Next
  End If
```

```
        WScript.Echo "    DNS domain: " & nic.DNSDomain

        If Not IsNull(nic.DNSDomainSuffixSearchOrder) Then
            For x = 0 To UBound(nic.DNSDomainSuffixSearchOrder)
                WScript.Echo "    DNS suffix search list: " & _
                    nic.DNSDomainSuffixSearchOrder(x)
            Next
        End If

    ' now display DHCP information

        WScript.Echo
        WScript.Echo "  DHCP Settings"
        WScript.Echo "  -------------"
        WScript.Echo "    DHCP enabled:        " & nic.DHCPEnabled
        WScript.Echo "    DHCP server:         " & nic.DHCPServer

        If Not IsNull(nic.DHCPLeaseObtained) Then
            utcLeaseObtained = nic.DHCPLeaseObtained
            strLeaseObtained = WMIDateStringToDate(utcLeaseObtained)
        Else
            strLeaseObtained = ""
        End If

        WScript.Echo "    DHCP lease obtained: " & strLeaseObtained

        If Not IsNull(nic.DHCPLeaseExpires) Then
            utcLeaseExpires = nic.DHCPLeaseExpires
            strLeaseExpires = WMIDateStringToDate(utcLeaseExpires)
        Else
            strLeaseExpires = ""
        End If
        WScript.Echo "    DHCP lease expires:  " & strLeaseExpires

    ' now display WINS configuration information
        WScript.Echo
        WScript.Echo "  WINS settings"
        WScript.Echo "  -------------"
        WScript.Echo "    Primary WINS server:   " & nic.WINSPrimaryServer
        WScript.Echo "    Secondary WINS server: " & nic.WINSSecondaryServer
        WScript.Echo

    ' move to the next adapter, if applicable
    n = n + 1
Next
```

```
' takes a UTC date string and displays it in a friendlier format
Function WMIDateStringToDate(utcDate)
  WMIDateStringToDate = CDate(Mid(utcDate, 5, 2)  & "/" & _
    Mid(utcDate, 7, 2)  & "/" & _
    Left(utcDate, 4)    & " " & _
    Mid (utcDate, 9, 2) & ":" & _
    Mid(utcDate, 11, 2) & ":" & _
    Mid(utcDate, 13, 2))
End Function
```

How It Works

One of the first steps you should take when troubleshooting a network connectivity issue is to get a snapshot of how your computer's TCP/IP connections are currently configured. Mistyping a default gateway or subnet mask can create troublesome errors that even the most seasoned of network professionals can overlook if they skip this simple step. Earlier client operating systems like Windows 95 and Windows 98 offered winipcfg, a GUI utility that would provide a snapshot of the current IP configuration; in NT, 2000, XP, and 2003 this has been replaced by command-line tools and scripting solutions.

Using a Command-Line Interface

In addition to the syntax listed here, both netsh and ipconfig can display a smaller subset of IP configuration information, and ipconfig can even be used to perform simple troubleshooting tasks. From the netsh interface ip command, you can append the following commands to display various IP addressing information:

show address: Displays IP address configuration only; no DNS or WINS info

show dns: Displays the configured DNS server addresses

show icmp: Displays ICMP statistics

show interface: Displays IP interface statistics

show ipstats: Displays IP statistics

show joins: Displays multicast groups joined

show wins: Displays the WINS server addresses

show /?: Displays all available views

See Also

- Chapter 9 for more on monitoring and troubleshooting

- Microsoft KB 169790: "How to Troubleshoot Basic TCP/IP Problems"

1-17. Enabling or Disabling the Windows Firewall

Problem

You want to enable or disable the built-in firewall on a Windows Server 2003 Service Pack 1 computer.

Solution

Using a Graphical User Interface

1. Open the Network Connections applet.

2. Double-click on the Local Area Connection icon.

3. From the Advanced tab, click Settings. This will launch the Windows Firewall Control Panel applet.

4. To enable the Windows Firewall, click the On radio button. To disable the Windows Firewall, click the Off radio button.

Using a Command-Line Interface

The following command disables the Windows Firewall on a Windows Server 2003 Service Pack 1 computer:

```
> netsh firewall set opmode mode=disable exceptions=disable profile=all
```

The following command enables the Windows Firewall on a Windows Server 2003 computer:

```
> netsh firewall set opmode mode=enable profile=all
```

Using Group Policy

Table 1-5 contains the Group Policy setting that enables or disables the Windows Firewall.

Table 1-5. *Windows Firewall Settings*

Path	Computer Configuration\Administrative Templates\Network\ Network Connections\Windows Firewall\Domain Profile
Policy name	Windows Firewall: Protect all network connections
Value	Enabled to turn on the Windows Firewall; Disabled to turn it off

Using the Registry

To enable the Windows Firewall on a Windows Server 2003 computer, configure the following Registry values:

```
[HKEY_LOCAL_MACHINE\SYSTEM\CurrentControlSet\Services\
SharedAccess\Parameters\FirewallPolicy\DomainProfile\]
"EnableFirewall"=dword:1

[HKEY_LOCAL_MACHINE\SYSTEM\CurrentControlSet\Services\
SharedAccess\Parameters\FirewallPolicy\StandardProfile\]
"EnableFirewall"=dword:1
```

To disable the Windows Firewall, set both of the previous Registry entry values to 0. You do not need to reboot after making these changes.

Using VBScript

This code enables or disables the Windows Firewall on the local computer.

```
' ------ SCRIPT CONFIGURATION ------
boolEnabled = TRUE  ' FALSE to disable
' ------ END CONFIGURATION ---------
Set firewall = CreateObject("HNetCfg.FwMgr")
Set firewallPolicy = firewall.LocalPolicy.CurrentProfile

firewallPolicy.FirewallEnabled = boolEnabled
WScript.Echo "Firewall enabled: " & boolEnabled
```

How It Works

The original Release To Manufacturing (RTM) version of the Windows Server 2003 operating system came preloaded with the Internet Connection Firewall (ICF), which provided a simple host-based firewall for the 2003 operating system. The drawback to ICF was that it was not enabled by default when 2003 was first installed, and it was fairly unintuitive to enable and configure. Windows Server 2003 Service Pack 1 (SP1) made some significant improvements to ICF, which was renamed the Windows Firewall. The Windows Firewall is now enabled when the operating system first boots, and you can make extensive configuration choices through netsh and Group Policy. We'll examine the Windows Firewall in depth in Chapter 3.

See Also

- Chapter 3 for more on Windows Firewall

- Microsoft TechNet: "Administering Windows Firewall" (http://www.microsoft.com/technet/prodtechnol/windowsserver2003/library/Operations/56b0f52e-61c0-4b85-99cb-911ea7b8bafe.mspx)

1-18. Enabling or Disabling TCP/IP Filtering

Problem

You want to enable or disable TCP/IP filtering on a Windows Server 2003 computer.

Solution

Using a Graphical User Interface

1. Open the Network Connections applet.

2. Double-click on the Local Area Connection icon.

3. Click on Internet Protocol (TCP/IP), and select Properties.

4. Click on Advanced. From the Options tab, select TCP/IP Filtering and select Properties.

5. To enable TCP/IP filtering, place a check mark next to Enable TCP/IP Filtering (All Adapters). To disable TCP/IP filtering, clear this check box.

6. Click OK when you're finished.

Using a Command-Line Interface

To configure this setting via the command line, you first need to create a .reg file containing the Registry key described in the next section, and then use Regedit to import the file into your local Registry.

You can use a shell script to automate the process of creating the Registry key as follows:

```
set TFILE=%TEMP%\HWIDfile.tmp
set ON=00000001
set OFF=00000000

echo Windows Registry Editor Version 5.00 >%TFILE%
echo >> %TFILE%
echo [HKEY_LOCAL_MACHINE\SYSTEM\CurrentControlSet\
    Services\Tcpip\Parameters\] >>%TFILE%
echo "EnableSecurityFilters"=dword:%ON% >>%TFILE%

:: regedit /s %TFILE%

del %TFILE% >null
```

Using the Registry

To enable TCP/IP filtering for all interfaces on a Windows Server 2003 computer, set the following Registry value:

```
[HKEY_LOCAL_MACHINE\SYSTEM\CurrentControlSet\Services\Tcpip\Parameters\]
"EnableSecurityFilters"=dword:1
```

To disable TCP/IP filters, set the previous DWORD key to 0. There is no need to reboot after making either of these changes.

Using VBScript

This code enables TCP/IP filtering on all interfaces in a Windows Server 2003 computer:

```
' ------ SCRIPT CONFIGURATION ------
strComputer = "."
' ------ END CONFIGURATION ---------

Set objWMIService = GetObject("winmgmts:\\" & strComputer & "\root\cimv2")
Set nicConfig = objWMIService.Get("Win32_NetworkAdapterConfiguration")

If Not nicConfig.IPFilterSecurityEnabled Then
  Filtering = nicConfig.EnableIPFilterSec(True)
    If Filtering = 0 Then
      WScript.Echo "Success! IP Filtering enabled."
    ElseIf Filtering = 1 Then
      WScript.Echo "Success! IP Filtering enabled, please reboot."
    Else
      WScript.Echo "Error! Unable to enable IP Filtering."
    End If
Else
  WScript.Echo "IP Filtering has already been enabled."
End If
```

How It Works

While it isn't as fully functional as using IP Security (IPSec), you can enable basic TCP/IP filtering on a Windows Server 2003 NIC to restrict network access to the local computer. By default, a 2003 NIC passes all TCP/IP traffic without any restriction, but you can enable TCP/IP filtering on a per-interface basis. To protect against connectivity loss while you're configuring filtering, IP filtering will allow all traffic to pass when it is first enabled. You'll then need to configure access to individual ports after enabling filtering for an interface, as you'll see in the next recipe.

See Also

- Recipe 1-19 for creating a TCP/IP filter

- Chapter 8 for more on Internet Protocol Security (IPSec)

- Brian Posey, "Filtering TCP/IP Packets" (http://www.brienposey.com/kb/filtering_tcp_ip_packets.asp)

- Microsoft KB 816792: "How to Configure TCP/IP Filtering in Windows Server 2003"

1-19. Creating a TCP/IP Filter

Problem

You want to create a TCP/IP filter for a Windows Server 2003 computer.

Solution

Using a Graphical User Interface

1. Open the Network Connections applet.

2. Double-click on the Local Area Connection icon.

3. Click on Internet Protocol (TCP/IP), and select Properties.

4. Click on Advanced. From the Options tab, select TCP/IP Filtering and select Properties.

5. To enable TCP/IP filtering, place a check mark next to Enable TCP/IP Filtering (All Adapters). To create a filter that allows only TCP port 80, select the radio button next to Allow Only in the TCP Ports Section. Click Add, and enter 80 in the TCP Port text box. Click OK when you're finished.

Using the Registry

To configure a TCP filter to allow traffic on ports 80 and 443, set the following Registry value, or enter the ports that you wish to configure for your environment:

```
[HKEY_LOCAL_MACHINE\SYSTEM\CurrentControlSet\Services\
Tcpip\Parameters\Interfaces\{<Interface GUID>}\]
"TcpAllowedPorts"=REG_MULTI_SZ: 80 443
```

Caution Entering 0 here indicates that all ports are allowed. Configuring this key with an empty list means that no traffic can pass.

To configure a User Datagram Protocol (UDP) filter, set the following Registry key:

```
[HKEY_LOCAL_MACHINE\SYSTEM\CurrentControlSet\Services\
Tcpip\Parameters\Interfaces\{<Interface GUID>}\
"UDPAllowedPorts"=REG_MULTI_SZ: "<UDP Port>"
```

To configure an IP filter, set the following key:

```
[HKEY_LOCAL_MACHINE\SYSTEM\CurrentControlSet\Services\
Tcpip\Parameters\Interfaces\{<Interface GUID>}\
"RawIPAllowedPorts"=REG_MULTI_SZ: "<IP Port>"
```

Note All of the values in this section can accept multiple entries separated by pressing the Enter key.

Using VBScript

This code configures a TCP/IP filter that will only allow TCP traffic on port 80. To enable TCP/IP filtering, use the script in Recipe 1-18.

```
' ------ SCRIPT CONFIGURATION ------
Const ALLOW_ALL = 0
Const HTTP = 80
TCPPorts = Array(HTTP)
UDPPorts = Array(ALLOW_ALL)
IPProtocols = Array(ALLOW_ALL)

strComputer = "."
' ------ END CONFIGURATION ---------

Set objWMIService = GetObject("winmgmts:\\" & strComputer & "\root\cimv2")
Set nics = objWMIService.ExecQuery _
 ("Select * From Win32_NetworkAdapterConfiguration Where IPEnabled = True")

For Each nic in nics
  intPorts = nic.EnableIPSec(TCPPorts, UDPPorts, IPProtocols)
  If intPorts = 0 Then
    WScript.Echo "Success! Filtering enabled for TCP port 80."
  ElseIf intIPSecReturn = 1 Then
    WScript.Echo "Success! Filtering enabled for TCP port 80, please reboot!"
  Else
    WScript.Echo "Error! Unable to enable IP filtering for TCP port 80."
  End If
Next
```

How It Works

Unlike Internet Protocol Security (IPSec), which provides granular control over the kinds of traffic that can pass over a particular interface, TCP/IP filtering only allows for the most basic "all-or-nothing" filtering for any interface on which it is enabled. (TCP/IP filtering was used in earlier versions of the Windows Server operating systems to provide basic filtering capabilities before the development of ICF and the Windows Firewall.) TCP/IP filtering will filter the following types of network traffic:

- TCP traffic

- UDP traffic

- IP traffic

In all three cases, TCP/IP filtering will either allow *all* traffic to pass through, or only the specific ports or protocols that you allow. So if you configure TCP/IP filtering to allow only port 80 for TCP traffic, then any traffic destined for an FTP server on port 21 or an HTTPS resource on port 443 will not reach the local computer—only HTTP traffic will be accepted once this filter is in place. In Chapter 7 we will look at the use of IPSec to create much more granular filtering controls for traffic on a Windows Server 2003 computer. TCP/IP filtering does not preclude the need for a more fully featured software- or hardware-based firewall, but it is one of many steps that you can take to reduce the overall attack surface on a network-connected computer.

See Also

- Recipe 7-3 for more on creating filters using IPSec
- Recipe 7-9 to learn about creating an IPSec policy

1-20. Configuring an IPv6 Address

Problem

You want to configure an IPv6 address on a Windows Server 2003 computer.

Solution

The following command enables IPv6 and configures an IP address of ea92::3162:c0fa:fe30:4357 with a DNS server address of FEDA::0:1:FFFF:9 (modify these values as necessary to suit your environment):

```
> netsh interface ipv6 install
> netsh interface ipv6 set address "Local Area Connection" ea92::3162:c0fa:fe30:4357
> netsh interface ipv6 add dns "Local Area Connection" FEDA::0:1:FFFF:9
```

■**Caution** You can disable IPv6 support by using the `netsh interface ipv6 uninstall` command. However, this will require a reboot to take effect.

How It Works

TCP/IP version 6, or IPv6, is the next generation of the IPv4 TCP/IP protocol that has existed almost unchanged since the early days of the Internet. One of the primary motivators behind the development of IPv6 was the fear that the 32-bit address space afforded by IPv4 would soon be exhausted. IPv6 offers a 128-bit address space that will not be exhausted within any reasonable timeframe. Instead of displaying IP addresses using dotted decimal format as we're familiar with in IPv4, IPv6 addresses use hexadecimal numbers to display address information in 16-bit chunks separated by colons.

■**Note** The IPv6 address syntax is referred to as *colon-hexadecimal*.

The concern about IP address conservation has become somewhat less urgent with the proliferation of network address translation (NAT) devices and proxy servers that have helped to reduce the consumption of publicly available IP addresses. However, IPv6 still offers a number of advances for internetworking, including built-in security and quality of service (QoS) functionality. IPv6 also has improved support for auto-configuration of IPv6 addresses—in many cases administrators won't even need to assign IPv6 addresses to machines on a single subnet, since the built-in auto-configuration support will take care of the heavy lifting.

Windows Server 2003 and Windows XP with a minimum of Service Pack 1 both offer complete support for IPv6 functions in production environments. This is an improvement over earlier IPv6 support that was not supported by Microsoft's Product Support Services (PSS) in anything other than a test or research environment.

Using a Command-Line Interface

If there is one drawback to IPv6 configuration in Windows Server 2003, it is that you can only perform it using the netsh utility: IPv6 configuration isn't currently available using WMI, VBScript, or a GUI interface. On the plus side, the commands available in the `netsh interface ipv6` context are nearly identical in syntax to those found under `netsh interface ip`.

■ **Caution** If you are migrating or upgrading from a Windows 2000 environment, you need to know that the `ipv6.exe` command-line utility is no longer supported in Windows Server 2003. All IPv6 configuration in Windows Server 2003 takes place using the `netsh` utility.

See Also

- Microsoft TechNet: "Introduction to IPv6" (`http://www.microsoft.com/technet/itsolutions/network/ipv6/introipv6.mspx`)

- Microsoft TechNet: "Migrating IPv6.exe Commands to Netsh Commands" (`http://www.microsoft.com/technet/itsolutions/network/ipv6/ipv62netshtable.mspx`)

- Microsoft KB 325449: "How to Install and Configure IP Version 6 in Windows Server 2003 Enterprise Server"

1-21. Renaming a Network Connection

Problem

You want to rename a network connection in a Windows Server 2003 computer to make it more easily recognizable within the Network Connections Control Panel applet.

Solution

Using a Graphical User Interface

1. Open the Network Connections applet.

2. Right-click on the connection that you want to change, and click Rename.

3. Type the new name for the network connection, and press Enter.

Using the Registry

To rename an individual network connection, set the following Registry value:

```
[HKEY_LOCAL_MACHINE\SYSTEM\CurrentControlSet\Control\Network\
{4D26E972-E325-11CE-BFC1-08002BE10318}\<Interface GUID>\Connection\]
"Name"=reg_sz:"<Connection Name>"
```

How It Works

When you are working with a multi-homed computer, the default names that are given to network connections in the Network Connections Control Panel applet ("Local Area Connection," "Local Area Connection 1," "Local Area Connection 2," and so on) can be somewhat inadequate to give you a clear picture of their purpose. To make it easier to manage a multi-homed server on a day-to-day basis, it's helpful to rename each network connection to a name that's indicative of its function in the server: you might have one connection named "LAN," one named "Heartbeat," and one named "VPN," for example. This is also useful when it comes time to troubleshoot a network connection in your Windows Server 2003 computer—to help ensure that you don't inadvertently disable or change a setting for the incorrect network connection.

1-22. Enabling or Disabling a Network Connection

Problem

You want to enable or disable a network connection in a Windows Server 2003 computer to control whether or not it is capable of passing network traffic.

Solution

Using a Graphical User Interface

1. Open the Network Connections applet.

2. Right-click on the connection that you want to modify. Click Disable to disable the connection, or Enable to bring the NIC back to a working state.

■**Note** You can also enable or disable a network connection using the Device Manager applet, or from the Network Connections status icon in your system tray if you've enabled it.

Using a Command-Line Interface

The following command will disable a particular network adapter in a Windows Server 2003 computer. This command uses the devcon.exe utility, which you can download from the Microsoft website from KB 311272. Devcon.exe requires the value of the PnpInstanceID REG_SZ key found in the HKEY_LOCAL_MACHINE\SYSTEM\CurrentControlSet\Control\Network\ {4D26E972-E325-11CE-BFC1-08002BE10318}\<*Interface GUID*>\Connection Registry key referenced in Recipe 1-21.

```
> devcon -r disable PCI\VEN_14E4&DEV_1677&SUBSYS_01791028&REV_01\4&1D
7EFF9E&0&00E0
```

How It Works

The reasons for enabling or disabling a network interface card are numerous. If you have unused NICs installed in a Windows Server 2003 computer, you can disable the ones that are not in use to simplify the configuration of your server. You might also want to temporarily disable network traffic while restoring files, performing a disaster recovery operation, or attempting to troubleshoot a hardware issue on the server.

The devcon.exe utility is a command-line equivalent to the Device Manager GUI, and it is freely downloadable from the Microsoft website. Devcon is a powerful utility that can enable and disable devices, update device drivers, and list the hardware resources that are being used by a particular device. But the power of devcon also means there is a potential hazard in using it: since you are able to enable or disable multiple devices at once through the use of the * wildcard, you need to be careful not to disable the wrong device, or more devices than you intend to. You can read the help information for devcon by typing devcon help at the command line.

1-23. Configuring a Network Bridge

Problem

You want to configure a network bridge on a Windows Server 2003 computer. Using a network bridge allows the Windows Server 2003 server to connect multiple LAN connections together, enabling communication between them without requiring additional or third-party router hardware or software.

Solution

Using a Graphical User Interface

1. Open the Network Connections applet.

2. Select the connections that you want to include in the network bridge.

3. Right-click the connections and select Bridge Connections.

■**Caution** Be certain that you do not create a bridged connection between your private network and a connection to a public network such as the Internet. Doing so will leave your network in a vulnerable state, where users on the public network can easily access internal resources.

Using Group Policy

While the network bridge is a useful technology for a home network or a small office, you will generally want to disable the ability to configure network bridging in a larger corporate environment. You can use Group Policy to disable the Bridge Connections menu option by configuring the setting shown in Table 1-6.

Table 1-6. *Network Bridge Settings*

Path	`Computer Configuration\Administrative Templates\Network\` `Network Connections`
Policy name	Prohibit installation and configuration of Network Bridge on your DNS domain network
Value	`Enabled` to prevent users from creating a network bridge

■**Caution** Enabling this setting in Group Policy will not remove a network bridge from a computer where one is already configured; this will simply prevent users from creating a *new* network bridge.

How It Works

Prior to the release of Windows XP and Windows Server 2003, the only way to connect a network that consisted of more than one LAN segment was to configure software- or hardware-based routing or bridging. (A *bridge* is necessary to connect networks using different media types, such as an Ethernet network and a network that uses wireless connectivity.) The network bridge that is built into Windows XP and Windows Server 2003 greatly simplifies this process; you simply need to select the connection to each separate network and click Bridge Connections on the right-click context menu. No further configuration is needed to enable communication between the two networks; it is all handled automatically by the bridge.

After you've configured the bridge, you'll see a new Network Bridge icon in the Network Connections applet. If you need to make a change to the configuration of any of the connections after they've been bridged, you'll use the Network Bridge icon to make the change—it has effectively taken over the network configuration of the bridged connections.

CHAPTER 2

■■■

Windows Internet Name Service (WINS)

The Windows Internet Name Service (WINS) is one of Microsoft's solutions to resolve computer names to their corresponding IP addresses. WINS is not a new technology; it was implemented in Windows NT 3.51 Server to facilitate name resolution when management of Lmhosts files became overwhelming.

WINS is one of the technologies that facilitates the "browsing" of a local area network to view other computers and ultimately access their resources. This is most noticeable when a user goes into My Network Places on his or her workstation and sees a list of all computers in the local subnet (or on other subnets that have registrations on the WINS server).

In a typical Windows domain environment, workstations register with a WINS server at boot time. They inform the WINS server that they are online and provide the computer name and respective IP address. In addition, administrators can create static WINS entries for systems that will not self-register.

Is WINS Obsolete?

Prior to the release of Windows 2000, NetBEUI was one of the two primary network protocols in use on Windows networks, the other being TCP/IP. NetBEUI is a lightweight, non-routable, broadcast-based protocol that requires little to no configuration. NetBEUI does not require the presence of WINS, since there are no IP addresses related to NetBIOS names.

Windows 2000 was released with much fanfare regarding its implementation of Active Directory and Domain Name Service (DNS). Administrators were told that they no longer needed to implement NetBEUI on their networks, that NetBIOS would be gradually phased out, and that WINS broadcasts would become a "thing of the past." All NetBIOS lookups would be replaced with pure DNS without any need for network broadcasts.

Although NetBEUI has indeed been removed from most networks, WINS and NetBIOS are still alive and well in Windows 2003 Server networks. Why is this?

DNS is certainly well-suited to locate network resources, especially if or when these resources have been registered in Active Directory. However, many applications still rely on NetBIOS name resolution for their basic functionality, and many users prefer the familiarity of being able to view a list of all computers on their network so that they can browse for the resource that they need. Therefore, we can conclude that WINS is not yet ready for the scrap heap. Perhaps in Windows Vista, or perhaps not.

The Anatomy of a WINS Network

Many small- and medium-sized businesses consist of a single-subnet network. In this environment, any server can be configured as a WINS server. The TCP/IP configuration of workstations can include the IP address of a WINS server so that the workstations will register their NetBIOS computer name and IP address when they boot. (See Recipe 1-13, "Managing WINS Server Lookups.")

The efficiency and redundancy of WINS networks can be enhanced by establishing multiple WINS servers, each of which can be configured to replicate another in a topology and over a time interval that is appropriate to the particular environment.

WINS replication is also important in environments that span multiple subnets, or even multiple geographic sites. Rather than having to query a non-local WINS server, workstations will query the closest one, which in turn has received its data through replication with other WINS servers. Not only does this allow for more efficient communication (which is most important to the network administrator), but it allows end users to browse resources that are located on the distant subnets. This is helpful for businesses that contain a central office and multiple remote sites, for example.

The overall network topology significantly affects WINS replication and network performance in general. You want replication to occur frequently enough so that network services will not be disrupted if a given WINS server is not available or does not contain the latest data, but not so often that it will become a disruption due to resource usage.

For small, non-routed LANs, bandwidth is not usually a major problem. In these environments, maintaining a persistent connection between servers and having replication occur relatively frequently will not produce a significant bottleneck in network communications.

However, larger organizations that may have sites separated by a large geographic distance and that may be connected by slow or inefficient WAN links must pay much closer attention to the network traffic generated by any service that is in operation over the network. To minimize network disruption, you should not enable persistent, WINS replication connections, and you should also consider increasing the interval at which replication occurs. For example, if you have one office in the United States and another in China, you may not need rapid replication. It may be sufficient to configure replication to occur only once or twice per day. In this chapter, we'll cover these tasks and many more related to managing a WINS environment.

Using a Graphical User Interface

All recipes that involve WINS management through a graphical user interface will refer to the WINS MMC snap-in utility, accessed from the Administrative Tools folder within the Start menu. In addition, you can access it directly at %systemroot%\system32\winsmgmt.msc.

Using a Command-Line Interface

In Windows Server 2003, the netsh command provides a command-line interface to manage WINS. In this chapter, all recipes with command-line solutions will be based on netsh. This syntax is documented on the Microsoft website and can be viewed by issuing the netsh help command.

To access the netsh interface for the local server, open a command prompt and issue the following commands, either one per line or all on a single line:

```
> netsh
> wins
> server
```

You can also connect to other WINS servers by appending the IP address or the server name to the third line, like this:

```
> server 10.0.0.2
```

or this:

```
> server \\WINS1
```

Additionally, you can view the full syntax of the netsh wins commands by appending /? at the end of any statement. For example, netsh wins server /? will bring up the detailed syntax of this command.

Only administrators on the WINS server are able to modify WINS settings through netsh wins. If you want to provide a user with read-only access to WINS via netsh wins, add the user to the server's WINS Users group.

Using the Registry

There are a number of entries in the Windows Registry that will allow you to modify parameters needed to configure WINS, with the exception of replication-related parameters. All entries are located at

```
HKEY_LOCAL_MACHINE\SYSTEM\CurrentControlSet\Services\Wins\Parameters
```

We provide the usual warning when editing the Registry: do so with care. Modifying the Registry incorrectly can leave your server in an unusable state.

Using VBScript

Unfortunately, there is not a built-in scripting interface through which to administer WINS at the server level. However, you can call the netsh wins command-line functions from a VBScript using the following syntax:

```
' This code will instantiate a WSH object and execute the desired command.
' ------ SCRIPT CONFIGURATION ------
' Enter the desired netsh wins command between the quotation marks,
' as in the example below
strCommand = "netsh wins server init scavenge"
' ------ END CONFIGURATION ---------
set objShell = CreateObject("WScript.Shell")
set objExec = objShell.Exec(strCommand)
' Run in a loop while the command is executing
```

```
Do While objExec.Status = 0
    WScript.Sleep 1000
Loop
' Delete the objects from memory once the command is completed.
Set objExec = Nothing
Set objShell = Nothing
```

Because this syntax is the same regardless of the `netsh wins` command or parameters, we will not discuss this method in each recipe. Instead, you should refer to the sections of recipes that describe using the command line and then place the appropriate command into the preceding script.

2-1. Installing WINS

Problem

You want to install the WINS service.

Solution

Using a Graphical User Interface

1. Start the Add or Remove Programs control panel applet.

2. Click the Add/Remove Windows Components button in the left pane.

3. When the Add/Remove Windows Components screen appears, scroll down to and select Networking Services and click the Details button.

4. Place a check in the check box next to Windows Internet Name Service (WINS).

5. Click OK to accept the selection, and then click Next to proceed with the installation.

6. Supply your original Windows installation media, or point to the location of the i386 directory, if prompted.

7. Manage your WINS server through the WINS Management console as follows:

   • Access the WINS Management console at the server console either from the Administrative Tools folder of the Start ➤ Run menu or by running `winsmgmt.msc` from `c:\windows\system32`.

   • Access the WINS Management console from a Windows XP workstation by installing the adminpak.msi utilities on your workstation. These are located on the server at `c:\windows\system32\adminpak.msi`. Once installed, follow the same procedure as if you were managing WINS at the server console.

Using a Command-Line Interface

You can install WINS or any other Windows service from the command line using the System Stand-Alone Optional Component Manager (sysocmgr.exe), which is built into Windows. Use this utility with the following syntax in a command prompt:

```
> sysocmgr /i:%windir%\inf\sysoc.inf /u:<path to answer file>
```

In this code, `<path to answer file>` is the only variable, and it represents a text file that you create. For example, create an answer file at c:\ocm.txt that contains the following two lines:

```
[NetOptionalComponents]
Wins=1
```

and then run the following command:

```
> sysocmgr /i:%windir%\inf\sysoc.inf /u:c:\ocm.txt
```

How It Works

The installation of WINS is fairly trivial and requires a minimal amount of time to complete. It is not necessary to restart the server after installing the service. Note that the WINS server should have a static IP address in order for WINS clients or replication partners to communicate with it without disruption of service.

See Also

- Microsoft KB 314978: "How to Use Adminpak.msi to Install a Specific Server Administration Tool in Windows." This provides a description of adminpak.msi and its components.

- Microsoft KB 222444: "How to Add or Remove Windows Components with Sysocmgr.exe." This provides the full syntax of the sysocmgr.exe utility, including other parameters that can be used to customize its operation.

2-2. Displaying Server Statistics

Problem

You want to display a summary of basic WINS statistics.

Solution

You can display general information about WINS using the following command:

```
> netsh wins server show info
```

The following is an example of the output from the show info command:

```
c:\>netsh wins server show info

***You have Read and Write access to the server widget.nuthaus.local***

WINS Database backup parameter
~~~~~~~~~~~~~~~~~~~~~~~~~~~~~~~~~~~~~~~~~~~~~~~~~~~~~~~~~~~~~~~~~~~~~~~

Backup Dir                      : c:\wins_bak
Backup on Shutdown              : Enabled

Name Record Settings(day:hour:minute)
~~~~~~~~~~~~~~~~~~~~~~~~~~~~~~~~~~~~~~~~~~~~~~~~~~~~~~~~~~~~~~~~~~~~~~~

Refresh Interval                : 000:00:40
Extinction(Tombstone) Interval  : 000:00:40
Extinction(Tombstone) TimeOut   : 001:00:00
Verification Interval           : 024:00:00

Database consistency checking parameters :
~~~~~~~~~~~~~~~~~~~~~~~~~~~~~~~~~~~~~~~~~~~~~~~~~~~~~~~~~~~~~~~~~~~~~~~

Periodic Checking               : Enabled
Max no. of records check each period  : 30000
Check database against          : Owner Server
Check database every            : 24 hours
Starting at(hour:minute:second) : 02:00:00

WINS Logging Parameters:
~~~~~~~~~~~~~~~~~~~~~~~~~~~~~~~~~~~~~~~~~~~~~~~~~~~~~~~~~~~~~~~~~~~~~~~

Log Database changes to JET log files : Enabled
Log details events to System Event Log : Disabled

Burst Handling Parameters :
~~~~~~~~~~~~~~~~~~~~~~~~~~~~~~~~~~~~~~~~~~~~~~~~~~~~~~~~~~~~~~~~~~~~~~~

Burst Handling State            : Enabled
Burst handing queue size        : 500

Start Version Counter ( in hex )
~~~~~~~~~~~~~~~~~~~~~~~~~~~~~~~~~~~~~~~~~~~~~~~~~~~~~~~~~~~~~~~~~~~~~~~
Start Version Count(High , Low)  :  0 , 0

Command completed successfully.
```

How It Works

There are many details that you may want to understand regarding the configuration of the WINS server. However, there are also times when a simple summary will be sufficient; for these cases, you can use the `netsh wins server show info` command.

If you require more detail than is provided by `netsh wins server show info`, you can append values other than `info` to the command, such as the following:

`Browser`: Displays all active domain master browser records for the indicated WINS server

`Database`: Displays the database and records for specified owner servers

`Name`: Displays detailed information about a specified record in the WINS database

`Partner`: Displays all replication partners for the given WINS server and indicates the associated replication type

`Server`: Displays the NetBIOS name and the IP address of the given WINS server

`Statistics`: Displays date statistics for WINS events, such as service start time and last replication time

`Version`: Displays the maximum version counter value for the given WINS server

For a complete list and a description of each item, run `netsh wins server show help` or `netsh wins server show /?`.

2-3. Checking the Consistency of the WINS Database

Problem

You want to force the database to update its statistics and verify its consistency at a regular interval and against a particular server.

Solution

Using a Graphical User Interface

1. Open the WINS MMC snap-in.

2. Right-click the server object in the left pane, and select Properties.

3. Enable the Automatically Update Statistics Every check box.

4. Enter the time interval at which you want to update the statistics.

5. Select the Database Verification tab.

6. Enable the Verify Database Consistency check box, and enter the interval in hours at which you want this to occur.

7. Set the start time for the initial verification by entering information in the Begin Verifying At fields.

8. Enter the maximum number of records that you want to verify, if appropriate.

9. Select an option to verify the database against the owner server or against a randomly selected partner.

10. Click OK to save changes.

Using a Command-Line Interface

You can use the `netsh wins server set periodicdbchecking` command to force the database to update its statistics and verify its consistency at a regular interval and against a particular server. Use the following syntax:

```
> netsh wins server set periodicdbchecking [[State=]{0 | 1}]
    [[MaxRec=]Value] [[CheckAgainst=]{0 | 1}] [[CheckEvery=]Value] [[Start=]Value]
```

Here is a description of the command-line options:

`State`: Required value to specify whether to check the database or not. A value of 0 will not check the database; a value of 1 will check it.

`MaxRec`: Optional parameter that specifies the number of records to check. The default value is 30,000.

`CheckAgainst`: Optional parameter that specifies where the consistency check should occur. A value of 0 will check against the owner-server; a value of 1 will check against a randomly selected server.

`CheckEvery`: Optional parameter that specifies the time interval, in hours, at which the consistency check should occur. The default interval is 24 hours.

`Start`: Optional parameter that specifies the time, in seconds, after which you want your first check to occur.

For example, use this command to check a maximum of 500 records in the database against the owner server every two hours and starting in one hour:

```
> netsh wins server set periodicdbchecking State=1
    MacRec=500 CheckAgainst=0 CheckEvery=2 Start=3600
```

Using the Registry

You can set the maximum number of records that are replicated during a database consistency check by creating or modifying the following Registry value:

```
[HKEY_LOCAL_MACHINE\SYSTEM\CurrentControlSet\Services\Wins\Parameters\]
"MaxRecsAtATime"=dword:<NumRecords>
```

Set the value of <NumRecords> in decimal mode as an integer with a minimum value of 1,000. The default value is 30,000 and there is no maximum value.

How It Works

A database consistency check is not a validation of the health of the database itself, but rather a check of the integrity of the records within the database, especially as compared to the databases of remote servers. If a remote record is identical to a local record, its time stamp is updated; however, if the remote record is newer than the local record, then the local record is marked for deletion and is replaced with the newer data.

The frequency at which you run this check depends on the overall health of your WINS environment. The default value of one check per day is sufficient for most organizations, as is the default value for the number of records to check.

See Also

Microsoft KB 167704: "Explanation of Windows NT 4.0 WINS Consistency Checking." This KB article was originally written for Windows NT 4.0 Server, but the process has remained relatively unchanged.

2-4. Configuring a Backup of the Database

Problem

You want to specify the path for a backup of the WINS database and enable it to be backed up whenever the server shuts down.

Solution

Using a Graphical User Interface

1. Open the WINS MMC snap-in.

2. Right-click the server object in the left pane, and select Properties. (The General tab should be selected by default.)

3. Enter or browse to the directory in which you want to store the database backup.

4. Select the Backup Database During Server Shutdown check box.

5. Click OK to save the changes.

Using a Command-Line Interface

You can configure backup parameters for the WINS database using the following command:

```
> netsh wins server set backuppath [Dir=]NewPath [[Shutdown=]{0 | 1}]
```

Here is a description of the command-line options:

Dir: Required parameter that specifies the folder in which you want to store the backup, such as C:\WinsBackup. The default path is simply c:\.

Shutdown: Optional parameter that specifies whether you want the backup to occur when the server shuts down. A value of 0 will disable automated backups; a value of 1 will enable them. The default value is 0.

For example, use the following command to tell the WINS server to back up its database each time the server shuts down and to store the backup in c:\wins_bak:

```
> netsh wins server set backuppath Dir=c:\wins_bak shutdown=1
```

Using the Registry

You can set the path to the backup folder by creating or modifying the following Registry value:

```
[HKEY_LOCAL_MACHINE\SYSTEM\CurrentControlSet\Services\WINS\Parameters\]
"BackupDirPath"="<BackupPath>"
```

Set the value of <BackupPath> to the actual path of the directory within the file system, such as c:\wins_bak.

You can set the option to back up the database whenever WINS stops by creating or modifying the following Registry value:

```
[HKEY_LOCAL_MACHINE\SYSTEM\CurrentControlSet\Services\WINS\Parameters\]
"DoBackupOnTerm"=dword:1
```

You can specify the time interval between consistency checks by creating or modifying the following Registry value, specified in seconds:

```
[HKEY_LOCAL_MACHINE\SYSTEM\CurrentControlSet\Services\WINS\Parameters\]
"TimeInterval"=dword:<Interval>
```

Specify <Interval> in decimal mode with a minimum value of 21,600, which corresponds to six hours.

How It Works

You might be wondering whether there really is a need to back up the WINS database.

In many small- to medium-sized businesses that have a single WINS server with only dynamically registered entries, the truth is that backups may not be necessary. If the server crashed and all data were lost, the server could be rebuilt, workstations could be restarted, and the registration process would populate the new database.

However, it is common to also include static entries for devices that might not have the ability to self-register, such as network printers or systems on a remote subnet. For those cases, recreating the database would be more time-consuming, as you would need to manually enter data into the database.

Even with simple database corruption, having a readily accessible database copy would greatly simplify and expedite the recovery process.

See Also

- See Recipe 2-5 for backing up the database.

- See Recipe 2-6 for restoring the database.

- Microsoft KB 251067: "WINS Registry Parameters for Windows 2000." This KB article was originally written for Windows 2000 Server, but the Registry entries also apply to Windows 2003.

2-5. Initiating a Backup of the Database

Problem

You want to manually start a backup of the WINS database.

Solution

Using a Graphical User Interface

1. Open the WINS MMC snap-in.

2. Right-click the server object in the left pane, and select Backup Database.

3. Browse to the folder in which you want to save the database, and click OK.

Using a Command-Line Interface

You can initiate a backup of the database using the following command:

```
> netsh wins server init backup [Dir=]BackupDir [Type=]{0 | 1}
```

Here is a description of the command-line options:

Dir: Optional parameter that specifies the path to the folder in which you want to store the backup. If omitted, the value specified in the WINS server's global properties will be used.

Type: Optional parameter that specifies the type of backup to perform. A value of 0 will provide a full backup; a value of 1 will provide an incremental backup. The default backup type is full.

For example, use this command to start an incremental backup and store it in c:\wins_bak:

```
> netsh wins server init backup dir=c:\wins_bak type=1
```

How It Works

This command is most useful when you cannot wait for the scheduled backup to occur. For example, if you are planning to apply a service pack or make other changes to the server, you will want to make certain that you have a fallback copy of the latest database.

Note that backups of remote servers are not supported through this command.

See Also

- Recipe 2-4 for configuring a backup of the database.

- Microsoft KB 251067: "WINS Registry Parameters for Windows 2000." This KB article was originally written for Windows 2000 Server, but the Registry entries also apply to Windows 2003.

2-6. Restoring the Database

Problem

You want to manually restore the WINS database.

Solution

Using a Graphical User Interface

1. Open the WINS MMC snap-in.

2. Stop the WINS service by right-clicking the server object and selecting All Tasks ➤ Stop to stop the service. (The option to restore the database will not be available unless this step is performed.)

3. Right-click the server object again, and select Restore Database.

4. Browse to the root of the database restore directory, typically c:\wins_bak, and click OK to restore the database.

Using a Command-Line Interface

You can restore the database from a saved copy using the following command:

```
> netsh wins server init restore [Dir=]RestoreDir
```

Dir is the only command-line option—it is a required parameter that specifies the folder from which you want to restore the backup, such as c:\wins_bak. This folder may also include a subdirectory of the same name, but this subdirectory should not be specified in the path. For example, use this command to restore the WINS database from c:\wins_bak:

```
> netsh wins server init restore dir=c:\wins_bak
```

How It Works

Restoring a database is typically done to recover from corruption. It is a fairly straightforward and quick process. Note the following points for correct database recovery:

- The command can only be executed on a server on which the WINS service is already stopped. Attempting to run it on an operational WINS server will result in failure.

- A database can only be restored locally; the command cannot be used to restore a database to a remote server.

- The path specified in the Dir parameter must match the path specified in the properties of the backup option.

See Also

- Microsoft KB 244810: "Restoring a Windows 2000 WINS Database from Other Backup Sources."

- Microsoft KB 235609: "Recovering a WINS Database from Other Backup Sources." This KB article describes the process of restoring a WINS database from third-party media.

2-7. Displaying All Records by Owner

Problem

You want to display all records registered to, or owned by, your WINS server.

Solution

Using a Graphical User Interface

1. Open the WINS MMC snap-in.

2. Expand the server object in the left pane.

3. Right-click the Active Registrations node in the left pane, and select Display Records. Perform step 4, 5, or 6 to filter the results, or simply proceed to step 7 to display the unfiltered results.

4. To filter results by record mapping, follow these steps:

   a. Select the Record Mapping tab.

   b. Select the Filter Records Matching This Name Pattern check box to restrict the query results to a single name.

   c. Select the Filter Records Matching This IP Address check box to restrict the query to a single IP address. Also select the Match the IP Address Based on This Subnet Mask check box if desired.

5. To filter results by record owner, follow these steps:

   a. Select the Record Owners tab.

   b. Select the check boxes corresponding to the owner-servers that you want to include in the query. (The owner-server is the server on which the WINS record was initially registered.)

   c. Clear the check boxes corresponding to the owner-servers that you want to exclude from the query.

   d. Click the Select Local button to select only the local server.

   e. Click the Select All or Clear All buttons as needed.

6. To filter results by record type, follow these steps:

   a. Select the Record Types tab.

   b. Select the check boxes corresponding to the record types that you want to include in the query.

   c. Clear the check boxes corresponding to the record types that you want to exclude from the query.

   d. Click the Select All or Clear All buttons as needed.

7. Click the Find Now button to process the query.

Using a Command-Line Interface

You can display the WINS database using the following command-line syntax:

```
> netsh wins server show database [Servers=]{IPAddresses}
    [[RecType=]{0 | 1 | 2}] [[Count=]Count] [[Start=]{0 | 1}]
    [[EndChar=]16thCharInHex] [[File=]FileName]
```

Here is a description of the command-line options:

Servers: Required parameter that specifies the IP addresses of the owner-server(s) that you want to query. (The owner-server is the server on which the WINS record was initially registered.) Place the values within the curly brackets. Multiple addresses must be separated with commas. Server NetBIOS names should not be used; they will result in failure of the command.

RecType: Optional parameter that specifies the type of record that you want to query. A value of 0 will query both static and dynamic records; a value of 1 will query only static records; and a value of 2 will query only dynamic records. The default query type is both static and dynamic.

Count: Optional parameter that specifies the maximum number of records that you want to return in your query. If omitted, all records within the subset of the RecType parameter will be returned.

Start: Optional parameter that specifies how you want to sort your query results. A value of 0 will sort records from the beginning of the database; a value of 1 will sort records from the end of the database. The default sort order is from the beginning of the database.

EndChar: Optional parameter that specifies the hexadecimal value of the 16th byte of the record type. If omitted, all record types will be returned.

File: Optional parameter that specifies a text file to which you want to save your results.

For example, use this command to generate the first 1,000 dynamic records for the WINS server at 192.168.2.2 and save the results in c:\temp\results.txt:

```
> netsh wins server show database servers={192.168.2.2} rectype=2
    count=1000 start=0 endchar=0 file=C:\temp\results.txt
```

The following output is from a sample netsh wins server show database command. Note the various columns that show data relevant to each record and record type.

```
c:\>netsh wins server show database servers={192.168.2.2}

***You have Read and Write access to the server widget.nuthaus.local***

Description of different fields in the Record Table
~~~~~~~~~~~~~~~~~~~~~~~~~~~~~~~~~~~~~~~~~~~~~~~~~~~~~~~
NAME             = Name of the Record. Upto 16 characters
T                = Type of Record : D - Dynamic, S - Static
S                = State of the Record : A - Active, R - Released,
                                     T - Tombstoned
VERSION          = LowPart ( in Hex)
G                = Address Group : U - Unique, N - Group, I - Internet,
                                 M - Multihomed, D - Domain Name.
IPADDRESS        = List of IP Addresses associated with the Name.
EXPIRATION DATE  = Expiration Time Stamp for the Name Record.

~~~~~~~~~~~~~~~~~~~~~~~~~~~~~~~~~~~~~~~~~~~~~~~~~~~~~~~~~~~~~~~~~~~~~~~~
      NAME         -T-S- VERSION -G-    IPADDRESS    -    EXPIRATION DATE
~~~~~~~~~~~~~~~~~~~~~~~~~~~~~~~~~~~~~~~~~~~~~~~~~~~~~~~~~~~~~~~~~~~~~~~~

Retrieving database from the Wins server 192.168.2.2
--__MSBROWSE__-[01h]-D-T- 2d2     -N- 192.168.2.2   -7/5/2005 8:02:08 AM
NUTHAUS        [1Bh]-D-A- 2b1     -U- 192.168.2.2   -7/4/2005 9:59:08 AM
40LOVE         [00h]-D-T- 2cf     -U- 192.168.2.3   -7/4/2005 10:26:00 PM
40LOVE         [20h]-D-T- 2d0     -U- 192.168.2.3   -7/4/2005 10:26:02 PM
NUTHAUS        [00h]-D-A- 6       -N- 192.168.2.2   -7/4/2005 9:59:08 AM
NUTHAUS        [1Ch]-D-A- 2ce     -I- 192.168.2.2   -7/4/2005 9:59:08 AM
NUTHAUS        [1Eh]-D-T- 2d1     -N- 192.168.2.2   -7/5/2005 8:02:08 AM
SPACECASE      [00h]-S-A- 29e     -U- 192.168.50.50 -Infinite
SPACECASE      [03h]-S-A- 29d     -U- 192.168.50.50 -Infinite
SPACECASE      [20h]-S-A- 29c     -U- 192.168.50.50 -Infinite
```

```
Total No of records retrieved for the server 192.168.2.2 : 10
Total No of records displayed : 10

Command completed successfully.
```

How It Works

One of the first tasks that an administrator typically performs when reviewing WINS settings or resolving issues is to display the WINS database. The database provides insight not only into the systems that are or have been on a network, but also into potential replication problems.

For organizations with hundreds or thousands of entries, viewing all the records of the database is not practical; for this scenario the administrator should use a filtered view.

Windows 2003 Server also allows you to export all records into a text file, which can then be manipulated as needed. This command is available in the graphical user interface and is accessed by right-clicking on the Active Registrations node and selecting Export List.

See Also

WINS help file: "Exporting WINS Console Data." This help file provides additional information on the data export process.

Note Access the help files from the WINS Management Console by selecting the top node of the console's left pane, and then pressing F1 for the help menu.

2-8. Creating a Mapping for a Static Host

Problem

You want to create a static WINS entry for a host that is unable to register dynamically, or for other reasons, such as for name resolution over WAN links in which replication may not occur.

Solution

Using a Graphical User Interface

1. Open the WINS MMC snap-in.

2. Expand the server object in the left pane.

3. Right-click the Active Registrations node in the left pane, and select New Static Mapping.

4. Enter the name of the computer or host in the Computer field.

5. Optionally enter the NetBIOS scope.

6. Enter the type of mapping. Available selections are Unique, Group, Domain Name, Internet Group, or Multihomed.

7. Enter the IP address of the host.

8. Click OK to save the information.

Using a Command-Line Interface

You can create a static mapping in the WINS database using the following command-line syntax:

```
> netsh wins server add name [Name=]ComputerName [[Scope=]ScopeName]
    [[EndChar=]16thCharInHex] [[RecType=]{0 | 1}] [[Group=]{0 | 1 | 2 | 3 | 4}]
    [[Node=]{0 | 1 | 2}] [IP=]{IPAddress1[,IPAddress2,IPAddress3]}
```

Here is a description of the command-line options:

Name: Required parameter that specifies the NetBIOS name of the computer that you want to add to the WINS database.

Scope: Optional parameter that specifies the name of the NetBIOS scope.

EndChar: Optional parameter that specifies the hexadecimal value of the 16th byte of the record type. If omitted, all record types will be returned.

RecType: Optional parameter that specifies the record type. A value of 0 will create a static record; a value of 1 will create a dynamic record. The default record type is static.

Group: Optional parameter that specifies the group type. A value of 0 specifies unique; a value of 1 specifies group; a value of 2 specifies Internet; a value of 3 specifies multi-homed; and a value of 4 specifies a domain name. The default group type is unique.

Node: Optional parameter that specifies the NetBIOS node type. A value of 0 indicates B-node; a value of 1 indicates P-node; and a value of 2 indicates H-node. The default type is P-node.

IP: Required parameter that specifies the IP address of the name record you are adding to the database. If the computer is multi-homed, place the different addresses within a single set of curly brackets and separate addresses with a comma.

For example, use this command to add a static mapping for the multi-homed host named MyNewHost in ScopeA that has IP addresses of 192.168.2.2 and 192.168.2.3:

```
> netsh wins server add name name=MyNewHost scope=ScopeA RecType=0
    Group=3 Node=1 IP={192.168.2.2,192.168.2.3}
```

How It Works

Adding static entries is required for computers or devices that are unable to dynamically register with the WINS server and for which you want name resolution at other systems. Examples of such systems might include network printers or other non-Windows hosts. Since the Windows-based hosts may need to resolve the names and addresses of the non-Windows hosts, it's necessary to perform this step.

Static mappings are also convenient for name resolution across different sites in which replication is not possible. For example, a remote, stand-alone office may need to resolve names across a virtual private network tunnel to a central office. If the two offices are not interconnected with WINS replication, static WINS entries may be an adequate solution for users in the remote office to resolve system names in the central office.

Care must be taken when adding static entries to a replicated WINS environment. Static entries will always overwrite dynamic entries. Therefore, creating a static entry on WINS Server A will overwrite a dynamic entry on WINS Server B. Once the replication cycle begins, the process of removing the erroneous entry becomes more tedious as additional WINS servers are considered.

See Also

- Microsoft KB 140064: "WINS Static Entry Descriptions." This article discusses the different types of host entries, including Unique, Group, Internet Group, and Multihomed.

- Recipe 2-11 for how to convert a static mapping to a dynamic one.

2-9. Deleting a Mapping for a Static Host

Problem

You want to delete the mapping of a static host in the WINS database.

Solution

Using a Graphical User Interface

1. Open the WINS MMC snap-in.

2. Expand the server object in the left pane, and select Active Registrations.

3. Right-click Active Registrations, and run a query to find all records or the particular record of interest (see Recipe 2-7, "Displaying All Records by Owner").

4. In the query results pane, right-click the record that you want to remove, and select Delete. (You can also select multiple records to be deleted simultaneously by holding down the Control key while you make your selections.)

5. Select the option to delete the record only from the current server, or to replicate the change to all servers.

6. Click OK to delete the record.

Using a Command-Line Interface

You can delete a static mapping from the WINS database using the following command:

```
> netsh wins server delete name [Name=]RegisteredName
    [EndChar=]16thCharInHex [[Scope=]ScopeName]
```

Here is a description of the command-line options:

`Name`: Required parameter that specifies the name of the computer that you want to delete from the WINS database.

`EndChar`: Required parameter that specifies the hexadecimal value of the 16th character of the name record that you want to delete.

`Scope`: Optional parameter that specifies the NetBIOS scope name of the record to be deleted.

For example, use this command to delete the messenger (`03`) record for `MyHost` from the WINS database:

```
> netsh wins server delete name name=MyHost endchar=03
```

How It Works

In a single WINS server environment, deleting a host record will permanently remove it from the WINS database. However, if there are multiple WINS servers in use (meaning it is a replicated environment), then the record may be recreated at the next replication interval even if it had been deleted at the owner-server (the WINS server at which the host initially registered). To avoid this scenario and to remove the record from all WINS servers, Windows offers the "tombstone" process.

A record marked as tombstoned is flagged as inactive or "extinct" on the owner-server. This flag is replicated to all other WINS servers so that the record will not be accessed for name resolution. Once the tombstone flag has been replicated to all partners in the network, and after a specific time interval, it will be officially removed from the database.

See Also

- Microsoft KB 177140: "How to Remove Static WINS Entries from All WINS Servers." This article describes techniques to remove static entries in a replicated environment. The article was originally written for Windows NT 4.0, but the concepts are still relevant.

- WINS help file: "Deleting Records." This help file provides a detailed description of the tombstoning process.

2-10. Importing a Lmhosts File

Problem

You want to create static mappings by importing entries from a Lmhosts or other text file.

Solution

Using a Graphical User Interface

1. Open the WINS MMC snap-in.

2. Expand the server object in the left pane, and select Active Registrations.

3. Right-click Active Registrations, and select Import Lmhosts File.

4. Browse to the location of your Lmhosts file and select Open. (By default, the Lmhosts file is located in `%SystemRoot%\system32\drivers\etc`.)

Using a Command-Line Interface

You can import data from your Lmhosts file using the following command:

```
> netsh wins server init import [File=]"ImportFile"
```

`File` is a required parameter that specifies the path to the Lmhosts file that contains the records to be imported into the WINS database.

For example, use this command to import the host information from the `ListOfAddresses` file located in `c:\temp`:

```
> netsh wins server init import file="c:\temp\ListOfAddresses"
```

How It Works

Adding records to the WINS database is a fairly straightforward matter (see Recipe 2-8), but it can be a time-consuming and error-prone inconvenience when multiple entries are needed. For this reason, Windows provides functionality to import these entries from a Lmhosts text file.

The minimum syntax for an entry in the Lmhosts file is as follows:

```
IP Address    DeviceName
```

For example:

```
192.168.0.2    MyServer
```

Each entry should be placed on its own line in the Lmhosts file. Do not precede the line with the pound (#) symbol, as this will flag the line as a comment rather than an actual entry or command.

See Also

- Microsoft KB 180094 and 314108: "How to Write an LMHOSTS File for Domain Validation and Other Name Resolution Issues." These articles describe the Lmhosts syntax.

- Microsoft KB 180099: "Troubleshooting LMHOSTS Name Resolution Issues." This article describes steps to take when name resolution fails.

2-11. Setting General Replication Properties and Automatic Partner Configuration

Problem

You want to set general or advanced global properties, or both, for replication partners.

Solution

Using a Graphical User Interface

1. Open the WINS MMC snap-in.

2. Right-click the Replication Partners subnode in the left pane, and select Properties.

3. On the General tab, specify whether you want to replicate only with configured partners, or with any WINS server.

4. On the General tab, specify whether you want to overwrite unique static mappings at this server (indicating that the static entries will be treated as if they were dynamic). This process is also referred to as "Migrate On."

5. Select the Advanced tab, and set the following options if needed:

   • Specify whether you want to accept or block records from a given server (by IP address or NetBIOS name).

   • Specify whether you want to enable automatic partner configuration.

   • Specify the multicast interval (hours and seconds) and time to live (TTL) to be used in automatic partner configuration.

6. Click OK to save the changes.

Using a Command-Line Interface

There are no commands that correspond to the settings on the General tab as described in the preceding section. However, you can use the following command to set the advanced configuration options, corresponding to automatic-replication partner configuration:

```
> netsh wins server set autopartnerconfig [[State=]{0 | 1}]
    [[Interval=]Value] [[TTL=]Value]
```

Here is a description of the command-line options:

State: Optional parameter that specifies whether you want to automate partner configuration. A value of 0 indicates no automatic configuration; a value of 1 will automate the configuration. The default state is no automatic configuration.

Interval: Optional parameter that specifies the multicast interval, in seconds.

TTL: Optional parameter that specifies the time-to-live value for multicasts between replication partners. The value must be an integer from 1 (minimum) to 32 (maximum) seconds.

For example, use this command to configure automatic partner configuration with a multicast interval of one hour and a time-to-live (TTL) value of 20:

```
> netsh wins server set autopartnerconfig state=1 interval=3600 ttl=20
```

Using the Registry

You can specify that static mappings be treated as dynamic during the replication process by creating or modifying the following Registry value:

```
[HKEY_LOCAL_MACHINE\SYSTEM\CurrentControlSet\Services\Wins\Parameters\]
"MigrateOn"=dword:1
```

You can specify the time interval, in seconds, at which the WINS server announces its presence through multicast announcements, by creating or modifying the following Registry value:

```
[HKEY_LOCAL_MACHINE\SYSTEM\CurrentControlSet\Services\Wins\Parameters\]
"McastIntvl"=dword:<Interval>
```

Specify <Interval> with a minimum value of 2,400 seconds, or 0x960 in hexadecimal format.

You can enable automatic partner configuration by creating or modifying the following Registry value:

```
[HKEY_LOCAL_MACHINE\SYSTEM\CurrentControlSet\Services\Wins\Parameters\]
"UseSelfFndPnrs"=dword:1
```

You can specify that only dynamic records are replicated by creating or modifying the following Registry value:

```
[HKEY_LOCAL_MACHINE\SYSTEM\CurrentControlSet\Services\Wins\Parameters\Push\➡
<IPAddress>]
"OnlyDynRecs"=dword:1
```

How It Works

You can configure your WINS server to automatically configure other WINS servers as replication partners using broadcast-and-discover functionality.

WINS servers periodically announce themselves using Internet Group Membership Protocol (IGMPv3) messaging on a standard address of 224.0.1.24. When you have enabled your WINS server to automatically configure other servers as replication partners, you have effectively configured your server to listen for these announcements, and when found, to configure the remote server as a replication partner. In addition, the server will be configured as both a push and a pull partner with pull replication set to occur every two hours.

Here are some important notes:

- Automatically configured partners will remain as partners only as long as WINS runs. If the service stops cleanly (perhaps because the server shuts down), the replication partners will be removed. The partners will be added again when the service restarts, generating a constant cycle of additions and removals. To enable persistent replication partner configuration, you should add the partners manually rather than rely on the automated process.

- The automated announcement and discovery process generates a significant amount of network traffic. This process is therefore recommended only for small networks containing a single subnet with one to three WINS servers.

See Also

Microsoft KB 151761: "WINS Server Sends IGMP Packets on Startup." This article discusses how to modify the automatic discovery process settings through the Registry.

2-12. Creating a Replication Partner

Problem

You want to create a replication partner for your WINS server and configure it as a push or pull partner, or both.

Solution

Using a Graphical User Interface

1. Open the WINS MMC snap-in.

2. Expand the server object in the left pane, right-click Replication Partners, and select New Replication Partner.

3. Enter the name or the IP address of the WINS server that you want to configure as a replication partner, or browse to that server and then click OK.

4. Right-click the newly created partner in the right pane, and select Properties.

5. Select the Advanced tab.

6. Modify the Replication Partner type (if required) by clicking the drop-down selection box. Select Push, Pull, or Push/Pull.

7. Click OK to save changes.

Using a Command-Line Interface

You can create a replication partner for your WINS server and configure it as a push, pull, or push/pull partner using the following command:

```
> netsh wins server add partner [Server=]IPAddress
    [[NetBIOS=]ServerNetBIOSName] [[Type=]{0 | 1 | 2}]
```

Here is a description of the command-line options:

Server: Required parameter that specifies the IP address of the WINS server that you want to add as a replication partner.

NetBIOS: Optional parameter that specifies the NetBIOS name of the server that you want to add as a replication partner.

Type: Optional parameter that specifies whether the server will be a push, pull, or push/pull replication partner. A value of 0 indicates pull replication; a value of 1 indicates push replication; and a value of 2 indicates both push and pull replication.

For example, use this command to add a push/pull replication partner named WINSB with an IP address of 10.0.0.3:

```
> netsh wins server add partner server=10.0.0.3 netbios=WINSB type=2
```

How It Works

WINS replication serves two fundamental purposes:

- **Redundancy:** In the event that a WINS server becomes unavailable, there will be another WINS server with a replica of the database available to serve clients.

- **Efficiency:** For sites connected by slow links, there is a need to minimize network traffic and conserve bandwidth, as well as to reduce the amount of time required for network queries.

WINS partners can be configured as push, pull, or push/pull partners.

A pull partner actively requests the updated records from its configured push partners so that it can update its database. Pull replication will occur when the WINS server starts, after an interval defined in the partner's properties. All replication changes are incremental, meaning that only the changes, rather than the entire database, are replicated.

A push partner actively notifies its pull partners that it has updated records available for their databases. Push replication can occur when the WINS server starts, when record IP addresses change, or when the version ID of a record is incremented.

When WINS servers replicate, there is an interval, known as the convergence time, before which all data is replicated to all servers. A dynamic registration request typically occurs faster than a release request. Therefore, depending on the replication topology, not all servers may have identical data records at a given time.

See Also

WINS help files: "WINS Push Partners Overview" and "WINS Pull Partners Overview." These help files offer a detailed discussion of the replication process.

2-13. Deleting a Replication Partner

Problem

You want to delete a WINS server as a replication partner.

Solution

Using a Graphical User Interface

1. Open the WINS MMC snap-in.

2. Expand the server object in the left pane, and select Replication Partners.

3. Right-click the replication partner in the right pane, and select Delete. Click Yes when prompted.

4. When prompted, click Yes if you want to delete all references to the selected WINS server, or No if you do not want to do so.

Using a Command-Line Interface

You can delete a WINS replication partner using the following command:

```
> netsh wins server delete partner [[Server=]IPAddress]
    [[Type=]{0 | 1 | 2}] [Confirm=]Y
```

Here is a description of the command-line options:

Server: Required parameter that specifies the IP address of the WINS server that you want to delete as a replication partner.

Type: Optional parameter that specifies the type of partner that you want to delete. A value of 0 indicates a pull partner; a value of 1 indicates a push partner; and a value of 2 indicates a push/pull partner. The default partner type is push/pull.

Confirm: Required parameter that specifies whether you want to be prompted for confirmation.

For example, use this command to delete the push/pull replication partner at 10.0.0.3 and confirm the deletion:

```
> netsh wins server delete partner server=10.0.0.3 type=2 confirm=Y
```

How It Works

There are various reasons to delete a replication partner. The partner may be decommissioned permanently, or just replaced with a new server. There may also be a change in overall network topology that mandates that replication will no longer be possible or even necessary.

Be certain when deleting replication partners that all systems that reference that WINS server have their TCP settings updated as well. For example, if a workstation is configured to use the WINS servers at 10.0.0.2 and 10.0.0.3, and you either demote 10.0.0.3 as a replication partner or you uninstall WINS from it entirely, you may need to update the WINS lookup parameters on the workstation or in the DHCP scope that provides the workstation's configuration so that the workstation will still have full name resolution capabilities.

2-14. Setting Global Pull-Replication Properties

Problem

You want to set global pull-replication parameters.

Solution

Using a Graphical User Interface

1. Open the WINS MMC snap-in.

2. Right-click the Replication Partners subnode in the left pane, and select Properties.

3. Select the Pull Replication tab.

4. Specify the replication start time (in hours, minutes, and seconds).

5. Specify the replication interval (in days, hours, and minutes).

6. Specify the number of retries on replication failure.

7. Select the check box to start pull replication at service startup, if desired.

8. Select the check box to use persistent connections for pull replication partners, if desired.

9. Click OK to save changes.

Using a Command-Line Interface

You can set the properties on a global scale for pull replication using the following command:

```
> netsh wins server set pullparam [[State=]{0 | 1}] [[Strtup=]{0 | 1}]
    [[Start=]Value] [[Interval=]Value] [[Retry=]Value]
```

Here is a description of the command-line options:

State: Required parameter that specifies whether you want to use persistent connections for replication. A value of 0 will disable persistent connections; a value of 1 will enable them.

Strtup: Optional parameter that specifies whether you want pull replication to occur at startup. A value of 0 indicates no replication at startup; a value of 1 will force WINS replication at startup. The default state is no replication at startup.

Start: Optional parameter that specifies the time period, in seconds, before which pull replication will occur.

Interval: Optional parameter that specifies the replication interval, in seconds.

Retry: Optional parameter that specifies the number of times to reattempt replication in the event of failure.

For example, use this command to configure the pull parameters for the WINS server such that pull replication will use persistent connections, occur at startup, send the pull trigger in 60 seconds, and occur every hour, with three attempts at replication:

```
> netsh wins server set pullparam state=1 strtup=1 start=60 interval=3600 retry=3
```

Using the Registry

You can set the WINS server to notify its pull-replication partners of its status when the service starts by creating or modifying the following Registry value:

```
[HKEY_LOCAL_MACHINE\SYSTEM\CurrentControlSet\Services\Wins\Parameters\Pull]
"InitTimeReplication"=dword:1
```

You can specify the maximum number of attempts a WINS server will make for pull replication by creating or modifying the following Registry value:

```
[HKEY_LOCAL_MACHINE\SYSTEM\CurrentControlSet\Services\Wins\Parameters\Pull]
"CommRetryCount"=dword:<NumAttempts>
```

Replace <NumAttempts> with the desired number of attempts. The default value is 3.

How It Works

Pull replication is the process in which a WINS server sends a trigger to one or more replication partners requesting that the partner push its updated records to the requesting WINS server, thereby ensuring a consistent and comprehensive database on each WINS server. This process may be manually initiated, or it can occur at regular, predefined intervals. You can configure pull replication to occur either when the WINS service starts or after a specific time interval.

Global replication parameters apply to the WINS server on which they are configured, and do not relate to any specific replication partner. In general, the replication parameters depend on the overall WINS topology. Considerations include the number of partners as well as their placement in the LAN or WAN and the integrity and speed of the connections between servers.

For slow or non-reliable links, you should specify a higher number of retries in the event that replication fails. Conversely, for reliable high-speed links, it may be acceptable to use persistent connections, since their impact on overall network performance will be minimized.

See Also

Microsoft KB 251067: "WINS Registry Parameters for Windows 2000." This article provides a comprehensive list of relevant Registry entries that can be used to configure global pull replication.

2-15. Setting Global Push-Replication Properties

Problem

You want to set global push-replication parameters.

Solution

Using a Graphical User Interface

1. Open the WINS MMC snap-in.

2. Right-click the Replication Partners subnode in the left pane, and select Properties.

3. Select the Push Replication tab.

4. Select the check box to start push replication at service startup, if desired.

5. Select the check box to start push replication when an IP address changes, if desired.

6. Specify the number of changes in the database's version ID before replication starts (the default is 0). This setting represents the number of record updates that can be made before replication occurs.

7. Select the check box to use persistent connections for push-replication partners, if desired.

8. Click OK to save changes.

Using a Command-Line Interface

You can set the properties on a global scale for push replication using the following command:

```
> netsh wins server set pushparam [State=]{0 | 1} [[Strtup=]{0 | 1}]
    [[AddChange=]{0 | 1}] [[Update=]Value]
```

Here is a description of the command-line options:

State: Required parameter that specifies whether you want to use persistent connections for replication. A value of 0 disables persistent connections; a value of 1 enables them.

Strtup: Optional parameter that specifies whether you want push replication to occur at startup. A value of 0 prevents replication at startup; a value of 1 will force replication at startup. The default is no replication at startup.

AddChange: Optional parameter that specifies whether you want replication to occur when an address changes in the WINS database. A value of 0 will not initiate replication; a value of 1 will initiate it. The default is not to initiate replication.

Update: Optional parameter that specifies the number of changes that should occur in the version ID before replication starts. This value represents the number of record updates that can be made before replication occurs.

For example, use this command to configure the push parameters for this WINS server such that push replication uses persistent connections and occurs at startup whenever an address changes or when the version ID has changed three times:

```
> netsh wins server set pushparam state=1 strtup=1 addchange=1 update=3
```

Using the Registry

You can specify the number of updates that are made to local records before partners are informed of the change by creating or modifying the following Registry value:

```
[HKEY_LOCAL_MACHINE\SYSTEM\CurrentControlSet\Services\Wins\Partners\Pull\]
"UpdateCount"=dword:<NumUpdates>
```

Replace <NumUpdates> with the number of updates you want to occur before a replication.

How It Works

Push replication is the process in which a WINS server sends its updated database records to a WINS server that is a replication partner and that has already sent a pull trigger to the push partner. This process may be manually initiated, or it can occur at regular, predefined intervals. You can configure push replication to occur when the WINS service starts, when an IP address in a name mapping changes, or when a defined number of changes in the version ID (the number of record updates) has occurred.

The configuration of global push-replication parameters follows a similar logic to that of global pull-replication parameters described in Recipe 2-14, "Setting Global Pull-Replication Properties."

Global push-replication parameters apply to the WINS server on which they are configured, and do not relate to any specific replication partner. In general, the replication parameters depend on the overall WINS topology. Considerations include the number of partners as well as their placement in the LAN or WAN and the integrity and speed of the connections between servers.

For slow or non-reliable links, you may want to specify a higher number of changes to the version ID prior to initiating replication, in order to reduce network traffic. Conversely, for reliable high-speed links, it may be acceptable to use persistent connections, since their impact on overall network performance will be minimized.

See Also

Microsoft KB 251067: "WINS Registry Parameters for Windows 2000." This article provides a comprehensive list of relevant Registry entries that can be used to configure global pull replication.

2-16. Configuring Push and Pull Replication for a Partner

Problem

You want to specify the parameters for push, pull, or push/pull replication with a given partner.

Solution

Using a Graphical User Interface

1. Open the WINS MMC snap-in.

2. Expand the server object in the left pane, and click Replication Partners.

3. Right-click the replication partner whose properties you want to specify, and select Properties.

4. Select the Advanced tab.

5. Modify the Replication Partner type (if required) by clicking the drop-down selection box. Select Push, Pull, or Push/Pull.

6. To configure pull-replication options, follow these steps:

   a. Select the check box to permit pull replication through a persistent connection if desired.

   b. Specify a start time for the pull trigger to be generated.

   c. Specify the replication interval.

7. To configure push-replication options, follow these steps:

   a. Select the check box to permit push replication through a persistent connection if desired.

   b. Specify the number of changes in the version ID (the number of record updates) that must occur before replication starts.

8. Click OK to save changes.

Using a Command-Line Interface

You can configure pull-replication parameters for a given partner using the following command:

```
> netsh wins server set pullpartnerconfig [[State=]{0 | 1}]
    [Server=]ServerName [[Start=]Value] [[Interval=]Value]
```

Here is a description of the command-line options:

State: Optional parameter that specifies whether you want to use persistent connections for replication. A value of 0 will not use persistent connections; a value of 1 will use them. The default connection type is persistent.

Server: Required parameter that specifies the IP address or the NetBIOS name of the pull-replication partner.

Start: Optional parameter that specifies the time after service startup, in seconds, at which you want replication to start.

Interval: Optional parameter that specifies the interval, in seconds, at which pull replication should occur.

For example, use the following command to configure the pull-replication parameters for the current server with the WINS server. Pull replication will occur one hour after service startup and occur every two hours; persistent connections will be used.

```
> netsh wins server set pullpartnerconfig state=1
    server=WINSB start=3600 interval=7200
```

You can configure push-replication parameters for a given partner using the following command:

```
> netsh wins server set pushpartnerconfig [[State=]{0 | 1}]
    [Server=]ServerName [Update=]Value
```

Here is a description of the command-line options:

State: Optional parameter that specifies whether you want to use persistent connections for replication. A value of 0 indicates not to use persistent connections; a value of 1 indicates to use them. The default connection type is persistent.

Server: Required parameter that specifies the IP address or the NetBIOS name of the pull-replication partner.

Update: Required parameter that specifies the number of changes in the version ID (the number of record updates) that must occur before replication starts.

For example, use this command to configure the push-replication parameters for the current server with the WINSB server. WINSB will be notified after three changes in the version ID:

```
> netsh wins server set pushpartnerconfig state=1 server=WINSB update=3
```

How It Works

You can configure replication parameters for a given partner in a single screen of the WINS Administrator console; however, two distinct commands are required to set these options through the command-line interface.

The version ID that has been referenced in this recipe can loosely be interpreted as the number of entries in the WINS database. More to the point, and as quoted in the Microsoft TechNet site, "the value in the version ID reflects the total number of replicable changes that occurred to owned entries for a particular WINS server. The value is incremented by hexadecimal 1 every time a replicable change occurs. For example, if WINSA is the owner for ClientA, which has a version ID of 4B3, and for ClientB, which has a version ID of 4C2, ClientB was the fifteenth replicated change in the WINSA database after the ClientA change."

Replication parameters must be configured on a per-replication-server basis; these are not global in nature. You should apply careful thought to the configuration of these replication parameters. For multisite environments, it is helpful to create a visual diagram that includes schematic representations of each site, as well as the intersite links. You should determine whether a hub-and-spokes replication topology is the most appropriate or whether you need a complete mesh. See "Configuring WINS Replication" in the WINS help file for a summary of replication and topology considerations.

The goal of the configuration of WINS replication is to minimize the convergence time and the impact on network performance. The convergence time is defined as the amount of time it takes for a change that occurs on one WINS server to propagate to all other WINS servers in the replication environment.

See Also

- Recipes 2-14 and 2-15 for the techniques to set global, rather than server-specific, parameters.

- WINS help file: "Configuring WINS Replication." This help file summarizes replication considerations and convergence issues.

2-17. Initiating Push/Pull Replication

Problem

You want to start a push/pull replication cycle between two partners.

Solution

Using a Graphical User Interface

There are two ways to initiate push/pull replication through the standard WINS console:

1. Open the WINS MMC snap-in.

2. Either right-click a server object in the left pane, or right-click a server object in the Replication Partners subnode of the server object, and then select Start Push Replication or Start Pull Replication, whichever is appropriate.

3. Enter the name or the IP address of the server with which you want to initiate replication.

4. Specify whether you want to initiate replication for that partner only, or whether you want to propagate replication to all partners.

5. Click OK to save the changes.

Using a Command-Line Interface

There are multiple commands that can be used to initiate push/pull replication through the command-line interface.

To initiate push/pull replication for the current server with all partners, use this command:

```
> netsh wins server init replicate
```

To initiate pull replication from a specified WINS server to the current server, use this command:

```
> netsh wins server init pull [Server=]{PullServerName | IPAddress}
```

Server is a required parameter that specifies either the server's IP address or the UNC of the server (\\ServerName).

For example, use this command to send a pull-replication trigger to the partner at 10.0.0.3:

```
> netsh wins server init pull server=10.0.0.3
```

To initiate push replication from the current server to a specified WINS server, use this command:

```
> netsh wins server init push [Server=]{\\PushServerName | IPAddress}
    [[PropReq=]{0 | 1}]
```

PropReq is an optional parameter that specifies whether you want to push propagation only to the specified partner or to all partners. A value of 0 will push only to the specified partner; a value of 1 will push to all partners. The default method is to push only to the specified partner.

For example, use this command to send a push-replication trigger to the partner at 10.0.0.3 and to propagate the trigger to its partners:

```
> netsh wins server init push server=10.0.0.3 propreq=1
```

To initiate pull replication from a specified server to another specified server, use this command:

```
> netsh wins server init pullrange [Owner=]OwnerServerIP
    [Server=]PullServerIP [MaxVer=]{High,Low} [MinVer=]{High,Low}
```

Here is a description of the command-line options:

Owner: Required parameter that specifies the IP address of the owner-server whose records you want to pull.

Server: Required parameter that specifies the IP address of the server from which you are pulling records.

MaxVer: Required parameter that specifies the maximum high and low values of the records that you want to pull. Separate the entries with a comma, and enclose them in braces.

MinVer: Required parameter that specifies the minimum high and low values of the records that you want to pull. Separate the entries with a comma, and enclose them in braces.

Note Set both MaxVer and MinVer arrays to {0,0} to pull all records.

For example, use this command to send a pull trigger from the WINS server at 10.0.0.2 to the one at 10.0.0.3 and to request all records owned by 10.0.0.3:

```
> netsh wins server init pullrange owner=10.0.0.3 server=10.0.0.2
    maxver={0,0} minver={0,0}
```

Using the Registry

You can instruct the WINS server to notify its pull partners when an address in the database changes by creating or modifying the following Registry value:

```
[HKEY_LOCAL_MACHINE\SYSTEM\CurrentControlSet\Services\...
    ...Wins\Partners\Push\<IPAddress>]
"RplOnAddressChg"=dword:1
```

Replace <IPAddress> with the IP address of the WINS server's pull partner.

How It Works

WINS replication is an automated process and will hopefully run without problems. However, there may occasionally be a need to manually initiate the replication process. For example, if a new server is brought online and you need all users on the network to have rapid access to it (via WINS resolution), you may not want to wait for the replication cycle to complete its process. You can instead initiate manual replication using one of the methods described in this section.

The command-line interface offers four different methods of triggering replication, whether through the push or the pull trigger. It may be sufficient in many cases to use only the `init replicate` command; however, you can reach much more granular levels with the other commands.

See Also

Microsoft TechNet: "WINS Best Practices" (http://technet2.microsoft.com/WindowsServer/ en/Library/ed9beba0-f998-47d2-8137-a2fc52886ed71033.mspx)

2-18. Scavenging Outdated Records

Problem

You want to initiate scavenging of obsolete records on your WINS server's database that were generated through replication with other WINS servers.

Solution

Using a Graphical User Interface

1. Open the WINS MMC snap-in.

2. Right-click the server object in the left pane, and select Scavenge Database.

Using a Command-Line Interface

You can initiate the WINS scavenging process using the following command:

```
> netsh wins server init scavenge
```

This command does not require any additional parameters.

How It Works

The WINS server automatically removes obsolete records from its database for registrations that it owns (meaning those for workstations registered with it and not with another WINS server). However, maintenance is periodically required to remove records that were created at other WINS servers and added to its database through the replication cycle. Scavenging will automatically remove those records.

See Also

WINS help file: "Maintaining the WINS Database." This help file provides a before-and-after discussion of the scavenging process.

2-19. Enabling Burst Handling

Problem

You want to enable burst handling to accommodate a high level of simultaneous WINS registrations.

Solution

Using a Graphical User Interface

1. Open the WINS MMC snap-in.

2. Right-click the server object in the left pane, and select Properties.

3. Select the Advanced tab.

4. Select the check box to enable burst handling.

5. Specify the level of handling. Options include Low, Medium, High, or Custom.

6. Click OK to save the changes.

Using a Command-Line Interface

You can enable burst handling using the following command:

```
> netsh wins server set burstparam [State=]{0 | 1} [[Value=]QueueSize]
```

Here is a description of the command-line options:

State: Required parameter that specifies whether you want to enable (or reset) burst handling. A value of 0 will disable or reset burst handling; a value of 1 will enable it.

Value: Optional parameter that specifies the number of simultaneous registrations that you want your WINS server to be able to accommodate. The value must be an integer from 50 to 5,000.

For example, use this command to enable burst handling once 2,000 registration or renewal requests have been received by the server:

```
> netsh wins server set burstparam state=1 value=2000
```

Using the Registry

You can configure WINS to use burst handling by creating or modifying the following Registry value:

```
[HKEY_LOCAL_MACHINE\SYSTEM\CurrentControlSet\Services\Wins\Parameters\]
"BurstHandling"=dword:1
```

You can also set the maximum number of queries that the WINS server will process before starting burst handling by setting the following Registry value:

```
[HKEY_LOCAL_MACHINE\SYSTEM\CurrentControlSet\Services\Wins\Parameters\]
"BurstQueSize"=dword:<MaxQueries>
```

Replace <MaxQueries> with the desired maximum as an integer from 50 to 5,000.

How It Works

A WINS "burst" occurs whenever there is a high number of simultaneous registrations at the server. This could occur, for example, if an organization's computers were all started at approximately the same time in the morning, or after a power failure has occurred and all workstations reboot.

By default, a WINS server can accommodate 500 simultaneous registration requests. (A burst value of 300 is considered low, 500 is considered medium, and 1,000 is considered high when comparing the GUI settings with values in the Registry.) However, this number may vary depending on the current server load and available resources. When a server reaches its burst threshold, it responds to all additional requests, in groups of 100, with an automatic "successful registration" response, though it actually puts the registration into a queue and assigns a five-minute time-to-live (TTL) value. Each additional batch of 100 requests receives the TTL of the previous batch plus an additional five minutes. If the TTL is exceeded, the registration request is dropped.

See Also

- Microsoft KB 251067: "WINS Registry Parameters for Windows 2000." This article provides a comprehensive list of relevant Registry entries that pertain to burst handling.

- WINS help file: "Burst Handling."

CHAPTER 3

■ ■ ■

Windows Firewall

The Windows Firewall is a feature of Windows Server 2003 Service Pack 1 that creates a protective boundary for Windows Server 2003; it monitors incoming connection attempts on the local computer and restricts information that travels between the local computer and a local area network (LAN) or the Internet. The Windows Firewall provides a way of protecting your server against malicious users or content on the Internet, or elsewhere on your network, that might try to access resources and information on your computer without your permission.

When Windows Server 2003 was first released, the Windows Firewall was known as the Internet Connection Firewall (ICF) and was a simple, host-based firewall for the Windows Server 2003 operating system. ICF was not enabled by default, and it was somewhat difficult to configure. With the release of Service Pack 1 (SP1), Windows Server 2003 now includes the same Windows Firewall that was introduced in Service Pack 2 for Windows XP. This improved firewall is much easier to configure and manage, both from the GUI as well as through Group Policy and the command line.

■**Note** All of the recipes in this chapter assume that you are running Windows Server 2003 Service Pack 1.

Windows Firewall functions by listening for unsolicited incoming requests to your server. A good example of this is a remote client attempting to access the web service running on a physical server. You can configure exceptions based on the name of a service or application, as well as on as the TCP/UDP port it uses to communicate. Using the Windows Firewall, you can configure which applications should be permitted to access your local computer, and which connection attempts should be rejected.

Another configuration improvement in the Windows Firewall is the ability to set up multiple profiles to control how the firewall should behave in different scenarios. You can create configuration items such as firewall exceptions to apply to one or both of the following profiles:

- **Domain profile:** This profile will take effect when your computer is logged onto a domain. The Windows Server 2003 operating system uses a process called *network determination* to figure out whether a computer is currently attached to a domain. This process involves checking the last time that a computer received a Group Policy update, as well as any connection-specific DNS suffixes that have been configured and whether a SLIP or PPP connection is enabled.

- **Standard profile:** In many cases, you will probably enable certain exceptions or other firewall features that should take effect when a computer is attached to a domain— exceptions that you would not want to take effect in a less controlled environment such as a laptop connected to a hotel's public broadband Internet connection. For this reason, many administrators will configure the standard profile with more stringent firewall settings than the domain profile.

When you make a configuration change to the Windows Firewall, you can specify that the change should apply to the domain profile, the standard profile, or all profiles.

Using a Graphical User Interface

Most of the configuration items you'll see in this chapter are done through the Windows Firewall Control Panel applet, which allows you to enable or disable the Windows Firewall, configure exceptions, and set other advanced options. In addition, Recipe 3-19, which discusses viewing event log entries associated with the Windows Firewall, makes use of the free EventCombMT utility, available for download from the Microsoft website as part of the Account and Lockout Management Tools at http://www.microsoft.com/downloads/details.aspx? FamilyID=7af2e69c-91f3-4e63-8629-b999adde0b9e&displaylang=en. This free utility allows you to collect and view Event Viewer entries from multiple computers, as well as querying Event Viewer data for specific entries. (The Event Viewer is the MMC snap-in that provides a view of any events that have been logged by a particular computer's auditing settings.)

Using a Command-Line Interface

The primary tool that you'll use to configure the Windows Firewall at the command line is netsh. Netsh has an entire subcontext devoted to the Windows Firewall, which allows you to perform the following configurations and more from the command line:

- Enable or disable the firewall

- Create, edit, or delete program and port exceptions

- Set Internet Control Message Protocol (ICMP) and logging options

In addition, Recipe 3-19, which discusses the Windows Firewall log file, makes use of the Microsoft Log Parser. This is a free utility available for download from the Microsoft website at http://www.microsoft.com/downloads/details.aspx?FamilyID= 890cd06b-abf8-4c25-91b2-f8d975cf8c07&displaylang=en. This free utility allows you to use a SQL-like query engine to parse information from a number of data sources, including the Windows Firewall log file, which stores information in the industry-standard W3C format.

Using a Group Policy

In addition to the Windows Firewall Control Panel applet introduced by Windows Server 2003 Service Pack 1, you now also have access to a number of options for configuring the firewall using Group Policy. Prior to Service Pack 1, the only configuration you could perform via Group Policy was to globally disable the use of ICF. With the Windows Firewall, you can now perform granular configuration of firewall options and exceptions in both the domain and standard profiles.

Depending on which profile you wish to configure, you'll find the Windows Firewall Group Policy entries in one of the following locations:

- Computer Configuration\Administrative Templates\Network\Network Connections\ Windows Firewall\Domain Profile

- Computer Configuration\Administrative Templates\Network\Network Connections\ Windows Firewall\Standard Profile

Using the Registry

When configuring the Windows Firewall via the Registry, you'll use one or both of the following keys, depending on which profile you wish to alter:

- `HKEY_LOCAL_MACHINE\SYSTEM\CurrentControlSet\Services\SharedAccess\Parameters\ FirewallPolicy\DomainProfile`

- `HKEY_LOCAL_MACHINE\SYSTEM\CurrentControlSet\Services\SharedAccess\Parameters\ FirewallPolicy\StandardProfile`

It's important to note here that these Registry keys are valid *only* if the computer you're working on is not receiving configuration data from Group Policy. If it is a Group Policy–enabled computer, these entries will be situated in a different Registry location, and any changes that you make will be overwritten the next time Group Policy refreshes itself. If your Windows Server 2003 computer is receiving its Windows Firewall configuration from Group Policy, it's best to make any changes there for the sake of consistency.

Using VBScript

With VBScript, you can manage the Windows Firewall using the following Windows Firewall interfaces:

- `INetFwOpenPort` provides access to the properties of a single port that you've opened within the Windows Firewall.

- `INetFwOpenPorts` provides access to the *collection* of ports that have been opened within the firewall.

- `INetFwService` provides access to the properties of a single service that's been enabled or disabled through the firewall.

- `INetFwServices` provides access to a *collection* of services that may be authorized to listen through the firewall.

- `INetFwRemoteAdminSettings` configures remote administration settings for utilities such as Computer Management and remote Registry editing.

- `INetFwAuthorizedApplication` allows you to configure the properties of a single application that's been authorized to receive traffic through the firewall.

- `INetFwAuthorizedApplications` provides access to the *collection* of authorized applications.

- `INetFwIcmpSettings` allows you to configure ICMP behavior through the Windows Firewall.

- `INetFwProfile` gives access to a particular firewall profile, either the domain profile, the standard profile, or the current profile that is in effect.

- `INetFwPolicy` provides access to a particular firewall policy.

- `INetFwMgr` provides access to the firewall settings for the local computer.

3-1. Enabling and Disabling the Windows Firewall

Problem

You want to enable or disable the built-in firewall on a Windows Server 2003 computer.

Solution

Using a Graphical User Interface

To enable the Windows Firewall, do the following:

1. Open the Network Connections applet.

2. Double-click on the Local Area Connection icon.

3. Click Settings from the Advanced tab; this will launch the Windows Firewall Control Panel applet.

4. Click the On radio button to enable the Windows Firewall, or Off to disable the firewall.

Using a Command-Line Interface

The following command enables the Windows Firewall on a Windows Server 2003 computer for all profiles:

```
> netsh firewall set opmode mode=enable exceptions=enable profile=all
```

The following command disables the Windows Firewall on a Windows Server 2003 computer:

```
> netsh firewall set opmode mode=disable exceptions=disable profile=all
```

Using Group Policy

Tables 3-1 and 3-2 contain the Group Policy settings that enable or disable the Windows Firewall for the domain and standard profiles respectively.

Table 3-1. *Enable or Disable Windows Firewall—Domain Profile*

Path	`Computer Configuration\Administrative Templates\Network\Network Connections\Windows Firewall\Domain Profile`
Policy name	Windows Firewall: Protect all network connections
Value	`Enabled` to enable the Windows Firewall for all interfaces in the domain profile. `Disabled` to turn off the Windows Firewall for all interfaces in the domain profile.

Table 3-2. *Enable or Disable Windows Firewall—Standard Profile*

Path	Computer Configuration\Administrative Templates\Network\Network Connections\Windows Firewall\Standard Profile
Policy name	Windows Firewall: Protect all network connections
Value	Enabled to enable the Windows Firewall for all interfaces in the standard profile. Disabled to turn off the Windows Firewall for all interfaces in the standard profile.

Using the Registry

To configure the Windows Firewall on a Windows Server 2003 computer, configure the following Registry values:

```
[HKEY_LOCAL_MACHINE\SYSTEM\CurrentControlSet\Services\SharedAccess\
    Parameters\FirewallPolicy\<Profile>]
"EnableFirewall"=dword:1
```

Set `<Profile>` to DomainProfile or StandardProfile. Set the dword value to 1 to enable the Windows Firewall or 0 to disable it.

Using VBScript

This code enables the Windows Firewall for the current profile.

```
Set firewall = CreateObject("HNetCfg.FwMgr")
Set firewallPolicy = firewall.LocalPolicy.CurrentProfile
firewallPolicy.FirewallEnabled = TRUE ' FALSE to disable
WScript.Echo("FirewallEnabled set to " & FirewallEnabled & "!")
```

How It Works

The original Release To Manufacturing (RTM) version of the Windows Server 2003 operating system came preloaded with the Internet Connection Firewall (ICF), which provided a simple host-based firewall. The drawback to ICF was that it was not enabled by default when Windows Server 2003 was first installed, and it was fairly unintuitive to enable and configure. Service Pack 1 for Windows Server 2003 made some significant improvements to ICF, which was renamed the Windows Firewall (WF). The Windows Firewall is now enabled when the operating system first boots, and you can make extensive configuration choices through the Windows Firewall Control Panel applet, netsh, and Group Policy.

In certain circumstances, though, you may find it necessary to disable the Windows Firewall. In most cases, this will be because your organization has already standardized on another software or hardware firewall solution, and you want to simplify the configuration of your Windows Server 2003 computers. Even if this is the case, however, the Windows Firewall is able to coexist with third-party products and might still be a useful tool to provide "defense in depth" for your Windows Server 2003 computers. This is especially true if you are relying on a hardware firewall at your network perimeter. These devices constitute the Maginot Line of network defense—if a single malware- or virus-infested PC comes online on the "safe" side of the firewall, your entire network will be at risk without another form of protection. You should also strongly consider enabling the Windows Firewall for the standard profile even if you disable it in the domain profile. In this way, any mobile users running Windows Server 2003 on their laptops (application developers, for example) will still have firewall protection for their laptop computers when they're not attached to the domain or are otherwise unable to rely on the protection of a corporate firewall.

Using a Command-Line Interface

When using netsh to configure the Windows Firewall, much of the verbiage is optional and can be skipped to save time when entering commands on the fly. For example, this command

```
netsh firewall set opmode mode = enable exceptions = enable profile = all
```

can be shortened to

```
netsh firewall set opmode enable enable all
```

or it can even be made as short as

```
netsh fi set op en en a
```

See Also

- Recipe 3-2 for more on configuring exception processing

- Microsoft: "Understanding Windows Firewall" (http://www.microsoft.com/windowsxp/ using/security/internet/sp2_wfintro.mspx)

3-2. Configuring Exception Processing

Problem

You want to manage rules and exceptions configured on the Windows Firewall.

Solution

Using a Graphical User Interface

1. Open the Network Connections applet.

2. Double-click on the Local Area Connection icon.

3. From the Advanced tab, click Settings. This will launch the Windows Firewall Control Panel applet.

4. From the General tab, place a check mark next to Don't Allow Exceptions if you want to prevent the Windows Firewall from allowing entries configured on the Exceptions tab to pass through the firewall. To allow these entries to be processed, remove the check mark next to Don't Allow Exceptions.

Using a Command-Line Interface

The following command enables the Windows Firewall and allows exception traffic to pass:

```
> netsh firewall set opmode mode = enable exceptions = enable
```

The following command enables the Windows Firewall and prevents exception traffic from passing through the firewall:

```
> netsh firewall set opmode mode = enable exceptions = disabled
```

Note If you do not specify a profile, netsh will assume a default value of `profile=current`.

Using Group Policy

Tables 3-3 and 3-4 contain the Group Policy settings that dictate whether Windows Firewall should allow traffic configured on the Exceptions tab in the domain and standard profiles respectively.

Table 3-3. *Configure Exception Processing—Domain Profile*

Path	Computer Configuration\Administrative Templates\Network\Network Connections\Windows Firewall\Domain Profile
Policy name	Windows Firewall: Do not allow exceptions
Value	Enabled to prevent WF from allowing exceptions. Disabled to allow exceptions.

Table 3-4. *Configure Exception Processing—Standard Profile*

Path	Computer Configuration\Administrative Templates\Network\Network Connections\Windows Firewall\Standard Profile
Policy name	Windows Firewall: Do not allow exceptions
Value	Enabled to prevent WF from allowing exceptions. Disabled to allow exceptions.

Using the Registry

To configure an individual computer to allow exceptions to pass through the Windows Firewall, set the following Registry values:

```
[HKEY_LOCAL_MACHINE\SYSTEM\CurrentControlSet\Services\SharedAccess\
    Parameters\FirewallPolicy\<Profile>]
"DoNotAllowExceptions"=dword:0
```

To configure an individual computer to prevent exceptions from passing through the Windows Firewall, set the following Registry values:

```
[HKEY_LOCAL_MACHINE\SYSTEM\CurrentControlSet\Services\
    SharedAccess\Parameters\FirewallPolicy\<Profile>]
"DoNotAllowExceptions"=dword:1
```

Using VBScript

This code allows exceptions to pass through the Windows Firewall *for the current profile*. Use LocalPolicy.DomainProfile or LocalPolicy.StandardProfile to alter a specific profile.

```
' ------ SCRIPT CONFIGURATION ------
boolNoExceptions = FALSE ' Set to TRUE to prevent exceptions
 ' from being passed
' ------ END CONFIGURATION ---------

Set firewall = CreateObject("HNetCfg.FwMgr")
Set firewallPolicy = firewall.LocalPolicy.CurrentProfile
firewallPolicy.ExceptionsNotAllowed = boolNoExceptions
WScript.Echo("ExceptionsNotAllowed set to " & boolNoExceptions & "!")
```

How It Works

The Windows Firewall is designed to protect your computer against malicious incoming traffic; whenever the firewall detects this kind of unsolicited request, it blocks the incoming connection and drops any packets associated with it. However, there are circumstances where an application may need to receive this type of traffic in order to function. This is quite common with Instant Messenger applications and network games, as well as server applications like Internet Information Server (IIS) that need to service incoming requests for information. In order to allow this incoming traffic to pass through the firewall, you need to configure a firewall exception based on the name of the application or the TCP/UDP port on which it communicates.

Depending on the network you are connecting to, you may need more or less firewall protection. In addition to enabling or disabling the Windows Firewall, you can also specify whether or not it should allow any exceptions that you've created. This is helpful if you're connecting to the Internet from an unprotected network, like a hotel broadband connection, using your Windows Server 2003 laptop. You can also disallow exceptions in a network emergency, such as if a zero-day virus or worm is circulating the Internet and your antivirus definitions have not yet been updated to detect it. When you configure the Don't Allow Exceptions option, whether through the GUI or another method, the Windows Firewall will block *all* unsolicited incoming traffic that's sent to your computer—this includes blocking any traffic that meets the definitions of any exceptions you've configured, as well as preconfigured services and applications like Remote Assistance, Remote Desktop, and File and Printer Sharing.

See Also

- Recipes 3-3 and 3-4 for more on configuring firewall exceptions

- Microsoft TechNet: "Known Issues for Managing Exceptions" (http://technet2.microsoft. com/WindowsServer/en/Library/b57b63fb-eb5c-4ca8-999e-e1e7e37fc0f11033.mspx)

3-3. Creating Program Exceptions

Problem

You want to create a program exception to allow a particular executable to pass through the Windows Firewall on a Windows Server 2003 computer.

Solution

Using a Graphical User Interface

1. Open the Network Connections applet.

2. Double-click on the Local Area Connection icon.

3. From the Advanced tab, click Settings. This will launch the Windows Firewall Control Panel applet.

4. In the Windows Firewall applet, select the Exceptions tab. To add a new program that should be allowed to traverse the firewall, select Add Program.

5. Select the executable from the prepopulated list, or click Browse to navigate to the file on your local hard drive.

6. To define the scope of the exception, click on Change Scope, and select from one of the following three options:

   • Any computer (including those on the Internet).

   • My network (local subnet).

   • Custom list. For this option, enter a single IP address using the syntax 192.168.1.151, and/or enter a range of addresses using the network ID of the range followed by its subnet mask, such as 192.168.1.1/255.255.255.0. Separate multiple entries using a comma.

7. Click OK when you're finished.

Using a Command-Line Interface

The following command allows standard.exe to pass through the Windows Firewall in the domain profile, but only for computers in the local subnet:

```
> netsh firewall add allowedprogram program = "C:\folder1\Standard.exe"
    name = Standard mode = ENABLE scope = SUBNET profile = DOMAIN
```

When enabling an exception through netsh, you can set mode to ENABLE or DISABLE; scope to ALL, SUBNET, or CUSTOM; and profile to CURRENT, DOMAIN, STANDARD, or ALL. If you set scope to CUSTOM, you also need to specify addresses = followed by a comma-separated list of IPv4 IP addresses.

Using Group Policy

Tables 3-5 and 3-6 contain the Group Policy settings that create program exceptions in the domain and standard profiles respectively.

Table 3-5. *Configure Program Exceptions—Domain Profile*

Path	Computer Configuration\Administrative Templates\Network\ Network Connections\Windows Firewall\Domain Profile
Policy name	Windows Firewall: Define program exceptions
Value	Enabled to configure a list of program exceptions. Disabled to remove any exceptions previously configured by Group Policy.

Table 3-6. *Configure Program Exceptions—Standard Profile*

Path	Computer Configuration\Administrative Templates\Network\ Network Connections\Windows Firewall\Standard Profile
Policy name	Windows Firewall: Define program exceptions
Value	Enabled to configure a list of program exceptions. Disabled to remove any exceptions previously configured by Group Policy.

Using the Registry

To configure an executable called standard.exe to pass through the Windows Firewall, set the following Registry values:

```
[HKEY_LOCAL_MACHINE\SYSTEM\CurrentControlSet\Services\SharedAccess\
    Parameters\FirewallPolicy\<Profile>\AuthorizedApplications\List]
"C:\folder1\Standard.exe":reg_sz:"C:\folder1\Standard.exe:*:Enabled:Standard.exe"
```

You can modify this Registry setting for your environment by adhering to the following syntax:

ProgramPath:*Scope*:Enabled|Disabled:*ApplicationName*

- ProgramPath allows you to enter the path and filename of the application. You can enter the path manually, or use environment variables such as %windir% or %ProgramFiles%.

- Scope specifies the scope of the exception. You can use * to specify the Any Computer setting, LocalSubnet to restrict the exception to your local network, or a single IP address or range of addresses to define a custom list. Create multiple entries by separating them with a comma, like this: LocalSubnet,10.0.0.151,10.112.25.0/255.255.255.0,10.121. 79.0/24.

- Use Enabled or Disabled to indicate whether this program should be enabled or disabled in the exception list.

- ApplicationName creates a friendly name for the application exception; this is the name that will appear on the Exceptions tab in the Windows Firewall Control Panel applet.

Using VBScript

This code creates a program exception for Standard.exe.

```
' ------ SCRIPT CONFIGURATION ------
Application.Name = "Standard"
Application.ProcessImageFileName = "c:\folder1\Standard.exe"
' ------ END CONFIGURATION ---------

Set firewall = CreateObject("HNetCfg.FwMgr")
Set firewallPolicy = firewall.LocalPolicy.CurrentProfile
Set Application = CreateObject("HNetCfg.FwAuthorizedApplication")

' IPVersion 2 stands for "any version of IP", this is the only correct value
Application.IPVersion = 2


' A scope of 0 allows the exception for all addresses
Application.Scope = 0

Application.Enabled = TRUE

Set Applications = firewallPolicy.AuthorizedApplications
Applications.Add(Application)
WScript.Echo("Program " & Application.Name & " added successfully!")
```

How It Works

One way to configure incoming traffic to pass through the firewall is by using a program exception. This allows a particular executable file to be accepted by the Windows Firewall, so long as exception processing is not disabled. By creating a program exception, Windows Firewall will only listen for traffic related to this exception if the program is running or active—if you close the application that requires the exception, traffic will not pass through the Windows Firewall even if it meets the criteria of the exception.

In addition to specifying the name of the application, you can also configure the *scope* of the exception. Scope options allow you to restrict which computers can communicate using the defined exception, rather than simply throwing it open to the entire world. You can choose from three options when configuring the scope of a program exception:

- **Any computer (including those on the Internet):** This setting will allow any computer on any network, including the Internet, to access your local computer by using the program exception you've defined. This is the least secure setting that you can configure, and it has the potential to expose your server to attacks from malicious users on untrusted networks.

- **My network (subnet) only:** This option will accept incoming requests only from computers that are on the same IPv4 or IPv6 subnet. For example, if your Windows Server 2003 computer has a single network connection to a private network with a network ID of 192.168.1.0 and a subnet mask of 255.255.255.0, this exception will be valid only for computers whose IP address falls within the range of 192.168.1.1 to 192.168.1.254.

> **Caution** The preceding setting can be deceptive, depending on how your server is configured. If you have a network connection to a private network, and are also directly connected to the Internet via a cable modem or other high-speed link, selecting the My Network (Subnet) Only option could potentially leave the exception open to all computers on your Internet service provider's network in addition to your own.

- **Custom list:** This option allows you to specify individual IPv4 addresses, ranges of IPv4 addresses, or any combination of the two. You can specify an individual IP address by simply entering its value, such as 10.0.0.151. You can specify a range of addresses using either of the following commonly accepted formats:

  - 10.0.0.0/255.0.0.0 indicates the 10.0.0.0 Class A network using the 255.0.0.0 subnet mask

  - 10.0.0.0/8 indicates the same network and subnet mask using classless interdomain routing (CIDR) notation, indicating that the first eight bits of the subnet mask (255.0.0.0) are used to indicate the network address.

> **Note** You cannot specify a custom list for IPv6 addresses, only IPv4.

Using Group Policy

In addition to enabling the Define Program Exceptions setting in Group Policy, you'll also need to define a list of programs that should be added to the exception list via Group Policy, as follows:

1. Enable the Define Program Exceptions setting in the Group Policy Object Editor, and then click Show.

2. Click Add to create a new program exception. In the Show Contents text box, enter the program exception using the following format (each portion of the string is explained next):

```
ProgramPath:Scope:Enabled|Disabled:ApplicationName
```

- ProgramPath allows you to enter the path and filename of the application. You can enter the path manually, or use environment variables such as %windir% or %ProgramFiles%.

- Scope specifies the scope of the exception. You can use * to specify the Any Computer setting, LocalSubnet to restrict the exception to your local network, or a single IP address or range of addresses to define a custom list. Create multiple entries by separating them with a comma, like this: LocalSubnet,10.0.0.151,10.112.25.0/255.255.255.0,10.121.79.0/24.

- Use Enabled or Disabled to indicate whether this program should be enabled or disabled in the exception list.

- ApplicationName creates a friendly name for the application exception; this is the name that will appear on the Exceptions tab in the Windows Firewall Control Panel applet.

Note You can create a program exception with a status of `Disabled` to prevent local administrators from enabling the program on an individual computer. The `Disabled` setting specified in Group Policy overrides any local settings.

An example of a complete Group Policy entry might look something like this:

```
C:\folder1\Standard.exe*:Enabled:Standard.exe
```

See Also

- Recipe 3-4 for information on configuring port exceptions

- Microsoft TechNet: "Configuring Scope Settings" (`http://technet2.microsoft.com/ WindowsServer/en/Library/94af04b3-140e-4108-8165-6d728470d5b21033.mspx`)

3-4. Creating Port Exceptions

Problem

You want to create a port exception to allow traffic on a particular TCP or UDP port to pass through the Windows Firewall on a Windows Server 2003 computer.

Solution

Using a Graphical User Interface

1. Open the Network Connections applet.

2. Double-click on the Local Area Connection icon.

3. From the Advanced tab, click Settings. This will launch the Windows Firewall Control Panel applet.

4. In the Windows Firewall applet, select the Exceptions tab. To add a new port that should be allowed to traverse the firewall, click Add Port.

5. Enter the name of the program or service in the Name text box. Enter the port number in the Port Number text box.

6. To define the scope of the exception, click on Change Scope, and select from one of the following three options:

   - Any computer (including those on the Internet).

   - My network (local subnet).

   - Custom list. For this option, enter a single IP address using the syntax `192.168.1.151`, and/or enter a range of addresses using the network ID of the range followed by its subnet mask, such as `192.168.1.1/255.255.255.0`. Separate multiple entries using a comma.

7. Click OK when you're finished.

Using a Command-Line Interface

The following command allows an application named FOO using TCP port 11065 to traverse the Windows Firewall. It restricts FOO to the local subnet, and configures it for the standard profile:

```
> netsh firewall add portopening protocol = TCP port = 11065
    name = FOO mode = ENABLE scope = SUBNET profile = STANDARD
```

Using Group Policy

Tables 3-7 and 3-8 contain the Group Policy settings that create port exceptions in the domain and standard profiles respectively.

Table 3-7. *Configure Port Exceptions—Domain Profile*

Path	Computer Configuration\Administrative Templates\Network\ Network Connections\Windows Firewall\Domain Profile
Policy name	Windows Firewall: Define port exceptions
Value	Enabled to configure a list of port exceptions. Disabled to remove any exceptions previously configured by Group Policy.

Table 3-8. *Configure Port Exceptions—Standard Profile*

Path	Computer Configuration\Administrative Templates\Network\ Network Connections\Windows Firewall\Standard Profile
Policy name	Windows Firewall: Define port exceptions
Value	Enabled to configure a list of port exceptions. Disabled to remove any exceptions previously configured by Group Policy.

Using the Registry

To configure an individual computer to allow an application called FOO using TCP port 11065 to traverse the Windows Firewall, set the following Registry value:

```
[HKEY_LOCAL_MACHINE\SYSTEM\CurrentControlSet\Services\SharedAccess\
    Parameters\FirewallPolicy\DomainProfile\AuthorizedApplications\List]
"11065:TCP":reg_sz:"11065:TCP:*:Enabled:FOO"
```

Note To restrict FOO traffic to the local subnet, change the "11065:TCP" reg_sz value to 11065:TCP:LocalSubNet:Enabled:FOO.

Using VBScript

This code allows an application named FOO using TCP port 11065 to traverse the Windows Firewall.

```
' ------ SCRIPT CONFIGURATION ------
 Set Firewall = CreateObject("HNetCfg.FwMgr")
 Set Policy = Firewall.LocalPolicy.CurrentProfile
 Set Port = CreateObject("HNetCfg.FwOpenPort")
' ------ END CONFIGURATION ---------

 Port.Port = 11065
 Port.Name = "FOO"
 Port.Protocol = NET_FW_IP_PROTOCOL_TCP
 Port.Enabled = TRUE

 set Ports = Policy.GloballyOpenPorts
 addedPorts = Ports.Add(Port)
WScript.Echo "Ports configured."
```

How It Works

Like program exceptions, port exceptions allow a certain type of traffic to traverse the Windows Firewall. Unlike program exceptions, which are based on a particular executable filename, port exceptions simply allow any traffic that is destined for a particular TCP or UDP port.

Another significant difference between port exceptions and program exceptions is that a program exception will only be active for as long as the program is running; if the program exits, the exception is no longer active. Contrast this with port exceptions, which will always listen for traffic on a particular port regardless of whether the associated application is running or not.

Because program exceptions lend themselves to more granular control of the Windows Firewall, you should try to enable program exceptions wherever possible. When necessary, however, you can enable port exceptions to listen continuously for incoming traffic bound for a particular port.

Using Group Policy

When defining program exceptions in Group Policy, ports should be added to the exception list as follows:

1. Enable the Define Port Exceptions setting in the Group Policy Object Editor, and then click Show.

2. Click Add to create a new program exception. In the Show Contents text box, enter the program exception using the following format (each portion of the string is explained next):

```
Port#:TCP|UDP:Scope:Enabled|Disabled:PortName
```

- Port# specifies the port number of the exception you're creating.

- Use TCP or UDP to specify the transport-level protocol being used by the port exception you're creating.

- Scope specifies the scope of the exception. You can use * to specify the Any Computer setting, LocalSubnet to restrict the exception to your local network, or a single IP address or range of IP addresses to define a custom list. Create multiple entries by separating them with a comma, like this: LocalSubnet,10.0.0.151,10.112.25.0/ 255.255.255.0,10.121.79.0/24

- Use Enabled or Disabled to indicate whether this port should be enabled or disabled in the exception list.

- PortName creates a user-friendly name for the port exception; this is the name that will appear on the Exceptions tab in the Windows Firewall Control Panel applet.

Note You cannot specify a custom scope for IPv6 addresses; it only supports * or LocalSubnet.

A complete Group Policy entry might look something like this:

```
8080:TCP:LocalSubnet:Enabled:IntranetApps
```

See Also

- Recipe 3-3 for more on creating program exceptions

- Microsoft TechNet: "Configuring Port Exceptions" (http://technet2.microsoft.com/ WindowsServer/en/Library/e53c01ac-1e0a-4693-af58-9242b884b5cd1033.mspx)

3-5. Managing Exceptions

Problem

You want to edit or delete an existing program or port exception on the Windows Firewall.

Solution

Using a Graphical User Interface

1. Open the Network Connections applet.

2. Double-click on the Local Area Connection icon.

3. From the Advanced tab, click Settings. This will launch the Windows Firewall Control Panel applet.

4. In the Windows Firewall applet, select the Exceptions tab. To edit an existing port or application exception, select the exception and click Edit. To remove the exception altogether, select the exception and click Delete.

Note When modifying a port exception, you can modify the name, scope, port number, and whether it uses TCP or UDP. When modifying a program exception, you can only modify its scope. If you need to change the executable name, you must delete the exception and create a new one.

Using the Registry

To modify an existing program or port exception, modify the appropriate reg_sz entry in the following location:

```
[HKEY_LOCAL_MACHINE\SYSTEM\CurrentControlSet\Services\SharedAccess\
    Parameters\FirewallPolicy\<Profile>\AuthorizedApplications\List]
```

Using a Command-Line Interface

The following command configures the Windows Firewall to permit an application named FOO using TCP port 11060. It restricts FOO to the local subnet and configures it for the domain profile:

```
> netsh firewall set portopening protocol = TCP port = 11060
    name = FOO mode = ENABLE scope = SUBNET profile = DOMAIN
```

The following command configures an existing application exception called Standard App to refer to an executable in the C:\Program Files\ directory:

```
> set allowedprogram program = "C:\Program FilesProgramFiles\Standard.exe"
    name = "Standard App" mode = ENABLE
```

The following two commands delete an existing application exception in the standard profile and delete an existing port exception from all profiles:

```
> netsh firewall delete allowedprogram program "C:\Program Files\Standard.exe"
    profile = STANDARD
> netsh firewall delete portopening protocol = TCP port = 11060 profile = ALL
```

Using Group Policy

To modify an exception that you've configured using Group Policy, delete the existing exception and re-create it using the instructions in Recipe 3-3 or 3-4.

Using VBScript

This code removes an existing application exception and re-creates it with new values.

```
' ------ SCRIPT CONFIGURATION ------
 Set Firewall = CreateObject("HNetCfg.FwMgr")
 Set Policy = Firewall.LocalPolicy
 Set Profile = Policy.GetProfileByType(1)
 strCurrentApp = "c:\program files\image\image123.exe"
 strNewApp = "c:\program files\image\imaging.exe"
' ------ END CONFIGURATION ---------

Set colApplications = Profile.AuthorizedApplications

For Each Application in colApplications
  If Application.ProcessImageFileName = strCurrentApp Then
    WScript.Echo "Removed " & Application.Name " from authorized list!"
    colApplications.Remove(Application)
  End If
Next

Set newApplication = CreateObject("HNetCfg.FwAuthorizedApplication")
newApplication.Name = "Imaging"
newApplication.IPVersion = 2
newApplication.ProcessImageFileName = strNewApp
newApplication.RemoteAddresses = "*"
newApplication.Scope = 0
newApplication.Enabled = True


colApplications.Add(objApplication)

WScript.Echo "Application " & strNewApp & " added successfully!"
```

How It Works

As an ongoing maintenance task, it's critical that you examine your Windows Firewall configuration on a regular basis to make sure that its configuration is up to date. At a minimum, you should remove any entries in the exception list that are out of date or not being used anymore, to prevent a malicious user or content from accessing your network via one of these "legitimate" entries. In addition, you can fine-tune your Windows Firewall configuration to limit the scope of your exceptions so that only legitimate users and computers can send unsolicited traffic to your Windows Server 2003 computer.

See Also

- Recipe 3-17 for more on configuring inbound connectivity

- Microsoft TechNet: "Help: Edit or Delete a Program Exception" (http://technet2.microsoft.com/WindowsServer/en/Library/ a433192f-6073-42a1-ab9b-de289d7e67951033.mspx)

- Microsoft TechNet: "Help: Edit or Delete a Port Exception" (http://technet2.microsoft.com/WindowsServer/en/Library/ c058566f-0d3f-41e4-9ff1-08c4409a17f51033.mspx)

3-6. Configuring Local Exceptions

Problem

You want to allow local administrators to create program or port exceptions in addition to those specified in Group Policy.

Solution

Tables 3-9 and 3-10 contain the Group Policy settings that allow local administrators to configure port or program exceptions in the domain profile.

Table 3-9. *Configure Local Program Exceptions—Domain Profile*

Path	Computer Configuration\Administrative Templates\Network\ Network Connections\Windows Firewall\Domain Profile
Policy name	Windows Firewall: Allow local program exceptions
Value	Enabled to allow local administrators to create exceptions. Disabled to prevent local administrators from changing firewall settings.

Table 3-10. *Configure Local Port Exceptions—Domain Profile*

Path	Computer Configuration\Administrative Templates\Network\ Network Connections\Windows Firewall\Domain Profile
Policy name	Windows Firewall: Allow local port exceptions
Value	Enabled to allow local administrators to create exceptions. Disabled to prevent local administrators from changing firewall settings.

Tables 3-11 and 3-12 contain the Group Policy settings that allow local administrators to configure port or program exceptions in the standard profile.

Table 3-11. *Configure Local Program Exceptions—Standard Profile*

Path	Computer Configuration\Administrative Templates\Network\ Network Connections\Windows Firewall\Standard Profile
Policy name	Windows Firewall: Allow local program exceptions
Value	Enabled to allow local administrators to create exceptions. Disabled to prevent local administrators from changing firewall settings.

Table 3-12. *Configure Local Port Exceptions—Standard Profile*

Path	`Computer Configuration\Administrative Templates\Network\` `Network Connections\Windows Firewall\Standard Profile`
Policy name	Windows Firewall: Allow local port exceptions
Value	`Enabled` to allow local administrators to create exceptions. `Disabled` to prevent local administrators from changing firewall settings.

How It Works

In a domain environment, the most efficient and effective way to configure the Windows Firewall is through the use of Group Policy objects (GPOs). This will ensure a consistent firewall configuration for all of the computers in your enterprise. However, you may need to allow local administrators to create their own exceptions for particular applications that they've deployed locally to a single Windows Server 2003 server. You can allow this by configuring the Allow Local Program/Port Exceptions settings in Group Policy.

Enabling this setting will allow the local administrator of a Windows Server 2003 computer to create a new exception for accepting inbound traffic. If you disable this setting, you have effectively prevented even your local administrators from altering the configuration of the Windows Firewall; the only exceptions that will be permitted are those defined by Group Policy.

See Also

- Recipes 3-3 and 3-4 for more on configuring exceptions

- Microsoft TechNet: "Help: Prevent Administrators from Configuring Local Program Exceptions" (`http://technet2.microsoft.com/WindowsServer/en/Library/134fedbd-2a53-4f70-893f-b8077a9328741033.mspx`)

- Microsoft TechNet: "Help: Prevent Administrators from Configuring Local Port Exceptions (`http://technet2.microsoft.com/WindowsServer/en/Library/1969e151-92bb-4108-b684-73f670e9c0521033.mspx`)

3-7. Configuring ICMP Traffic

Problem

You want to configure how Internet Control Message Protocol (ICMP) traffic is passed through or blocked by the Windows Firewall.

Solution

Using a Graphical User Interface

1. Open the Network Connections applet.

2. Double-click on the Local Area Connection icon.

3. From the Advanced tab, click Settings. This will launch the Windows Firewall Control Panel applet.

4. From the Advanced tab, click the Settings button in the ICMP section.

5. In the ICMP Settings section, place a check mark next to the ICMP packets that you want to allow:

   - Allow incoming echo request

   - Allow incoming timestamp request

   - Allow incoming mask request

   - Allow incoming router request

   - Allow outgoing destination unreachable

   - Allow outgoing source quench

   - Allow outgoing parameter problem

   - Allow outgoing time exceeded

   - Allow redirect

   - Allow outgoing packet too big

6. Click OK when you're finished.

Using a Command-Line Interface

The following command allows all ICMP traffic to pass through the Windows Firewall for the standard profile:

```
> netsh firewall set icmpsetting type = ALL mode = ENABLE profile = STANDARD
```

You can set mode to ENABLE or DISABLE; profile to CURRENT, DOMAIN, STANDARD, or ALL. For type, you can specify one or more of the following:

   2: Allow outbound packet too big

   3: Allow outbound destination unreachable

   4: Allow outbound source quench

   5: Allow redirect

   8: Allow inbound echo request

   9: Allow inbound router request

   11: Allow outbound time exceeded

   12: Allow outbound parameter problem

   13: Allow inbound timestamp request

17: Allow inbound mask request

ALL: All types

You can use commas or dashes to specify multiple exceptions, such as type = 2, 13, 11 or type = 2-5, 9.

Using Group Policy

Tables 3-13 and 3-14 show the settings that control ICMP traffic handling in the domain and standard profiles respectively.

Table 3-13. *Configure ICMP Traffic—Domain Profile*

Path	Computer Configuration\Administrative Templates\Network\ Network Connections\Windows Firewall\Domain Profile
Policy name	Windows Firewall: Allow ICMP exceptions
Value	Enabled to allow ICMP exceptions; Disabled to prevent them.

Table 3-14. *Configure ICMP Traffic—Standard Profile*

Path	Computer Configuration\Administrative Templates\Network\ Network Connections\Windows Firewall\Standard Profile
Policy name	Windows Firewall: Allow ICMP exceptions
Value	Enabled to allow ICMP exceptions; Disabled to prevent them.

Using the Registry

To configure an individual computer to allow various types of ICMP traffic through the Windows Firewall, set the following Registry values:

```
[HKEY_LOCAL_MACHINE\SYSTEM\CurrentControlSet\Services\SharedAccess\
    Parameters\FirewallPolicy\<Profile>\IcmpSettings\]
"AllowInboundEchoRequest"=dword:1
"AllowInboundRouterRequest"=dword:1
"AllowInboundTimestampRequest"=dword:1
"AllowInboundMaskRequest"=dword:1
"AllowOutboundDestinationUnreachable"=dword:1
"AllowOutboundSourceQuench"=dword:1
"AllowOutboundTimeExceeded"=dword:1
"AllowOutboundParameterProblem"=dword:1
"AllowOutboundPacketTooBig"=dword:1
"AllowRedirect"=dword:1
```

■**Note** When the Windows Firewall is enabled, all ICMP exceptions are turned off by default.

Using VBScript

This code enables all ICMP traffic to pass through the Windows Firewall.

```
Set Firewall = CreateObject("HNetCfg.FwMgr")
Set Policy = Firewall.LocalPolicy.CurrentProfile

Set ICMPSettings = Policy.ICMPSettings

ICMPSettings.AllowInboundEchoRequest = TRUE
ICMPSettings.AllowInboundMaskRequest = TRUE
ICMPSettings.AllowInboundRouterRequest = TRUE
ICMPSettings.AllowInboundTimestampRequest = TRUE
ICMPSettings.AllowOutboundDestinationUnreachable = TRUE
ICMPSettings.AllowOutboundPacketTooBig = TRUE
ICMPSettings.AllowOutboundParameterProblem = TRUE
ICMPSettings.AllowOutboundSourceQuench = TRUE
ICMPSettings.AllowOutboundTimeExceeded = TRUE
ICMPSettings.AllowRedirect = TRUE
WScript.Echo "Settings enabled"
```

How It Works

The Internet Control Message Protocol (ICMP) is used by TCP/IP utilities such as ping and tracert to assist in network troubleshooting and diagnostics. By default, the Windows Firewall will block any incoming ICMP traffic destined for the local computer, since ICMP can be misused as part of a number of network attacks. If you do not enable ICMP exceptions, you will not be able to use any network utilities that rely on ICMP to contact your Windows Server 2003 computer.

However, if you open TCP port 445, the Windows Firewall will automatically allow incoming ICMP echo messages, even if the Allow ICMP Exceptions setting is disabled through Group Policy. This will occur if you specifically create a port exception for TCP port 445, or if you enable the file and printer sharing or remote administration exceptions.

Using a Command-Line Interface

If you want to enable only specific ICMP message types using netsh, you'll need to specify a number associated with the message type in the `type =` parameter. The numeric values associated with the ICMP message types are as follows:

  2: Allow outbound packet too big

  3: Allow outbound destination unreachable

  4: Allow outbound source quench

  5: Allow redirect

8: Allow inbound echo request

9: Allow inbound router request

11: Allow outbound time exceeded

12: Allow outbound parameter problem

13: Allow inbound timestamp request

17: Allow inbound mask request

To enable individual ICMP message types, you'll need to issue a separate `netsh` command for each message type that you want, or use `type = ALL` to allow all ICMP messages.

Using Group Policy

In addition to enabling the Allow ICMP Exceptions Group Policy setting, you'll also need to place a check mark next to the individual ICMP message types that you wish to allow. For this setting, at least, the Group Policy user interface is essentially identical to the Windows Firewall Control Panel applet; it does not require you to manually enter a complex configuration string.

■ Note Enabling ICMP exceptions overrides any locally configured ICMP settings on a Windows Server 2003 computer. If you *disable* this setting in Group Policy, local administrators will be unable to define any ICMP exceptions locally.

See Also

- Microsoft TechNet: "Help: Configure ICMP Exceptions" (http://technet2.microsoft. com/WindowsServer/en/Library/b07dd75f-ab62-475a-be2e-709f67416c201033.mspx)

- Microsoft TechNet: "Block and Unblock ICMP Messages" (http://technet2.microsoft. com/WindowsServer/en/Library/c65c9cdc-0613-411c-a474-b779dac4d1881033.mspx)

- MSDN: "Configuring ICMP Settings in Windows Firewall" (http:// msdn.microsoft.com/library/default.asp?url=/library/en-us/xpehelp/ html/xeconfiguringicmpsettingsinwindowsfirewall.asp)

3-8. Configuring Remote Administration Through the Windows Firewall

Problem

You want to configure the Windows Firewall to allow remote administration of a Windows Server 2003 computer.

Solution

Using a Command-Line Interface

The following command enables the remote administration exception for the local subnet in the domain profile:

```
> netsh firewall set service type = REMOTEADMIN mode = ENABLE
    scope = SUBNET profile = DOMAIN
```

As with other exceptions that you enable through netsh, you can set mode to ENABLE or DISABLE; scope to ALL, SUBNET, or CUSTOM; and profile to CURRENT, DOMAIN, STANDARD, or ALL. If you set the scope to CUSTOM, you also need to specify addresses = followed by a comma-separated list of IPv4 IP addresses.

Using Group Policy

Tables 3-15 and 3-16 contain the Group Policy settings that enable remote administration through the Windows Firewall in the domain and standard profiles respectively.

Table 3-15. *Configure Remote Administration Exception—Domain Profile*

Path	Computer Configuration\Administrative Templates\Network\ Network Connections\Windows Firewall\Domain Profile
Policy name	Windows Firewall: Allow remote administration exception
Value	Enabled to allow remote administration. Disabled to prevent it.

Table 3-16. *Configure Remote Administration Exception—Standard Profile*

Path	Computer Configuration\Administrative Templates\Network\ Network Connections\Windows Firewall\Standard Profile
Policy name	Windows Firewall: Allow remote administration exception
Value	Enabled to allow remote administration. Disabled to prevent it.

Using the Registry

To configure an individual computer to allow for remote administration through the Windows Firewall, set the following Registry value:

```
[HKEY_LOCAL_MACHINE\SYSTEM\CurrentControlSet\Services\SharedAccess\
    Parameters\FirewallPolicy\<Profile>\RemoteAdminSettings\]
"Enabled"=dword:1
"RemoteAddresses=reg_sz:"IpAddress, IpAddress, localsubnet"
```

Using VBScript

This code enables the remote administration exception for the current profile.

```
Set Firewall = CreateObject("HNetCfg.FwMgr")
Set Policy = Firewall.LocalPolicy.CurrentProfile
Set AdminSettings = Policy.RemoteAdminSettings
AdminSettings.Enabled = TRUE
WScript.Echo "Setting enabled"
```

How It Works

In a domain environment, you'll often want to remotely administer server and workstations using tools such as Computer Management or Windows Management Instrumentation (WMI). This is because most of the administration tools you'll use need to make unsolicited incoming connections to the computer that you're trying to administer, using TCP port 445 and the svchost.exe and lsass.exe executables. As such, you'll need to open the necessary ports on the Windows Firewall to allow you to use these tools on machines in your environment.

Caution The ports and executables used by the remote administration exception are well-known attack vectors. Be sure to only open this exception selectively to trusted hosts that require access to it.

In order to enable remote administration through the Windows Firewall, you'll need to enable the appropriate setting in Group Policy, the Windows Registry, or VBScript; you cannot make this change in the Windows Firewall Control Panel applet.

In addition to enabling the remote administration exception through Group Policy, you need to specify the IPv4 addresses that are permitted to make remote administration connections. As with other Windows Firewall Group Policy settings, you can use LocalSubnet to specify the local subnet, * to specify all hosts, or a custom list of addresses. For IPv6 addresses, you can only specify LocalSubnet or *; you can't create a custom exception list.

See Also

- Recipes 3-3 and 3-4 for more on enabling program and port exceptions

- Microsoft TechNet: "Windows Firewall Settings: Remote Administration Tools" (http://technet2.microsoft.com/WindowsServer/en/Library/ 62d661cc-8267-4440-aacc-55358c602a081033.mspx)

3-9. Configuring File and Print Sharing Through the Windows Firewall

Problem

You want to configure the Windows Firewall to allow file and printer sharing.

Solution

Using a Graphical User Interface

1. Open the Network Connections applet.

2. Double-click on the Local Area Connection icon.

3. From the Advanced tab, click Settings. This will launch the Windows Firewall Control Panel applet.

4. From the Exceptions tab, place a check mark next to File and Printer Sharing.

5. To define the scope of the exception, click on Edit, followed by Change Scope, and select from one of the following three options:

   • Any computer (including those on the Internet).

   • My network (local subnet).

   • Custom list. For this option, enter a single IP address using the syntax 192.168.1.151, and/or enter a range of addresses using the network ID of the range followed by its subnet mask, such as 192.168.1.1/255.255.255.0. Separate multiple entries using a comma.

6. Click OK when you're finished.

Using a Command-Line Interface

The following command enables the file and printer sharing exception.

```
> netsh firewall set service type = fileandprint mode = ENABLE
```

Using Group Policy

Tables 3-17 and 3-18 show the settings that control the file and printer sharing exception within the Windows Firewall in the domain and standard profiles respectively.

Table 3-17. *Configure File and Printer Sharing Exception—Domain Profile*

Path	Computer Configuration\Administrative Templates\Network\ Network Connections\Windows Firewall\Domain Profile
Policy name	Windows Firewall: Allow file and printer sharing exception
Value	Enabled to allow file and printer sharing. Disabled to prevent it.

Table 3-18. *Configure File and Printer Sharing Exception—Standard Profile*

Path	Computer Configuration\Administrative Templates\Network\ Network Connections\Windows Firewall\Standard Profile
Policy name	Windows Firewall: Allow file and printer sharing exception
Value	Enabled to allow file and printer sharing. Disabled to prevent it.

Using VBScript

This code enables the file and printer sharing exception for the current firewall profile.

```
' ------ SCRIPT CONFIGURATION ------
 Set Firewall = CreateObject("HNetCfg.FwMgr")
 Set Policy = Firewall.LocalPolicy.CurrentProfile
' ------ END CONFIGURATION ---------
Set Services = Policy.Services
Set Service = Services.Item(0)
Service.Enabled = TRUE
WScript.Echo "Setting enabled"
```

How It Works

Before the Windows Firewall was available through Service Pack 1 for Windows Server 2003, enabling file and printer sharing meant that you needed to manually open UDP ports 137 and 138, TCP ports 139 and 445, and the ICMP echo message. In the Windows Firewall, you can simply enable or disable the preconfigured file and printer sharing exception in the GUI, the Registry, or using netsh or VBScript.

Like the remote administration exception, file and printer sharing opens several well-known ports that are often used by malicious users to engage in network attacks. You should therefore configure the scope of the file and printer sharing exception carefully to ensure that only authorized users can access these ports on your Windows Server 2003 computer.

Though both the remote administration and file and printer sharing exceptions open TCP port 445, you can enable and disable them independently of each other. However, enabling the file and printer sharing exception will enable ICMP echo messages even if you've disabled the ICMP exception.

In addition to enabling the file and printer sharing exception in Group Policy, you need to specify the IPv4 addresses that are permitted to make remote administration connections. As with other Windows Firewall settings, you can use LocalSubnet to specify the local subnet, * to specify all hosts, or a custom list of addresses. For IPv6 addresses, you can only specify LocalSubnet or *; you can't create a custom exception list.

Note If you disable the file and printer sharing exception without allowing local exceptions as described in Recipe 3-5, local administrators will not be able to enable the exception on any computers that they administer.

See Also

- Recipe 3-8 to configure the remote administration exception

- Eric Cross's Networking: "Configure Windows Firewall Settings for File and Printer Sharing" (http://ecross.mvps.org/howto/firewall.htm)

- Microsoft TechNet: "Help: Enable or Disable the File and Printer Sharing Exception" (http://www.microsoft.com/technet/prodtechnol/windowsserver2003/library/ServerHelp/267c6000-957e-4fb4-8698-e41d4439fb58.mspx)

3-10. Configuring Remote Assistance Through the Windows Firewall

Problem

You want to configure the Windows Firewall to allow Remote Assistance on a Windows Server 2003 computer.

Solution

1. Open the Network Connections applet.

2. Double-click on the Local Area Connection icon.

3. From the Advanced tab, click Settings. This will launch the Windows Firewall Control Panel applet.

4. From the Exceptions tab, place a check mark next to Remote Assistance.

5. To define the scope of the exception, click on Edit, followed by Change Scope, and select from one of the following three options:

   • Any computer (including those on the Internet).

   • My network (local subnet).

   • Custom list. For this option, enter a single IP address using the syntax 192.168.1.151, or enter a range of addresses using the network ID of the range followed by its subnet mask, such as 192.168.1.1/255.255.255.0. Separate multiple entries using a comma.

6. Click OK when you're finished.

Using a Command-Line Interface

The following command enables Remote Assistance requests to pass through the Windows Firewall

```
> netsh firewall set service type = remotedesktop mode = ENABLE
```

Using Group Policy

Tables 3-19 and 3-20 show the settings that control the Remote Assistance exception within the Windows Firewall in the domain and standard profiles respectively.

Table 3-19. *Configure Remote Assistance Exception—Domain Profile*

Path	Computer Configuration\Administrative Templates\Network\ Network Connections\Windows Firewall\Domain Profile
Policy name	Windows Firewall: Allow remote desktop exception
Value	Enabled to allow incoming remote desktop traffic. Disabled to prevent it.

Table 3-20. *Configure Remote Assistance Exception—Standard Profile*

Path	`Computer Configuration\Administrative Templates\Network\` `Network Connections\Windows Firewall\Standard Profile`
Policy name	Windows Firewall: Allow remote desktop exception
Value	`Enabled` to allow incoming remote desktop traffic. `Disabled` to prevent it.

Using VBScript

This code allows Remote Assistance to traverse the Windows Firewall.

```
Set Firewall = CreateObject("HNetCfg.FwMgr")
 Set Policy = Firewall.LocalPolicy.CurrentProfile
 Set Port = CreateObject("HNetCfg.FwOpenPort")

 Port.Port = 3389
 Port.Name = "Remote Desktop"
 Port.Protocol = NET_FW_IP_PROTOCOL_TCP
 Port.Enabled = TRUE

 set Ports = Policy.GloballyOpenPorts
 addedPorts = Ports.Add(Port)
WScript.Echo "Ports configured."
```

How It Works

Remote Assistance is a feature in Windows XP and Windows Server 2003 that lets you share control of your computer with another user. Unlike a Terminal Services session, this grants you direct access to view and manipulate a user's desktop to offer them support. Creating a Remote Assistance connection requires the permission of the user to whose computer you're trying to connect.

To enable Remote Assistance connections prior to Windows Server 2003 Service Pack 1, you needed to manually configure the following program exceptions:

- `%WINDIR%\PCHealth\HelpCtr\Binaries\Helpsvc.exe`

- `%WINDIR%\PCHealth\HelpCtr\Binaries\Helpctr.exe`

- `%WINDIR%\SYSTEM32\Sessmgr.exe`

Additionally, you needed to enable access to TCP port 135.

On Windows Server 2003 computers with Service Pack 1 installed, you simply need to enable the preconfigured Allow Remote Desktop Exception setting; there is not a separate exception to enable for Remote Assistance. As with other exceptions, you should restrict the scope of this exception to protect your systems against attacks targeted at the well-known Remote Procedure Call (RPC) port, TCP 135.

See Also

- Recipes 3-3 and 3-4 for more on configuring program and port exceptions

- Microsoft TechNet: "Configuring System Service Exceptions" (http://
www.microsoft.com/technet/prodtechnol/windowsserver2003/
library/Operations/9a29df7b-235a-42fd-9c25-13f6be94ad9a.mspx)

3-11. Configuring UPnP Through the Windows Firewall

Problem

You want to configure the Windows Firewall to allow Universal Plug and Play (UPnP) on a
Windows Server 2003 computer.

Solution

Using a Graphical User Interface

1. Open the Network Connections applet.

2. Double-click on the Local Area Connection icon.

3. From the Advanced tab, click Settings. This will launch the Windows Firewall Control
   Panel applet.

4. From the Exceptions tab, place a check mark next to UPnP Framework.

5. To define the scope of the exception, click on Edit, followed by Change Scope, and
   select from one of the following three options:

   - Any computer (including those on the Internet).

   - My network (local subnet).

   - Custom list. For this option, enter a single IP address using the syntax 192.168.1.151,
     or enter a range of addresses using the network ID of the range followed by its subnet
     mask, such as 192.168.1.1/255.255.255.0. Separate multiple entries using a comma.

6. Click OK when you're finished.

Using a Command-Line Interface

The following command enables UPnP to pass through the Windows Firewall:

```
> netsh firewall set service type = upnp mode = ENABLE
```

Using Group Policy

Tables 3-21 and 3-22 show the settings that control the UPnP exception within the Windows Firewall in the domain and standard profiles respectively.

Table 3-21. *Configure UPnP Exception—Domain Profile*

Path	`Computer Configuration\Administrative Templates\Network\` `Network Connections\Windows Firewall\Domain Profile`
Policy name	Windows Firewall: Allow UPnP framework exception
Value	`Enabled` to allow incoming UPnP traffic. `Disabled` to prevent it.

Table 3-22. *Configure UPnP Exception—Standard Profile*

Path	`Computer Configuration\Administrative Templates\Network\` `Network Connections\Windows Firewall\Standard Profile`
Policy name	Windows Firewall: Allow UPnP framework exception
Value	`Enabled` to allow incoming UPnP traffic. `Disabled` to prevent it.

Using VBScript

This code allows UPnP traffic to traverse the Windows Firewall.

```
Set Firewall = CreateObject("HNetCfg.FwMgr")
Set Policy = Firewall.LocalPolicy.CurrentProfile
Set TcpPort = CreateObject("HNetCfg.FwOpenPort")
Set UdpPort = CreateObject("HNetCfg.FwOpenPort")

TcpPort.Port = 2869
TcpPort.Name = "UPnP Framework"
TcpPort.Protocol = NET_FW_IP_PROTOCOL_TCP
TcpPort.Enabled = TRUE

UdpPort.Port = 1900
UdpPort.Name = "UPnP Framework"
UdpPort.Protocol = NEW_FW_IP_PROTOCOL_UDP
UdpPort.Enabled = True

set Ports = Policy.GloballyOpenPorts
addedPorts = Ports.Add(TcpPort)
addedPorts = Ports.Add(UdpPort)
WScript.Echo "Ports configured"
```

How It Works

The Universal Plug and Play (UPnP) framework extends the functionality of Plug-and-Play devices to allow device discovery and driver installations over a local area network or the Internet. Using UPnP, a device can automatically connect to a network and discover other network devices, allowing them to communicate directly without requiring administrator configuration or intervention.

UPnP requires the ability to make unsolicited connections on TCP port 2869 and UDP port 1900. If you choose to enable UPnP on your network, be sure to restrict the scope of the exception to only authorized computers, using comma-separated IP addresses or the LocalSubnet parameter.

See Also

- Recipe 3-4 for more on configuring port exceptions

- Microsoft KB 886257: "How Windows Firewall Affects the UPnP Framework in Windows XP Service Pack 2"

3-12. Configuring Firewall Notifications

Problem

You want to control how the Windows Firewall notifies the user of a Windows Server 2003 computer about events relating to the Windows Firewall.

Solution

Using a Graphical User Interface

1. Open the Network Connections applet.

2. Double-click on the Local Area Connection icon.

3. From the Advanced tab, click Settings. This will launch the Windows Firewall Control Panel applet.

4. From the Exceptions tab, place a check mark next to Display a Notification When Windows Firewall Blocks a Program to enable Windows Firewall notification. Remove this check box to disable notifications.

Using a Command-Line Interface

The following command enables the Windows Firewall to notify the local user of any programs it blocks in both the standard and domain profiles:

```
> netsh firewall set notifications mode = ENABLE profile = ALL
```

Using Group Policy

Tables 3-23 and 3-24 show the settings that control program notifications within the Windows Firewall in the domain and standard profiles respectively.

Table 3-23. *Configure UPnP Exception—Domain Profile*

Path	Computer Configuration\Administrative Templates\Network\ Network Connections\Windows Firewall\Domain Profile
Policy name	Windows Firewall: Prohibit notifications
Value	Enabled to disallow notifications; Disabled to allow notifications.

Table 3-24. *Configure UPnP Exception—Standard Profile*

Path	Computer Configuration\Administrative Templates\Network\ Network Connections\Windows Firewall\Standard Profile
Policy name	Windows Firewall: Prohibit notifications
Value	Enabled to disallow notifications; Disabled to allow notifications.

Using the Registry

To configure an individual computer to allow the Windows Firewall to notify the local user when it blocks a particular program, set the following Registry value:

```
[HKEY_LOCAL_MACHINE\SYSTEM\CurrentControlSet\Services\SharedAccess\
    Parameters\FirewallPolicy\<Profile>\]
"DisableNotifications"=dword:0
```

Using VBScript

This code enables firewall notifications.

```
Set Firewall = CreateObject("HNetCfg.FwMgr")
Set Policy = Firewall.LocalPolicy.CurrentProfile
Policy.NotificationsDisabled = FALSE ' set this to TRUE to disable notifications
WScript.Echo "Notifications enabled"
```

How It Works

When most applications request an open port, Windows Firewall adds the program to the program exceptions list with the default status value of Disabled. If you enable this policy setting, notifications are not displayed, and the status value for the program exception remains Disabled until manually changed.

If you disable or do not configure this policy setting, Windows Firewall displays notification messages.

If the user is not a local administrator, the message informs them that they might need to contact a network administrator, which can alert the network administrator about possible malicious programs on the network.

If the user is a local administrator, and you have either enabled the Windows Firewall: Allow Local Program Exceptions setting or you have not configured the Windows Firewall: Define Program Exceptions setting, the notification message allows the user to specify whether to enable the application. If you disable the Windows Firewall: Define Program Exceptions setting, the user will not be notified unless the policy is enabled locally.

See Also

- Recipe 3-19 for more on auditing Windows Firewall events

- Microsoft TechNet: "Managing Windows Firewall Notifications"
  (http://technet2.microsoft.com/WindowsServer/en/Library/
  b3440a22-ae9c-45a3-8a61-da3f8a2c791f1033.mspx)

- Microsoft TechNet: "Known Issues for Managing Windows Firewall Notifications"
  (http://technet2.microsoft.com/WindowsServer/en/Library/
  2e3c1981-39fb-4979-bd16-c38ec6bf29fb1033.mspx)

3-13. Allowing IPSec Traffic

Problem

You want to allow IPSec traffic to pass through the Windows Firewall on a Windows Server 2003 computer.

Solution

Using Group Policy

Table 3-25 contains the Group Policy setting that allows IPSec traffic to bypass the Windows Firewall.

Table 3-25. *Configure IPSec Traffic Exception*

Path	Computer Configuration\Administrative Templates\Network\ Network Connections
Policy name	Windows Firewall: Allow authenticated IPSec bypass
Value	Enabled to allow authenticated IPSec traffic to bypass the Windows Firewall. Disabled to prevent it.

How It Works

By default, the Windows Firewall will allow Internet Key Exchange (IKE) packets to pass through the firewall on UDP ports 500 and 4500. You have the additional option to allow *all* IPSec-protected traffic to bypass the Windows Firewall. To configure this, you can use the Allow Authenticated IPSec Bypass Group Policy setting to allow incoming, unsolicited IPSec traffic to bypass the Windows Firewall.

In order for this feature to work effectively, you need to specify which computers should be allowed to communicate this way. You'll do this in the Group Policy setting listed in Table 3-25 by listing a Security Descriptor Definition Language (SDDL) string that contains a list of the computers or groups of computers that should be exempt from the Windows Firewall blocking rules. An SDDL string is formatted as follows:

```
O:DAG:DAD:(A;;RCGW;;;<SID>)
```

In this syntax, `<SID>` refers to the Security Identifier (SID) of the computer or group of computers to which this policy should apply.

You can obtain the SID of an object within Active Directory by using the getsid.exe utility from Windows Support Tools. To obtain the SID for a group of computers called `DOMAINPCS`, for example, you would use the following syntax:

```
getsid \\<domain_controller> DOMAINPCS \\<domain_controller> DOMAINPCS
```

Getsid will return a numeric SID that looks something like this:

```
S-1-5-21-3475798998-36396922571-9412747344-3157
```

You would then enter the following SDDL string into Group Policy in the `Define IPSec Peers to be exempted from firewall policy` text box:

```
O:DAG:DAD:(A;;RCGW;;; S-1-5-21-3475798998-36396922571-9412747344-3157)
```

To enter multiple computers or groups of computers, use a single SDDL string with the following syntax:

```
O:DAG:DAD:(A;;RCGW;;;<SID1>) (A;;RCGW;;;<SID2>) (A;;RCGW;;;<SID3>)...
```

Caution If you configure an SDDL in Group Policy and subsequently disable the Allow Authenticated IPSec Bypass setting, the SDDL will be deleted.

See Also

Microsoft TechNet: "Help: Allow IPSec Traffic to Bypass Windows Firewall" (http://www.microsoft.com/technet/prodtechnol/windowsserver2003/library/ServerHelp/c7dd775d-00e9-4957-beba-3d82f1d829ad.mspx)

3-14. Controlling Broadcast and Multicast Traffic

Problem

You want to configure how the Windows Firewall responds to broadcast and multicast traffic on a Windows Server 2003 computer.

Solution

Using a Command-Line Interface

The following command enables the local computer to respond to broadcast or multicast traffic while using the domain profile:

```
> netsh firewall set multicastbroadcastresponse mode = ENABLE profile = DOMAIN
```

Using Group Policy

Tables 3-26 and 3-27 show the settings that control multicast and broadcast traffic behavior in the domain and standard profiles respectively.

Table 3-26. *Configure Multicast and Broadcast Traffic—Domain Profile*

Path	Computer Configuration\Administrative Templates\Network\ Network Connections\Windows Firewall\Domain Profile
Policy name	Windows Firewall: Prohibit unicast response to multicast or broadcast requests
Value	Enabled to disallow responses to broadcast/multicast traffic; Disabled to allow the local computer to respond.

Table 3-27. *Configure Multicast and Broadcast Traffic—Standard Profile*

Path	Computer Configuration\Administrative Templates\Network\ Network Connections\Windows Firewall\Standard Profile
Policy name	Windows Firewall: Prohibit unicast response to multicast or broadcast requests
Value	Enabled to disallow responses to broadcast/multicast traffic; Disabled to allow the local computer to respond.

Using the Registry

To configure an individual computer not to respond to multicast or broadcast traffic, set the following Registry value:

```
[HKEY_LOCAL_MACHINE\SYSTEM\CurrentControlSet\Services\SharedAccess\
    Parameters\FirewallPolicy\<Profile>\]
"DisableUnicastResponsesToMulticastBroadcast"=dword:1
```

Using VBScript

This code disables unicast responses to broadcast or multicast traffic.

```
Set Firewall = CreateObject("HNetCfg.FwMgr")
Set Policy = Firewall.LocalPolicy.CurrentProfile
Policy. UnicastResponsestoMulticastBroadcastDisabled = TRUE
' set this to FALSE to enable broadcast/multicast responses
WScript.Echo "Unicast disabled"
```

How It Works

When a Windows Server 2003 computer sends a multicast or broadcast packet, it will drop any unicast packets sent in response to the broadcast that are not received within three seconds. By enabling the Prohibit Unicast Response to Multicast or Broadcast Requests setting, Windows Firewall will drop any packet received in response to broadcast or multicast traffic. (The default setting for this behavior is Not Configured.)

The exception to this setting is that Windows Firewall will permit traffic associated with a DHCP lease request. However, this setting can interfere with broadcast-based NetBIOS name resolution, since responses to a NetBIOS broadcast will be dropped, preventing the computer from resolving a NetBIOS name to an IP address using broadcasts. If your network uses WINS for NetBIOS name resolution, this problem will be alleviated.

See Also

Microsoft TechNet: "Computer Names Do Not Resolve When Used in a UNC Path" (http://technet2.microsoft.com/WindowsServer/en/Library/ b8b1438d-8871-406d-a366-75f1f3a815e91033.mspx)

3-15. Resetting the Windows Firewall

Problem

You want to reset the Windows Firewall to its default protection settings.

Solution

Using a Graphical User Interface

1. Open the Network Connections applet.

2. Double-click on the Local Area Connection icon.

3. From the Advanced tab, click Settings. This will launch the Windows Firewall Control Panel applet.

4. From the Advanced tab, click the Restore Defaults button in the Default Settings section. Click Yes to acknowledge the warning message stating that this will delete all settings of Windows Firewall that you have made since Windows was installed.

5. Click OK when you're finished.

Using a Command-Line Interface

The following command resets the Windows Firewall to its default settings:

```
> netsh firewall reset
```

Using VBScript

This code restores the Windows Firewall to its default settings.

```
Set Firewall = CreateObject("HNetCfg.FwMgr")
Firewall.RestoreDefaults()
WScript.Echo "Default settings restored."
```

How It Works

As an ongoing administrative task, you should monitor and audit your firewall settings to ensure that any existing settings, such as port and program exceptions, are still applicable to your current environment. This ensures that your network is not exposed to any unnecessary risks caused by unused or out-of-date firewall exceptions being enabled.

By using the RestoreDefaults() method, you can erase all user-defined program and port exceptions that you've created, and restore the Windows Firewall to its default setting of Enabled with appropriate exceptions permitted.

Note As a precaution, you should take a Registry backup before performing this procedure.

See Also

- The RestoreDefault() method in the Windows Firewall

- Microsoft TechNet: "Restore Windows Firewall Default Settings"
  (http://technet2.microsoft.com/WindowsServer/en/Library/
  22623f4a-4699-4a59-8365-97783d117bd81033.mspx)

3-16. Configuring Per-Interface Protection

Problem

You want to enable or disable the Windows Firewall for individual network interface cards (NICs) installed in a Windows Server 2003 computer.

Solution

Using a Graphical User Interface

1. Open the Network Connections applet.

2. Double-click on the Local Area Connection icon.

3. From the Advanced tab, click Settings. This will launch the Windows Firewall Control Panel applet.

4. From the Advanced tab, remove the check mark next to the interface name that should not be protected by the Windows Firewall in the Network Connections Settings section. To re-enable Windows Firewall protection for a particular interface, place a check mark next to it.

5. Click OK when you're finished.

Note This option is only available if you have more than one NIC installed in your Windows Server 2003 computer. For a single-homed computer, you can enable or disable the Windows Firewall using the steps in Recipe 3-1.

Using a Command-Line Interface

The following command disables the Windows Firewall for the NIC associated with the Local Area Connection.

```
> netsh firewall set opmode mode = DISABLE interface = "Local Area Connection"
```

Note If you are enabling or disabling the Windows Firewall for an individual interface, you cannot specify either the profile or the exceptions switch.

How It Works

When you are working with a multi-homed Windows Server 2003 computer, you may need to enable or disable the Windows Firewall on a per-interface basis, rather than globally for the entire server. You may wish to enable unfettered connectivity on a private network, for example, or you may have a hardware-based firewall protecting the NIC attached to a public network such as the Internet. Even if this is the case, however, the Windows Firewall is able to coexist with third-party products, and might still be a useful tool to provide "defense in depth" for your Windows Server 2003 computers, since the Windows Firewall will take effect before any third-party applications you've installed.

When working from the command line, you cannot use the `profile=` or `exceptions=` parameters in conjunction with the `interface=` parameter. To configure exceptions for an individual interface, you can use the `netsh firewall set portopening` command, which we will discuss in the next recipe.

See Also

- Recipe 3-1 for more on enabling and disabling the Windows Firewall

- Microsoft TechNet: "Help: Understanding Windows Firewall Exceptions" (http://technet2.microsoft.com/WindowsServer/en/Library/ 7a19b261-840a-449e-b2b3-38b136d7bd591033.mspx)

3-17. Enabling Per-Interface Inbound Connectivity

Problem

You want to configure the Windows Firewall to allow external users to connect to the local computer.

Solution

Using a Graphical User Interface

1. Open the Network Connections applet.

2. Double-click on the Local Area Connection icon.

3. From the Advanced tab, click Settings. This will launch the Windows Firewall Control Panel applet.

4. From the Advanced tab, select the interface that should be listening for inbound traffic in the Network Connections Settings section. Click Settings to configure the applications that this interface should be listening for connections on.

5. The Windows Firewall is preconfigured to enable inbound traffic for any of the following applications:

- FTP Server

- Internet Mail Access Protocol (IMAP) version 3

- Internet Mail Access Protocol (IMAP) version 4

- Internet Mail Server (SMTP)

- Post Office Protocol version 3 (POP3)

- Remote Desktop

- Secure Web Server (HTTPS)

- Telnet Server

- Web Server (HTTP)

Place a check mark next to the protocol(s) that you want to enable for inbound traffic.

6. To create a new port for inbound connectivity, click on Add and follow these steps:

   a. Enter the name of the service or application in the Description of Service text box.

   b. Enter the DNS name or IP address of the computer that's hosting this service in the Name text box.

   c. Select the appropriate radio button next to TCP or UDP.

   d. Enter the external port number on which this application or service listens in the External Port Number for This Service text box.

   e. Enter the internal port number (if you are translating port numbers on your internal network, for example) in the Internal Port Number for This Service text box.

7. Click OK when you are finished.

Using a Command-Line Interface

The following command enables inbound connectivity on TCP port 80 for the Local Area Network interface:

```
> netsh firewall set portopening protocol = TCP port = 80 name = WEB
   mode = ENABLE interface = "Local Area Network"
```

Note You can also enable per-interface ICMP exceptions by using the netsh firewall set icmpsettings command with the interface= parameter.

How It Works

When you are working with a multi-homed server—a server containing more than one network interface card (NIC) and attached to more than one network segment—you may have Windows Firewall exceptions that are only applicable to a particular interface.

For example, you may have a Windows Server 2003 that is attached to a private network as well as the Internet, on which you've installed the Internet Information Server (IIS) to host your company's public website. In this case, the NIC that is connected to the Internet should be configured to listen for unsolicited incoming requests on the HTTP port, TCP port 80. However, you may wish to restrict access to this port to the public-facing NIC only, while the NIC attached to your private network should not accept unsolicited HTTP traffic. In this case, you'll need to configure only the Internet-connected NIC with an exception for the HTTP port; this exception should not apply to the NIC attached to the private network.

Because this is a common reason to enable per-connection Windows Firewall settings, the Windows Firewall Control Panel applet allows you to easily select several preconfigured services for per-connection exceptions, including the FTP service, telnet server service, IMAP, SMTP, and HTTP/HTTPS for Web traffic.

See Also

- Recipe 3-7 for more on configuring ICMP exceptions

- Microsoft TechNet: "Help: Add a System Service to the Windows Firewall Exceptions List" (http://technet2.microsoft.com/WindowsServer/en/Library/ 34cfba8e-d564-4a8c-9f4c-58120bed441d1033.mspx)

3-18. Configuring Firewall Logging

Problem

You want to control how the Windows Firewall logs information on a Windows Server 2003 computer.

Solution

Using a Graphical User Interface

1. Open the Network Connections applet.

2. Double-click on the Local Area Connection icon.

3. From the Advanced tab, click Settings. This will launch the Windows Firewall Control Panel applet.

4. From the Advanced tab, click the Settings button in the Security Logging section.

5. In the Logging Options section, place a check mark next to one or both of the following settings:

- Log dropped packets

- Log successful connections

6. In the Log File Options section, specify the filename and directory path of the log file in the Name text box. Specify the maximum size of the file in the Size Limit (KB) window.

7. Click OK when you're finished.

Using a Command-Line Interface

The following command enables Windows firewall logging for dropped packets with a maximum file size of 8,192 bytes:

```
> netsh firewall set logging c:\logs\wfirewall.log droppedpackets = ENABLE
    maxfilesize = 8192
```

Using Group Policy

Tables 3-28 and 3-29 contain the Group Policy settings that dictate whether Windows Firewall should log firewall activity for the domain and standard profiles respectively.

Table 3-28. *Configure Firewall Logging—Domain Profile*

Path	Computer Configuration\Administrative Templates\Network\ Network Connections\Windows Firewall\Domain Profile
Policy name	Windows Firewall: Allow logging
Value	Enabled to turn on logging. Disabled to turn off logging.

Table 3-29. *Configure Firewall Logging—Standard Profile*

Path	Computer Configuration\Administrative Templates\Network\ Network Connections\Windows Firewall\Standard Profile
Policy name	Windows Firewall: Allow logging
Value	Enabled to turn on logging. Disabled to turn off logging.

How It Works

When you enable logging, the Windows Firewall creates a text file containing information about any packets that it drops or accepts. By default, the file is stored as c:\windows\ pfirewall.log with a maximum file size of 4096 bytes (4MB). Once the file reaches its maximum size, Windows will begin logging to a new file called pfirewall.log.1.

The log file itself is recorded in the W3C Extended Log File Format. This is an industry standard format that will allow you to analyze the log file in a simple text editor like Notepad, or to import log information into a database for analysis with third-party tools. The file begins with a header that lists the fields that are recorded, as follows:

```
#Version: 1.5
#Software: Microsoft Windows Firewall
#Time Format: Local
#Fields: date time action protocol src-ip dst-ip src-port dst-port size
    tcpflags tcpsyn tcpack tcpwin icmptype icmpcode info path
```

After the header, the body of the log file begins. Each line in the body records a packet that was either dropped or allowed to pass through the firewall. Each field in the body of the file corresponds to the title listed in the header; a dash (-) indicates that there was no information to record in that field. For example, a log file entry that records a dropped packet would resemble the following:

```
2005-07-15 11:26:36 DROP UDP 10.1.7.30 255.255.255.255
    1522 14000 104 - - - - - - - - RECEIVE
```

Note You can also analyze the Windows Firewall log file with the Microsoft Log Parser, which we'll discuss further in Recipe 3-19.

See Also

- Recipe 3-19 for more on auditing Windows Firewall events.

- Microsoft TechNet: "W3C Extended Log File Format (IIS 6.0)" (http:// www.microsoft.com/technet/prodtechnol/WindowsServer2003/Library/IIS/ 676400bc-8969-4aa7-851a-9319490a9bbb.mspx).

- Microsoft TechNet: "Log Parser 2.2" (http://www.microsoft.com/technet/scriptcenter/ tools/logparser/default.mspx). This article discusses the free Microsoft Log Parser tool.

3-19. Auditing Windows Firewall Events

Problem

You want to view and manage the Windows event log entries created by the Windows Firewall.

Solution

Using a Graphical User Interface

1. Open the EventCombMT Utility. Be sure that your domain name is listed in the Domain text box.

2. Right-click in the Select to Search/Right-click to Add text box, and select Add Single Server.

3. Type the name of your server in the Server Name text box and select Add Server, or click Browse to select the server from My Network Places. Click Close when you've selected the name of the server.

4. In the Choose Log Files to Search section, place a check mark next to Security.

5. In the Event Types section, place a check mark next to the following event types:

   - Error

   - Informational

   - Warning

   - Success Audit

   - Failure Audit

   - Success

6. Enter the following event IDs in the From and To text boxes:

   - 848

   - 861

7. Click on Search to begin querying for event log entries that match these criteria. By default, the results will be stored in a comma-separated values (CSV) file called `<ComputerName>-Security_LOG.txt`.

Using Group Policy

Tables 3-30 and 3-31 contain the Group Policy settings that enable the Windows Event viewer to track events related to the Windows Firewall. As with other Windows auditing events, auditing `Success` events means that the Event Viewer will create an entry if someone attempts to perform a particular action and is able to do so. Auditing `Failure` events will create an Event Viewer entry if someone attempts an action and is unsuccessful.

Table 3-30. *Audit Process Tracking Settings*

Path	`Computer Configuration\Windows Settings\Security Settings\` `Local Policies\Security Options`
Policy name	Audit Process Tracking
Value	`Success, Failure`

Table 3-31. *Audit Policy Change Settings*

Path	Computer Configuration\Windows Settings\Security Settings\ Local Policies\Security Options
Policy name	Audit Policy Change
Value	Success, Failure

■**Note** If you are not in an Active Directory environment, you can enable auditing on an individual Windows Server 2003 computer by using the Local Security Policy MMC snap-in available in the Administrative Tools folder.

Using a Command-Line Interface

The following command uses the logparser.exe command-line utility to parse the Security log for events relating to the Windows Firewall:

```
> LogParser "SELECT TimeGenerated, SourceName,
EventCategoryName, Message INTO report.txt FROM Security WHERE
EventID > 847 AND EventID < 862" -resolveSIDs:ON
```

■**Note** Notice that logparser.exe doesn't support the "greater than or equal to" or "less than or equal to" operators (<= and >=), so instead we're searching for event IDs that are greater than 847 and less than 862.

How It Works

One of the greatest challenges of system administration is the maintenance and analysis of the auditing data that is generated by a network or domain full of Windows computers. In the spirit of the "tree falling in the forest" question, many administrators find themselves wondering if a security breach or configuration error has actually taken place somewhere on their network and they simply haven't spotted the event log entry that will alert them to it.

To help combat this, Microsoft has released a number of free utilities to help you to analyze and monitor event log data. One of these tools, EventCombMT, has been around since the days of Windows NT 4.0 and is used to collect Event Viewer entries from numerous computers into a single location to allow you to monitor and view them more efficiently. EventCombMT is now available within a larger bundle of free tools called the Account Lockout and Management Tools, available for download from http://www.microsoft.com/downloads/details.aspx? FamilyID=7AF2E69C-91F3-4E63-8629-B999ADDE0B9E&displaylang=en.

Another free tool that hasn't received quite the same publicity as EventCombMT is the Microsoft Log Parser. This was first released as a free Resource Kit utility with very little supporting documentation, but it has developed a large grassroots following with strong Internet community support. In a nutshell, the Microsoft Log Parser allows you to use a SQL-like query engine to extract data from any number of common log file sources, including Windows event logs,

IIS logs, firewall logs in the W3C standard log file format, and even metadata stored by the operating system about files and folders on a Windows hard drive. In this case, the Windows Firewall creates a log file in the W3C file format that can be easily queried by the Microsoft Log Parser.

While you cannot parse a log file or the Event Viewer using Group Policy, you can (and should) use a Group Policy object (GPO) to enable event auditing for your Windows computers wherever possible. This ensures that all of your Windows Server 2003 computers are recording the same types of data, to ensure that no security-related events go unnoticed because they are not being audited.

See Also

- Microsoft TechNet: "Events and Errors Message Center" (`http://www.microsoft.com/technet/support/ee/ee_advanced.aspx`).

- EventID.net (`www.eventid.net`): This site provides detailed information on Windows Event Viewer entries.

The Unofficial Log Parser Support Site (`www.logparser.com`).

CHAPTER 4

■ ■ ■

Routing and Remote Access Service (Remote Access)

Routing and Remote Access Services (RRAS) was officially born in 1996 when Microsoft released the service to replace the more basic Remote Access Service (RAS) in Windows NT 4.0. As its name implies, RRAS provides services for network routing and remote access.

In Chapter 5, we will discuss the configuration of RRAS as a full-featured network router. In this chapter, however, we will discuss how remote access services work; remote access services are an integral part of RRAS, yet they are deserving of their own chapter.

Remote access services come in many forms. Generally, remote access refers to any method that an end user can employ to connect to a non-local site. We will focus on two common scenarios in this chapter:

- An end user manually establishes a remote connection in order to access data on the remote network. The end user may be at home, at an airport, or at a customer's business location.

- Two remote sites are connected by a dedicated or on-demand link. No end user intervention is required to establish or restore the link.

In today's computing environment, with so much emphasis placed on Internet access, security has (or should) become a driving factor in any network implementation. Whether your users and administrators select a remote-control solution, such as Microsoft's Remote Desktop, Terminal Services, or Symantec's pcAnywhere, the implementation must be considered with security in mind in order to reduce the risk of unauthorized intrusion, data or identity theft, or any compromise of the internal (trusted) network.

Creating virtual private networks (VPNs) is one method that can be used to secure remote connections. VPNs are frequently described as "tunnels" through an untrusted network (typically the Internet) that securely connect two points. These endpoints include the end user requesting the remote access and the RRAS server providing the service; it may alternatively consist of two RRAS servers connected to each other through the Internet.

VPNs operate over one of two protocols: Point-to-Point Tunneling Protocol (PPTP) or Layer-2 Tunneling Protocol (L2TP). Microsoft RRAS supports both protocols. In general, PPTP connections are easier for an end user to configure, but they are less secure than L2TP connections due to the fundamental design of the protocol. As a system administrator, you should consider which implementation is best for you by identifying not only the systems you are trying to protect, but also from what or whom you are trying to protect them, and what the implications are for your organization if these systems are compromised.

We could certainly devote many chapters just to the implementation of security. However, we will assume that you have already weighed these considerations and put appropriate safeguards into place prior to working with Microsoft RRAS to create and support your VPN connections.

Using a Graphical User Interface

All recipes that involve RRAS management through a graphical user interface will refer to the Routing and Remote Access MMC snap-in, accessed from the Administrative Tools folder within the Start menu. In addition, you can access it directly at %systemroot%\system32\rrasmgmt.msc.

Using a Command-Line Interface

In Windows Server 2003, the netsh ras command provides a command-line interface for managing RRAS. In this chapter, all recipes with command-line solutions will be based on netsh ras.

To access the netsh ras interface for the local server, open a command prompt and issue the following command:

```
> netsh ras
```

To access the help menu for the netsh ras syntax, just append the help parameter to the command:

```
> netsh ras help
```

Using the Registry

There are a number of entries in the Windows Registry that will allow you to modify parameters needed to configure remote access services. All entries are located at

```
HKEY_LOCAL_MACHINE\SYSTEM\CurrentControlSet\Services\RemoteAccess\
```

As usual, edit the Registry with care. Changing a value or key incorrectly can leave your server in an unusable state.

Using VBScript

Unfortunately, there is no built-in scripting interface through which to administer RRAS. However, you can call the netsh ras command-line functions from a VBScript using the following syntax:

```
' This code will instantiate a WSH object and execute the desired command.
' ------ SCRIPT CONFIGURATION ------
' 'Enter the desired netsh ras command between the quotation marks
'      in the line below, for example:
strCommand = "netsh ras add registeredserver domain=acmecorp.local server=voyager"
```

```
' ------ END CONFIGURATION ---------
set objShell = CreateObject("WScript.Shell")
set objExec = objShell.Exec(strCommand)
' Run in a loop while the command is executing
Do While objExec.Status = 0
         WScript.Sleep 1000
Loop
' Delete the objects from memory once the command is completed.
Set objExec = Nothing
Set objShell = Nothing
```

Because this syntax is the same regardless of the `netsh ras` command or parameters, we will not discuss this method in each recipe. Instead, you should refer to the sections of recipes that describe using a command line and then place the appropriate command into the preceding script.

4-1. Enabling or Disabling Windows Server 2003 As a Remote Access Server

Problem

You want to enable your server to provide remote access services.

Solution

Routing and remote access services are installed by default in Windows Server 2003. They are not like other networking components such as WINS or DNS that can be added or removed. Rather, RRAS just needs to be enabled and configured.

Using a Graphical User Interface

1. Start the Routing and Remote Access Services administrative console from the Administrative Tools folder in the Start menu, or directly from %systemroot%\ system32\rrasmgmt.msc.

2. If your server is not already listed in the console, then add it by right-clicking Routing and Remote Access in the left pane and selecting Add Server. Select the first option, This Computer.

Note If you are enabling Routing and Remote Access on a remote server, you can add those servers to this console by selecting The Following Computer, All Routing and Remote Access Servers, or Browse Active Directory rather than the This Computer option.

---

3. Right-click on the server name in the left pane, and select Configure and Enable Routing and Remote Access.

4. Click the Next button when the Routing and Remote Access Server Setup Wizard starts.

5. Select the option that describes your environment and then click the Next button to proceed. The options are:

   • **Remote Access (Dial-up or VPN):** Use this option to enable remote clients to connect to the server through either a dial-up or VPN connection. Your server must have at least two network adapters: one for the LAN and one for the WAN (Internet).

   • **Network Address Translation:** This option does not apply to this chapter. This feature allows internal clients to access the Internet over a single public IP address.

   • **Virtual Private Network (VPN) Access and NAT:** Use this option to enable remote clients to connect to the server through a VPN connection and to permit local clients to access the Internet through a single common IP address on the server.

   • **Secure Connection Between Two Private Networks:** Use this option to configure this server as one endpoint in a connection with another server. This is known as a site-to-site VPN.

   • **Custom Configuration:** Use this option to configure this server as a VPN server when none of the preceding options apply. Also use this option when you are already connected to the Internet, such as through a firewall or router, and your only goal is to enable this server to provide VPN services.

6. If you selected Remote Access (Dial-up or VPN), then do the following:

   a. Select the check box next to VPN and click the Next button.

   b. Select the network card that connects your server to the WAN (Internet), and click the Next button to proceed. (Optionally, you may also select to enable packet-filtering security on the WAN card.)

   c. Select the network card that connects your server to the internal network to which you want your remote clients to have access, and then click the Next button to proceed.

   d. Select whether you want to use DHCP to provide addresses to remote clients or whether you want to configure a static pool of addresses. Then click the Next button to proceed.

   e. If you selected to use a static pool of addresses, configure them now and click the Next button to proceed.

   f. Select the option to use a RADIUS server for authentication, if desired; click the Next button to proceed.

   g. If you chose to use a RADIUS server, configure it now and click the Next button to proceed.

   h. Click Finish to complete and exit the wizard.

7. If you selected Virtual Private Network (VPN) Access and NAT, then follow the same procedure as in step 6, but skip step 6a.

8. If you selected Secure Connection Between Two Private Networks, then do the following:

   a. Select Yes, the option to enable demand-dial connections.

   b. Select whether you want to use DHCP to provide addresses to remote clients or whether you want to configure a static pool of addresses. Then click the Next button.

   c. If you chose to use a static pool of addresses, configure them now, and click the Next button.

   d. Click Finish to complete and exit the wizard.

9. If you selected Custom Configuration, then do the following:

   a. Select the check box corresponding to VPN Access. Click the Next button.

   b. Click the Finish button to complete and exit the wizard.

After you have completed the preceding steps, the configuration wizard will prompt you with a Yes/No dialog box to start the service. You should start it at this point.

Using the Registry

You can enable Routing and Remote Access Services by setting the following Registry value:

```
[HKEY_LOCAL_MACHINE\SYSTEM\CurrentControlSet\Services\RemoteAccess\]
"ConfigurationFlags"=dword:00000001
```

Note that this Registry value will enable the RRAS service, but it will not actually start it. You can manually start the service by using the Services Control Panel applet or any other technique at your disposal.

If you want to enable RRAS to accept incoming connections, then also add the following Registry entry:

```
[HKEY_LOCAL_MACHINE\SYSTEM\CurrentControlSet\Services\RemoteAccess\Parameters]
"IcConfigured"=dword:00000001
```

How It Works

Remote access provides significant benefits to businesses, permitting workers to remain productive when on the road. If your business plans to deploy remote access, spend some time planning and testing your implementation before enabling it for end users. Each of the five options described in step 5 of the "Using a Graphical User Interface" section of this recipe deserve careful consideration regarding functionality and security. You should take great care that you do not inadvertently expose your systems to unauthorized access.

Although there are a number of excellent VPN appliance solutions, one that deserves mention is Microsoft's Internet Security and Acceleration Server (ISA Server). ISA Server takes control of the Routing and Remote Access Services, so if you use both, take care when making adjustments in either. We strongly recommend that you use the wizards built into ISA Server for the initial configuration of a VPN or dial-in server. However, once you are comfortable in the RRAS and ISA Server environment, you can use the RRAS graphical user interface or other scripts described in this chapter to fine-tune your advanced settings.

See Also

- Microsoft KB 311953: "How to Enable the Routing and Remote Access Service Silently from a Command Prompt." This article describes the technique for setting Registry parameters from the command line. This is useful if you want to run command-line scripts to enable or disable the service.

- Microsoft KB 838374: "Interoperability of Routing and Remote Access and Internet Security and Acceleration Server 2004." This article describes the interactions between RRAS and ISA Server.

- Microsoft TechNet: "Virtual Private Networking with Windows Server 2003: Deploying Remote Access VPNs" (www.microsoft.com/technet/prodtechnol/windowsserver2003/ technologies/networking/vpndeplr.mspx). This article describes the VPN deployment process, issues to consider, and issues that may be encountered.

- ISAServer.org (http://www.isaserver.org). This site provides FAQs and technical "how to" articles for Microsoft ISA Server 2000 and 2004.

- Chapter 6 of this book for information on RADIUS servers and Internet Authentication Services (IAS).

4-2. Starting and Stopping the Routing and Remote Access Service

Problem

You want to start or stop Routing and Remote Access Services.

Solution

Using a Graphical User Interface

1. Start the Services control panel applet from the Administrative Tools folder in the Start menu.

2. Select the Routing and Remote Access Services.

3. Select the Action menu, and then select the option to start, stop, or restart the service, whichever is appropriate.

Using a Command-Line Interface

To start RRAS, type the following in the command window:

```
> net start remoteaccess
```

To stop the service, type the following in the command window:

```
> net stop remoteaccess
```

Using VBScript

To stop RRAS on the local computer, use the following code:

```
'This code will stop the Routing and Remote Access Services
'---SCRIPT CONFIGURATION ---
strComputer = "."
'---END CONFIGURATION---
Set objWMIService = GetObject("winmgmts:" _
    & "{impersonationLevel=impersonate}!\\" & strComputer & "\root\cimv2")
Set colServiceList = objWMIService.ExecQuery _
        ("Select * from Win32_Service where Name='remoteaccess'")
For each objService in colServiceList
     errReturn = objService.StopService()
Next
WScript.Echo ("RRAS service has been stopped.")
```

To start RRAS on the local computer, use the following similar code instead:

```
'This code will start the Routing and Remote Access Services
'---SCRIPT CONFIGURATION---
strComputer = "."
'---END CONFIGURATION---
Set objWMIService = GetObject("winmgmts:" _
    & "{impersonationLevel=impersonate}!\\" & strComputer & "\root\cimv2")
Set colServiceList = objWMIService.ExecQuery _
        ("Select * from Win32_Service where Name='remoteaccess'")
Set colServiceList = objWMIService.ExecQuery _
    ("Select * from Win32_Service where Name='remoteaccess'")
For each objService in colServiceList
     errReturn = objService.StartService()
Next
WScript.Echo ("RRAS service has been started.")
```

To restart RRAS on the local computer, combine the previous two code segments into a single one, as follows:

```
'This code will restart the Routing and Remote Access Services
'---SCRIPT CONFIGURATION---
strComputer = "."
'---END CONFIGURATION---
Set objWMIService = GetObject("winmgmts:" _
    & "{impersonationLevel=impersonate}!\\" & strComputer & "\root\cimv2")
Set colServiceList = objWMIService.ExecQuery _
        ("Select * from Win32_Service where Name='remoteaccess'")
```

```
For each objService in colServiceList
    errReturn = objService.StopService()
Next
Set colServiceList = objWMIService.ExecQuery _
    ("Select * from Win32_Service where Name='remoteaccess'")
For each objService in colServiceList
    errReturn = objService.StartService()
Next
WScript.Echo ("RRAS service has been restarted.")
```

Note   Make certain that you check the system event log after you have run this code to verify that the service has started. Look for events 7035 and 7036.

Note that even though the preceding code sends the command to the local computer, you can manage RRAS for any remote computer to which you have access and administrative rights by modifying the value of strComputer. So if the remote computer is named RRAS2 then you would modify the first line to read:

```
strComputer = "RRAS2"
```

How It Works

You may want to stop and start RRAS if you have made changes to the server configuration and these changes are not visible to clients. Even though most changes ideally should not require that the service be restarted, the reality is that this is necessary on occasion.

4-3. Registering, Deleting, and Viewing Remote Access Servers in Active Directory

Problem

You want to publish (register) your RRAS server in Active Directory or remove (unregister) it from Active Directory, or you want to display status information about the server.

Solution

Using a Graphical User Interface

You can register your RRAS server in Active Directory by doing the following:

1. Start the Active Directory Users and Computers administrative console from the Administrative Tools folder in the Start menu, or directly from %systemroot%\system32\dsa.msc.

2. Expand the tree in the left pane, and select the Users node.

3. Double-click RAS and IAS Servers in the right pane.

4. Select the Members tab, and click the Add button.

5. Click the Advanced button, and then click the Object Types button. Enable the check box to search on Computers. Click OK and then click the Find Now button to search all computers.

6. Select your computer in the Search Results pane, and click OK until you see your server listed as a member of the group.

7. Click the OK button to complete the task.

You can unregister your RRAS server from Active Directory using a procedure similar to the preceding:

1. Start the Active Directory Users and Computers administrative console from the Administrative Tools folder in the Start menu, or directly from %systemroot%\ system32\dsa.msc.

2. Expand the tree in the left pane, and select the Users node.

3. Double-click RAS and IAS Servers in the right pane.

4. Select the Members tab.

5. Select the RRAS server that you wish to remove from Active Directory, and click the Remove button. Click Yes when prompted for confirmation of this action.

6. Click the OK button to complete the task.

Using a Command-Line Interface

You can register your RRAS server in Active Directory using netsh ras add registeredserver:

```
> netsh ras add registeredserver domain=<YourDomainName> server=<YourServerName>
```

These are the parameters used:

Domain: Optional parameter that specifies the Windows domain name in which you want to register the server. If omitted, the server will be registered in its primary domain. Specify the fully qualified domain name (FQDN).

Server: Optional parameter that specifies the name of the server if it is not the local host. You may substitute the server name with its corresponding IP address.

For example, use the following command to register the remote access server named Remote1 in the TechOps.local domain:

```
> netsh ras add registeredserver domain=TechOps.local server=Remote1
```

You can unregister your RRAS server in Active Directory. To do so, use netsh ras delete registeredserver:

```
> netsh ras delete registeredserver domain=<YourDomainName> server=<YourServerName>
```

The parameters used are identical to those for netsh ras add registeredserver.

Note User accounts are cached by Internet Authentication Service (IAS) and RRAS; therefore, these services must be restarted to complete the removal of the RRAS server from Active Directory.

For example, to unregister the server named Remote1 in the TechOps.local domain, run the following command and then restart the RRAS service:

```
> netsh ras delete registeredserver domain=TechOps.local server=Remote1
```

You can also display the status of your RRAS server once it has been registered in Active Directory. To do so, use netsh ras show registeredserver:

```
> netsh ras show registeredserver [domain=]<YourDomainName>
[server=]<YourServerName>
```

The parameters used are identical to those for netsh ras add registeredserver.

Note The output of this function indicates whether the server is registered or not registered in Active Directory.

As an example, you would run the following command to display statistics of the server named Remote1 in the TechOps.local domain:

```
> netsh ras show registeredserver domain=TechOps.local server=Remote1
```

The output of the command will look like the following:

```
c:\>netsh ras show registeredserver
```

```
The following Remote Access server is registered:
  Remote Access Server:   Remote1
  Domain:                 techops.local
```

How It Works

The primary purpose of registering a RRAS server in Active Directory is that the registration provides the server with the ability to access the dial-in properties of user accounts to determine whether the user should be granted or denied access, or whether the server should refer this decision to policies defined within the remote access server. Without this level of authentication, and in the absence of a Remote Authentication Dial-In User Service (RADIUS) server, the remote access server would only be able to authenticate against local accounts, which is impractical for many organizations.

4-4. Configuring Authentication Providers

Problem

You want to configure the method of authentication by your RRAS server.

Solution

Using a Graphical User Interface

1. Start the Routing and Remote Access Services administrative console from the Administrative Tools folder in the Start menu, or directly from %systemroot%\system32\ rrasmgmt.msc.

2. Right-click the name of the RRAS server that you want to manage in the left pane, and select Properties.

3. Select the Security tab.

4. Click the arrow in the Authentication Provider drop-down list and select whether you want to use RADIUS Authentication or Windows Authentication.

5. If you selected to use RADIUS Authentication, configure the settings to connect to the RADIUS server as follows:

   a. Click the Configure button next to the Authentication Provider drop-down list.

   b. Click the Add button to select your RADIUS server.

   c. Type your RADIUS server name in the Server Name field.

   d. If your RADIUS server uses a secret phrase, click the Secret button next to the corresponding field and enter the phrase. Click OK when complete.

   e. Set the idle timeout value, specified in seconds. The default value is 5.

   f. Set the initial score (priority) for your RADIUS server. The default value is 30.

   g. Set the port on which your RADIUS server listens for authentication requests. The default port is 1812.

   h. Check the check box if you want to always use the message authenticator.

   i. Click OK when complete.

   j. Repeat steps b through i for any additional RADIUS servers on your network.

6. Click the Authentication Methods button to configure the various authentication protocols.

7. Enable the authentication methods that you want to enable for your RRAS server, or disable those that you do not want to use. The options are:

- Extensible Authentication Protocol (EAP): enabled by default

- Microsoft Encrypted Authentication v2 (MS-CHAP v2): enabled by default

- Microsoft Encrypted Authentication (MS-CHAP): enabled by default

- Encrypted Authentication (CHAP)

- Shiva Password Authentication Protocol (SPAP)

- Unencrypted Password (PAP)

8. You may optionally configure your RRAS server to allow remote clients to connect without any level of authentication.

9. Click OK when complete.

Using a Command-Line Interface

You can configure your RRAS server's authentication parameters from the command line using the `netsh ras` syntax.

To display the authentication protocols used by your RRAS server, run the following command:

```
> netsh ras show authtype
```

The output will look like this:

```
>netsh ras show authtype
```

```
Enabled Authentication Types:
Code         Meaning
MSCHAP       Microsoft Challenge-Handshake Authentication Protocol.
MSCHAPv2     Microsoft Challenge-Handshake Authentication Protocol version 2.
EAP          Extensible Authentication Protocol.
```

To configure the authentication protocol used by your RRAS server, run the `netsh ras add authtype` command:

```
> netsh ras add authtype {pap|spap|md5chap|mschap|mschapv2|eap}
```

This command must be issued once for each authentication protocol that you want to add. These are the options:

- `PAP`: Unencrypted password

- `SPAP`: Shiva Password Authentication Protocol

- `MD5CHAP`: Encrypted Authentication

- `MSCHAP`: Microsoft Encrypted Authentication

- MSCHAPV2: Microsoft Encrypted Authentication v2

- EAP: Extensible Authentication Protocol

For example, to add mschapv2 to the authentication protocol list, run the following command:

```
> netsh ras add authtype mschapv2
```

You can remove an authentication protocol by using the similar netsh ras delete authtype command:

```
> netsh ras delete authtype {pap|spap|md5chap|mschap|mschapv2|eap}
```

The parameters are the same as for the netsh ras add authtype command.

By default, your RRAS server is configured to use Windows Authentication; however, you may also configure it to use RADIUS authentication. You can determine the authentication mode by issuing this command:

```
> netsh ras AAAA show authentication
```

You can configure the server to authenticate using a RADIUS server by running the netsh ras AAAA add authserv command:

```
> netsh ras AAAA add authserv [name=]<ServerID> [[secret=]<SharedSecret>]
    [[init-score=]<ServerPriority>] [[port=]<Port>] [[timeout=]<Seconds>]
    [[signature] {enabled | disabled}]
```

The parameters used by this command are as follows:

Name: Required parameter that specifies the name of the RADIUS server. You may enter this value as either the DNS name of the server or its IP address.

Secret: Optional parameter that specifies the shared secret.

Init-Score: Optional parameter that specifies the initial score or server priority. If omitted, the default score of 30 will be assumed.

Port: Optional parameter that specifies the port on which the RADIUS server listens for authentication requests. If omitted, the default port of 1812 will be assumed.

Timeout: Optional parameter that specifies the timeout value, specified in seconds. If omitted, the default timeout of 5 seconds will be assumed.

Signature: Optional parameter that specifies whether to use digital signatures. This parameter may only take values of enabled or disabled.

Note If you have already configured these settings and just want to modify their properties, replace netsh RAS AAAA add authserv with netsh RAS AAAA set authserv.

For example, to configure RRAS to authenticate requests against the RADIUS1 server with a shared secret of NCC1701A with digital signatures enabled, use the following command:

```
> netsh ras AAAA add authserv name=RADIUS1 secret=NCC1701A signature enabled
```

■**Note** You can add additional RADIUS servers by issuing the `netsh ras AAAA add authserv` command with appropriate parameters for each RADIUS server.

To delete a RADIUS server against which your RRAS server authenticates, run the `netsh ras AAAA delete authserv` command:

```
> netsh ras AAAA delete authserv [name=]<ServerID>
```

■**Note** You can configure your RRAS server to use Windows Authentication by deleting all listed RADIUS servers.

How It Works

As described in this recipe, there are seven authentication protocols that can be used by RRAS. As the system administrator, you are obligated to determine which protocol is the most appropriate for your organization, and whether you should permit multiple authentication types.

When negotiating a connection request from a remote user, the server will attempt the authentication starting with the most secure protocol and proceeding to the least secure until both the client and the server agree on the authentication type. Once they have reached this agreement, the connection request can proceed. On the other hand, if no agreement is reached, the request will be terminated by the server.

These are the seven authentication methods:

- **Extensible Authentication Protocol (EAP):** EAP is considered to be the most secure authentication protocol of the seven that are supported. EAP interacts with a certificate authority (CA) or a smart-card system to provide mutual authentication. As described in Microsoft KB 259880, "to use EAP with a VPN, the server must be configured to accept EAP authentication as a valid authentication method and it must have a user certificate (X.509). The client must be configured to use EAP, and either have a SmartCard (with a SmartCard Certificate installed) or a user certificate."

  EAP is preferable to other methods because it cannot be compromised by brute-force or password dictionary attacks, unlike methods such as MS-CHAP or CHAP.

- **Microsoft Challenge Handshake Authentication Protocol v2 (MS-CHAP v2):** MS-CHAP v2 provides mutual authentication between the server and the remote client using a transmitted and a received session key, both of which are based on the user's password and an arbitrary string value. The key will be different for every authentication session.

  MS-CHAP v2 is supported by Windows versions 2003, 2000, XP, NT 4.0, ME, and 98. It is supported for Windows 95 when used for VPN connections, but not for dial-in connections.

If your server does not integrate with certificate services, and your clients are all Windows-based with a version of Win9x or later, you will want to use MS-CHAP v2 as your authentication protocol.

- **Microsoft Challenge Handshake Authentication Protocol (MS-CHAP):** MS-CHAP is the predecessor to MS-CHAP v2. Unlike, MS-CHAP v2, MS-CHAP provides only one-way authentication; it is not mutual. A single session key is created that is based only on the user's password and is the same for every session by that user. Unless you have pre-Win9x clients on your network, there should not be much call for this protocol.

- **Challenge Handshake Authentication Protocol (CHAP):** CHAP is less secure than MS-CHAP or MS-CHAP v2. Unlike the other protocols, however, CHAP is frequently accessible to non-Windows clients and is therefore supported by Windows 2003 Server to maintain a broader level of client support. During the CHAP authentication process, the password is not actually sent from the client to the server; rather a representation of the password is generated and used.

- **Shiva Password Authentication Protocol (SPAP):** SPAP is an authentication protocol supported by Shiva remote access servers that provides a simple level of encryption for passwords.

- **Unencrypted Password (PAP):** PAP, the simplest of the authentication protocols, and formally known as Password Authentication Protocol, transmits passwords in clear text, making them visible to monitoring and hacking utilities. This method of authentication is not recommended unless absolutely required by the server.

- **Unauthenticated access:** Unauthenticated access permits "guest" level access to the remote server. Any user can connect without providing any credentials.

In addition to selecting an authentication protocol, you must also select whether you want to use Windows or RADIUS authentication. If you use Windows authentication, all requests are authenticated against the local accounts database, Active Directory, or even an NT 4 domain database.

You should consider using RADIUS instead of Windows authentication if you have more than one RRAS server. RADIUS provides centralized authentication and auditing of remote access connections. Management of remote access policies is also simplified with RADIUS servers; in fact, once you configure your RRAS server to authenticate against a RADIUS server, you will no longer be able to configure policies on the remote access server itself.

See Also

- MSDN: "Certificate Services" (http://msdn.microsoft.com/library/default.asp?url=/library/en-us/seccrypto/security/certificate_services.asp). This article provides details on Microsoft Certificate Services necessary to implement the Extensible Authentication Protocol (EAP).

- Microsoft TechNet: "Authentication Protocols and Methods" (http://technet2.microsoft.com/WindowsServer/f/?en/Library/4e9baec7-dafc-4f9f-8fb4-660284a645391033.mspx). This article describes each of the authentication protocols that we have discussed in this recipe.

- Microsoft KB 826156: "How to Configure Unauthenticated Access for the Routing and Remote Access Service or for Internet Authentication Service." This article describes the techniques to configure unauthenticated access and also demonstrates a method for changing the user account that is used to grant the guest-level access.

4-5. Configuring Accounting (Logging) Methods

Problem

You want to configure the accounting (logging) method used by your RRAS server.

Solution

Using a Graphical User Interface

1. Start the Routing and Remote Access Services administrative console from the Administrative Tools folder in the Start menu, or directly from `%systemroot%\system32\rrasmgmt.msc`.

2. Right-click the name of the RRAS server that you want to manage in the left pane, and select Properties.

3. Select the Security tab.

4. Click the arrow in the Accounting Provider drop-down list, and select whether you want to use RADIUS Accounting or Windows Accounting.

5. If you chose to use RADIUS accounting, configure the settings to connect to the RADIUS server as follows:

   a. Click the Configure button next to the Authentication Provider drop-down list.

   b. Click the Add button to select your RADIUS server.

   c. Type your RADIUS server name in the Server Name field.

   d. If your RADIUS server uses a secret phrase, click the Secret button next to the corresponding field and enter the phrase. Click OK when complete.

   e. Set the idle timeout value, specified in seconds. The default value is 5.

   f. Set the initial score (priority) for your RADIUS server. The default value is 30.

   g. Set the port on which your RADIUS server listens for authentication requests. The default port is 1813.

   h. Check the check box if you want to enable RADIUS accounting ON and OFF messages.

   i. Click OK when complete.

   j. Repeat steps *b* through *i* for any additional RADIUS servers on your network.

6. Click OK when complete.

Using a Command-Line Interface

You can configure your RRAS server's accounting parameters from the command line using the `netsh ras AAAA` syntax.

To display the accounting methods used by your RRAS server, run the following command:

```
> netsh ras AAAA show acctserv [[name=]ServerID]
```

In this code, `name` is an optional parameter that specifies the fully qualified domain name (FQDN) or IP address of the server whose accounting method you want to display. If omitted, the command will return results on all configured accounting servers.

The output will look like this:

```
> netsh ras AAAA show acctserv
```

Name	Address	Port	Score	Timeout	Messages
RADIUS1	RADIUS1	1813	30	5	enabled

Note The table will not contain any data if Windows accounting is used.

To configure the accounting method used by your RRAS server, run the `netsh ras AAAA add acctserv` command:

```
> netsh ras AAAA add acctserv [name=]<ServerID> [[secret=]<SharedSecret>]
    [[init-score=]<ServerPriority>] [[port=]<Port>] [[timeout=]<Seconds>]
    [[messages=] {enabled | disabled}]
```

The parameters used by this command are as follows:

`Name`: Required parameter that specifies the name of the RADIUS server. You may enter this value as either the DNS name of the server or its IP address.

`Secret`: Optional parameter that specifies the shared secret.

`Init-Score`: Optional parameter that specifies the initial score or server priority. If omitted, the default score of 30 will be assumed.

`Port`: Optional parameter that specifies the port on which the RADIUS server listens for authentication requests. If omitted, the default port of 1812 will be assumed.

`Timeout`: Optional parameter that specifies the timeout value, specified in seconds. If omitted, the default timeout of 5 seconds will be assumed.

`Messages`: Optional parameter that specifies whether to send accounting ON and OFF messages.

For example, to configure RRAS to send accounting details to the `RADIUS1` server with a shared secret of `NCC1701A`, use the following command:

```
> netsh ras AAAA add acctserv name=RADIUS1 secret=NCC1701A messages=enabled
```

Note You can add additional RADIUS servers by issuing the `netsh ras AAAA add acctserv` with appropriate parameters for each RADIUS server.

To delete a RADIUS server to which your RRAS server sends its accounting data, run the `netsh ras AAAA delete acctserv` command:

```
> netsh ras AAAA delete acctserv [name=]<ServerID>
```

Note You can configure your RRAS server to use Windows accounting by deleting all listed RADIUS servers.

How It Works

If you chose to use Windows accounting, your RRAS log files will be stored in the folder specified in the console, as described in Recipe 4-8, "Configuring the Logging Level." If you specified RADIUS as the accounting method, however, all logging information is sent to the RADIUS server, which processes it accordingly.

See Also

- Recipes in Chapter 6, "Internet Authentication Service (IAS)," for details relating to RADIUS management.

- Microsoft TechNet: "Remote Access RADIUS Attributes" (`http://technet2.microsoft.com/WindowsServer/en/Library/25bf4449-283f-4e70-846a-dc2f724a42571033.mspx`). This article lists all attributes that may be logged by a RADIUS server.

- IETF: "RFC 2866" (`http://www.ietf.org/rfc/rfc2866.txt`). This RFC provides a technical description of the RADIUS accounting protocol.

4-6. Configuring IP Settings

Problem

You want to configure IP routing to provide access either to the entire LAN or just to the remote access server, and you want to configure the method by which the server allocates IP addresses to remote clients and how clients resolve resource names.

Solution

Using a Graphical User Interface

1. Start the Routing and Remote Access Services administrative console from the Administrative Tools folder in the Start menu, or directly from %systemroot%\system32\ rrasmgmt.msc.

2. Right-click the name of the RRAS server that you want to manage in the left pane, and select Properties.

3. Select the IP tab.

4. Select the Enable IP Routing check box to allow remote access clients to access resources beyond the remote access server. This is enabled by default.

5. Select the Allow IP-Based Remote Access and Demand-Dial Connections check box to specify that the Internet Protocol Control Protocol (IPCP) is negotiated for PPP connections. This is enabled by default.

6. Select the radio button corresponding to the method of IP address allocation that you desire. The default selection is to use DHCP, but you may also select a static address pool.

7. If you chose to use a static address pool in step 6, do the following:

    a. Click the Add button.

    b. Enter the starting and ending addresses of the desired range. Note that the total number of addresses will be automatically calculated. Alternatively, you can enter the starting address and the total number of addresses that you want; the ending address will instead be calculated for you.

    c. Click the OK button to complete the IP address range entry.

    d. Repeat steps *a* through *c* for any additional ranges that you want to add.

8. Select the Enable Broadcast Name Resolution check box if you want remote access clients to be able to resolve NetBIOS names on a single-subnet LAN without the benefit of a WINS or DNS server.

9. Select the network adapter over which you want your RRAS server to provide IP addresses, WINS and DNS server addresses to your clients. By default, the setting is configured to allow the server to select the adapter.

10. Click OK when complete.

Using a Command-Line Interface

You can display your RRAS server's IP settings at any time by running the following command:

```
> netsh ras ip show config
```

The results will look as follows:

```
> netsh ras ip show config
```

RAS IP config

```
Negotiation mode:      deny
Access mode:      serveronly
Address request mode:      deny
Broadcast name resolution:      enabled
Assignment method:      pool
Pool:
     192.168.2.200 to 192.168.2.250
```

▪Note In the preceding results, Negotiation mode corresponds to the Allow IP-Based Remote Access and Demand-Dial Connections setting in the graphical user interface. Access mode corresponds to the Enable IP Routing setting, and Address request mode, which is set to deny by default, refers to the ability of clients to request a specific IP address, a feature not available in the graphical user interface. Broadcast name resolution is the same as its graphical counterpart, and Assignment method refers to the selection of static addresses (pool) or DHCP (auto).

There are a number of commands for configuring the IP settings. Use the following commands to make the indicated configuration changes.

To set the negotiation method, use this command:

```
> netsh ras ip set negotiation {allow | deny}
```

A value of allow will permit IP-based remote access and demand-dial connections.

To set the access mode, use this command:

```
> netsh ras ip set access {all | serveronly}
```

A value of all will permit the remote client to access the entire LAN, or whatever segment has been made accessible; a value of serveronly restricts the client to resources on the RRAS server.

To set the ability of clients to request a specific IP address, use this command:

```
> netsh ras ip set addrreq {allow | deny}
```

A value of allow will enable this feature; a value of deny (the default) will disable it.

To enable clients to use NetBIOS over TCP/IP broadcasts to resolve names without a WINS or DNS server, use this command:

```
> netsh ras ip set broadcastnameresolution {enabled | disabled}
```

A value of enabled will permit clients to resolve names.

To configure RRAS to allocate addresses using DHCP or from a static address table, use this command:

```
> netsh ras ip set addrassign {auto | pool}
```

A value of auto enables RRAS to allocate addresses from DHCP; a value of pool implies a static address table.

To add a range of addresses, use this command:

```
> netsh ras ip add range [from=]<StartingIPAddress> [to=]<EndingIPAddress>
```

Both the from and to parameters are required. Replace StartingIPAddress with the first address in your range; replace EndingIPAddress with the final address in the range.

To delete a range of addresses, use this command:

```
> netsh ras ip delete range [from=]<StartingIPAddress> [to=]<EndingIPAddress>
```

This command takes the same parameters and value format as the preceding netsh ras ip add range.

To delete all ranges of addresses in the static address table, use this command:

```
> netsh ras ip delete pool
```

For example, to configure your RRAS server to permit IP routing and IP-based remote access and demand-dial connections with access to the entire LAN, to enable broadcast resolution, and to configure two static address pools, one from 192.168.0.10 to 192.168.0.20 and one from 192.168.0.110 to 192.168.0.120, use the following set of commands:

```
> netsh ras ip set negotiation allow
> netsh ras ip set access all
> netsh ras ip set broadcastnameresolution enabled
> netsh ras ip set addrassign pool
> netsh ras ip add range from=192.168.0.10 to=192.168.0.20
> netsh ras ip add range from=192.168.0.110 to=192.168.0.120
```

Using the Registry

You can modify your RRAS server's IP settings at any time by creating or modifying the following Registry values:

```
[HKEY_LOCAL_MACHINE\SYSTEM\CurrentControlSet\Services\RemoteAccess\Parameters\IP]
```

- To permit clients to request a particular IP address, use

    "AllowClientIPAddresses"=dword:1

- To disable NetBIOS over TCP/IP remote access connections, use

    "DisableNetBIOSOverTCPIP"=dword:1

- To enable IP remote access connections, use

    "EnableIn"=dword:1

- To enable clients to use NetBIOS broadcasts in the absence of a WINS or DNS server, use

    "EnableNetbtBcastFwd"=dword:1

- To enable access to the entire LAN, use

  `"EnableRoute"=dword:1`

- To specify the use of a DHCP server, use

  `"UseDHCPAddressing"=dword:1`

- To specify the start and end range of a static IP address pool, use

  ```
  [HKEY_LOCAL_MACHINE\SYSTEM\CurrentControlSet\Services\RemoteAccess\...
        ...Parameters\IP\StaticAddressPool\<PoolNumber>]
  "From"=dword:<StartAddress>
  "To"=dword:<EndAddress>
  ```

  Replace `StartAddress` and `EndAddress` with the appropriate values in hexadecimal notation. Do not enter the IP address in dotted decimal notation, such as `192.168.2.50`; use its hexadecimal equivalent, which would be `C0A80232`.

Note There are a number of online utilities to convert IP addresses between dotted decimal and hexadecimal notations. One example can be found at `http://www.subnetonline.com/subnet/subnet.html`.

How It Works

Your selections relating to IP routing will have important security implications, so you should understand all concepts related to this topic. For example, you should consider carefully whether you want your remotely connected users to access the entire LAN, or whether they should be restricted to the remote access server, which could also contain the resources (data) that they need.

It is helpful to also understand the DHCP process as it relates to remote access clients. If you have configured your server to use DHCP to provide addresses, the server will automatically request a block of ten addresses from the DHCP server and place them into its cache. This is done in order to shorten the remote connection process. You can adjust the number of addresses that are cached by modifying the following Registry value:

```
[HKEY_LOCAL_MACHINE\SYSTEM\CurrentControlSet\Services\RemoteAccess\Parameters\IP\]
InitialAddressPoolSize=dword:<SizeOfPool>
```

Replace `<SizeOfPool>` with the number of addresses that you want to request from the DHCP server for caching purposes. The default value is 10.

One other issue that you may encounter is support calls from remote users who think they cannot access network resources even though they have established a connection. Many users are accustomed to locating network resources by browsing through My Network Places or Windows Explorer. However, unlike LAN-based clients, remote access clients do not receive WINS, DNS, and other options directly from the DHCP server; they receive only an IP address and a subnet mask, which may have been prefetched from the DHCP server (as was just described) or may have been predefined in a static pool. WINS and DNS addresses, on the other hand, are pulled directly from the configuration of the RRAS server's network adapters if they are configured with these values.

If the WINS and DNS lookups provided by the RRAS server's NIC configuration are not sufficient to access resources on the remote network, and if you want quick name resolution beyond what you can achieve by enabling the Enable Broadcast Name Resolution option, consider using Hosts and/or Lmhosts files on a case-by-case basis for clients, or you can use client-based logon scripts to map network drives. These are not ideal solutions, and they will require a lot of administrative overhead, but they are still viable options that will typically get the job done.

See Also

- Microsoft KB 232651: "How to Prevent Routing and Remote Access from Assigning WINS and DNS Addresses to Clients." This article will instruct you to modify two Registry keys if you do not want your remote access clients to receive WINS and/or DNS server settings during the DHCP address allocation process.

- Microsoft KB 216805: "RAS Server Behavior When Configured to Use DHCP to Assign IP Addresses." This article describes the allocation process of IP addresses when RRAS is configured to use DHCP to obtain addresses.

- Microsoft KB 160699: "Understanding DHCP IP Address Assignment for RAS Clients." This article explains the parameters that are passed to the remote access client and the mechanisms that are used to do this. The parameters that are discussed include IP address, subnet, WINS, DNS, NetBIOS scope ID, and node type.

- Microsoft KB 292822: "Name Resolution and Connectivity Issues on a Routing and Remote Access Server That Also Runs DNS or WINS." This article covers issues related to the coinstallation of WINS Server and/or DNS Server on the RRAS server.

4-7. Configuring Point-to-Point Protocol (PPP)

Problem

You want to configure PPP options for your server.

Solution

Using a Graphical User Interface

1. Start the Routing and Remote Access Services administrative console from the Administrative Tools folder in the Start menu, or directly from %systemroot%\system32\ rrasmgmt.msc.

2. Right-click the name of the RRAS server that you want to manage in the left pane, and select Properties.

3. Select the PPP tab.

4. Select the Multilink Connections check box if you want to allow clients and demand-dial routers to combine multiple physical links into a single logical connection.

5. If you enabled Multilink Connections in step 4, select the Dynamic Bandwidth Control Using BAP or BACP check box to enable the dynamic addition or removal of connections using the Bandwidth Allocation Protocol (BAP) or Bandwidth Allocation Control Protocol (BACP).

6. Select the Link Control Protocol (LCP) Extensions check box to allow the server to send Time-Remaining and Identification packets and request a callback during the negotiation phase.

7. Select the Software Compression check box to allow the Microsoft Point-to-Point Compression Protocol (MPPC) to compress data over the remote connection.

Using a Command-Line Interface

You can manage your PPP link settings by running several `netsh ras` commands.

To display the link properties that PPP will negotiate, use this command:

```
> netsh ras show link
```

The results will look like the following:

```
> netsh ras show link
```

```
Enabled Link Options:
Code          Meaning
SWC           Provides software compression (MPPC).
LCP           Provides Link Control Protocol extensions from the PPP suite
              of protocols.
```

To enable or disable a link property that PPP will negotiate, use this command:

```
> netsh ras {add | delete} link {swc | lcp}
```

The parameters and values are as follows:

Add | Delete: Required parameter that specifies whether you want to enable (add) or disable (delete) the given value.

SWC | LCP: Required parameter that specifies the protocol on which you want to take the given action. SWC enables or disables software compression; LCP enables or disables LCP extensions.

For example, to enable LCP extensions but disable software compression, run the following commands:

```
> netsh ras add link lcp
> netsh ras delete link swc
```

You can display the multilink properties using this command:

```
> netsh ras show multilink
```

The results will look like this:

```
> netsh ras show multilink
```

```
Enabled Multilink Options:

Code           Meaning
MULTI          Provides multilink PPP sessions.
BACP           Provides Bandwidth Allocation Control Protocol.
```

To enable or disable a multilink property, use this command:

```
> netsh ras {add | delete} multilink {multi | bacp}
```

The parameters and values are as follows:

Add | Delete: Required parameter that specifies whether you want to enable (add) or disable (delete) the given value.

Multi | BACP: Required parameter that specifies the result of your action. Multi enables or disables multilink PPP sessions; BACP enables or disables Bandwidth Allocation Control Protocol (BACP).

For example, to enable multilink connections but disable BACP, run the following commands:

```
> netsh ras add multilink multi
> netsh ras delete multilink bacp
```

How It Works

The Point-to-Point Protocol (PPP) allows interoperability between different vendors of remote access software. Unlike the earlier Serial Line Interface Protocol (SLIP) that was common in the early 1990s, PPP permits multiple authentication protocols, compression, and encryption. In addition, PPP supports connections for multiple protocols such as TCP/IP, IPX/SPX, and AppleTalk, and it allows the entire logon sequence to be automated.

By specifying PPP options on the RRAS server, you are able to grant remote access clients the right to combine multiple physical lines into a single logical connection, as well as take advantage of bandwidth-conserving techniques and data compression.

See Also

- Microsoft KB 315253: "The Point-to-Point Protocol Dial-Up Sequence." This article explains the sequence of events that occurs when a remote access client negotiates a PPP session.

- Microsoft Windows 2000 Resource Kit: Series of articles under "Point-to-Point Protocol" (`http://www.microsoft.com/resources/documentation/Windows/2000/server/reskit/en-us/Default.asp?url=/resources/documentation/Windows/2000/server/reskit/en-us/w2rkbook/default.asp`). These articles give a comprehensive description of the function, architecture, and configuration of PPP.

- Microsoft TechNet: "PPP Operation and Protocols" (`http://technet2.microsoft.com/WindowsServer/f/?en/Library/372d813d-91ae-41b5-a20a-a57d58357ea91033.mspx`).

4-8. Configuring the Logging Level

Problem

You want to configure the level of logging detail for RRAS events.

Solution

Using a Graphical User Interface

1. Start the Routing and Remote Access Services administrative console from the Administrative Tools folder in the Start menu, or directly from `%systemroot%\system32\rrasmgmt.msc`.

2. Right-click the name of the RRAS server that you want to manage in the left pane, select Properties, and then click the Logging tab.

3. Select the level of logging that you want to configure. These are the options:

   - Log Errors Only

   - Log Errors and Warnings (Default)

   - Log All Events

   - Do Not Log Any Events

4. Select the check box to Log Additional Routing and Remote Access Information if you want to log all RRAS details and events. This is most useful for debugging purposes.

5. Click OK when complete.

6. Select the Remote Access Logging folder in the left pane.

7. If you want to configure logging to the file system, double-click Local File in the right pane. Then follow these steps:

    a. Select the Settings tab if it is not already selected.

    b. Check the Accounting Requests check box if you want to log accounting requests such as on, off, start, and stop.

    c. Check the Authentication Requests check box if you want to log requests for authentication by clients.

    d. Check the Periodic Status check box if you want to log interim accounting requests. Note that this will result in a high level of logging and may consume significant hard disk space.

    e. Select the Log File tab.

    f. Specify or browse to the directory in which you want to store your logs. The default value is %systemroot%\system32\LogFiles.

    g. Select either the IAS or Database-Compatible format for your logs.

    h. Specify the frequency at which you want to create new log files. This may be daily, weekly, monthly, never, or only when the log reaches a specific size, which you can specify in megabytes.

    i. Select the option to delete old log files if a disk-full situation is encountered.

    j. Click the OK button when complete.

Using a Command-Line Interface

You can enable detailed logging of events (components) in RRAS, which is equivalent to enabling the check box in step 4 in the "Using a Graphical User Interface" section, by running the following commands.

    To show a list of all possible components and their current logging status, use this command:

```
> netsh ras show tracing
```

To enable or disable logging of a particular event (component), use this command:

```
> netsh ras set tracing [component=]<ComponentToLog> [state=] {enabled | disabled}
```

For ComponentToLog, specify one of the components that you obtained from the netsh ras show tracing command.

    Here are some examples. To enable detailed logging of all PPP events, use this command:

```
> netsh ras set tracing component=ppp state=enabled
```

This command disables detailed logging of Extensible Authentication Protocol (EAP) events:

```
> netsh ras set tracing component=eap state=disabled
```

This command enables tracing of all events:

```
> netsh ras set tracing component=*
```

Using the Registry

There are a large number of RAS-specific protocols, services, and events whose logging can be enabled or disabled in the Registry. You can view a list of these keys beneath the following Registry key:

```
HKEY_LOCAL_MACHINE\Software\Microsoft\Tracing\
```

Once you select the desired item to log, enable it by navigating to the appropriate key and modifying the `EnableConsoleTracing` and `EnableFileTracing` values. Each subkey has an identical structure.

For example, you can enable verbose logging of PPP events by modifying this key:

```
[HKEY_LOCAL_MACHINE\Software\Microsoft\Tracing\PPP\]
"EnableConsoleTracing"=dword:1
"EnableFileTracing"=dword:1
```

Or you can enable verbose logging of EAP events by modifying this key:

```
[HKEY_LOCAL_MACHINE\Software\Microsoft\Tracing\RASEAP\]
"EnableConsoleTracing"=dword:1
"EnableFileTracing"=dword:1
```

How It Works

Under normal operating conditions, you really only need to record error and warning events. However, two conditions mandate a higher level of logging:

- **Debugging:** You are experiencing configuration or connection problems and need to view the details of connection events as a step in the troubleshooting process.

- **Security:** You suspect that unauthorized users are attempting to access your system; you want to record all details as a means to record and block these connections.

If you enable verbose logging, pay close attention to the size of the log files on the disk. They can quickly grow to fill the disk! Also, make certain to save log files in a format that you are able to parse and put into a readable form, since log files can be extremely long and difficult to follow.

See Also

Microsoft TechNet: "Log Parser 2.2" (`http://www.microsoft.com/technet/scriptcenter/tools/logparser`). The Log Parser utility is designed to query text-based log files and generate easy-to-read reports and tables.

4-9. Creating Remote Access Policies

Problem

You want to create a remote access policy to apply to users or security groups.

Solution

Creating a remote access policy involves using the New Remote Access Policy Wizard to create a typical policy (for a common scenario) or a custom policy for your specific environment. Both will be explained.

Note There is no convenient or practical way to create policies through a command-line interface or VBScript.

To start the New Remote Access Policy Wizard, follow these steps:

1. Start the Routing and Remote Access Services administrative console from the Administrative Tools folder in the Start menu, or directly from `%systemroot%\system32\rrasmgmt.msc`.

2. Expand the server tree in the left pane.

3. Right-click the Remote Access Policies node, and select New Remote Access Policy.

4. Click the Next button to start the New Remote Access Policy Wizard.

At this point in the wizard, you will be prompted to either create a typical policy for a common scenario or to create a custom policy.

To create a typical policy for a common scenario, follow these steps:

1. Select the option to Use the Wizard to Set Up a Typical Policy for a Common Scenario, and provide a convenient name for the policy in the field below. Then click the Next button.

2. Select the method that your clients will use to connect to the network, and then click the Next button. These are the options:

   - **VPN:** This policy will apply to all VPN types. (To configure a policy for specific VPN protocols or parameters, create a custom policy as discussed later in this section.)

   - **Dial-up:** Use this policy for dial-up modems or ISDN lines.

   - **Wireless:** Use this policy for remote wireless connections.

   - **Ethernet:** Use this policy for standard Ethernet connections.

3. Select the option to specify that policy permissions are defined in the user account settings or to specify particular groups to which you want this policy to apply. Click the Next button when complete.

4. Select the method that you want to use to authenticate your remote users to the server, and click the Next button when complete. These are the options:

- **Extensible Authentication Protocol (EAP):** This option applies to certificate-based authentication.

- **Microsoft Encrypted Authentication v2 (MS-CHAP v2):** If you select this option, remote users will be required to supply a password. This option is enabled by default. This option is not available for wireless access policies.

- **Microsoft Encrypted Authentication (MS-CHAP):** This option is less secure than MS-CHAP and should only be used on networks that include operating systems that do not support MS-CHAP v2. This option is not available for wireless access policies.

Note   If you select EAP, you must also select whether you want to use Protected EAP (PEAP) or a smart card or other certificate.

---

5. Select the level of encryption that you want to use on your connections, and click the Next button when complete. These are the options:

- **Basic:** IPSec 56-bit DES or MPPE 40-bit

- **Strong:** IPSec 56-bit DES or MPPE 56-bit

- **Strongest:** IPSec Triple DES or MPPE 128-bit

- **No Encryption:** All data is sent in clear-text. This option is not available when configuring VPN policies, but it is available for dial-up policies.

6. Click the Finish button to complete the wizard.

To create a custom policy, follow these steps:

1. Select the option to Setup a Custom Policy, and provide a convenient name for the policy in the field below. Then click the Next button.

2. Specify the conditions that you want to enforce for this policy. Click the Add button to view a list of predefined conditions. For each condition that you select, click its Add button to specify the restrictions and parameters. When complete, click the Next button. These are the options:

- **Authentication Type:** Specifies the authentication scheme that is used to verify the user

- **Called Station ID:** Specifies the phone number dialed by the user

- **Calling Station ID:** Specifies the phone number from which the call originated

- **Client Friendly Name:** Specifies the friendly name for the RADIUS client, if applicable

- **Client IP Address:** Specifies the IP address of the RADIUS client

- **Client Vendor:** Specifies the manufacturer of the RADIUS proxy

- **Day and Time Restrictions:** Specifies a time window during which the remote connections will be allowed

- **Framed Protocol:** Specifies the allowed protocols

- **MS RAS Vendor:** This description is a placeholder and is not yet defined

- **NAS Identifier:** Specifies the description of the network access server (NAS) that originated the request

- **NAS IP Address:** Specifies the IP address of the NAS that originated the request

- **NAS Port Type:** Specifies the type of port that is used on the NAS that originated the request

- **Service Type:** Specifies the type of service that the user has requested

- **Tunnel Type:** Specifies restrictions on VPN protocols

- **Windows Groups:** Specifies that only certain security groups are allowed to establish connections

3. Select the option to define whether the user will be granted or denied remote access if the request meets the policy's conditions. Click the Next button.

4. Click the Edit button to specify additional, advanced options, or click the Next button to complete and exit the wizard.

5. If you proceeded to edit the policy that you were in the process of creating, you can now specify additional, advanced options, including the following:

   - **Dial-In Constraints:** You can restrict the hours during which remote connections will be accepted; you can accept connections only to specific phone numbers; and you can permit connections only from specific media types, such as wireless, cable, Ethernet, and others.

   - **IP:** You can restrict the method of IP address assignment, such as whether the client has the ability to request a particular IP address. You can also configure inbound and outbound address filters. Addresses matching the criteria specified in the filters will not be permitted to establish a connection; they will be discarded.

   - **Multilink:** You can restrict whether and how multilink connections are permitted, and you can configure Bandwidth Allocation Protocol (BAP).

   - **Authentication:** You can force connections to authenticate via specific authentication protocols, such as EAP, MS-CHAP v2, or MS-CHAP. You can also disable the requirement for any form of authentication if desired.

   - **Encryption:** You can enforce the level of encryption used for the remote session.

   - **Advanced:** You can specify additional parameters, including the dial-up modem type, the network protocol, specific VPN parameters, and others.

How It Works

Remote access policies permit connections based on criteria such as these:

- Remote access permission
- Group membership
- Type of connection
- Time of day
- Authentication methods

They also permit connections based on advanced conditions, such as these:

- Access server identity
- Access client phone number or MAC address
- Whether user account dial-in properties are ignored
- Whether unauthenticated access is allowed

After the connection is granted, remote access policies can also be used to specify connection restrictions based on criteria such as these:

- Idle timeout time
- Maximum session time
- Encryption strength
- IP packet filters

Advanced connection restrictions include the following:

- IP address for PPP connections
- Static routes

For example, you can have policies that permit remote access only to the Engineering group but deny it to the HR group. You could also restrict relevant groups to access during normal business hours and specify that the connection should be terminated if left idle for more than 15 minutes.

In order to take full advantage of remote access policies, your Windows 2000 or 2003 domain must be running in native mode. If you are still operating in mixed mode, your restrictions are limited to allowing or denying access on a per-user basis.

If a particular user is configured such that the account properties explicitly grant or deny dial-in permissions, then the server-based remote access policy will be ignored unless an advanced restriction is defined on the server that specifies that the user account properties should be ignored.

Group permissions can only be created and managed using server policies; it is not possible to allow or deny access to a group in a manner analogous to a specific user account. However, if you do configure a server policy that is based on group membership, you should be certain that the individual members of that group are configured to use policies; do not specify the option to explicitly allow or deny dial-in access.

If your server is configured to use Windows authentication, you can manage policies from the RRAS console, but the policies will apply only to connections made to that particular server. On the other hand, if your server is configured to use RADIUS authentication, you will no longer be able to manage the policies at the RRAS server; all policies must be managed at the RADIUS server. The advantage to managing policies on a RADIUS server, however, is that you will be able to apply the policies to any number of RRAS servers on your network.

As described in this recipe, there is a rich selection of options that you can use for the basis of your policy. Review each option and select the ones that meet the needs of your organization, whether those needs are to conserve bandwidth or to enforce a particular time of day to permit connections.

See Also

Microsoft KB 816522: "How to Create and Enforce a Remote Access Security Policy in Windows Server 2003." This article provides details relating to policies and their troubleshooting.

4-10. Specifying Additional Details of Remote Access Policies

Problem

You want to fine-tune your remote access policies, specifying additional levels of detail and prioritizing one policy against another.

Solution

Manage your remote access policies by following these steps:

1. Start the Routing and Remote Access Services administrative console from the Administrative Tools folder in the Start menu, or directly from `%systemroot%\system32\rrasmgmt.msc`.

2. Expand the server tree in the left pane.

3. Right-click the Remote Access Policies node in the left pane.

4. Right-click the policy that you want to edit in the right pane, and select Properties.

5. Click the Add button to specify additional connection criteria. (These criteria are detailed in Recipe 4-9, "Creating Remote Access Policies," in step 2 of the instructions for creating a custom policy.)

6. Specify the details of the criteria when prompted. For example, if you choose to specify Day and Time Restriction as a criterion, the wizard will prompt you to specify the actual days and times to which you want to limit remote access. Click the OK button when complete.

7. If you want to edit or delete a restriction, select the restriction and click the Edit or Remove button, as appropriate. Click the OK button when complete.

8. Select the appropriate radio button to either grant or deny remote access to the user if the connection matches the specified criteria.

9. Click the Edit button to edit the dial-in profile. (The settings are the same as described in Recipe 4-9, "Creating Remote Access Policies," in step 5 of the instructions for creating a custom policy.)

10. Click the OK button when complete.

To prioritize one policy over another, follow these steps:

1. Expand the server tree in the left pane.

2. Right-click the Remote Access Policies node in the left pane.

3. Right-click the policy in the right pane that you want to prioritize, and select the option to either Move Up or Move Down with respect to other policies.

How It Works

The policy with the lowest order number is processed before those with higher numbers. Once a connection request meets the criteria specified by a policy, the connection is either allowed or denied based on the configuration of that policy; subsequent policies are not processed. Because of this, it is important to consider the order in which policies are applied so that you do not inadvertently allow or deny someone remote access inappropriately.

If the connection request does not meet the criteria of any of the policies, the request will be denied.

See Also

Microsoft KB 816522: "How to Create and Enforce a Remote Access Security Policy in Windows Server 2003." This article provides additional information relating to the enforcement of remote access security policies in a Windows Server 2003-based native-mode domain.

4-11. Managing User-Specific Permissions and Settings

Problem

You want to control the method by which user accounts are granted or denied remote access connectivity.

Solution

Using a Graphical User Interface

1. Start the Active Directory Users and Computers administrative console from the Administrative Tools folder in the Start menu, or directly from %systemroot%\system32\dsa.msc.

2. Expand the Active Directory tree in the left pane until you can see the desired user accounts in the right pane.

3. Double-click the user account of interest, and select the Dial-in tab.

4. Select whether you want to explicitly allow or deny remote access, or whether you want remote access policies to make this determination.

5. Select the Verify Caller-ID check box if you want to grant remote access to users only if they dial-in from a specific number. Enter that phone number in the associated field.

Note The Caller ID verification option is only available when a Windows 2000 or Windows 2003 Active Directory is running in native mode.

---

6. Specify any callback options if desired. You may specify the following options:

   • **No Callback:** Callback will not be permitted

   • **Set by Caller (Routing and Remote Access Service Only):** Callback can be requested by the user

   • **Always Callback To:** Forces callback to the number that you provide

7. Enable the check box to Assign a Static IP Address if you want to force a particular address to the remote user. This option will override policy settings and is available only in Windows 2000 or Windows 2003 native mode. Enter the desired IP address in the provided field.

8. Click OK when complete.

Using a Command-Line Interface

You can display the remote access properties of a specific user by running the following command. If you omit the parameters, the properties of all users on the system will be displayed.

```
> netsh ras show user [name=<UserName>] [[mode=] {permit | report}]
```

The parameters and values are as follows:

Name: Optional parameter that specifies the account name (logon name) of the account whose remote access properties you want to view. If omitted, the command will return information for all accounts.

Mode: Optional parameter that specifies whether the properties will be displayed for all users or only for those that have been explicitly granted access. A value of permit will display properties for explicitly defined users; a value of report will display properties for all users.

For example, this command will display remote access properties for all users:

```
> netsh ras show user
```

A sampling of the results will look as follows:

```
> netsh ras show user
```

User name:	Administrator
Dialin:	policy
Callback policy:	none
Callback number:	
User name:	BDinerman
Dialin:	permit
Callback policy:	admin
Callback number:	508-555-1234

To configure remote access parameters for a specified user, run the following command:

```
> netsh ras set user [name=]<UserName> [dialin] {permit | deny | policy}
    [cbpolicy] {none | caller | admin [cbnumber=]<CallbackNumber>}
```

The parameters and values are as follows:

Name: Required parameter that specifies the account name (user ID) of the account whose remote access properties you want to configure.

Dialin: Required parameter that specifies how you want to manage dial-in privileges. Specify permit to explicitly grant permission; specify deny to forbid it; or specify policy if you want a remote access policy to make the decision. Note that in a mixed-mode Active Directory, policy is not an option, but the resultant behavior will be as if policy were set to deny.

CBPolicy: Required parameter that specifies how you want to handle user callback policies. Specify none to prohibit user callback; specify caller to allow the caller to set the callback number; or specify admin to force a callback number.

CBNumber: Required parameter only if the CBPolicy parameter has been given a value of admin. This parameter specifies the callback number to use for the given user.

As an example, if you want to explicitly grant the EPresley user account dial-in rights with a callback number set to 1-800-555-1234, you could run the following command:

```
> netsh ras set user EPresley permit admin 18005551234
```

How It Works

Callback occurs after the user has authenticated to the remote access server. Once the authentication process has successfully completed, the server will disconnect the session and reinitiate the connection to the user.

Callback policies offer two key advantages:

- **Security:** By specifying a callback number, unauthorized users cannot connect remotely to your system from their own location. All calls will be connected only at the location (phone number) to which the server returns the call.

- **Cost savings:** The remote user will only make a brief call to the remote access server. The remote access server will then place a call back to the user, meaning that the organization providing the server will pay for any time-based connection charges rather than the end-user having to pay these charges.

■**Note** Callback is offered only for dial-in connections; it is not available for VPN connections.

Another feature of user-based remote access settings is the ability to assign a static IP address to the user that will be consistent at each remote access session. This setting is one way to overcome the fact that remote access clients do not truly query the DHCP server for addresses, and can therefore not take advantage of DHCP reservations to receive the same IP address for each session. If you want your end users to consistently receive the same address, you can configure your user account settings to provide this.

RRAS caches IP addresses received in batches from the DHCP server but does not cache the usual DHCP scope options, such as WINS and DNS server lookups. See Recipe 4-6, "Configuring IP Settings," for more information relating to this topic.

■**Note** The ability to assign static IP addresses to remote access users exists only in native-mode Windows 2000 or Windows 2003 domains. If you run in a mixed mode, this feature will be disabled.

See Also

- Microsoft KB 303684: "How to Configure IP Reservations for RRAS Clients in Windows 2000." This article provides a summary of the IP address reservation process when using RRAS.

- Microsoft Windows XP Professional Product Documentation: "Callback" (http://www.microsoft.com/resources/documentation/windows/xp/all/proddocs/en-us/using_callback.mspx).

- Microsoft TechNet: "Callback" (http://technet2.microsoft.com/WindowsServer/f/?en/Library/ed9c2d7e-2752-4abb-ac71-a63e184c9e391033.mspx). This article describes the callback mechanism as viewed by the server.

4-12. Configuring and Managing a Remote Access Account Lockout Policy

Problem

You want to protect your network by creating a lockout policy for failed authentication attempts by remote access clients.

Solution

Remote access lockout policies can only be created and managed through the Windows Registry. There is not an equivalent graphical user interface or command-line option for this technique.

Using the Registry

You can create (enable) a remote access lockout policy by modifying the following Registry key:

```
[HKEY_LOCAL_MACHINE\SYSTEM\CurrentControlSet\Services\...
    ...RemoteAccess\Parameters\AccountLockout\]
"MaxDenials"=dword:<Limit>
"ResetTime"=dword:<Duration>
```

In these keys, Limit corresponds to the number of allowed attempts that you will permit before locking a user account to remote access connections. A value of 0 will disable account lockout.

■Note Locking a user account from remote access connectivity will not lock the actual user account in Active Directory. These entries relate only to remote access.

Duration is the amount of time, in minutes, after which you want a locked account to be re-enabled. Specify the duration in decimal format. The default value is 2,880 minutes, or two days.

For example, to enable remote access account lockout after five failed logon attempts, and to automatically unlock the account after 60 minutes, create or modify the following keys:

```
[HKEY_LOCAL_MACHINE\SYSTEM\CurrentControlSet\Services\...
    ...RemoteAccess\Parameters\AccountLockout\]
"MaxDenials"=dword:5
"ResetTime"=dword:60
```

You can also unlock an account by modifying the Registry. To do so, use Regedit.exe and select the following key:

```
HKEY_LOCAL_MACHINE\SYSTEM\CurrentControlSet\Services\...
    ...RemoteAccess\Parameters\AccountLockout\
```

In the right pane, locate the value given by <DomainName:UserName>, which corresponds to the locked-out user, and delete that entry.

Using VBScript

You can create (enable) a remote access lockout policy by running the following script. In this script, we will configure the remote access server named RRAS1 to lock the account after five failed authentication attempts, and to unlock the account after 60 minutes.

```
' This code configures the account lockout threshold and
' lockout duration for a remote access server
' ------ SCRIPT CONFIGURATION ------
strComputer = "RRAS1"
dMaxDenials = "5"
dLockoutDuration = "60"
' ------ END CONFIGURATION ---------
Const HKEY_LOCAL_MACHINE = &H80000002
strKeyPath = _
"SYSTEM\CurrentControlSet\Services\RemoteAccess\Parameters\AccountLockout"
Set objReg=GetObject("winmgmts:{impersonationLevel=impersonate}!\\" & _
    strComputer & "\root\default:StdRegProv")
dValueName = "MaxDenials"
objReg.SetStringValue HKEY_LOCAL_MACHINE,strKeyPath,dValueName,dMaxDenials
dValueName = "Reset Time(mins)"
dValue = dLockoutDuration
objReg.SetDWORDValue HKEY_LOCAL_MACHINE,strKeyPath,dValueName,dValue
WScript.Echo "Values set"
```

How It Works

Configuring an account and an RRAS lockout policy is part of any solid security implementation. If your server is connected to or accessible from the Internet, you can safely assume that it will be a target for unauthorized users, whether the targeting is specifically aimed at your organization or whether you are instead the victim of scanning tools that automatically scan entire subnets looking for vulnerable systems.

Whatever the case, you should decide on limits for account lockout that do not negatively impact your business operations yet keep you reasonably secure from password-guessing tools, disgruntled employees, and malicious hackers. For example, configuring a policy that locks out a user after only one failed attempt would certainly seem to secure your system, yet it would be counterproductive for your company because any user who mistypes a password would be locked out, and would have to ask an administrator to unlock the account so that he or she could try again, and could only then reattempt the logon (hopefully successfully) and finally get to work.

See Also

- Microsoft KB 816118: "How to Configure Remote Access Client Account Lockout in Windows Server 2003"

- Microsoft TechNet: "Remote Access Account Lockout" (http://technet2.microsoft.com/WindowsServer/f/?en/Library/ c03f130b-ecc8-4f71-8bb2-cf447a438a181033.mspx)

4-13. Viewing Client Connections

Problem

You want to know who is connected to your remote access server and view statistics about that user's connection.

Solution

Using a Graphical User Interface

1. Start the Routing and Remote Access Services administrative console from the Administrative Tools folder in the Start menu, or directly from %systemroot%\system32\ rrasmgmt.msc.

2. Expand the tree in the left pane, and select the Remote Access Clients node under the server object.

3. View connected clients in the right pane. The default view includes the following:

   - **User Name:** The user account through which the remote user connected

   - **Duration:** The amount of time that has passed since the connection was established

   - **Number of Ports:** The number of dial-in ports used by this connection

4. Double-click any client in the right pane to view additional statistics about that connection, including the following:

   - **Statistics:** The number of bytes and frames in and out, as well as the compression ratio

   - **Errors:** The number of errors that have occurred during this connection, including cyclic redundancy check (CRC), time-out, alignment, framing, hardware overruns, and buffer overruns

   - **Network Registration:** The IP, IPX, or AppleTalk address assigned to the connection, or the NetBIOS name of the associated device

5. While in the additional statistics screen, you can also take the following actions:

   • Click the Refresh button to view the latest data; this screen is not dynamic.

   • Click the Reset button to reset all statistics and errors to zero.

   • Click the Disconnect button to terminate the user's remote session.

   • Click Close to close this screen and return to the previous view.

6. You can send console messages to connected users from the default view. Right-click a connected user in the right pane, and select one of the following options:

   • **Send Message:** Send a message to the connected user. You will be prompted to enter the text of the message that you want to send.

   • **Send to All:** Send a message to all connected clients. You will be prompted to enter the text of the message that you want to send.

Note In order to send messages to remote clients, the Messenger service must be running on the target computer and you must have administrative permissions to use it. Note also that the Messenger service refers to the built-in Windows service, and not to the "chat" application of similar name.

Using a Command-Line Interface

To view a list of connected clients, run the following command:

```
> netsh ras show client
```

The results will look like this:

```
> netsh ras show client
```

```
User:             EPresley
Domain:           GRACELAND
Connected from:   KINGPC
Duration:         0 days 0 hours 22 mins 8 secs
```

How It Works

The ability to see in real time the users that are connected to your system, as well as statistics about their connections, is fundamental to the proper management of your system. Not only does this ability allow you to know who is connected in the event that you need to disconnect them (for a planned server reboot, for example), but it also gives you insight into who may be connected when they shouldn't be! In the event that this latter situation occurs, you may need to fine-tune your remote access policies.

4-14. Configuring Connection Profiles for End Users Using the Connection Manager Administration Kit (CMAK)

Problem

You want to create a profile or package that contains preconfigured connectivity parameters for end users to connect to your remote access server.

Solution

The Connection Manager Administration Kit (CMAK) provides an easy-to-use wizard that will build a profile that you can then distribute to your end users. This profile will allow the users to connect to your remote access server using settings and information that you have already specified for them.

Before you can start using the CMAK, you must verify that it is installed on your server. You can easily check this in the Add/Remove Windows Components applet (within Management and Monitoring Tools); you should also have a shortcut icon located in your Administrative Tools folder.

Once you have verified that it is installed, proceed to build the profile by starting the wizard, clicking the Next button, and going through each of the following screens. Much of the information in the screens is optional.

1. **Service Profile Selection:** Select the option for New Profile if you are creating a new profile. If you are editing an existing one, select that option as well as the appropriate profile. Click the Next button to proceed.

2. **Service and File Names:** Enter the Service Name, which is just a friendly name for the profile. For example, enter Widgets Plus, Inc. Also enter a name that will be used for the resulting profile file. The name must be eight characters or fewer. For example, you could call it `MyWidget`. Click the Next button to proceed.

3. **Realm Name:** Enter a domain name, realm name, or domain suffix if your remote access server requires that it be entered. For example, you could enter `Widgets\` to precede the user name, or `@widgets.com` to follow it. Click the Next button to proceed.

4. **Merging Profile Information:** Merge information from other profiles that you've already configured, if desired, by selecting the existing profile and clicking the Add button. Click the Next button to proceed.

5. **VPN Support:** If this profile will connect you to a VPN server, select either the Phone Book from This Profile and/or the Phone Books from the Merged Profiles check boxes. Enter the full DNS name of the VPN server or its IP address, such as `remote.widgets.com`. If desired, also set the option to force the same logon credentials for both VPN and dial-up connections. Click the Next button to proceed.

6. **VPN Entries:** Edit the current VPN entry or create a new one by clicking the Edit or New button, respectively. Then configure the parameters in each of the following three tabs.

7. **VPN Entries ➤ General**

   - Provide a friendly name for this VPN entry, such as Widgets VPN.

   - Select the check box to disable file and printer sharing over the VPN connection, if desired.

   - Select the check box to enable clients to log on to a remote network.

8. **VPN Entries ➤ TCP/IP Settings**

   - Select how the remote client will obtain its DNS and WINS settings. Select the option to either obtain these through DHCP, or enter them manually.

   - Select the check box to Make This Connection the Client's Default Gateway, if desired. Enabling this option means that all Internet access from the client will go through the VPN connection. *Split tunnels*, in which the client can access the Internet through its own connection at the same time that it can access the remote site, will not be permitted.

   - Select the check box to Use IP Header Compression, if desired.

9. **VPN Entries ➤ Security**

   - Select whether you want to use Basic, Advanced, or both Basic and Advanced security settings.

   - Configure the basic settings. These include the Authentication Method and the VPN Strategy (protocol). The options for VPN Strategy include PPTP or L2TP/IPSec. If you select the latter, you also have the option to force a preshared key for the connection.

   - Configure the advanced settings. These include an option for Data Encryption, the method of Logon Security (EAP or other methods such as MS-CHAP v2), and the VPN Strategy.

10. Once you have finished with the three VPN tabs, click OK to proceed.

■Note The VPN Strategy in this step differs from that in the previous one in that now you may select a strategy priority. You may, for example, configure the connection to try one protocol first and then fallback to the other.

---

11. **Phone Book:** Enter a phone book file if you want to include it with the connection profile. You can also configure the profile to automatically download phone book updates from a location that you will specify in the next step, and you can add extra access numbers if desired. Click the Next button to proceed.

12. **Phone Book Updates:** If you enabled the auto-download option for phone books in the previous step, you can now specify a phone book name and the URL for the Connection Point Services server. Click the Next button to proceed.

13. **Dial-Up Networking Entries:** Configure any dial-up entries here, with the same options available for configuration as those under VPN Entries. Click the Next button to proceed.

14. **Routing Table Update:** Specify custom routing table entries if you want these to be available to your remote client. If enabled, you can select routing data from a text file or provide a URL from which the client can download the entries. If you choose to download the routing table from a URL, you also have the option of forcibly disconnecting the client in the event that the URL is not accessible. Click the Next button to proceed.

15. **Automatic Proxy Configuration:** You have the option of specifying custom proxy settings to be applied to the client's web browser on connection. These proxy settings will be imported from a file that you specify. You also have the option of restoring the browser's proxy settings upon termination of the remote connection. Click the Next button to proceed.

16. **Custom Actions:** You can specify programs to start automatically before, during, or after the remote connection. You also have the option of specifying the type of remote connection to which these actions should apply, including VPN or dial-up. Click the Next button to proceed.

17. **Logo Bitmap:** Specify a graphic that will be displayed in the logon dialog box. Click the Next button to proceed.

18. **Phone Book Bitmap:** Specify a graphic that will be displayed in the phone book dialog box. Click the Next button to proceed.

19. **Icons:** Specify icons that will be displayed in the Connection Manager interface. Click the Next button to proceed.

20. **Notification Area Shortcut Menu:** You may add commands to be displayed and run from the System Tray icon that appears following a successful connection. Click the Next button to proceed.

21. **Help File:** You can choose to include the default help file or a custom one. Click the Next button to proceed.

22. **Support Information:** You may include a phone number, URL, or any other relevant support contact information. Click the Next button to proceed.

23. **Connection Manager Software:** Enable this setting to install the Connection Manager software on remote clients if they do not already have it. Earlier versions of Connection Manager will be automatically upgraded when you use this option. Click the Next button to proceed.

24. **License Agreement:** You can specify that a text file containing license information or acceptable usage policies be displayed when the user installs this profile. Click the Next button to proceed.

25. **Additional Files:** Specify any additional files that you want to include with this profile, such as any required by custom actions that you defined earlier. Click the Next button to proceed.

26. **Ready to Build the Service Profile:** Click the Next button to build the profile. The profile will typically be saved to `c:\program files\cmak\profiles\<ProfileName>\<ProfileFileName>.exe`.

27. Distribute the profile to users so that they can connect to the remote access server.

How It Works

Use of the Connection Manager Administration Kit has two key advantages for the system administrator:

- **Reduced number of help desk calls:** By creating a CMAK profile, you have specified all the information that the end user should need to connect to your remote access server. The user only needs to install the package and provide logon credentials. Without a CMAK profile, you will undoubtedly have to spend significant time creating documentation and working with end users over the phone because they are uncertain how to properly configure their workstations for remote access.

- **Enhanced security:** You specify the level of security and other key settings in the CMAK profile. Users will not have the ability to relax the security settings and compromise the security policies that you have put into place.

As previously described, there are many settings that can be configured in the profile. You will probably use a small number of these (such as VPN-related settings) the majority of the time, and many others (such as logo bitmaps) only on rare occasions.

If you plan to distribute phone books with your CMAK profile, you should also install Connection Point Services from the Add/Remove Programs ➤ Add/Remove Windows Components wizard to enable their distribution.

See Also

- Microsoft TechNet: "Connection Manager Administration Kit" series of articles (http://technet2.microsoft.com/WindowsServer/f/?en/Library/be5c1c37-109e-49bc-943e-6595832d57611033.mspx). These articles provide a complete description of the service as well as its configuration and use.

- Microsoft TechNet: "Connection Point Services" series of articles (http://technet2.microsoft.com/WindowsServer/f/?en/Library/abbc6145-06ed-428c-8fb6-44a3f22033411033.mspx). These articles provide a complete description of the service as well as its configuration and use.

4-15. Configuring Site-to-Site VPNs

Problem

You want to connect two sites through a virtual private network.

Solution

1. Start the Routing and Remote Access Services administrative console from the Administrative Tools folder in the Start menu, or directly from `%systemroot%\system32\rrasmgmt.msc`.

2. If your server is not already listed in the console, add it by right-clicking Routing and Remote Access in the left pane and selecting Add Server. Select the first option, This Computer.

Note If you are enabling Routing and Remote Access Services on a remote server, you can add those servers to this console by selecting The Following Computer, All Routing and Remote Access Servers, or Browse Active Directory, rather than selecting the This Computer option.

---

3. If Routing and Remote Access Services are not yet enabled and configured on your server, right-click on the server name in the left pane, and select Configure and Enable Routing and Remote Access.

Note If Routing and Remote Access Services has already been enabled and configured, expand the tree beneath the server name. Right-click Network Interfaces, select New Demand-Dial Interface, and proceed to step 10.

---

4. Click the Next button after the Routing and Remote Access Server Setup Wizard starts.

5. Select the option for Secure Connection Between Two Private Networks and click the Next button.

6. Select Yes to enable demand-dial connections and click the Next button.

7. Select whether you want to use DHCP to provide addresses to remote clients or whether you want to configure a static pool of addresses, and click the Next button to proceed.

8. If you chose to use a static pool of addresses, configure the pool now and click the Next button.

9. Click Finish to complete the first phase of the wizard.

10. Click the Next button when the Demand-Dial Interface Wizard automatically starts.

11. In the Interface Name window, enter a convenient name for the interface. A good selection may be the name of the company or organization to which you are connecting. Click the Next button to proceed.

12. In the Connection Type window, select the option to Connect Using Virtual Private Networking (VPN), and click the Next button to proceed.

13. In the VPN Type window, select the type of VPN interface to create, and then click the Next button to proceed. The interface options are:

    • Automatic Selection (RRAS will select the protocol for you)

    • Point-to-Point Tunneling Protocol (PPTP)

    • Layer-2 Tunneling Protocol (recommended for a higher level of security)

14. In the Destination Address window, enter the DNS name or the public IP address of the host to which you want to connect. Click the Next button to proceed.

15. In the Protocols and Security window, select the check box to Route IP Packets on This Interface. Because credentials must be specified to make the connection, you can also select the check box to Add a User Account So a Remote User Can Dial In. Click the Next button to proceed.

16. In the Static Routes for Remote Networks window, create the static route for the remote network. The two required values are the Destination and the Network Mask. You may also add a Metric if you have multiple static routes defined on your server.

Note The Destination represents the remote network, not just the remote host. For example, if the remote host is at 192.168.20.2 on a network (subnet) mask of 255.255.255.0, you would enter the remote network as 192.168.20.0.

---

17. In the Dial-In Credentials window, enter the credentials, including domain, account, and password that you will pass for authentication to the remote server. If you enabled the option to add a user account in step 15 of this section, the wizard will create the account on your server at this time. Click the Next button to proceed.

18. Click the Finish button to complete the wizard.

19. Repeat steps 1–18 on the remote server as well. Make certain to enable the same protocols and security settings.

20. After the remote access servers have been configured at both sites, test your connection by issuing a PING command from one server to the other. Ping first by IP address, and if that is successful, ping by DNS or NetBIOS name to test name resolution.

You can access configuration parameters and management tasks by right-clicking on the interface that you just created and selecting the following options:

• **Set Credentials:** Modifies the credentials passed by the local server to the remote server.

• **Connect:** Establishes the site-to-site link.

- **Disconnect:** Terminates the site-to-site link until a user action reestablishes it.

- **Enable:** Enables the site-to-site link. If the link is disabled, no action can establish the connection.

- **Disable:** Disables the site-to-site link.

- **Unreachability Reason:** Reports the reason for the last failed connection attempt.

- **Dial-Out Hours:** Limits the site-to-site link to specific hours.

- **Delete:** Permanently removes the site-to-site link.

- **Properties:** Displays other properties of this link. The relevant properties include:

  - **General:** Sets the host name or IP address of the remote server.

  - **Options:** Sets a timeout period after which an idle connection will be broken, or configures a persistent connection.

  - **Networking:** Sets the network clients or protocols that you want to enable through the site-to-site link.

How It Works

Demand-dial VPN connections are easy links to create between two distinct sites, such as a branch office and a central office. Although an administrator could certainly configure each workstation in the remote office to connect to the central server with its own VPN client, this will undoubtedly place a significant demand on IT Help Desk staff; it can also be an inconvenience to the remote users who just want to have a transparent connection that is available when needed. A site-to-site VPN, on the other hand, creates a connection that will be available when needed without asking the end user to take additional steps to establish the link.

As described in this recipe, the administrator can choose to use either Point-to-Point Tunneling Protocol (PPTP) or Layer-2 Tunneling Protocol (L2TP) for the connection.

PPTP, first supported in Windows NT 4.0 and Windows 98, takes advantage of the authentication and encryption techniques of PPP. It relies on Microsoft Point-to-Point Encryption (MPPE) to encrypt the PPP packets, and then encapsulates the encrypted data into a larger data packet.

L2TP was first supported in Windows 2000 and is now the preferred method to establish VPN tunnels. L2TP relies on Internet Protocol Security (IPSec) for its encryption rather than MPPE. The combination of IPSec and L2TP is frequently labeled "L2TP over IPSec." IPSec provides the security; L2TP provides the transport mechanism. In addition to authentication and encryption, L2TP over IPSec also provides enhanced compression.

By default, RRAS installs 128 PPTP and 128 L2TP ports when initially configured for VPN usage; however, it can be configured to support (in theory) a maximum of 1,000 ports for each protocol.

Note Windows Server 2003 Web Edition will support only a single VPN connection.

In general, PPTP is easier to configure for both the system administrator and the end user. If a sufficiently strong password is used for authentication, PPTP may be considered to be "good enough" by many organizations. PPTP is also supported by non-Windows operating systems. Macintosh clients, for example, can connect to a Windows RRAS server using its own PPTP VPN client.

L2TP over IPSec, however, is more difficult to configure, since it involves knowing the endpoint configuration ahead of time. However, once configured, it is much more secure than PPTP. L2TP over IPSec is less interoperable with other operating systems and devices. For example, it may not be possible to connect a Windows XP client with a SonicWALL or Cisco VPN server.

See Also

- Routing and Remote Access Services Help menu: "Troubleshooting Demand-Dial Routing." This explains techniques to troubleshoot poor or failed VPN connections.

- Microsoft TechNet: "Components of Virtual Private Networking" (http://technet2.microsoft.com/WindowsServer/f/?en/Library/ c991adc2-1ed0-457e-896b-ea2819a031a81033.mspx). This article explains the architecture of PPTP and L2TP and how it works.

■ ■ ■

CHAPTER 5

Routing and Remote Access Service (Routing)

Routing and Remote Access Services, or RRAS, was born in 1996 when Microsoft released the service to replace the more basic Remote Access Service (RAS) in Windows NT 4.0. As its name implies, RRAS provides services for network routing and remote access.

In this chapter, we will focus on the first *R* of RRAS: routing. We will provide recipes that will help you configure your Windows 2003 Server as a full-featured router, including network address translation (NAT), basic firewall configuration, and DHCP and DNS services. In Chapter 4, we focused on the functionality and configuration of remote access services as a component of RRAS; there is some overlap of content since both routing and remote access services are ultimately tied into the same management console and have complementary functionality.

Network routing can be an extremely complex topic that can involve a very large number of protocols, techniques, and configurations. Many experienced Windows administrators or engineers are humbled when confronted with routing concepts or with the multivolume publications devoted to learning them and passing various industrial certifications.

The objective of this chapter is not to provide a tutorial on network routing. Rather, we will provide recipes to assist you in the fundamental configuration of Windows Server 2003 as a network router, assuming that you are already familiar with the basic concepts.

Routing and remote access services are installed by default in Windows Server 2003. They are not like other networking components, such as WINS or DNS, that can be installed or uninstalled. Rather, RRAS just needs to be enabled and configured. Recipes 5-1 through 5-4 will describe the methods to enable and configure these services.

Using a Graphical User Interface

All recipes that involve RRAS management through a graphical user interface will refer to the Routing and Remote Access MMC snap-in utility, accessed from the Administrative Tools folder within the Start menu. In addition, you can access it directly at %systemroot%\system32\rrasmgmt.msc. You must have administrator-level permissions on the server in order to fully use this console.

Using a Command-Line Interface

In Windows Server 2003, the netsh routing command provides a very comprehensive command-line interface for managing RRAS. In this chapter, all recipes with command-line solutions will be based on netsh routing. This syntax is documented on the Microsoft website and can be viewed by issuing the netsh routing help command. You must have administrator-level permissions on the server in order to fully use these commands.

To access the netsh routing interface for the local server, open a command prompt and issue the following command:

```
> netsh routing
```

To access the help menu for netsh routing, just append the help parameter to the command:

```
> netsh routing help
```

Using VBScript

Unfortunately, there is no built-in scripting interface through which to administer RRAS. However, you can call the netsh routing command-line functions from a VBScript using the following syntax:

```
' This code will instantiate a WSH object and execute the desired command.
' ------ SCRIPT CONFIGURATION ------
' Enter the desired netsh routing command between the quotation marks
' in the line below, for example:
strCommand = "netsh routing ip reset"
' ------ END CONFIGURATION ---------
set objShell = CreateObject("WScript.Shell")
set objExec = objShell.Exec(strCommand)
' Run in a loop while the command is executing
Do While objExec.Status = 0
    WScript.Sleep 1000
Loop
' Delete the objects from memory once the command is completed.
Set objExec = Nothing
Set objShell = Nothing
WScript.Echo ("Command completed successfully")
```

Because this syntax is the same regardless of the netsh routing command or parameters, we will not discuss this method in each recipe. Instead, you should refer to the sections of recipes that describe using a command line and then place the appropriate command into the previous script.

5-1. Enabling and Configuring a Network Address Translation Router

Problem

You want to enable RRAS and provide a method for your internal clients to access the Internet using a single, public IP address.

Solution

1. Start the Routing and Remote Access Services administrative console from the Administrative Tools folder in the Start menu, or directly from %systemroot%\system32\ rrasmgmt.msc.

2. If your server is not already listed in the console, add it by right-clicking Routing and Remote Access in the left pane and selecting Add Server. Select the first option, This Computer.

Note If you are enabling RRAS on a remote server, you can add those servers to this console by selecting The Following Computer, All Routing and Remote Access Servers, or Browse Active Directory rather than This Computer.

---

3. Right-click on the server name in the left pane, and select Configure and Enable Routing and Remote Access.

4. Click the Next button when the Routing and Remote Access Server Setup Wizard starts.

5. Select the Network Address Translation option. Click the Next button to proceed.

6. You can now select whether to use an existing interface or to create a demand-dial interface to connect to the Internet. Configure the following options as appropriate for your network, and click the Next button to proceed:

   • If you have a server with two or more network cards, and one is attached to the untrusted network (typically the Internet), select Use This Public Interface to Connect to the Internet. Also select the particular network card that is configured with the public address.

   • If you do not have a network interface attached to the untrusted network, as described in the previous step, but you do have a modem or a Point-to-Point Protocol Over Ethernet (PPPoE) connection, select Create a New Demand-Dial Interface to the Internet.

   • Select the check box if you want to enable a basic firewall on the public interface.

7. Select the interface for the network segment (typically the LAN) that needs access to the Internet. Click the Next button to proceed.

8. Click the Finish button when complete.

Note If you selected the option to create a new demand-dial interface to connect to the Internet in step 6, the Demand-Dial Interface Wizard will automatically start. Proceed to Recipe 5-3, "Enabling and Configuring a Demand-Dial Interface," for the steps relating to this configuration.

How It Works

Configure network address translation (NAT) on your network when you want to provide a rough level of anonymity on the Internet. Rather than each client having its own public IP address, all requests that are sent out from your LAN will appear to come from the same address—that of your NAT router.

In addition, network address translation is useful because it saves you the expense of paying an Internet service provider for a large block of addresses. After all, for most businesses, there is just no technical need for a public IP address on each node of the network. On a more global scale, there would certainly be no IPv4 addresses left if every workstation had a public address.

Not only does NAT provide translation of IP addresses and TCP/UDP port numbers for data packets transferred between the trusted (LAN) and the untrusted (WAN) networks, but it also provides both addressing using the DHCP Allocator (comparable to DHCP Server) and name resolution using the DNS proxy to devices on the LAN.

See Also

- Microsoft KB 324286: "How To Set Up Internet Connection Sharing in Windows Server 2003." This article discusses NAT via Internet Connection Sharing (ICS) in a small- or home-office environment.

- Microsoft TechNet: "Understanding Network Address Translation" (http://technet2.microsoft.com/WindowsServer/en/Library/321780ff-6027-4906-b1e5-3701f3105f0c1033.mspx).

- Microsoft TechNet: "Setting Up Network Address Translation" (http://technet2.microsoft.com/WindowsServer/f/?en/Library/931361cf-ee8a-4c88-8854-039bb3a0d7861033.mspx). This article discusses design and deployment considerations.

- Microsoft TechNet: "Troubleshooting Network Address Translation" (http://technet2.microsoft.com/WindowsServer/f/?en/Library/b91c88e4-17f8-4ad3-87d0-6c5c20d9ac651033.mspx).

- RFC 1918 (http://www.faqs.org/rfcs/rfc1918.html). This RFC explains the IP addressing scheme on private networks.

5-2. Enabling and Configuring a Network Address Translation Router with VPN Support

Problem

You want to enable RRAS and provide a method for your internal clients to access the Internet using a single IP address. You also want to permit inbound VPN connections.

Solution

1. Start the Routing and Remote Access Services administrative console from the Administrative Tools folder in the Start menu, or directly from %systemroot%\system32\ rrasmgmt.msc.

2. If your server is not already listed in the console, add it by right-clicking Routing and Remote Access in the left pane and selecting Add Server. Select the first option, This Computer.

Note If you are enabling RRAS on a remote server, you can add those servers to this console by selecting The Following Computer, All Routing and Remote Access Servers, or Browse Active Directory rather than This Computer.

---

3. Right-click on the server name in the left pane, and select Configure and Enable Routing and Remote Access.

4. Click the Next button when the Routing and Remote Access Server Setup Wizard starts.

5. Select the Virtual Private Network (VPN) Access and NAT option. Click the Next button to proceed.

6. Select the network interface that connects this server to the Internet. Optionally, enable security on the interface by selecting the check box to set up a basic firewall. Click the Next button to proceed.

7. Select the network interface to which you want remote VPN clients to have access. Click the Next button to proceed.

8. Select the method that you want to use to assign addresses to VPN clients. You choose to use DHCP or a specified range of addresses. Click the Next button to proceed.

9. If you chose to use a specified range of addresses in the previous step, create the range now. You can create multiple noncontiguous ranges. Click the Next button to proceed.

10. Select the network interface on the internal or private network that contains the clients that require access to the Internet. Click the Next button to proceed.

11. If you have multiple remote access servers, you can configure your remote access server to interact with a RADIUS server for authentication purposes. Specify whether you want to use a RADIUS server in this step. Click the Next button to proceed.

12. If you enabled RADIUS authentication in the previous step, provide the name or IP address of the RADIUS server as well as a shared secret here. Click the Next button to proceed.

13. Click the Finish button to complete the wizard.

How It Works

Configure a network address translation router with VPN support when you want to allow workstations on your LAN to access the Internet through a single connection (the router) and you also want to host a VPN server so that your mobile users, business partners, and home-office employees can connect securely from the Internet and access resources on the LAN.

Design and security considerations for network address translation (NAT) are the same as those described in Recipe 5-1, "Enabling and Configuring a Network Address Translation Router." Design and security considerations for VPNs, however, could easily be the subjects for their own books. Rather than attempt to identify all the issues relating to this topic, we will point out a few that deserve particular attention:

- **The "health" of the remote client:** Once a client establishes a VPN tunnel to your network, that client is now part of the network in the same way that any workstation on your LAN is on the network. If the client has any malware installed, including viruses, worms, or spyware, that malware may be capable of spreading to the rest of the network. Therefore, as a system administrator, you should make certain that the VPN-connected clients have up-to-date virus protection, have operating systems and applications that are fully patched, and have users behind the keyboard who are trained on security best-practices. You may also want to configure a network quarantine zone in which your remote clients will be confined until a policy gives them a clean bill of health and permits them to access the rest of the LAN.

- **Split-tunnel VPNs:** For enhanced security, configure your VPNs so that the remote clients cannot access other networks (especially the Internet) when connected to your network. When a client can access both your network through the VPN at the same time as the Internet (a scenario known as "split tunneling"), the client is susceptible to compromise by man-in-the-middle attacks and other known hacking techniques.

- **Password and other remote access policies:** When a user connects via VPN, that user has a direct connection into your network along with all rights and privileges granted to that user account. Therefore, you must make certain that you have strong password policies in place to prevent unauthorized users from accessing the network based on the trusted user's credentials.

See Also

- Microsoft KB 816573: "How to Configure a VPN Server to Act as a Router in Windows Server 2003." This article provides general information regarding the configuration of an existing VPN server as a router.

- Microsoft KB 867483: "Network Configuration in ISA Server 2004." This article provides information relating to NAT and VPNs in conjunction with Microsoft ISA Server 2004.

- Microsoft: "ISA Server 2004 VPN Deployment Kit" (http://www.microsoft.com/isaserver/techinfo/Guidance/2004/configuration.mspx). This article provides in-depth documentation relating to VPNs and RRAS in an ISA Server 2004 environment.

- Microsoft TechNet: "Security Issues for VPN" (http://technet2.microsoft.com/WindowsServer/f/?en/Library/09b02d03-ac5d-4a9f-96a2-abde22a714191033.mspx). This article discusses security considerations regarding virtual private networks.

5-3. Enabling and Configuring a Demand-Dial Interface

Problem

You want to create a demand-dial connection to connect two routers, such as in a central-to-branch office scenario.

Solution

Note If you are in the process of enabling RRAS, you may be creating the demand-dial interface with a wizard that has automatically started. If that is the case, begin with step 5. Otherwise, start the wizard manually as described here.

---

1. Start the Routing and Remote Access Services administrative console from the Administrative Tools folder in the Start menu, or directly from %systemroot%\system32\ rrasmgmt.msc.

2. Expand the console tree and right-click on the server object.

3. Select the General tab and verify that LAN and Demand-Dial Routing is enabled. If it is not enabled, enable it and restart the service when prompted.

4. Right-click the Interfaces node in the left pane, and select New Demand-Dial Interface to start the wizard. Click the Next button to proceed through the steps of the wizard.

5. In the Interface Name window, enter a convenient name for the interface. A good choice may be the name of the company or organization to which you are connecting. Click the Next button to proceed.

6. In the Connection Type window, select the option to Connect Using a Modem, ISDN Adapter, or Other Physical Device or to Connect Using PPP Over Ethernet (PPPoE) and click the Next button to proceed.

7. Depending on your choice in step 6, do one of the following and click the Next button to proceed:

   • If you chose to use a modem, ISDN adapter, or other physical device, select the appropriate device and enter the phone number or address of the service to which you need to connect.

   • If you chose to use PPPoE, you can optionally provide a service name or let Windows automatically provide one for you.

8. In the Protocols and Security window, select the check boxes that apply to your situation:

   • **Route IP Packets on This Interface:** Select this option to enable routing over this interface.

   • **Add a User Account So a Remote Router Can Dial In:** This option is enabled only if you chose to use a modem or other physical device. Select this option to provide credentials that remote routers will use when connecting to this interface.

- **Send a Plain-Text Password If That Is the Only Way to Connect:** Use this option only if encrypted passwords cannot be sent, but beware that the passwords are highly vulnerable to exposure.

- **Use Scripting to Complete the Connection with the Remote Router:** Select this option if you need or want to run a script during the connection process.

9. In the Static Routes for Remote Networks window, create a static route for the remote network to which you want to connect your demand-dial interface. Enter the remote network address and its subnet.

Note Make sure that you enter the address of the remote network and not of a particular host on the network. For example, you may be connecting to a RRAS server at the remote address of 192.168.50.2. In this case, the remote network is specified as 192.168.50.0, assuming a subnet of 255.255.255.0.

---

10. If you enabled the option to use scripting in step 8, you can identify in the Router Scripting window the script that you want to run. You can select from a number of preconfigured scripts supplied with the operating system, or you can create your own and use that instead. All scripts, including the ones supplied with Windows, can be customized for your environment. Click the Next button to proceed once you have selected your script.

11. If you selected the option to add a user account in step 8, provide the password in the Dial-In Credentials window. (The wizard will automatically create and name the account.) Click the Next button to proceed.

12. In the Dial-Out Credentials window, set the credentials that this interface will use when connecting to a remote router. The credentials that you specify here must match credentials configured on the remote router. Click the Next button to proceed.

13. Click the Finish button to complete the wizard.

How It Works

You should create a demand-dial connection when you do not have a dedicated link to your remote site but need to access resources on that site. The demand-dial connection is activated only when data is sent to the remote network. Once activated, it remains connected until a timeout period has elapsed, after which the connection drops until requested again.

Although your users could certainly create individual VPN connections to the remote site, this is not practical when more than a few users require the connections. Administration is more complex, since you must maintain VPN settings for each user that needs to connect. Demand-dial connections are a better solution, since you only need to maintain the connection on the two servers (routers), and all clients can then access resources on the remote network with nearly the same effort as if they were on the local network. The amount of Help Desk support that you will need to provide to individual users will be greatly reduced.

See Also

- Microsoft TechNet: "Understanding Demand-Dial Routing"
  (http://technet2.microsoft.com/WindowsServer/f/?en/Library/
  48757b3c-9211-48b6-a057-7ec71406f44a1033.mspx). This article discusses the basic
  concepts and issues behind demand-dial routing.

- Microsoft KB 278880: "The Demand-Dial Interface Does not Disconnect When Network
  Address Translation Is Installed." This article provides information regarding the DNS
  proxy and its effect on demand-dial connections.

- Microsoft TechNet: "Setting Up Demand-Dial Routing"
  (http://technet2.microsoft.com/WindowsServer/f/?en/Library/
  bdfca0ed-a4a1-4cec-859d-b0c26b1afb451033.mspx). This series of articles discusses
  demand-dial design and security considerations.

- Microsoft TechNet: "Troubleshooting Demand-Dial Routing"
  (http://technet2.microsoft.com/WindowsServer/f/?en/Library/
  0cb97fcf-ca9f-40fb-b543-5ed93696c8861033.mspx).

- Recipe 5-4 for more on configuring demand-dial interfaces.

5-4. Configuring Advanced Properties
for Demand-Dial Interfaces

Problem

You want to modify additional properties for existing demand-dial interfaces.

Solution

1. Start the Routing and Remote Access Services administrative console from the
   Administrative Tools folder in the Start menu, or directly from %systemroot%\system32\
   rrasmgmt.msc.

2. Expand the console tree and click on the server object to expand its tree structure.

3. Select the Network Interfaces node in the left pane.

4. Right-click the interface whose properties you want to modify in the right pane, and
   select Properties.

5. Select the General tab and set one of the following:

   - If this interface uses a modem, ISDN, or other dial-out device, click the Configure
     button to set the properties of the device. Also modify the phone number as needed.

   - If this interface uses PPPoE, modify the Service Name as needed.

6. Select the Options tab and set the following options as necessary:

   - **Connection Type:** Specify whether this interface is activated on demand or whether it is persistent.

   - **Dialing Policy:** Specify the number of attempts the system will make to complete the connection, as well as the interval between connection attempts.

   - **Callback:** Click the Callback button to specify any callback numbers for this connection. Click OK to accept the changes and proceed.

   - **X.25:** If this interface uses a modem, ISDN, or other dial-out device, you can configure X.25 options. Click the X.25 button to specify an X.25 network provider and the X.121 address of the remote server. Click OK to accept the changes and proceed.

Note For a discussion of X.25 and X.121, see the explanations in Wikipedia (`http://en.wikipedia.org/wiki/X.25` and `http://en.wikipedia.org/wiki/X.121`).

---

7. Select the Security tab and select the level of security that you want to configure. You can select either Typical (Recommended) or Advanced (Custom Settings).

8. If you selected Typical (Recommended) in step 7, choose the method of identity verification. The available options are to verify with either a secured or unsecured (plain text) password. Additionally, if you enforce a secured password, you can also specify that the data sent during the connection attempt must be encrypted.

Note If you enforce data encryption, the server will disconnect the session if it detects unencrypted communications.

---

9. If you selected Advanced (Custom Settings) in step 7, select the following options:

   - **Data Encryption:** Select whether you want to enforce, recommend, or prevent encrypted sessions.

   - **Logon Security:** Select whether you want to use Extensible Authentication Protocol (EAP), or whether you want to allow PAP, SPAP, CHAP, MS-CHAP, or MS-CHAP v2. You can select as many of the latter protocols as needed, but if you use EAP, you cannot select any of the others.

10. If this interface uses a modem, ISDN, or other dial-out device, you can also enable script processing by enabling the appropriate check box. Select the script that you want to run from the drop-down list, or click the Browse button to browse to the location of the script.

11. Select the Networking tab, and set the options in much the same way that you would configure any network interface:

   - Click the Settings button to configure PPP options, including the use of LCP extensions, software compression, and multilink negotiation. Click OK to accept the changes.

   - Add, remove, enable, or disable components that you want to use with this interface, including protocol (TCP/IP, IPX, or network monitor driver), client (Client for Microsoft Networks or Client Service for NetWare), or service (QoS Packet Scheduler, Network Load Balancing, or Service Advertising Protocol). Additionally, select any of the components and click the Properties button to specify additional details of each.

12. Click the OK button to accept all changes.

How It Works

The term *demand-dial* routing can be somewhat misleading. Demand-dial connections are typically initiated when a user on the local network requests resources from the remote network. However, the connections can actually be configured as persistent ones that form when the service is started and that never terminate (under normal operating conditions). This option may be very convenient for organizations that do not need to worry about the expense of an always-on connection and that want an always-ready connection.

As with any connection over the Internet, security should be a major concern. For this reason, RRAS allows you to configure the method of authentication that you want to enable on your connections. Always select the most secure method that can be implemented without causing undue hardship to your end users. For example, if your remote users use Macintosh clients, it does not make sense to use MS-CHAP v2 as the only allowed protocol, since this protocol is not currently supported by the Macintosh operating system, and the users will not be able to connect.

Make certain you have a solid knowledge of each authentication type and the ramifications of selecting one over another before you make the system available to end users.

See Also

- Microsoft TechNet: "Understanding Demand-Dial Routing" (http://technet2.microsoft.com/WindowsServer/f/?en/Library/48757b3c-9211-48b6-a057-7ec71406f44a1033.mspx). This article discusses the basic concepts and issues behind demand-dial routing.

- Microsoft KB 278880: "The Demand-Dial Interface Does not Disconnect When Network Address Translation Is Installed." This article contains information regarding the DNS proxy and its effect on demand-dial connections.

- Microsoft TechNet: "Troubleshooting Demand-Dial Routing" (http://technet2.microsoft.com/WindowsServer/f/?en/Library/0cb97fcf-ca9f-40fb-b543-5ed93696c8861033.mspx).

- Recipe 5-3 for basic information on configuring demand-dial interfaces.

5-5. Configuring Global IP Routing Parameters

Problem

You want to configure settings that are global to all IP routing interfaces, including logging level, route source preferences, and multicast scopes.

Solution

Using a Graphical User Interface

1. Start the Routing and Remote Access Services administrative console from the Administrative Tools folder in the Start menu, or directly from %systemroot%\system32\ rrasmgmt.msc.

2. Expand the console tree below the server object until you have selected IP Routing ➤ General.

3. Right-click General and select Properties.

4. Select the Logging tab and set the level of error logging that meets your needs. These are the options:

   • Log Errors Only

   • Log Errors and Warnings

   • Log the Maximum Amount of Information

   • Disable Event Logging

5. Select the Preference Levels tab to set the relative preference of each source. Click the Move Up or Move Down buttons to change the relative ordering of each source. Routes from sources at lower ranks are preferred over sources with higher ranks.

6. Click the Multicast Scopes tab to create a multicast scope.

7. Click the Add button to create the scope, click the Edit button to modify a scope, or click the Remove button to delete a scope. Each scope must have a name, address, and mask.

Note A multicast scope is a named range of IP multicast addresses that is expressed with an IP address and mask. Multicast scopes must be in the range 239.0.0.0 through 239.254.255.255. You can use these scopes later when configuring IP routing interfaces.

---

8. Click the OK button when complete.

Using a Command-Line Interface

You can use the `netsh routing ip` command to display or set configuration information.
To display the logging level, use this command:

```
> netsh routing ip show loglevel
```

To display the preference levels of the routing protocols, use this command:

```
> netsh routing ip show preferenceforprotocol
```

The results will look like this:

```
> netsh routing ip show preferenceforprotocol
```

```
Priority Information for Routing Protocols
Protocol              Priority (Lower value = higher priority)
------------------------------------------------------------
Local                  1
Static                 3
Non-DOD Static         5
Autostatic             7
NetMgmt                10
OSPF                   110
RIP                    120
```

To add or delete a preference level for a specified routing protocol, use this command:

```
> netsh routing ip add|delete preferenceforprotocol
    [proto=] autostatic|local|netmgmgt|nondod|ospf|rip|static [preflevel=]<integer>
```

Here is a description of the command-line options:

Add|Delete: Parameter that specifies whether you want to add or delete the routing protocol

Proto: Required parameter whose value specifies the routing protocol to add or delete.

PrefLevel: Required parameter whose value is the preference level of the specified protocol

For example, to add the Open Shortest Path First (OSPF) protocol with a preference level of 110, use the following command:

```
> netsh routing ip add preferenceforprotocol proto=ospf preflevel=110
```

To display the multicast boundaries, use this command:

```
> netsh routing ip show scope
```

To add or delete multicast boundaries, use this command:

```
> netsh routing ip add scope [grpaddr=]<IP address>
    [grpmask=]<IP subnet mask> [scopename=]<string>
```

Here is a description of the command-line options:

GrpAddr: Required parameter whose value is the group IP address

GrpMask: Required parameter whose value is the subnet mask of the multicast scope

ScopeName: Required parameter whose value is the name of the multicast scope

For example, to create a multicast scope with an IP address of 239.1.1.1, a subnet mask of 255.255.255.224, and a name of My Favorite Scope, use the following command:

```
> netsh routing ip add scope 239.1.1.1 255.255.255.225 "My Favorite Scope"
```

How It Works

Multicasting is the process of delivering a data packet to a group of hosts rather than to a single host on a TCP/IP-based network. When data must be delivered to multiple hosts, multicasting is preferred over unicasting or broadcasting. Broadcasting is nonroutable and unicasting is less efficient, since it requires multiple data packets.

Note For an explanation of the IPv4 multicasting protocol, see the Microsoft TechNet article "What Is IPv4 Multicasting" (http://technet2.microsoft.com/WindowsServer/en/Library/a8ae022c-a00b-4b0f-ba59-3b476853025c1033.mspx).

RRAS uses IGMP as an IP routing protocol component. Router interfaces are configured in one of two operating modes: IGMP router mode or IGMP proxy mode. The purpose of IGMP router mode is to forward multicast traffic in a single-router intranet. The purpose of IGMP proxy mode is to connect a single-router intranet to a multicast-capable intranet or the Internet.

See Also

- Microsoft TechNet: "Understanding Multicasting" (http://technet2.microsoft.com/WindowsServer/f/?en/Library/93175810-b5bf-4c45-b962-6bc45c3012641033.mspx). This article contains information on the multicast routing process.

- Microsoft TechNet: "Using the IP Multicasting Utilities" (http://technet2.microsoft.com/WindowsServer/f/?en/Library/094959ee-b18c-4e3c-b8e2-4511cde49d301033.mspx). This article describes utilities that can diagnose and troubleshoot multicast issues.

- Recipe 5-11 for more on IGMP, the protocol required to support multicasting.

5-6. Managing the IP Routing Table and Static Routes

Problem

You want to view entries in the IP routing table.

Solution

Using a Graphical User Interface

1. Start the Routing and Remote Access Services administrative console from the Administrative Tools folder in the Start menu, or directly from %systemroot%\system32\rrasmgmt.msc.

2. Expand the console tree below the server object until you have selected IP Routing ➤ Static Routes.

From here you can display the routing table or add, delete, or modify a static route:

- **Display the routing table:** Right-click Static Routes in the left pane and select Show IP Routing Table. The results will appear in a pop-up window. Click any of the column headers to sort the data by that criterion.

- **Add a static route:**

    a. Right-click Static Routes in the left pane and select New Static Route.

    b. Select the interface to which you want to add the static route.

    c. Enter the IP address of the destination network.

    d. Enter the network (subnet) mask of the destination network.

    e. Enter the IP address of the local gateway to the destination network.

    f. Select the metric value of this static route.

    g. Click the OK button to complete the static route configuration.

- **Delete a static route:** Right-click the interface in the right pane and select Delete. (You will not be prompted to confirm the action.)

- **Modify a static route:** Right-click the interface in the right pane and select Properties. Configure the same settings as those specified when you created the static route.

Using a Command-Line Interface

You can manipulate the IP routing table using the route command. The basic syntax is as follows:

```
> route [-f] [-p] [command [destination] [Mask <netmask>]
    [gateway] [Metric <metricvalue>]  [Interface <interfacenumber>]
```

Here is a description of the command-line options:

-f: Parameter that clears the routing tables of all gateway entries. If this is used in conjunction with one of the commands, the tables are cleared prior to running the command.

-p: Parameter that permanently adds a route, even after the computer is restarted. This option can only be used with the add command; it will be ignored if used with any other command.

Command: Parameter that specifies a particular action to take on a route. Possible values include Print, Add, Change, and Delete.

Destination: Parameter whose value specifies the address of the destination network. You can specify the destination using the wildcard character (*) if the command is print or delete.

Mask: Parameter whose value specifies the subnet mask of the destination network. A value of 255.255.255.255 is implied if this parameter is omitted.

Gateway: Parameter whose value specifies the address of the gateway to the destination network. You can specify the gateway using the wildcard character (*) if the command is print or delete.

Metric: Parameter whose value specifies the relative metric, or cost, of the gateway.

Interface: Parameter whose value specifies the interface number for the specified route.

To display the routing table, use the following simple command:

```
> route print
```

The results will look like the following:

```
> route print
```

```
IPv4 Route Table
===========================================================================
Interface List
0x1 ........................ MS TCP Loopback interface
0x2 ...00 60 73 e1 82 ba ...... SonicWALL VPN Adapter
0x10004 ...00 02 b3 be 28 84 ...... Intel(R) PRO/1000 XT Server Adapter
===========================================================================
===========================================================================
Active Routes:
Network Destination        Netmask          Gateway       Interface  Metric
        0.0.0.0          0.0.0.0      192.168.2.1      192.168.2.2      1
      127.0.0.0        255.0.0.0        127.0.0.1        127.0.0.1      1
    169.254.0.0      255.255.0.0      192.168.2.2      192.168.2.2     30
    192.168.2.0    255.255.255.0      192.168.2.2      192.168.2.2     20
    192.168.2.2  255.255.255.255        127.0.0.1        127.0.0.1     20
  192.168.2.255  255.255.255.255      192.168.2.2      192.168.2.2     20
   192.168.50.0    255.255.255.0          0.0.0.0         ffffffff      1
   192.168.60.0    255.255.255.0          0.0.0.0         ffffffff      1
      223.1.1.0    255.255.255.0      223.1.1.128      223.1.1.128     30
    223.1.1.128  255.255.255.255        127.0.0.1        127.0.0.1     30
    223.1.1.255  255.255.255.255      223.1.1.128      223.1.1.128     30
      224.0.0.0        240.0.0.0      192.168.2.2      192.168.2.2     20
      224.0.0.0        240.0.0.0      223.1.1.128      223.1.1.128     30
255.255.255.255  255.255.255.255      192.168.2.2      192.168.2.2      1
```

```
    255.255.255.255  255.255.255.255      223.1.1.128     223.1.1.128      1
Default Gateway:        192.168.2.1
===========================================================================
Persistent Routes:
  None
```

In the preceding output, the entry that has both a network destination and a netmask of 0.0.0.0 and a metric of 1 represents the default static route. All data to routes not otherwise specified in the routing table will be directed through the gateway of 192.168.2.1.

A common use of route print is to create a static route with parameters similar to the following:

- Destination network: 192.168.100.0

- Destination subnet: 255.255.255.0

- Gateway: 192.168.0.10

- Metric: 2

Use the following command to add this route.

```
> route add 192.168.100.0 mask 255.255.255.0 192.168.0.10 metric 2
```

Or, use the delete command to remove the static route to the 192.168.100.0 network:

```
> route delete 192.168.100.0
```

How It Works

Add static routes to the IP routing table when you need to connect with a nonlocal network through a router that is not also the default gateway. One very common scenario is an organization that has a connection to the Internet but also a separate connection (gateway) to a branch office. Create a static route to the branch office so that workstations will be able to access resources at that site.

Line entries in the routing table fall into one of three categories:

- **Network route:** Specifies the path to a particular network. This type of route is more common than a host route.

- **Host route:** Specifies the path to a particular host, rather than to the entire network. Use a host route when you need to optimize network performance.

- **Default route:** Provides a fallback when no routes are explicitly defined for the packets being sent.

The metric value specified in the routing table entries are defined such that the route to a particular destination will be selected based on the lowest metric value. For example, if two routes exist for the same destination network, the route with the lower metric value will be selected before that with the higher value.

See Also

- Microsoft TechNet: "Setting Up a Static Routed IP Internetwork" (http://technet2.microsoft.com/WindowsServer/f/?en/Library/2f31b4c2-b1ba-4d20-a18f-b7c9eb11649c1033.mspx). This article discusses design and security considerations when deploying static routes.

- Microsoft TechNet: "Understanding the IP Routing Table" (http://technet2.microsoft.com/WindowsServer/f/?en/Library/e17c9aaa-f857-46d9-8428-b1d2563b7e361033.mspx). This article describes each of the entries in the IP routing table.

5-7. Adding an IP Interface

Problem

You want to create a new IP interface.

Solution

1. Start the Routing and Remote Access Services administrative console from the Administrative Tools folder in the Start menu, or directly from %systemroot%\system32\rrasmgmt.msc.

2. Expand the console tree below the server object until you have selected IP Routing ➤ General.

3. Right-click the General node and select New Interface.

4. Select the adapter on which you want this IP interface to run, and click the OK button to proceed.

At this point you can configure general settings, the method of IP address allocation, the multicast boundaries, or a multicast heartbeat.

To configure general settings, follow these steps:

1. Select the General tab.

2. Check the IP Router Manager check box in the General tab to enable the interface.

3. Check the Router Discovery Advertisements check box if you want to enable ICMP router discovery advertisements on this interface. If you enable this option, you must also set the following options:

   - Advertisement Lifetime, specified in minutes

   - Level of Preference

   - Minimum Time Interval, specified in minutes, for advertisements to be sent

   - Maximum Time Interval, specified in minutes, for advertisements to be sent

4. Click the Inbound Filters or Outbound Filters buttons to configure packet filters on this interface. See Recipe 5-9, "Managing Packet Filters," for details on configuring packet filters.

5. Check the Fragmentation Checking check box if you want the router to discard all fragmented IP packets that do not correspond to traffic permitted by the filters on this interface.

To configure the method of IP address allocation, follow these steps:

1. Select the Configuration tab.

2. Specify an IP address, subnet, and gateway for this interface, or configure the interface to obtain addressing values from a DHCP server.

3. Click the Advanced button if you want to add additional IP addresses or gateways to the interface.

To configure multicast boundaries, follow these steps:

1. Select the Multicast Boundaries tab.

2. Select the scope that you want to configure from the drop-down list, and click the Add button to enable it.

3. Check the Time-To-Live (TTL) check box if you want to disable the forwarding of IP multicast traffic out of the interface if it has a TTL less than a desired value. Also specify the TTL value and the rate limit, in KB/s.

Note In order to complete step 2 (scope selection), you must have already created the scope. See Recipe 5-5, "Configuring Global IP Routing Parameters," to create a multicast scope.

To configure a multicast heartbeat, follow these steps:

1. Select the Multicast Heartbeat tab.

2. Check the Multicast Heartbeat Detection check box if you want to listen for periodic multicast traffic.

3. Enter the IP address of the multicast heartbeat group in the text field.

4. Enter a desired quiet time, in minutes, before you want to generate an alert.

5. Click the OK button when complete. Close and restart the RRAS management console in order to view the changes.

How It Works

As described in this recipe, there are a number of options that can be configured for IP interfaces. Two options that have not yet been discussed in this chapter are router discovery advertisements and multicast heartbeats.

- **Router discovery advertisements:** Enabling this feature specifies that ICMP advertisements are enabled on an interface. Router discovery clients use these messages to configure their default gateways.

- **Multicast heartbeats:** Enabling this feature specifies that a router will listen for regular notifications (the "heartbeats") that are sent to a specified group address. If the heartbeat is not observed after a specified amount of time, the router will set the heartbeat status to inactive.

See Also

- Microsoft TechNet: "Understanding Multicasting" (`http://technet2.microsoft.com/WindowsServer/f/?en/Library/93175810-b5bf-4c45-b962-6bc45c3012641033.mspx`). This article discusses multicast forwarding, routing, boundaries, and heartbeats.

- IETF: "ICMP Router Discovery Messages" (`http://www.ietf.org/rfc/rfc1256.txt`). This article offers a formal description of the router discovery process according to the IETF Network Working Group, RFC 1256.

- Microsoft TechNet: "ICMP Router Discovery" (`http://technet2.microsoft.com/WindowsServer/f/?en/Library/75a81f60-f527-4ae7-be20-c6cdcc2ff02b1033.mspx`). This article describes router advertisements and router solicitations.

5-8. Adding a Routing Protocol

Problem

You want to add a routing protocol.

Solution

1. Start the Routing and Remote Access Services administrative console from the Administrative Tools folder in the Start menu, or directly from `%systemroot%\system32\rrasmgmt.msc`.

2. Expand the console tree below the server object until you have selected IP Routing ➤ General.

3. Right-click the General node, and select New Routing Protocol.

4. Select the protocol that you want to add, which may include DHCP Relay Agent, IGMP Router and Proxy, Open Shortest Path First (OSPF), or RIP v2 for Internet Protocol.

5. Click the OK button when complete.

How It Works

You can only add each protocol once to the list of active protocols. When you add a protocol, it will become a node under IP Routing in the management console. Note that this chapter provides recipes for the DHCP Relay Agent and the IGMP router and proxy. The remaining two protocols, Open Shortest Path First (OSPF) and Routing Information Protocol, version 2 (RIP v2) are beyond the scope of this chapter; you can find information on these protocols in Microsoft TechNet or in any number of texts dedicated to these topics.

See Also

- Microsoft TechNet: "IP Routing Protocols" (http://technet2.microsoft.com/WindowsServer/en/Library/7a817de6-a3bb-4bfb-8e73-464c97324c2e1033.mspx). This article describes RIP and the OSPF protocol.

- Recipe 5-11 for more on configuring an IGMP interface.

- Recipe 5-15 for more on adding or removing a DHCP Relay Agent.

5-9. Managing Packet Filters

Problem

You want to manage inbound and/or outbound packet filters on an interface.

Solution

Note The Inbound Filters and Outbound Filters buttons appear at different times and in different locations of the router configuration screens, as we will describe throughout this chapter. This section will describe how to configure these filters, regardless of where these buttons are displayed.

Using a Graphical User Interface

1. Click the Inbound Filters button if you want to control which packets are accepted from the external to the internal network, or the Outbound Filters button if you want to control the packets that are forwarded from the internal to the external network. The configuration process is the same for both options.

2. Click the New button to create a new filter.

3. Check the Source Network check box if you want to inspect packets arriving from specific networks. Provide the network address and the subnet mask of the source network.

4. Check the Destination Network check box if you want to inspect packets destined for specific networks. Provide the network address and the subnet mask of the destination network.

5. Specify a network protocol that you want to inspect. The default value is ANY. These are the other values:

- **TCP:** Specify the source and/or destination port

- **TCP (Established):** Specify the source and/or destination port

- **UDP:** Specify the source and/or destination port

- **ICMP:** Specify the ICMP type and code

- **Other:** Specify the protocol number

6. Click the OK button to complete the packet filter configuration.

7. Create additional packet filters, if desired, by repeating the preceding steps.

8. Select the option that specifies that you want packets to be accepted or dropped if they meet your filter criteria.

9. Click the OK button to complete the configuration of the filters.

Using a Command-Line Interface

To display packet filter information, use this command:

```
> netsh routing ip show filter
```

To configure packet filters, use the following command. (The command is wrapped for readability.)

```
> netsh routing ip add|delete filter [name=]<InterfaceName>
     [filtertype=]{INPUT|OUTPUT|DIAL} [srcaddr=]<IP address>
     [srcmask=]<IP subnet mask> [dstaddr=]<IP address> [dstmask=]<IP subnet mask>
{[proto=] ANY|
 [proto=] TCP|TCP-EST|UDP} [srcport=]<integer> [dstport=]<integer> |
 [proto=] ICMP [type=]<integer> [code=]<integer>}
```

Here is a description of the command-line options:

Add|Delete: Required parameter that specifies whether you want to add or delete the packet filter.

Name: Required parameter whose value specifies the name of the interface to which the filter will apply.

FilterType: Required parameter that specifies whether the filter pertains to inbound or outbound packets, or to a dial-up interface.

SrcAddr: Parameter whose value specifies the source IP address of the packets. Specify this value as 0.0.0.0 to filter packets from any address.

SrcMask: Parameter whose value specifies the subnet corresponding to the source IP address. Specify this value as 0.0.0.0 to filter packets from any subnet.

DstAddr: Parameter whose value specifies the destination of the packets.

DstMask: Parameter whose value specifies the subnet mask of the packets.

Proto: Parameter whose value specifies the protocol type. Possible values are Any, TCP, TCP-EST (Established TCP), or UDP.

SrcPort: Parameter whose value specifies the source port of the packet. This parameter is required only if TCP, TCP-EST, or UDP were specified as the protocol type. Specify the value as 0 to indicate any port.

DstPort: Parameter whose value specifies the destination port of the packet. This parameter is required only if TCP, TCP-EST, or UDP were selected as the protocol type. Specify the value as 0 to indicate any port.

Type: Parameter whose value specifies the ICMP type of the data packet. Specify the value as 255 to indicate any type.

Code: Parameter whose value specifies the ICMP code of the data packet. Specify the value as 255 to indicate any code.

For example, you can create an inbound filter applied to Local Area Connection #2 that inspects packets of any protocol type using the following command. The filter will inspect packets from any source destined for the 169.254.0.0 network with a subnet of 255.255.0.0.

```
> netsh routing ip add filter name="Local Area Connection #2" filtertype=input
    srcaddr=0.0.0.0 srcmask=0.0.0.0 dstaddr=169.254.0.0
    dstmask=255.255.0.0 proto=any
```

How It Works

Network firewalls are critical to help protect any organization's infrastructure. Although routers, including the Windows Server 2003 router that we are discussing in this chapter, support packet filters (one of the basic features of a firewall), you should make a decision whether you want the router to provide this functionality, or whether you want to offload this work to a full-featured firewall such as Microsoft ISA Server or any number of products from other vendors.

The latest generation of firewalls supports stateful packet inspection, network address and port translation, application filtering, virus and spyware protection, content filtering, VPN management, and much, much more. Is this too much functionality for a single device to handle? Only you can make that decision based on the power of the device and the anticipated traffic. If appropriate, use a single device. If not, configure your protection in layers with multiple devices.

See Also

- Microsoft TechNet: "Packet Filtering" (http://technet2.microsoft.com/WindowsServer/en/Library/04025562-6f81-4272-a345-d694711c83b91033.mspx). This article describes packet filtering and also includes a list of ports and protocols used by common services.

- Internet Assigned Numbers Authority (IANA): "Port Numbers" (http://www.iana.org/assignments/port-numbers). This is an easy-to-use list that indicates what ports are used by which services. This site is very convenient if you know that you want to enable a packet filter for DNS (for example) but cannot remember what ports it uses.

5-10. Displaying TCP/IP Statistics

Problem

You want to display TCP/IP statistics for your router.

Solution

1. Start the Routing and Remote Access Services administrative console from the Administrative Tools folder in the Start menu, or directly from %systemroot%\system32\ rrasmgmt.msc.

2. Expand the console tree below the server object until you have selected IP Routing ➤ General.

3. Right-click General, and select Show TCP/IP Information.

4. The TCP/IP statistics will appear in a pop-up window. These are the default statistics:

   - IP Routes

   - IP Datagrams Received

   - IP Datagrams Forwarded

   - UDP Datagrams Received

   - UDP Datagrams Sent

   - TCP Connect-Attempts Failed

   - TCP Connections Reset

   - TCP Connections

   - ICMP Messages Received

   - ICMP Messages Sent

5. Right-click anywhere in the window and select Select Columns to view a list of additional parameters whose statistics you can also display. These are a few of the many parameters available:

   - IP incoming header errors

   - IP incoming address errors

   - IP output request

- IP packets requiring reassembly

- TCP active opens

- ICMP input errors

- ICMP outgoing redirects

6. Close the pop-up window when complete.

How It Works

View TCP/IP statistics when you want to troubleshoot issues such as network bottlenecks or to provide a basic level of monitoring of the traffic that is being directed through your router. The statistics window in the GUI provides a snapshot of the statistics at the time the window was requested. You can right-click anywhere on the window to refresh the statistics.

If you want a real-time view of TCP/IP statistics, you should consider using Windows' built-in Performance Monitor. You can run this from the Performance icon in the Administrative Tools folder, or from the Start ➤ Run menu by typing perfmon.exe. All of the counters that were described in this recipe are also available in Performance Monitor within the IPv4 and the ICMP objects.

If you suspect that your router is not functioning properly or that there is a problem with the traffic being directed through or at your router, you may want to analyze the various metrics. Let's look at the case of IP traffic as an example. One of the first statistics you will want to look at is IP Datagrams Received. This represents the total number of datagrams that were received on an interface, including those datagrams that may have been problematic. Compare this to IP Datagrams Forwarded, which represents the datagrams that were forwarded by the router to a different network, or IP Datagrams Failing, and you will obtain a sense for the flow of traffic on this interface.

Of course, it is a lot more helpful when troubleshooting if you first have baseline statistics for comparison purposes. Spend some time immediately after installing your router, during a time of "average" traffic, to view the statistics. Use these later when measuring the router's performance to determine if it has degraded or if the amount and nature of the traffic has changed significantly.

See Also

Microsoft TechNet: "IP Object" (http://technet2.microsoft.com/WindowsServer/en/Library/046ed8bf-9f3d-42a7-b56a-f279495203f11033.mspx). This article provides a list of IP performance-counter objects and their descriptions.

5-11. Configuring an IGMP Interface

Problem

You want to configure an IGMP interface to support multicasts.

Note This recipe assumes that you have already configured RRAS to support IGMP router and proxy as a routing protocol. If you have not completed this step, you should first review Recipe 9-8, "Adding a Routing Protocol."

Solution

Using a Graphical User Interface

1. Start the Routing and Remote Access Services administrative console from the Administrative Tools folder in the Start menu, or directly from %systemroot%\system32\ rrasmgmt.msc.

2. Expand the console tree below the server object until you have selected IP Routing ➤ IGMP.

3. Right-click IGMP and select New Interface.

4. Select the interface to which you want to bind IGMP, and click the OK button.

5. Check the Enable IGMP check box to enable this interface to listen for or forward IGMP broadcasts.

6. Select the appropriate Mode option to configure the interface to operate as either an IGMP router or proxy.

7. Select the version of IGMP that you want to enable. The options are Version 1, Version 2, and Version 3. The default is Version 3.

8. If you configured this interface as a proxy, click the OK button to complete the configuration. However, if you configured this interface as a router, select the Router tab and complete the following steps.

9. Specify the value of the Robustness Variable that you want to use. The default value is 2, with a range of 1–7.

10. Specify the Query Interval in seconds. The default value is 125.

11. Specify the Query Response Interval in seconds. The default value is 10.

12. Specify the Last Member Query Interval in milliseconds. The default value is 1,000.

13. Check the Automatically Recalculate Defaults check box if you want the startup query interval, startup query count, and last member query count to be automatically configured based on your selections in steps 9 through 12. If you do not check this check box, you can manually specify these values.

14. Click the OK button when complete.

To display the global IGMP group table, follow these steps:

1. Start the Routing and Remote Access Services administrative console from the Administrative Tools folder in the Start menu, or directly from %systemroot%\system32\ rrasmgmt.msc.

2. Expand the console tree below the server object until you have selected IP Routing ➤ IGMP.

3. Right-click IGMP and select Show Group Table. A pop-up window will appear that will display addresses for the interface, the group, and the last reporter.

To display the group table for a specific interface, follow these steps:

1. Start the Routing and Remote Access Services administrative console from the Administrative Tools folder in the Start menu, or directly from %systemroot%\system32\ rrasmgmt.msc.

2. Expand the console tree below the server object until you have selected IP Routing ➤ IGMP.

3. Right-click the desired interface in the right pane, and select Show Interface Group Table. A pop-up window will appear that will include the following statistics:

   • Group Address

   • Last Reporter

   • Expiry Time

   • Uptime

   • Flags

   • Mode

4. Close the pop-up window when complete.

Using a Command-Line Interface

You can manage IGMP routers and proxies through the netsh routing ip igmp command.
To install the IGMP routing protocol and specify the logging level, use this command:

```
> netsh routing ip igmp install [[LogLevel=]{none | error | warn | info}]
```

If the LogLevel parameter is omitted, logging will occur for errors only.
To uninstall the IGMP routing protocol, use this command:

```
> netsh routing ip igmp uninstall
```

This command takes no parameters.

To display the global IGMP parameters, including the version number and logging level, use this command:

```
> netsh routing ip igmp show global
```

This command takes no parameters.

To configure the logging level, use this command:

```
> netsh routing ip igmp set global [[LogLevel=]{none | error | warn | info}]
```

If the LogLevel parameter is omitted, logging will occur for errors and warnings.

To display IGMP-related information for a particular interface, use this command:

```
> netsh routing ip igmp show interface [InterfaceName=]InterfaceName
```

If the InterfaceName parameter is omitted, information will be displayed for all interfaces. This command produces output like the following:

```
> netsh routing ip igmp show interface
```

```
IGMP Interface Configuration Information for "Server Local Area Connection"
-------------------------------------------------------
Version                         : 0x301
IGMP Router Type                : IGMP ver-3 Router
Interface Enabled Flag          : enable
Robustness Variable             : 2
Startup Query Interval          : 31   (sec)
Startup Query Count             : 2
General Query Interval          : 125  (sec)
General Query Max Response Time  : 10   (sec)
Last Mem Query Interval         : 1000 (msec)
Last Mem Query Count            : 2
Other Querier Present Interval  : 255  (sec)
Group Membership Timeout        : 260  (sec)
AcceptNonRtrAlertPkts  Flag     : YES
Num Static Groups               : 0
```

To bind IGMP to a particular interface, use this command:

```
> netsh routing ip igmp add interface [InterfaceName=]<InterfaceName>
    [[IgmpPrototype=]{igmprtrv1 | igmprtrv2 | igmprtrv3 | igmpproxy}]
    [[IfEnabled=]{enable | disable}] [[RobustVar=]<Integer>]
    [[GenQueryInterval=]<Integer>] [[GenQueryRespTime=]<Integer>]
    [[StartUpQueryCount=]<Integer>] [[StartUpQueryInterval=]<Integer>]
    [[LastMemQueryCount=]<Integer>] [[LastMemQueryInterval=<Integer>]
    [[AccNonRtrAlertPkts=]{yes | no}]
```

Here is a description of the command-line options:

InterfaceName: Required parameter whose value specifies the name of the interface to which you want to bind the IGMP routing protocol.

IGMPPrototype: Optional parameter whose value specifies the type of protocol to be configured on the interface. The values reflect IGMP v1, IGMP v2, IGMP v3, and IGMP Proxy, respectively. The default value is igmprtrv2.

IfEnabled: Optional parameter whose value specifies whether the protocol is enabled or disabled. The default value is enable.

RobustVar: Optional parameter whose value specifies the robustness variable. The default value is 2, with an overall range of 1–7.

GenQueryInterval: Optional parameter whose value specifies the interval, in seconds, at which general queries should be sent on the interface. The default value is 125.

GenQueryRespTime: Optional parameter whose value specifies the maximum time, in seconds, in which a host should respond to a query. The default value is 10 seconds.

StartUpQueryCount: Optional parameter whose value specifies the number of queries that are sent at startup. The default number is 2.

StartUpQueryInterval: Optional parameter whose value specifies the interval, in seconds, between general startup queries. The default value is 31 seconds.

LastMemQueryCount: Optional parameter whose value specifies the number of group-specific queries sent when a host announces that it is leaving the group. The default value is 2.

LastMemQueryInterval: Optional parameter whose value specifies the interval, in milliseconds, between group-specific queries. The default value is 1000 milliseconds.

AccNonRtrAlertPkts: Optional parameter whose value specifies whether the router should accept IGMP packets that do not have the alert option set. The default value is yes.

For example, to add an IGMP interface to Local Area Connection #2 with the default values but a general query response time of 100 seconds, run the following command:

```
> netsh routing ip igmp add interface "Local Area Connection #2"
    genqueryresptime=100
```

To modify the IGMP parameters on an interface already configured for IGMP, use this command:

```
> netsh routing ip igmp set interface InterfaceName=<InterfaceName>
    [[IgmpPrototype=]{igmprtrv1 | igmprtrv2 | igmprtrv3 | igmpproxy}]
    [[IfEnabled=]{enable | disable}] [[RobustVar=]<Integer>]
    [[GenQueryInterval=]<Integer>] [[GenQueryRespTime=]<Integer>]
    [[StartUpQueryCount=]<Integer>] [[StartUpQueryInterval=]<Integer>]
    [[LastMemQueryCount=]<Integer>] [[LastMemQueryInterval=<Integer>]
    [[AccNonRtrAlertPkts=]{yes | no}]
```

The parameters are identical to those used with the netsh routing ip igmp add interface command.

To delete (unbind) the IGMP protocol from a particular interface, use this command:

```
> netsh routing ip igmp delete interface InterfaceName=<InterfaceName>
```

InterfaceName is a required parameter.

How It Works

IGMP is the protocol responsible for maintaining entries in the multicast forwarding table. There are two possible ways to configure IGMP: in router mode or proxy mode.

Configure IGMP in *router mode* if you want your system to listen for IGMP membership report packets and track group membership. Configure IGMP in *proxy mode* if you just want to forward membership report messages to a device or interface running in router mode.

There are three versions of IGMP that are relevant in Windows Server 2003:

- **Version 1:** Hosts can join multicast groups. There are no messages generated when a host leaves a group. Routers use a time-out period to discover which groups are no longer relevant and which should be dropped.

- **Version 2:** Version 2 adds to version 1 by generating messages when a host leaves a group.

- **Version 3:** Hosts can specify a list of hosts from which they want to receive traffic. Traffic from all other hosts will be blocked.

There are a number of terms that are used in this recipe that may not be familiar to many system administrators and therefore deserve a definition:

- **Robustness variable:** Indicates the relative quality of the subnet that the interface is connected to. Lossy subnets have high robustness variables. Microsoft recommends that you set this variable to a value of 2 or higher for efficient operation.

- **Query interval:** The duration between IGMP queries sent by the router.

- **Query response interval:** Specifies the amount of time that the router will wait before it gives up on its general query response.

- **Last member query interval:** Specifies the amount of time after which the router will give up waiting for a response to a query focused at a specific group.

- **Startup query interval:** Specifies the amount of time between successive general query messages that a IGMP router sends when it starts.

- **Startup query count:** Specifies the number of general query messages that an IGMP router sends when it starts.

- **Last member query count:** Specifies the number of queries that a router sends at a particular group before it assumes there are no remaining hosts in the group on a particular interface.

See Also

- Microsoft TechNet: "Understanding Multicasting" (`http://technet2.microsoft.com/WindowsServer/en/Library/93175810-b5bf-4c45-b962-6bc45c3012641033.mspx`). This article discusses multicast forwarding, routing, boundaries, and heartbeats.

- Connected: An Internet Encyclopedia: "Internet Group Management Protocol (IGMP)" (`http://www.freesoft.org/CIE/RFC/1112/18.htm`). This article describes IGMP and its relation to multicasting.

- Connected: An Internet Encyclopedia: "Multicast Addresses" (`http://www.freesoft.org/CIE/RFC/1700/5.htm`). This article lists Internet multicast addresses.

5-12. Configuring Global NAT and Firewall Options

Problem

You want to configure the logging level, timeout values, address assignment methods, or name resolution methods.

Solution

Using a Graphical User Interface

1. Start the Routing and Remote Access Services administrative console from the Administrative Tools folder in the Start menu, or directly from %systemroot%\system32\rrasmgmt.msc.

2. Expand the console tree below the server object until you have selected IP Routing ➤ NAT/Basic Firewall.

3. Right-click NAT/Basic Firewall, and select Properties.

4. Select the General tab and set the level of error logging that meets your needs. These are the options:

   - Log Errors Only (this is the default)

   - Log Errors and Warnings

   - Log the Maximum Amount of Information

   - Disable Event Logging

5. Select the Translation tab and set the following two values:

   - Set the timeout value, in minutes, for dynamic TCP mappings. The default value is 1440.

   - Set the timeout value, in minutes, for dynamic UDP mappings. The default value is 1.

6. Select the Address Assignment tab to configure the DHCP Allocator. (See Recipe 5-14, "Configuring a DHCP Allocator," for the details of this procedure.)

7. Click the Name Resolution tab to configure a DNS proxy. (See Recipe 5-16, "Configuring a DNS Proxy," for this procedure.)

8. Click the OK button when complete.

Using a Command-Line Interface

You can manage global options for NAT interfaces on your router by using the `netsh routing ip nat` command.

To display the global options, run the following command:

```
> netsh routing ip nat show global
```

The output will look similar to the following:

```
> netsh routing ip nat show global
```

```
NAT Configuration Information
-----------------------------
TCP Timeout (minutes)    : 1440
UDP Timeout (minutes)    : 1
Logging Level            : Errors Only
```

Configure the global options by running the following command:

```
> netsh routing ip nat set global
    {[[TCPTimeoutMins=]Integer] |
    [[UDPTimeoutMins=]Integer] |
    [[LogLevel=]{none | error | warn | info}]}
```

Here is a description of the command-line options:

TCPTimeoutMins: Optional parameter whose value, specified in minutes, provides the timeout for dynamic TCP mappings.

UDPTimeoutMins: Optional parameter whose value, specified in minutes, provides the timeout for dynamic UDP mappings.

LogLevel: Optional parameter whose value sets the level of logging that will occur to the system log. Possible values are none (no logging), error (log errors only), warn (log errors and warnings), and info (verbose logging).

For example, to configure NAT interfaces to provide verbose logging, and to specify a TCP timeout value of 500 minutes and a UDP timeout value of 2 minutes, you would run the following command:

```
> netsh routing ip nat set global tcptimeoutmins=500 udptimeoutmins=2 loglevel=info
```

How It Works

The level of logging that you configure depends on your particular need or concern. For most administrators, it should be sufficient to log just errors, or perhaps warnings as well, to verify that your system is functioning properly. We don't recommend disabling logging entirely; you will not be alerted to problems when they occur and will run the risk of unanticipated failure. Configure detailed logging if you know that there is a problem and are actively troubleshooting the system. All events are written into the Windows system event log.

If your network already has an accessible DHCP server, do not configure the router as a DHCP Allocator. There can only be a single provider of DHCP services on a given network segment. When possible, use the built-in Windows DHCP Server service instead; it provides much more functionality. Some networks may also have a firewall appliance between the router and the network hosts, which will probably include a full-featured DHCP server. As you can see, there are many options to provide this service.

See Also

- Recipe 5-15 for more on adding or removing a DHCP Relay Agent

- Recipe 5-16 for more on configuring a DNS proxy

5-13. Managing NAT Interfaces and Basic Firewalls

Problem

You want to add or delete a NAT interface, or manage the properties of an existing one.

Solution

Note This recipe assumes that you have already configured RRAS to support network address translation (NAT). If you have not completed this step, you should first review Recipe 5-1, "Enabling and Configuring a Network Address Translation Router," or 5-2, "Enabling and Configuring a Network Address Translation Router with VPN Support."

Using a Graphical User Interface

To add or manage a NAT interface:

1. Start the Routing and Remote Access Services administrative console from the Administrative Tools folder in the Start menu, or directly from %systemroot%\system32\rrasmgmt.msc.

2. Expand the console tree below the server object until you have selected IP Routing ➤ NAT/Basic Firewall.

3. If you are creating a new interface, right-click NAT/Basic Firewall and select New Interface. Select the adapter that you want to configure to support NAT, and click the OK button. However, if you are modifying an existing interface, right-click the interface object in the right pane, and select Properties.

4. Specify the type of interface with which you want to configure this adapter. The options are as follows:

   • **Private Interface Connected to a Private Network:** Select this option if this interface will connect one private network to another private network.

   • **Public Interface Connected to the Internet:** Select this option if this interface is connected to the untrusted network (typically the Internet).

   • **Basic Firewall Only:** Select this option to configure basic firewall capabilities on the interface. This option will not configure the interface for network address translation.

5. Configure the packet filters. Click the Inbound Filters button if you want to manage the packets that are permitted from the external to the internal network, or the Outbound Filters button if you want to manage the packets that are passed from the internal to the external network. See Recipe 5-9, "Managing Packet Filters," for a description of filter-management procedures and techniques.

6. The following steps configure additional settings. If you chose the Private Interface Connected to a Private Network option in step 4, you do not need to take any further action. Click the OK button to complete the configuration of the interface.

7. If you selected the Public Interface Connected to the Internet option in step 4, check the Enable NAT on This Interface check box to permit clients on the private network to access the untrusted network (the Internet). This forces the router to perform TCP and UDP port translation in addition to IP address translation. Continue with step 9.

8. If you selected the Basic Firewall Only option in step 4, check the Enable a Basic Firewall on This Interface check box to configure the firewall to block unsolicited inbound traffic.

9. Select the Address Pool tab. Click the Add button to enter the range of public (routable) IP addresses that have been assigned to you by your Internet service provider and that you want to add to this interface. Click the OK button when you have entered the address range.

10. Click the Reservations button if you want to map one of your public addresses (configured in the previous step) to a host on the private network. Specify the public address and the private address of the appropriate host, and enable the option to allow incoming sessions to this host to make it publicly accessible. Click the OK button to accept the configuration.

11. Select the Services and Ports tab. Select the services on your network to which you want to provide access for Internet users. When you select a service, you will automatically be presented with the service configuration dialog box. You must specify the IP address of the internal host to which you want the respective packets forwarded. Click the OK button when you have specified the address, and then check the check box next to the service name.

12. Click the Add button if you want to create a custom service. You will need to provide the following information to create the service. Click the OK button when you have finished creating the service.

    a. Description of Service: Provide a convenient name for the service, such as `MyWidgetService`.

    b. Public Address: Specify the public address that will be associated with the particular service.

    c. Protocol: Specify whether the service uses TCP or UDP.

    d. Incoming Port: Specify the incoming port number used by the data packet. For example, if you are hosting an internal Web server, the internal port will most likely be 80.

    e. Private Address: Specify the IP address of the host on your internal network to which the service requests will be forwarded. For example, if your web server has an internal address of `192.168.40.3`, enter that information here.

    f. Outgoing Port: Specify the port number used by this service for outbound traffic.

13. Select the ICMP tab and specify the requests for information from the Internet to which RRAS will respond. For example, select Incoming Echo Request to enable RRAS to respond to ping requests. These are the options:

- **Incoming Echo Request:** The server will repeat data back to the sending system.

- **Incoming Timestamp Request:** The server will confirm that it has received data sent to it by responding with a timestamp.

- **Incoming Mask Request:** The server will answer requests that have been sent to it regarding its public network.

- **Incoming Router Request:** The server will answer requests that have been sent to it regarding the routes of which it is aware.

- **Outgoing Destination Unreachable:** When it cannot reach a destination, the server will respond by providing a message describing the failure.

- **Outgoing Source Quench:** When it cannot accommodate the amount of incoming data, the server will ask the sender to reduce its rate of transmission.

- **Outgoing Parameter Problem:** The server will inform the sender if the data that it receives has bad header information.

- **Outgoing Time Exceeded:** The server will respond with a message if the amount of time required to process the data is more than is permitted.

- **Redirect:** The server will reroute data if its default path changes.

14. Click the OK button to complete the configuration of the interface.

To delete a NAT interface, do the following:

1. Right-click the interface object in the right pane, and select Delete.

Using a Command-Line Interface

You can manage NAT interfaces on your router by using the `netsh routing ip nat` command. To display the NAT interfaces already configured, run the following command:

```
> netsh routing ip nat show interface
```

The output will look similar to the following:

```
> netsh routing ip nat show interface
```

```
NAT Server Local Area Connection Configuration
---------------------------
Mode                : Private Interface

NAT Local Area Connection #2 Configuration
---------------------------
Mode                : Address and Port Translation with Firewall Enabled

NAT Internal Configuration
---------------------------
Mode                : Private Interface
```

There are four distinct commands for adding NAT interfaces. First, to create a NAT interface, use this command:

```
> netsh routing ip nat add interface [InterfaceName=]<InterfaceName>
    [[Mode=]{full | addressonly | private | fullfirewall |
        addressonlyfirewall | firewallonly}]
```

The command-line options are as follows:

InterfaceName: Required parameter whose value specifies the interface on which you want to configure NAT. The value must match the name of the interface as it has been specified in Network Connections. Put the value in quotation marks if there are spaces in the name.

Mode: Optional parameter whose value specifies the interface mode. Specify full to enable both address and port translation for an interface connected to the Internet; specify addressonly to enable IP address translation without port translation when connected to the Internet; specify private to enable the interface to connect to a private network rather than the Internet; specify fullfirewall to enable full translation with a firewall; specify addressonlyfirewall to enable a firewall in address-only mode; specify firewallonly to configure a firewall without translation.

For example, to configure an interface on Local Area Connection #2 to provide both address and port translation with firewall capabilities, run the following command:

```
> netsh routing ip nat add interface "Local Area Connection #2" fullfirewall
```

Second, to map a public address to a private address in the NAT address pool, use this command:

```
> netsh routing ip nat add addressmapping [InterfaceName=]<InterfaceName>
    [public=]<IPAddress> [private=]<IPAddress>
    [inboundsessions=]{enable | disable}
```

The command-line options are as follows:

InterfaceName: Required parameter whose value specifies the interface on which you want to configure NAT. The value must match the name of the interface as it has been specified in Network Connections. Put the value in quotation marks if there are spaces in the name.

Public: Required parameter whose value specifies the public IP address of the interface.

Private: Required parameter whose value specifies the private IP address to which you want to map the public address.

InboundSessions: Required parameter whose value specifies whether to allow or prohibit inbound requests. The two possible values are enable (permit inbound requests) and disable (prohibit inbound requests).

For example, to map the public IP address of 209.132.64.128 to the private address of 192.168.30.2 on Local Area Connection #2, but to prohibit inbound requests on the interface, run the following command:

```
> netsh routing ip nat add addressmapping
    "Local Area Connection #2" 209.132.64.128 192.168.30.2 disable
```

Third, to add an address range to address pool for the specified NAT interface, use this command:

```
> netsh routing ip nat add addressrange [InterfaceName=]InterfaceName
    [start=]<IPAddress> [end=]<IPAddress> [mask=]<SubnetMask>
```

The command-line options are as follows:

InterfaceName: Required parameter whose value specifies the interface on which you want to configure NAT. The value must match the name of the interface as it has been specified in Network Connections. Put the value in quotation marks if there are spaces in the name.

Start: Required parameter whose value specifies the first IP address in the range.

End: Required parameter whose value specifies the final IP address in the range.

Mask: Required parameter whose value specifies the subnet mask of the range.

For example, to add the range 10.10.10.1 through 10.10.10.254 to the Local Area Connection #2 interface using a subnet mask of 255.255.255.0, run the following command:

```
> netsh routing ip nat add addressrange
     "Local Area Connection #2" 10.10.10.1 10.10.10.254 255.255.255.0
```

Fourth, to add a port mapping to a specified interface, use this command:

```
> netsh routing ip nat add portmapping [InterfaceName=]<InterfaceName>
     [proto=]{tcp | udp} [publicip=]{IPAddress | 0.0.0.0}
     [publicport=]<Integer> [privateip=]<IPAddress> [privateport=]<Integer>
```

The command-line options are as follows:

InterfaceName: Required parameter whose value specifies the interface on which you want to configure NAT. The value must match the name of the interface as it has been specified in Network Connections. Put the value in quotation marks if there are spaces in the name.

Proto: Required parameter whose value specifies whether the mapping will use TCP or UDP.

PublicIP: Required parameter whose value specifies an external IP address on the public network. Alternatively, you may use 0.0.0.0 to indicate any IP address that is not already part of the private network.

PublicPort: Required parameter whose value specifies the public protocol port number. The port number must be an integer ranging from 0 to 9999.

PrivateIP: Required parameter whose value specifies an IP address within the private address range.

PrivatePort: Required parameter whose value specifies the private protocol port number. The port number must be an integer from 0 to 9999.

For example, to map TCP port 80 on all public addresses to port 80 on an internal address of 192.168.25.2 over the Local Area Connection #2 interface, use the following command:

```
> netsh routing ip nat add portmapping
     "Local Area Connection #2" TCP 0.0.0.0 80 192.168.25.2 80
```

You can also delete interfaces from the command line. Use the following commands, each of which is a counterpart to the commands previously described. The descriptions for the parameters are identical to those previously presented.

To delete a NAT interface, use this command:

```
> netsh routing ip nat delete interface [InterfaceName=]<InterfaceName>
```

To delete an address mapping on a NAT interface, use this command:

```
> netsh routing ip nat delete addressmapping
     [InterfaceName=]<InterfaceName> [[public=]<IPAddress>]
```

If the public parameter is omitted, all mappings will be deleted from the interface.
To delete an address range from a NAT interface, use this command:

```
> netsh routing ip nat delete addressrange
     [InterfaceName=]<InterfaceName> [start=]<IPAddress>
```

To delete a port mapping from a NAT interface, use this command:

```
> netsh routing ip nat delete portmapping
    [InterfaceName=]<InterfaceName> [[proto=]{tcp | udp}]
    [publicip=]{IPAddress | 0.0.0.0}] [[publicport=]<Integer>]
    [[privateip=]<IPAddress>] [privateport=]<Integer>]
```

How It Works

If you are a system administrator for a small- or medium-sized business, there is a good probability that you will be configuring your Windows Server 2003 router to provide Internet access to the hosts on your LAN using network address translation.

If this is the case, and if you do not have a firewall between the router and the LAN, be certain to enable the Basic Firewall on the interface. Although it is far from a full-featured firewall appliance that might also contain anti-spyware, anti-virus, or other features, it certainly provides a starting point for your perimeter defense. The Basic Firewall is distinct from the Windows Firewall discussed in Chapter 3.

When configuring services and ports (as defined in the graphical user interface section) or port mappings (as defined in the command-line section), be aware that these services and ports are not those to which users on your LAN have access. Rather, they define the services on your network to which users on the Internet are permitted access. In other words, each service or port that you open on the firewall represents one additional channel into your network that an unauthorized user can attempt to exploit.

Note By default, users on the LAN have outbound access to all protocols, services, and ports unless explicitly prohibited.

See Also

- Microsoft TechNet: "Basic Firewall" (http://technet2.microsoft.com/WindowsServer/ en/Library/7c9a082b-0c5c-49d1-a1a8-5bfccc0eeb5c1033.mspx). This article provides a brief discussion of how the Basic Firewall works, as well as factors to consider when using this in conjunction with another firewall.

- Microsoft TechNet: "Understanding Network Address Translation" (http://technet2.microsoft.com/WindowsServer/en/Library/ 321780ff-6027-4906-b1e5-3701f3105f0c1033.mspx). This article describes the three key components: translation, addressing, and name resolution.

- Microsoft TechNet: "Network Address Translation Design Considerations" (http://technet2.microsoft.com/WindowsServer/en/Library/ b0b24722-8e44-416b-97a6-d24f861a21ba1033.mspx). This article discusses private vs. public addressing, single vs. multiple addresses, inbound connections, and application and service configuration.

5-14. Configuring a DHCP Allocator

Problem

You want to configure your router to provide IP address assignments to clients on your private network.

Solution

Using a Graphical User Interface

1. Start the Routing and Remote Access Services administrative console from the Administrative Tools folder in the Start menu, or directly from %systemroot%\system32\rrasmgmt.msc.

2. Expand the console tree below the server object until you have selected IP Routing ➤ NAT/Basic Firewall.

3. Right-click NAT/Basic Firewall, and select Properties.

4. Select the Address Assignment tab.

5. Check the Automatically Assign IP Addresses by Using the DHCP Allocator check box.

6. Enter the network address and subnet mask of the addresses to distribute.

7. If you want to exclude certain addresses from being distributed, click the Exclude button, and follow these steps:

   a. Click the Add button.

   b. Enter the IP address to exclude.

   c. Click the OK button.

   d. Repeat steps *a–c* to create additional exclusions.

8. Click the OK button when complete.

Additionally, you can view DHCP Allocator statistics at any time:

1. Start the Routing and Remote Access Services administrative console from the Administrative Tools folder in the Start menu, or directly from %systemroot%\system32\rrasmgmt.msc.

2. Expand the console tree below the server object until you have selected IP Routing ➤ NAT/Basic Firewall.

3. Right-click NAT/Basic Firewall and select Show DHCP Allocator Information. A pop-up window will appear that will include the following statistics:

- Messages Ignored

- DECLINE Messages Received

- DISCOVER Messages Received

- INFORM Messages Received

- RELEASE Messages Received

- REQUEST Messages Received

- ACK Messages Sent

- BOOTP Replies Sent

- NAK Messages Sent

- OFFER Messages Sent

4. Close the window when complete.

Using a Command-Line Interface

The command-line interface provides a richer environment for DHCP Allocator configuration than the graphical user interface. You can manage the DHCP Allocator using the netsh routing ip autodhcp commands described in this section.

To install or uninstall the DHCP Allocator, use this command:

```
> netsh routing ip autodhcp {install | uninstall}
```

To show the global options for the DHCP Allocator, use this command:

```
> netsh routing ip autodhcp show global
```

The results of this command will look like the following:

```
> netsh routing ip autodhcp show global
```

```
DHCP Allocator Configuration Information
----------------------------------------
Scope Network          : 192.168.0.0
Scope Mask             : 255.255.255.0
Lease Time (minutes)   : 10080
Logging Level          : Errors Only
```

To configure global options for the DHCP Allocator, use this command:

```
> netsh routing ip autodhcp set global
    {[[scopenetwork=]<IPAddress>] | [[scopemask=]<SubnetMask>] |
    [[leasetime=]<Minutes>] | [[loglevel=]{none | error | warn | info}]}
```

Here is a description of the command-line options:

ScopeNetwork: Optional parameter whose value specifies the network address of the DHCP range.

ScopeMask: Optional parameter whose value specifies the subnet mask of the DHCP range.

LeaseTime: Optional parameter whose value, specified in minutes, provides the duration of the DHCP lease.

LogLevel: Optional parameter whose value specifies the level of logging by the DHCP Allocator. You can configure this value for no logging (none), logging for errors only (error), warnings and errors (warn), or all events (info).

For example, to configure a DHCP range for the 192.168.0.0 network with a subnet mask of 255.255.255.0, with addresses having a 60 minute lease time, run the following command:

```
> netsh routing ip autodhcp set global 192.168.0.0 255.255.255.0 60
```

To display the DHCP Allocator configuration for a specific interface, use this command:

```
> netsh routing ip autodhcp show interface [InterfaceName=]<InterfaceName>
```

To set the DHCP Allocator configuration for a specific interface, use this command:

```
> netsh routing ip autodhcp set interface
    [InterfaceName=]<InterfaceName> [mode=]{enable | disable}
```

Here is a description of the command-line options:

InterfaceName: Required parameter whose value is the name of the interface to which you want to bind the DHCP Allocator service. This value must match the name of the interface as it appears in Network Connections.

Mode: Required parameter whose value either enables or disables the protocol on this interface.

For example, to bind the DHCP Allocator to Server Local Area Connection #2, run the following command:

```
> netsh routing ip autodhcp "Server Local Area Connection #2" enable
```

To add or remove an exclusion, use this command:

```
> netsh routing ip autodhcp {add | delete} exclusion <IPAddress>
```

Here is a description of the command-line options:

Add | Delete: Required parameter whose value specifies whether you want to add or delete the exclusion.

Exclusion: Required parameter whose value is the IP address of the excluded system.

For example, to add an exclusion for the IP address of 192.168.0.15, use the following command:

```
> netsh routing ip autodhcp add exclusion 192.168.0.15
```

How It Works

Configure the DHCP Allocator when you want to assign addresses to clients on your local area network. This service is not required if you already have a DHCP server on your network. It is not as full-featured as the DHCP Server service provided with Windows Server 2003, 2000, or even NT 4. The only options that you can configure or that are distributed by the DHCP Allocator are the range of IP addresses, the subnet mask, the default gateway, and the DNS server. You cannot issue other settings such as WINS servers, MX records, or domain names.

See Also

Recipe 5-15 for more on adding or removing a DHCP Relay Agent

5-15. Adding or Removing a DHCP Relay Agent

Problem

You want to configure your router to relay DHCP requests to a DHCP server.

Solution

Using a Graphical User Interface

Note The following steps assume that you have already added the DHCP Relay Agent as a routing protocol. If you have not done so, install the protocol. See Recipe 5-8, "Adding a Routing Protocol," for the details of this procedure.

---

1. Start the Routing and Remote Access Services administrative console from the Administrative Tools folder in the Start menu, or directly from %systemroot%\system32\rrasmgmt.msc.

2. Expand the console tree below the server object until you have selected IP Routing ➤ DHCP Relay Agent.

3. Right-click DHCP Relay Agent and select Properties.

4. Specify the IP address of the DHCP server to which you want to send requests and click the Add button, or select the IP address of the server that you want to remove and click the Remove button.

5. Click the OK button when complete.

Using a Command-Line Interface

The command-line interface providers a richer environment for DHCP Relay Agent configuration than the graphical user interface. You can manage the Relay Agent using the `netsh routing ip relay` commands.

To add or delete a DHCP server to or from the list of servers to which DHCP requests are relayed, use this command:

```
> netsh routing ip relay {add | delete} dhcpserver <IPAddress>
```

For example, to relay DHCP requests to the server at `192.168.60.5`, use the following command:

```
> netsh routing ip relay add dhcpserver 192.168.60.5
```

To display global settings for the Relay Agent, use this command:

```
> netsh routing ip relay show global
```

This command will generate results as follows:

```
> netsh routing ip relay show global
```

```
DHCP Relay Global Configuration Information
-------------------------------------------------------
Logging Level                   : Errors Only
Max Receive Queue Size          : 1048576
Server Count                    : 1
```

The preceding results of the `netsh routing ip relay show global` command show that only errors are logged, the queue size is limited to 1,048,576 DHCP packets, and that there is only a single DHCP server in the global list.

To set logging criteria for the Relay Agent, use this command:

```
> netsh routing ip relay set global [LogLevel=]{none | error | warn | info}
```

For example, to set logging to record warning messages, use the following command:

```
> netsh routing ip relay set global warn
```

To enable or disable the Relay Agent on an interface, use this command:

```
> netsh routing ip relay {add | delete} interface
    [InterfaceName=]<InterfaceName>
```

For example, to enable the DHCP Relay Agent on the interface named `Local Area Connection #2`, use the following command:

```
> netsh routing ip relay add interface "Local Area Connection #2"
```

To display configuration information for the Relay Agent on an interface, use this command:

```
> netsh routing ip relay show ifconfig
    [[Index=]<InterfaceIndex>] [[Rr=]<RefreshRate>]
```

There are two command-line parameters:

Index: Optional parameter whose value specifies the index number of the interface. If omitted, the command will return results for all interfaces.

Rr: Optional parameter whose value specifies the refresh rate, given in seconds, of the statistics to display.

The command will return results like the following:

```
> netsh routing ip relay add interface "Server Local Area Connection"
```

```
DHCP Relay Agent Interface Config for : Server Local Area Connection
----------------------------------------------------
State                            Bound and Enabled
Relay Mode                       ENABLED
Max Hop Count                    4
Minimum Seconds Since Boot       4
```

To edit the Relay Agent configuration for an interface, use this command:

```
> netsh routing ip relay set interface [InterfaceName=]<InterfaceName
    [relaymode=]{enable | disable}
    [[maxhop=]<Integer>] [[minsecs=]<Integer>]
```

These are the command-line parameters:

InterfaceName: The name of the interface whose configuration you want to edit. The name must be identical to the name of the interface as specified in Network Properties.

RelayMode: Required parameter whose value specifies whether you want to enable or disable the agent on the interface.

MaxHop: Optional parameter whose value specifies the number of hops that a DHCP packet can make before it should be dropped and no longer relayed.

MinSecs: Optional parameter whose value, specified in seconds, indicates the amount of time from system boot that must appear in a DHCP packet before it is relayed to a DHCP server.

For example, to enable the DHCP Relay Agent on the interface named Local Area Connection #2 with a maximum hop count of 16 and a minimum interval of 4 seconds from boot time, use the following command:

```
> netsh routing ip relay set interface "Local Area Connection #2" enable 16 4
```

To display statistics for an interface, use this command:

```
> netsh routing ip relay show ifstats [[Index=]<Integer>] [[Rr=]<Integer>]
```

If you omit the refresh rate parameter, the results will display in a non-dynamic table. Include the refresh rate parameter to open a real-time, dynamic table of results.

For example, to show statistics for all interfaces and refresh the display every 5 seconds, use this command:

```
> netsh routing ip relay show ifstats rr=5
```

```
DHCP Relay Agent Interface Stats for :  Server Local Area Connection
---------------------------------------------------
State                            Bound and Enabled
Send Failures                    0
Receive Failures                 0
ARP Update Failures              0
Requests Received                0
Requests Discarded               0
Replies Received                 0
Replies Discarded                0
```

How It Works

You cannot install or configure the DHCP Relay Agent on a server that is running DHCP Server, NAT with the DHCP Allocator service enabled, or Internet Connection Sharing (ICS).

DHCP is not a routable protocol. Therefore, use the DHCP Relay Agent when the DHCP server is located on a different subnet than the clients so that you can relay requests between the clients and the server.

See Also

- Microsoft TechNet: "DHCP Relay Agent" (http://technet2.microsoft.com/ WindowsServer/en/Library/b18e9fb8-fec8-4d47-9869-0cbe55d438d21033.mspx)

- Recipe 5-14 for more on configuring a DHCP Allocator.

5-16. Configuring a DNS Proxy

Problem

You want to configure your router to relay DNS requests on behalf of clients on its private network.

Solution

Using a Graphical User Interface

1. Start the Routing and Remote Access Services administrative console from the Administrative Tools folder in the Start menu, or directly from %systemroot%\system32\ rrasmgmt.msc.

2. Expand the console tree below the server object until you have selected IP Routing ➤ NAT/Basic Firewall.

3. Right-click NAT/Basic Firewall and select Properties.

4. Select the Name Resolution tab.

5. If you want this router to relay DNS requests for clients on the private network, check the check box to resolve IP addresses for Clients Using Domain Name System (DNS).

6. If you want to use a demand-dial interface to connect to a DNS server on the public network, check the check box to Connect to the Public Network When a Name Needs to Be Resolved. You will be prompted to select the demand-dial interface if you enable this option.

7. Click the OK button when complete.

Additionally, you can view DNS proxy statistics at any time. Follow these steps:

1. Start the Routing and Remote Access Services administrative console from the Administrative Tools folder in the Start menu, or directly from %systemroot%\system32\ rrasmgmt.msc.

2. Expand the console tree below the server object until you have selected IP Routing ➤ NAT/Basic Firewall.

3. Right-click NAT/Basic Firewall and select Show DNS Proxy Information. A pop-up window will appear displaying these statistics:

   • Messages Ignored

   • Queries Received

   • Responses Received

   • Queries Sent

   • Responses Sent

4. Close the window when complete.

Using a Command-Line Interface

The command-line interface provides a richer environment for DNS proxy configuration than the graphical user interface. You can manage the proxy configuration using the `netsh routing ip dnsproxy` commands.

To configure the router to proxy DNS requests, use this command:

```
> netsh routing ip dnsproxy {install | uninstall}
```

For example, to configure your router to proxy DNS requests:

```
> netsh routing ip dnsproxy install
```

This command will not provide any feedback if it has been successful. The cursor in the command prompt will simply move to the next line.

To display global parameters related to the DNS proxy, use this command:

```
> netsh routing ip dnsproxy show global
```

This command takes no parameters. It will display a table that resembles the following:

```
> netsh routing ip dnsproxy show global
```

```
DNS Proxy Configuration Information
-----------------------------------
DNS Proxy Mode          : ENABLED
Query Timeout (seconds)  : 3
Logging Level           : Errors Only
```

To configure the global settings for the DNS proxy, use this command:

```
> netsh routing ip dnsproxy set global [querytimeout=]<Integer>
   [[dnsmode=]{enable | disable}] [[loglevel=]{none | error | warn | info}]
```

The command-line parameters are as follows:

QueryTimeout: Required parameter whose value specifies the timeout period, in seconds, of the DNS request.

DNSMode: Optional parameter whose value specifies whether DNS proxy operation is enabled or disabled.

LogLevel: Optional parameter whose value specifies which events should be logged. As in previous recipes in this chapter, the possible values are none, error, warn, and info.

For example, to enable DNS proxy operation with a query timeout value of 5 seconds and to log only warning events, run the following command:

```
> netsh routing ip dnsproxy set global 5 enable warn
```

To display the status of the DNS proxy on a particular interface, use this command:

```
> netsh routing ip dnsproxy show interface name=<InterfaceName>
```

As in previous recipes in this chapter, InterfaceName is a required value that must match the name of the interface as specified in Network Properties.

To enable or disable the DNS proxy on a particular interface, use this command:

```
> netsh routing ip dnsproxy set interface name=<InterfaceName
    [[mode=]{enable | disable | default}
```

If you set the mode to a value of default, it will use the global setting (enabled or disabled) of the DNS proxy as specified in the netsh routing ip dnsproxy set global command shown earlier in this recipe.

How It Works

The DNS proxy is not a DNS server. Rather, when a client on the LAN cannot resolve a host name, the DNS proxy will relay the request to the DNS server specified in the server's network properties.

If you are running Active Directory, you are already running DNS Server on the domain. You are probably using the root hints or have configured forwarders for nonlocal name resolution. If that is the case, you do not need to configure the DNS proxy on the router; the exception is if there are devices on your local network that do not look to the server's DNS server for name resolution.

See Also

Microsoft KB 816567: "How To Troubleshoot DNS Name Resolution on the Internet in Windows Server 2003." This article discusses name resolution troubleshooting techniques.

5-17. Starting and Stopping RRAS

Problem

You want to start or stop RRAS.

Solution

Using a Graphical User Interface

1. Start the Services Control Panel applet from the Administrative Tools folder in the Start menu.

2. Select the Routing and Remote Access service.

3. Select the Action menu, and then select the option to start, stop, or restart the service, whichever is appropriate.

Using a Command-Line Interface

To start RRAS, type the following in the command window:

```
> net start remoteaccess
```

To stop the service, type the following in the command window:

```
> net stop remoteaccess
```

Using VBScript

To stop RRAS on the local computer, put the following code into a VBScript file:

```
'This code will stop the Routing and Remote Access service
'---SCRIPT CONFIGURATION ---
strComputer = "."
'---END CONFIGURATION---
Set objWMIService = GetObject("winmgmts:" _
    & "{impersonationLevel=impersonate}!\\" & strComputer & "\root\cimv2")
Set colServiceList = objWMIService.ExecQuery _
        ("Select * from Win32_Service where Name='remoteaccess'")
For each objService in colServiceList
    errReturn = objService.StopService()
Next
WScript.Echo ("Service stopped.")
```

To start the service on the local computer, use the following similar code instead:

```
'This code will start the Routing and Remote Access service
'---SCRIPT CONFIGURATION---
strComputer = "."
'---END CONFIGURATION---
Set objWMIService = GetObject("winmgmts:" _
    & "{impersonationLevel=impersonate}!\\" & strComputer & "\root\cimv2")
Set colServiceList = objWMIService.ExecQuery _
        ("Select * from Win32_Service where Name='remoteaccess'")
Set colServiceList = objWMIService.ExecQuery _
    ("Select * from Win32_Service where Name='remoteaccess'")
For each objService in colServiceList
    errReturn = objService.StartService()
Next
WScript.Echo ("Service started.")
```

To restart the service on the local computer, combine the previous two code segments into a single one, as follows:

```
'This code will start the Routing and Remote Access service
'---SCRIPT CONFIGURATION---
strComputer = "."
'---END CONFIGURATION---
Set objWMIService = GetObject("winmgmts:" _
    & "{impersonationLevel=impersonate}!\\" & strComputer & "\root\cimv2")
Set colServiceList = objWMIService.ExecQuery _
        ("Select * from Win32_Service where Name='remoteaccess'")
For each objService in colServiceList
    errReturn = objService.StopService()
```

```
Next
Set colServiceList = objWMIService.ExecQuery _
    ("Select * from Win32_Service where Name='remoteaccess'")
For each objService in colServiceList
    errReturn = objService.StartService()
Next
WScript.Echo ("Service restarted.")
```

Note that even though the preceding code sends the command to the local computer, you can perform this action against any computer to which you have access and permission by modifying the value of strComputer. So if you are at your workstation and want to manage the remote computer named RRAS2, you would modify the first line to read as follows:

```
strComputer = "RRAS2"
```

How It Works

You may want to stop and start RRAS if you have made changes to the server configuration and these changes are not visible to clients. Even though most changes should not ideally require that the service be restarted, the reality is that this is necessary on occasion.

Also, keep in mind that the service can be neither started nor restarted if RRAS is not yet configured, implying that the service state is set to disabled.

5-18. Troubleshooting Your Windows Server 2003 Routing Environment

Problem

You want to troubleshoot routing issues on your network.

Solution

Due to the complexity of routing, it is not possible to enumerate all the problems that may occur or even the tools that are available to diagnose and solve them. However, some problems occur much more frequently than others, and some tools or utilities should be used for initial troubleshooting.

"Troubleshooting Routing" in Microsoft TechNet (http://technet2.microsoft.com/ WindowsServer/en/Library/b1468dee-95b1-4ff8-9e13-a2b20d82b66c1033.mspx) lists a number of common problems and methods to diagnose and correct them, such as the following:

- Common routing problems

  - The server running Routing and Remote Access is not properly forwarding traffic

- Troubleshooting network address translation

  - The network address translation (NAT) computer is not properly translating packets

  - Private network hosts are not receiving IP address configuration

  - Name resolution for private network hosts is not working

- Troubleshooting the DHCP Relay Agent

    - The DHCP Relay Agent is not providing relay services for DHCP clients on a network segment

- Troubleshooting IP multicast

    - The IGMP router does not work correctly

- Troubleshooting demand-dial routing

    - On-demand connection is not made automatically

    - Unable to make a demand-dial connection

    - Unable to reach locations beyond the calling router or answering router

    - Auto-static updates are not working

There are a number of utilities, including the most basic system event log, that are a part of Windows Server 2003 and that should be included in any IT administrator's toolkit. These can be very useful for diagnosing routing issues: ping, tracert, pathping, mrinfo, and tracing.

Ping

Ping is probably the most fundamental and well-known command for diagnosing routing and connectivity issues. Ping hosts by IP address to determine whether they are active and reachable. Ping them by host name to verify that name resolution is working properly.

Most administrators should be familiar with the basic syntax:

```
> ping Destination
```

There are additional parameters available. A comprehensive ping syntax includes the following:

```
> ping [-t] [-a] [-n count] [-l size] [-f] [-i TTL] [-w timeout]
    [-R] [-S srcaddr] [-4] [-6] Destination
```

The parameters are described by typing ping /? at a command prompt:

-t	Pings the specified host until stopped; to see statistics and continue, type Ctrl-Break; to stop type Ctrl-C.
-a	Resolves addresses to hostnames
-n count	Specifies the number of echo requests to send
-l size	Specifies the send buffer size
-f	Sets the Don't Fragment flag in packet (IPv4-only)
-i TTL	Sets the time to live
-v TOS	Sets the type of service (IPv4-only)
-r count	Records the route for count hops (IPv4-only)

-s *count*	Specifies the timestamp for counting hops (IPv4-only)
-j *host-list*	Specifies a loose source route along the host-list (IPv4-only)
-k *host-list*	Specifies a strict source route along the host-list (IPv4-only)
-w *timeout*	Specifies the time in milliseconds to wait for each reply
-R	Traces the round-trip path (IPv6-only)
-S *srcaddr*	Specifies source address to use (IPv6-only)
-4	Forces using IPv4
-6	Forces using IPv6

Tracert

The tracert command will report the path that a connection request follows as it passes along a routed network from a source to its destination. Use this command when a user calls you to report that "the Internet is broken," and you suspect that there is really a router that may be inaccessible somewhere between you and the final destination.

Many administrators are familiar with the basic syntax:

```
> tracert Destination
```

There are also additional parameters available. The full tracert syntax is as follows:

```
> tracert [-d] [-h maximum_hops] [-w timeout]
    [-R] [-S srcaddr] [-4] [-6] Destination
```

The parameters are described by typing tracert /? at a command prompt:

-d	Specifies that tracert will not resolve addresses to hostnames
-h *maximum_hops*	Specifies the maximum number of hops to search for target
-j *host-list*	Specifies a loose source route along host-list (IPv4-only)
-w *timeout*	Specifies the wait time in milliseconds for each reply
-R	Traces the round-trip path (IPv6-only)
-S *srcaddr*	Specifies the source address to use (IPv6-only)
-4	Forces using IPv4
-6	Forces using IPv6

Pathping

The pathping command combines some aspects of ping and some of tracert, and throws in a few other goodies for good measure. Pathping, similar to tracert, displays and resolves the routers between the source and the destination, but after this process is complete, it will take some time to analyze and return the relative packet loss that occurs at each router hop.

For example, the following command runs the pathping command to microsoft.com without resolving host names:

```
> pathping -n microsoft.com
```

```
Tracing route to microsoft [157.54.1.196]
over a maximum of 30 hops:
  0   172.16.87.35
  1   172.16.87.218
  2   192.168.52.1
  3   192.168.80.1
  4   157.54.247.14
  5   157.54.1.196

Computing statistics for 125 seconds...
              Source to Here   This Node/Link
Hop   RTT    Lost/Sent = Pct  Lost/Sent = Pct  Address
  0                                             172.16.87.35
                                 0/ 100 =  0%   |
  1   41ms    0/ 100 =   0%     0/ 100 =  0%   172.16.87.218
                                13/ 100 = 13%   |
  2   22ms   16/ 100 =  16%     3/ 100 =  3%   192.168.52.1
                                 0/ 100 =  0%   |
  3   24ms   13/ 100 =  13%     0/ 100 =  0%   192.168.80.1
                                 0/ 100 =  0%   |
  4   21ms   14/ 100 =  14%     1/ 100 =  1%   157.54.247.14
                                 0/ 100 =  0%   |
  5   24ms   13/ 100 =  13%     0/ 100 =  0%   157.54.1.196
Trace complete.
```

In this example, 13 percent of the packets are dropped at the link between hop 1 and hop 2, indicating possible router problems. The pipe symbol (|) indicates a link.

Mrinfo

The mrinfo command will contact a multicast router with an IGMP message to display its configuration information. The response from the router will contain a version number, a list of interfaces and neighbors, time-to-live (TTL) values, and other flags. The full syntax is as follows:

```
> mrinfo [-n] [-i address] [-r retry_count] [-t timeout_count]
    multicast_router_destination
```

The parameters are listed by typing mrinfo /? at a command prompt:

-n   Displays IP addresses in numeric format

-i *address*   Specifies address of local interface to send query out

-t *seconds*	Specifies timeout in seconds for IGMP queries (default is 3 seconds)
-r *retries*	Specifies the number of extra times to send the SNMP queries (default is 0)
destination	Specifies the address or name of destination

The following example runs the `mrinfo` command against a multicast router at `10.1.0.1`:

```
> mrinfo 10.1.0.1
10.1.0.1(test1.microsoft.com) [version 18.55,mtrace,snmp]:
10.1.0.1 -> 0.0.0.0 (local) [1/0/querier/leaf]
10.2.0.1 -> 10.2.0.2 (test2.microsoft.com) [1/0]
10.2.0.1 -> 10.2.0.3 (test3.microsoft.com) [1/0]
10.3.0.1 -> 0.0.0.0 (local) [1/0/querier/leaf]
```

The first line of the preceding output shows the configuration of the multicast router at `10.1.0.1`, including its version number and the fact that it supports both `mtrace` and SNMP. If the multicast router is a Windows Server router running RRAS, the version number represents the build number of the operating system.

Additional lines display the interfaces on the router and the neighbors on each interface. In the second and fifth lines of the results, we see that there are interfaces at `10.1.0.1` and at `10.3.0.1`, but that they do not have any neighbors, as indicated by the value `0.0.0.0`. In the third and fourth lines, we see an interface at `10.2.0.1` which has neighbors at `10.2.0.2` and `10.2.0.3`.

Tracing

Tracing is a form of logging. It provides a wealth of information for troubleshooting purposes. Unfortunately, the logs produced by tracing can be so complex that they are valuable only to those with extensive skills in interpreting them.

Tracing can use significant system resources, such as disk space, and should therefore be used only when necessary. Microsoft recommends that you disable tracing whenever it is not required and never leave it running on multiprocessor systems.

Tracing is enabled or disabled by modifying specific Registry keys, or by using a utility described in the "See Also" section of this recipe. We provide the usual warning about editing the Registry: Do so with care. Changing a value or key incorrectly can leave your server in an unstable or unusable state. All tracing keys are located at `HKEY_LOCAL_MACHINE\SOFTWARE\Microsoft\Tracing`.

You can enable or disable tracing for each routing protocol, and you can do so while the router is running. Each protocol has its own subkey in the branch indicated previously. For example, to enable tracing for the IGMP v2 routing protocol, set the following value:

```
[HKEY_LOCAL_MACHINE\Software\Microsoft\Tracing\IGMPv2]
"EnableFileTracing"=dword:00000001
```

Set the folder in which to save the IGMP log (trace) files as follows:

```
[HKEY_LOCAL_MACHINE\Software\Microsoft\Tracing\IGMPv2]
"FileDirectory"=expand_sz:<path>
```

In the preceding key, <path> is the absolute path to the folder in which you want to save the log files. The default location is %systemroot%\tracing.

Set the size of the IGMP log file as follows:

```
[HKEY_LOCAL_MACHINE\Software\Microsoft\Tracing\IGMPv2]
"MaxFileSize"=dword:<FileSize>
```

In this key, <FileSize> is the size of the file specified in either hexadecimal or decimal notation. The default value is 1048576 (bytes, specified in decimal notation).

How It Works

Troubleshooting routing can be as simple as issuing a tracert command, or as complex as determining problems with interface configuration, router bottlenecks, and any number of problems outside the control of your own network. Utilize the commands described in this recipe as a first step toward diagnosing and correcting common routing problems.

See Also

- Microsoft KB 323388: "How To Diagnose and Test TCP/IP or NetBIOS Network Connections in Windows Server 2003." This article reviews of the basic troubleshooting tools and syntax.

- Microsoft TechNet: "Common Routing Problems" (http://technet2.microsoft.com/ WindowsServer/en/Library/9f68c37b-02b6-4e1b-b898-c25389dba4f41033.mspx). This article discusses frequently observed problems and their solutions.

- WindowsNetworking.com: "Routing Troubleshooting Primer" (http://www. windowsnetworking.com/articles_tutorials/Router-Troubleshooting-Primer.html).

- Microsoft 2000 Resource Kit Tool: Trace Enable (traceenable.exe) (http://www.microsoft.com/downloads/ details.aspx?FamilyID=ae22c39c-7165-45bc-8d77-39b6987a6530&displaylang=en). This is a free, downloadable utility that provides a graphical interface for enabling or disabling tracing of various components. This utility is part of the Windows 2000 Resource Kit, but also works with Windows Server 2003. It is discussed as part of the Small Business Server 2000 Resource Kit (http://www.microsoft.com/technet/ prodtechnol/sbs/2000/reskit/sbrkapxf.mspx).

CHAPTER 6

■ ■ ■

Internet Authentication Service (IAS)

The Internet Authentication Service (IAS) is the Microsoft Remote Authentication Dial-In User Service (RADIUS) server implementation, which can serve as both a RADIUS server and a RADIUS proxy. When configured as a RADIUS server, IAS can perform authentication (determining the identity of a user), authorization (determining what a user is allowed to access), and accounting (keeping track of a user's actions) for different types of network access. IAS can be used to configure and secure wireless local area networks (WLANs), as well as virtual private network (VPN) connections. In addition, you can use IAS to create a "quarantine" zone that will prevent remote clients from accessing your network until they have passed certain health checks, such as verifying patch levels and the status of antivirus software. You can also configure IAS to function as a RADIUS proxy, which means that IAS can forward authentication requests and accounting information to other RADIUS servers located elsewhere on your network.

IAS supports a number of authentication algorithms, ranging from unauthenticated access to Challenge Handshake Authentication Protocol (CHAP), MS-CHAP, MS-CHAPv2, and the Extensible Authentication Protocol (EAP), which allows for smart card and certificate-based authentication. You can configure both remote access policies and connection request policies to control whether incoming connection requests are permitted or denied, and what type of information is passed on to other RADIUS servers when IAS is configured as a RADIUS proxy.

Using a Graphical User Interface

When you install IAS on a Windows Server 2003 computer, the IAS MMC snap-in is automatically added to the Administrative Tools folder of the local computer. This snap-in is a "one-stop shop" for administering IAS. You can use it to start and stop the IAS service; create, modify, and delete RADIUS clients and server groups; and configure all aspects of the IAS service.

Using a Command-Line Interface

As with most of the technologies discussed in this book, the primary command-line utility used to configure IAS is netsh, using the netsh aaaa context. The most important task that this context allows you to perform is importing and exporting IAS configuration information from one server to another. In addition, you can configure RADIUS clients at the command line using the addradiusclients.exe utility, which is downloadable from the Microsoft website at http://www.microsoft.com/technet/security/topics/cryptographyetc/peap_d.mspx. (This utility requires the .NET Framework.)

6-1. Registering an IAS Server

Problem

You want to register an IAS server in Active Directory. This is a necessary step before the server can accept incoming client connections in an Active Directory environment.

Solution

Using a Graphical User Interface

1. Open the IAS MMC snap-in on the server being authorized or on a workstation with the Administrative Tools installed.

2. Right-click the Internet Authentication Service node and select Register Server in Active Directory.

3. In the Register Internet Authentication Service in Active Directory dialog box, click OK.

Using a Command-Line Interface

The following command will register the local server in the default Active Directory domain:

```
> netsh ras add registeredserver
```

Using VBScript

The following script will register the local server in Active Directory:

```
' This script will register the local IAS Server
' in Active Directory

' Now execute the netsh command
set wshShell = CreateObject("WScript.Shell")
set oExec = wshShell.Exec("netsh ras add registeredserver")

' Sit in a loop while the command is running
Do While oExec.Status = 0
  WScript.Sleep 1000
Loop

WScript.Echo("Server registration complete!")
```

How It Works

As with Dynamic Host Configuration Protocol (DHCP) and Remote Access Service (RAS) servers, you need to authorize an IAS server in Active Directory before it will be able to accept incoming connections. This feature was added to Active Directory networks as a way to protect against *rogue* servers; that is, servers that may have been installed by illegitimate or malicious users to steal data or stage denial-of-service attacks against your network.

Registering an IAS server within your current domain is a simple matter; just right-click the server node in the IAS MMC snap-in and select Register Server in Active Directory. (There is also a command-line option in netsh.)

Another option is to add the IAS server's computer account to the RAS and IAS Servers security group in the appropriate Active Directory domain. If you need to authorize the server in a remote Active Directory domain, you have two options:

- Add the computer account to the RAS and IAS Servers group in the remote domain.

- Modify the netsh syntax as follows:

  netsh add registeredserver *RemoteDomainName ServerName*

RAS and IAS do not have a Windows Management Instrumentation (WMI) provider specifically, but you can execute netsh commands via the Windows Scripting Host (WSH) Exec() method.

See Also

Microsoft TechNet: "Running Programs from WSH Scripts" (http://www.microsoft.com/technet/community/columns/scripts/sg1002.mspx)

6-2. Starting and Stopping IAS

Problem

You want to start or stop the IAS service on a local or remote computer.

Solution

Using a Graphical User Interface

1. Open the Services MMC snap-in. Scroll down to the Internet Authentication Service entry.

2. Right-click the entry and select one of the following:

   - Stop to stop IAS

   - Start to start IAS

   - Restart to restart IAS

Note You can also start and stop the IAS service from within the IAS MMC snap-in.

Using a Command-Line Interface

The following command stops IAS:

```
> net stop "Internet Authentication Service"
```

The following command starts IAS:

```
> net start "Internet Authentication Service"
```

Using VBScript

The following script will stop IAS on the local computer:

```
' The following script stops the IAS service on the local computer

strComputer = "."

Set objWMIService = GetObject("winmgmts:" _
    & "{impersonationLevel=impersonate}!\\" & strComputer & "\root\cimv2")

Set colServiceList = objWMIService.ExecQuery _
 ("Select * from Win32_Service where Name='Internet Authentication Service'")
For Each objService in colServiceList
    errReturn = objService.StopService() ' change the method name to
                                         ' StartService() to start
                                         ' the service instead.

  If errReturn Then
    WScript.Echo("Service started/stopped successfully!")
  Else
    WScript.Echo("Error starting/stopping service.")
  End If
Next
```

How It Works

You will occasionally need to manually start and stop IAS. This may be necessary for trouble-shooting purposes, or to bring down the service for scheduled or emergency maintenance. Because IAS is a standard Windows service, there are a number of options to start and stop the service from the graphical user interface or command-line, or through VBScript.

When starting and stopping IAS, you can use either the IAS or Services MMC snap-in to accomplish this task. However, you should be aware of one caveat when you have both of these snap-ins open at the same time: If you start or stop the IAS service using the Services MMC snap-in while the IAS snap-in is open, the IAS snap-in will not reflect the change until you've manually refreshed its view. Because of this, you should use care in using both of these options at the same time, so that you do not inadvertently lose any configuration changes to the IAS server.

While IAS does not have its own WMI provider, you can still start and stop the service using the `Win32_Service` class of the `root\cimv2` namespace. This class has the built-in methods called `StopService()` and `StartService()`, which you can use to affect any Windows service listed in the Services MMC snap-in.

See Also

MSDN: Information on the `Win32_Service` class, particularly the `StartService()` and `StopService()` methods

6-3. Configuring IAS Ports

Problem

You want to change the ports that are used by IAS for authentication and accounting traffic.

Solution

1. Open the IAS MMC snap-in.

2. Right-click the Internet Authentication Service node and select Properties.

3. Select the Ports tab.

4. In the Authentication text box, enter the port numbers that IAS should use for authentication traffic. You can enter one or more port numbers, separated by commas.

5. In the Accounting text box, enter one or more port numbers (again separated by commas) to be used for accounting traffic.

6. Click OK to save your changes.

Note You must restart IAS for the new port numbers to take effect. See Recipe 6-2.

How It Works

By default, IAS uses UDP ports 1812 and 1645 for authentication, and ports 1813 and 1646 for accounting. You may need to change the default ports, for example, if you are working with proprietary network access server (NAS) hardware that uses its own port numbers.

Keep in mind that if you change the ports, you must ensure that all relevant devices on your network are communicating using the new values. If any RADIUS clients are still using the default ports to transmit authentication and accounting information, they will not be able to communicate with your IAS server after you've made your modifications.

Remember that you can enable multiple port numbers for both authorization and accounting traffic by separating them with commas, as in "1812, 1645, 1135, 353." So if you need to enable additional authorization ports to support legacy or proprietary hardware, you can enable your

IAS computer to use *both* the RADIUS defaults and the legacy ports by entering the port information.

See Also

FreeRADIUS.org, Internet Engineering Task Force (IETF) RFCs that relate to RADIUS (`http://www.freeradius.org/rfc/`)

6-4. Enabling Event Logging for IAS

Problem

You want to enable event logging for IAS.

Solution

1. Open the IAS MMC snap-in.

2. Right-click the Internet Authentication Service node and select Properties.

3. On the General tab, place a check mark next to one or both of the following event types that you wish to log:

   • Rejected authentication requests

   • Successful authentication requests

4. Click OK to save your changes.

How It Works

As both a security and troubleshooting measure, it's critical that you enable and maintain event logging on any computers on your network that are running IAS. By monitoring rejected authentication requests, you can troubleshoot remote clients that are unable to connect to the IAS server, or you can be alerted to a potential attacker who is trying to gain access to your network. In addition, you can use a log of successful authentication requests to chart usage of your RADIUS servers to plan for future expansion and growth.

See Also

• Recipe 6-5 for more on customizing event logging for IAS

• Microsoft Download Center, "Securing Wireless LANs with Certificate Services" (`http://www.microsoft.com/downloads/details.aspx?FamilyId=CDB639B3-010B-47E7-B234-A27CDA291DAD&displaylang=en`)

6-5. Customizing Event Logging for IAS

Problem

You want to customize how events are logged by IAS.

Solution

Using Local File Logging

To configure IAS to use local file logging, do the following:

1. Open the IAS MMC snap-in.

2. Select the Remote Access Logging node.

3. Double-click Local File.

4. On the Settings tab, under Log the Following Information, place a check mark next to one or more of the following:

   - Accounting Requests (for example, accounting start or stop)

   - Authentication Requests (for example, access accept or access reject)

   - Periodic Status (for example, interim accounting requests)

5. On the Log File tab, enter the name of the directory where log files will be stored in the Directory Name text box, or click Browse to locate the directory.

6. Under the Format section, select either the IAS or Database-Compatible radio button.

7. Under the Create a New Log File section, specify how frequently IAS should create a new log file. Choose one of the following options:

   - Daily

   - Weekly

   - Monthly

   - Never (unlimited file size)

   - When the Log File Reaches This Size (and enter the maximum log size in megabytes)

8. Optionally, place a check mark next to When Disk Is Full Delete Older Log Files.

9. Click OK to save your settings.

Logging Information to a SQL Server

To configure IAS to log information to a SQL Server database, do the following:

1. Open the IAS MMC snap-in.

2. Select the Remote Access Logging node.

3. Double-click SQL Server.

4. On the Settings tab, under Log the Following Information, place a check mark next to one or more of the following:

   • Accounting Requests (for example, accounting start or stop)

   • Authentication Requests (for example, access accept or access reject)

   • Periodic Status (for example, interim accounting requests)

5. Enter the maximum number of connections that should be made to the SQL Server at any time.

6. Under the Data Source section, click Configure.

7. On the Connection tab, enter the fully qualified domain name (FQDN) or IP address of ´ the server in the Select or Enter a Server Name text box.

8. Under the Enter Information to Log onto the Server section, choose one of the following:

   • Use Windows NT Integrated Security (Windows Authentication)

   • Use a Specific Username and Password (SQL Authentication)

9. If you selected SQL authentication, enter the SQL username and password. Optionally, place a check mark next to Blank Password or Allow Saving Password.

10. Choose a database to which to connect by selecting one of the following:

    • Select the database on the server

    • Attach a database as a filename

11. Click Test Connection to make sure that you can connect to the SQL Server successfully.

12. Click OK to save your settings.

How It Works

When logging IAS-related data, you can store information in two possible locations: a file on the local hard drive or in a SQL Server or Microsoft SQL Server Database Engine (MSDE) database. When logging information to the local hard drive, you can customize how the information is stored, similar to the way that you can customize logs for Internet Information Services.

Local File Logging

Depending on how much traffic your IAS server handles, you may want to create a new log file on a daily, weekly, or monthly basis, or begin a new log file when the existing one reaches a certain size. You can also record logs in either the IAS log file format or a database-compatible format. The IAS log file format stores accounting entries in the following format:

```
IPAddress,UserID,Date,Time,Service,ServerName,RadiusAttributesList
```

The following is an example of an IAS log file entry:

```
10.0.0.151,jsmith,05/23/2005,13:16:29,IAS,SERVER3,6,2,7,1,5,9,61,5,64,1,65,1,31,1
```

Each line item consists of a number of comma-separated entries that correspond to the following information:

IPAddress: The IP address of the network access server to which the client is connecting (10.0.0.151 in the preceding example).

UserID: The username being used to authenticate (jsmith in the preceding example).

Date, Time: The date and time of the incoming connection request (05/23/2005,13:16:29 in the preceding example).

Service: The name of the service being requested (IAS in the preceding example).

ServerName: The name of the server that received the connection request (SERVER3 in the preceding example).

RadiusAttributesList: Correspond to RADIUS attributes such as the Service-Type (6,2,7,1,5,9,61,5,64,1,65,1,31,1 in the preceding example).

The database-compatible format creates log entries in the following format:

```
ComputerName,Service,Record-Date,Record-Time,Packet-Type,Username,
Fully-Qualified-Username,Called-Station-ID,Calling-Station-ID,Callback-Number,
Framed-IP-Address,NAS-Identifier,NAS-IP-Address,NAS-Port,Client-Vendor,
Client-IP-Address,Client-Friendly-Name,Event-Timestamp,Port-Limit,NAS-Port-Type,
Framed-Protocol,Service-Type,Authentication-Type,NP-Policy-Name,Reason-Code,
Class,Session-Timeout,Idle-Timeout,Termination-Action,EAP-Friendly-Name,
Acct-Status-Type,Acct-Delay-Time,Acct-Input-Octets,Acct-Output-Octets,
Acct-Session-ID,Acct-Authentic,Acct-Session-Time,Acct-Input,Packets,
Acct-Output-Packets,Acct-Terminate-Cause,Acct-Multi-Ssn-ID,Acct-Link-Count,
Acct-Interim-Value,Tunnel-Type,Tunnel-Medium-Type,Tunnel-Client-Endpt,
Tunnel-Server-Endpt,Acct-Tunnel-Connection,Tunnel-Pvt-Group-ID,
Tunnel-Assignment-ID,Tunnel-Preference,MS-Acct-Auth-Type,MS-Acct-EAP-Type,
MS-RAS-Version,MS-CHAP-Error,MS-CHAP-Domain,MS-MPPE-Encryption-Types,
MS-MPPE-Encryption-Policy
```

The following is an example of a database log entry. Notice that any headers that do not contain data are denoted by comma delimiters.

```
"SERVER3","IAS",05/23/2005,13:16:29,1,"jsmith",,,,,,,,,,9,"10.0.0.151","iasclient"
,,,,,,,1,,0,,,,,,,,,,,,,,,,,,,,,,,,,,,,,,,,,,
```

Logging Information to a SQL Server

For a more flexible and extensible data storage option, you can log information to a SQL Server database. This option requires you to specify the name of the SQL Server and database file to which to connect. In addition, you need to specify the type of authentication you're using to connect to the server:

- Windows authentication, which uses the Windows credentials of the user connecting to the server

- SQL authentication, which maintains a separate username and password combination within the SQL Server database

See Also

- Microsoft TechNet: "Logging" (http://www.microsoft.com/technet/prodtechnol/ windowsserver2003/library/ServerHelp/bacb2431-b9c1-4c10-ae83-dc8e9caa5dbe.mspx)

- Microsoft TechNet: "Interpreting Database-Import Log Files" (http://www. microsoft.com/technet/prodtechnol/windowsserver2003/library/ServerHelp/ b583bb8c-f90d-4c52-a748-7bd5c41df564.mspx)

- Microsoft TechNet: "Importing IAS Log Files into a Database" (http://www. microsoft.com/technet/prodtechnol/windowsserver2003/library/ServerHelp/ 53915e23-bae4-4801-82d1-a3e284eb256f.mspx)

- MSDN: Information on SQL Server authentication methods

6-6. Managing RADIUS Clients

Problem

You want to add or delete a RADIUS client on your IAS server, or modify the configuration of an existing RADIUS client.

Solution

Using a Graphical User Interface

To create a new RADIUS client, do the following:

1. Open the IAS MMC snap-in.

2. Right-click RADIUS Clients and click New RADIUS Client.

3. In the Friendly Name text box, enter the name of the client as it will be displayed in the IAS MMC snap-in.

4. In the Client Address (IP Address or DNS Name) text box, enter either the numeric IP address or the FQDN of the client.

5. In the Client-Vendor drop-down box, enter the name of the vendor of the RADIUS client software.

6. Optionally, if you want to manually create the shared secret to be used by the client, enter it in the Shared Secret text box and confirm it in the Confirm Shared Secret text box.

7. Optionally, place a check mark next to Request Must Contain the Message Authenticator Attribute.

8. Click Finish to create the new RADIUS client.

To delete a RADIUS client, do the following:

1. Open the IAS MMC snap-in.

2. In the RADIUS Clients node, right-click the target client and select Delete. Click Yes to confirm the deletion.

To modify the configuration of an existing RADIUS client, do the following:

1. Open the IAS MMC snap-in.

2. In the RADIUS Clients node, right-click the target client and select Properties.

3. In the dialog box, make any desired changes:

   • Use the Client-Vendor drop-down box to modify the name of the vendor of the RADIUS client.

   • Enter the shared secret to be used by the client in the Shared Secret text box and confirm it in the Confirm Shared Secret text box.

   • Add or remove the check mark next to Request Must Contain the Message Authenticator attribute.

4. Click OK to save your changes.

Using a Command-Line Interface

The addradiusclients.exe executable is a free download from the Microsoft website, installed as part of the TechNet "Securing Wireless LANs with PEAP and Passwords" solution, using the following syntax:

```
> addradiusclient -name:FriendlyName -address:ClientIPAddress
    -secret:strClientSecret
```

The following command adds a RADIUS client with a friendly name of CLIENT1, an IP address of 10.0.0.151, and a shared secret of cj4!5jksdt53!%^#$kcntST^s:

```
> addradiusclient.exe -name:CLIENT1 -address:10.0.0.151
    -secret: cj4!5jksdt53!%^#$kcntST^s:
```

Note Unfortunately, there is not a command-line equivalent to delete an existing RADIUS client.

Using VBScript

The following script adds a RADIUS client:

```
' The following script adds a RADIUS client with a friendly
' name of CLIENT1, an IP address of 10.0.0.151, and a shared
' secret of cj4!5jksdt53!%^#$kcntST^s

strComputer = "."

strFriendlyName = "CLIENT1"
strIPAddres = "10.0.0.151"
strSecret = " cj4!5jksdt53!%^#$kcntST^s"

' Now execute the netsh command
set wshShell = CreateObject("WScript.Shell")
set oExec = wshShell.Exec("netsh aaaa show config > " & strOutputFile)

set oExec = wshShell.Exec("addradiusclient.exe -name:" & strFriendlyName _
  & " -address:" & strIPAddress & " -secret:" & strSecret

' Sit in a loop while the command is running
Do While oExec.Status = 0
  WScript.Sleep 1000
Loop

WScript.Echo("Client added successfully!")
```

How It Works

Before a RADIUS client such as an NAS can connect to an IAS server, it must be configured in the IAS MMC. If the NASs that you are using support the use of the Message Authenticator or Signature attribute, you can specify that incoming client connections must contain that attribute. Enabling the use of the Message Authenticator attribute provides additional security for PAP, CHAP, MS-CHAP, and MS-CHAPv2 authentication. (EAP authentication uses the Message Authenticator by default.)

Keep in mind that the Standard Edition of Windows Server 2003 can support a maximum of 50 RADIUS clients and a maximum of 2 remote RADIUS server groups. The Enterprise and Datacenter Editions place no limit on the number of RADIUS clients and remote RADIUS server groups that you can configure. With those editions, you are limited only by the memory and CPU speed of your server hardware. In addition, the Enterprise and Datacenter Editions will allow you to configure clients using a network address if you have a number of RADIUS clients on a single subnet, as long as all of the clients within that range have the same configuration information, including the same shared secret. Windows Server 2003 will allow you to specify only one client at a time using an IP address or a FQDN.

See Also

- Microsoft TechNet: "Securing Wireless LANs with PEAP and Passwords" (http://www.microsoft.com/technet/security/topics/cryptographyetc/peap_d.mspx)

- Microsoft TechNet: "Add RADIUS Clients" (http://www.microsoft.com/technet/prodtechnol/windowsserver2003/library/ServerHelp/ce2709b9-4dc5-4d10-86bc-0d05a2c52acf.mspx)

6-7. Configuring a Remote Access Policy

Problem

You want to create a remote access policy to define who can remotely access a network via the IAS server and under what conditions.

Solution

Configuring a Policy for a Common Scenario

To configure a policy to match a typical remote access scenario, do the following:

1. Open the IAS MMC snap-in.

2. Right-click Remote Access Policies and select New Remote Access Policy.

3. Click Next on the wizard's initial Welcome screen.

4. On the Policy Configuration Method screen, select the Use the Wizard to Set Up a Policy for a Common Scenario radio button. Enter a descriptive name in the Policy Name text box. Then click Next.

5. On the Access Methods screen, select one of the following scenarios:

   - **VPN:** Use for all VPN connections. (To create a policy for a specific VPN type, see the following set of instructions, "Configuring a Custom Policy.")

   - **Dial-up:** Use for dial-up connections that use a traditional phone line or an Integrated Services Digital Network (ISDN) line.

   - **Wireless:** Use for WLAN connections only.

   - **Ethernet**: Use for Ethernet connections, such as connections that use a switch.

6. On the User or Group Access page, select one of the following:

   - **User:** User access permissions are specified in the user account.

   - **Group**: Individual user permissions override group permissions.

7. If you selected Group access in step 6, click Add to select the Windows groups who should be given access.

8. Click Next to continue.

9. On the Authentication Methods screen, place a check mark next to as many of the following methods as needed:

   • **Extensible Authentication Protocol (EAP):** If you select this method, you need to select one of two EAP types, based on your method of access and your network configuration. From the Type drop-down box, select either the Protected EAP (PEAP) option or the Smart Card or Other Certificate option.

   • **Microsoft Encrypted Authentication version 2 (MS-CHAPv2):** Select this option if your users supply a password for authentication.

   • **Microsoft Encrypted Authentication (MS-CHAP):** MS-CHAP is less secure than MS-CHAPv2. Select this option only if your network runs operating systems that do not support MS-CHAPv2.

10. Click Next when you've finished selecting and configuring authentication methods.

11. On the Policy Encryption screen, select the level of encryption that the server will accept from incoming client connections. Choose one or more of the following:

    • Basic Encryption (IPSec 56-bit DES or MPPE 40-bit)

    • Strong Encryption (IPSec 56-big DES or MPPE 56-bit)

    • Strongest Encryption (IPSec Triple DES or MPPE 128-bit)

12. Click Next to continue.

13. Click Finish to create a typical remote access policy.

Configuring a Custom Policy

To create a remote access policy based on a custom set of criteria, do the following:

1. Open the IAS MMC snap-in.

2. Right-click Remote Access Policies and select New Remote Access Policy.

3. Click Next on the wizard's initial Welcome screen.

4. On the Policy Configuration Method screen, select the Set Up a Custom Policy radio button. Enter a descriptive name in the Policy Name text box. Then click Next.

5. On the Policy Conditions screen, click Add. Specify one or more conditions that this remote access policy should check, based on the following list:

   • Authentication-Type

   • Called-Station-Id

   • Calling-Station-Id

   • Client-Friendly-Name

- Client-IP-Address

- Client-Vendor

- Day-And-Time-Restrictions

- Framed-Protocol

- NAS-Identifier

- NAS-IP-Address

- NAS-Port-Type

- Service-Type

- Tunnel-Type

- Windows-Groups

6. Click Add to select a profile condition. For each condition that you add, you will be prompted to configure the appropriate information for that condition. For example, if you select Day-And-Time-Restrictions, you'll be prompted to configure the days and times during which this policy should apply. If you select Windows-Groups, you'll be prompted for the groups that should be included.

7. Click Next when you've finished configuring remote access conditions.

8. On the Permissions screen, select either Grant Remote Access Permission or Deny Remote Access Permission. This will determine whether users who meet the criteria specified by this policy should be granted or denied access to the IAS server. Click Next to continue.

9. On the Profile screen, click Edit Profile to modify any additional settings that should apply to this policy, including the following:

- On the Authentication tab, specify the authentication methods that you will permit for this connection, including EAP, MS-CHAPv2, MS-CHAP, CHAP, PAP, SPAP, and Unauthenticated Access.

- On the Encryption tab, specify the encryption levels that you will accept from incoming clients, including Basic (MPPE 40-bit), Strong (MPPE 56-bit), Strongest (MPPE 128-bit), or No Encryption.

- On the Dial-in Constraints tab, specify idle timeouts, the maximum length of a session, and similar settings.

- On the IP tab, specify how remote access clients receive a valid IP address, as well as any inbound or outbound packet filtering for the remote connection.

- On the Multilink tab, specify whether remote clients can use multilink connections, as well as configure the Bandwidth Allocation Protocol (BAP).

- On the Advanced tab, configure RADIUS-specific attributes.

10. Click OK when you've configured the remote access profile.

11. Click Next to continue.

12. Click Finish to create the new policy.

13. If there are multiple policies configured for the IAS server, right-click the policy and click Move Up or Move Down as necessary to place it in the correct processing order.

How It Works

The IAS MMC snap-in allows you to create remote access policies that are nearly identical to those created for the RAS. You can configure remote access policies for RADIUS clients that are connecting directly to the IAS server. These policies will establish a specific set of conditions under which remote clients will (or will not) be permitted to connect to the server. You can configure remote access policies to allow or disallow client connections based on a number of conditions, including the type of authentication used by the remote client, the IP address of the remote client, the day and time of the connection attempt, and many others. You can configure multiple remote access policies to create extremely granular connection rules, such as the following:

- Disallow any client that does not connect using strong encryption.

- Allow members of the VicePresident security group to connect to the RAS server at any time of day.

- Disallow members of the Contractors security group to connect any time other than Monday through Friday 9 a.m. to 6 p.m.

An RAS or IAS server will evaluate all remote access policies in order; the server will stop as soon as it finds a matching policy.

See Also

- Recipe 5-16 for more on configuring remote access policies

- Microsoft KB 816522: "How to Enforce a Remote Access Security Policy in Windows Server 2003"

6-8. Re-creating the Default Remote Access Policy

Problem

You want to re-create the default remote access policy for an IAS server. The default remote access policy will deny all incoming remote access connection attempts.

Solution

1. Open the IAS MMC snap-in.

2. Right-click Remote Access Policies and select New Remote Access Policy.

3. Click Next on the wizard's initial Welcome screen.

4. On the Policy Configuration Method screen, select the Set Up a Custom Policy radio button. Enter **Default** in the Policy Name text box.

5. On the Policy Conditions screen, click Add. Select Day-and-Time-Restrictions. Click Add again.

6. On the Time of Day constraints screen, select the Permitted radio button, and then click OK. Click Next to continue.

7. On the Permissions screen, select the Deny Remote Access Permission radio button, and then click Next.

8. On the Profile screen, click Next (do not modify the profile associated with this policy).

9. Click Finish to complete the configuration of the policy.

10. Make sure that this policy is listed first in the processing order. Right-click the policy and select Move Up, if necessary.

How It Works

Windows Server 2003 RAS and IAS servers are configured with a default remote access policy that denies incoming connections to all remote access clients. To allow incoming connections, you need to configure additional policies that will allow specific clients to connect remotely. If you need to re-create the default policy as a troubleshooting measure or to temporarily disable remote access connectivity, simply create a policy that uses the following conditions:

- Day and time restrictions, configured for all available times

- Deny remote access permissions

- No profile information

Since remote access policies are processed in order, you then need to make sure that this policy appears first in the policy list if there is more than one policy in place.

See Also

- Microsoft TechNet: "Recreate the Default Remote Access Policy" (http://www.microsoft.com/technet/prodtechnol/windowsserver2003/library/ServerHelp/94d64ae4-fde3-4b20-9319-9f19d72313bd.mspx)

- Microsoft TechNet: "Configure a Remote Access Policy to Grant or Deny Access" (http://www.microsoft.com/technet/prodtechnol/windowsserver2003/library/ServerHelp/7f8ab3bf-fc25-4464-8024-ffc9f0404519.mspx)

6-9. Configuring Connection Request Policies

Problem

You want to configure a connection request policy on an IAS server. Connection request policies are similar to remote access policies, but they are specifically intended to manage RADIUS traffic to determine whether it should be handled locally or forwarded to a remote RADIUS server.

Solution

Configuring a Typical Connection Request Policy

To configure a typical connection request policy, do the following:

1. Open the IAS MMC snap-in.

2. Expand the Connection Request Processing node in the left pane.

3. Right-click Connection Request Policies and select New Connection Request Policy.

4. Click Next on the wizard's initial Welcome screen.

5. On the Policy Configuration Method screen, select the A Typical Policy for a Common Scenario radio button. Enter a descriptive name for the policy in the Policy Name text box. Then click Next.

6. On the Request Authentication screen, specify where connection requests that meet the criteria of this policy should be authenticated. Select one of the following options:

   • Authenticate connection requests on this server

   • Forward connection requests to a remote RADIUS server for authentication

7. If you configure this policy to authenticate requests locally, you must also specify the way in which remote users connect to the IAS server. Select from one of the following options:

   • Users connect to this server through an Internet service provider (ISP)

   • Users dial directly into this server or connect through a virtual private network (VPN)

8. Click Next to continue.

■**Note** If your users will be dialing directly into the IAS server or connecting through a VPN, the New Connection Request Policy Wizard will skip steps 9 and 10.

---

9. If you have configured this connection request policy to forward connection requests to a remote server in step 6, or if users will be connecting to this server via an ISP (step 7), you will see the Realm Name screen next. Specify the realm name that should be used to identify incoming connections. This can be in the form of a prefix, such as DOMAIN\user1, or in the form of user1@domain. If the realm name is an identifier, that is added to the existing Windows username so that Windows can authenticate the request. In that case, place a check mark next to Before Authentication, Remove the Realm Name from the User Name.

10. If you chose to have authentication requests forwarded to a remote server in step 6, select the appropriate name from the Server Group drop-down list, or click New Group to configure a new RADIUS group (see Recipe 6-10).

11. Click Next to continue.

12. Click Finish to create a new connection request policy.

13. If there are multiple policies configured for the IAS server, right-click the policy and select Move Up or Move Down as necessary to place it in the desired processing order.

Configuring a Custom Connection Request Policy

To configure a custom connection request policy, do the following:

1. Open the IAS MMC snap-in.

2. Expand the Connection Request Processing node in the left pane.

3. Right-click Connection Request Policies and select New Connection Request Policy.

4. Click Next on the wizard's initial Welcome screen.

5. On the Policy Configuration Method screen, select the A Custom Policy Radio button. Enter a descriptive name for the policy in the Policy Name text box. Then click Next.

6. On the Policy Conditions screen, select one or more conditions that incoming requests must match before being processed by the policy. Choose conditions from the following list:

   • Called-Station-Id

   • Calling-Station-Id

   • Client-Friendly-Name

   • Client-Vendor

   • Day-And-Time-Restrictions

   • Framed-Protocol

   • NAS-Identifier

   • NAS-IP-Address

- Service-Type

- Tunnel-Type

- User-Name

- Client-IP-Address

- NAS-Port-Type

7. Click Add to select a profile condition. For each condition that you add, you will be prompted to configure the appropriate information for that condition. For example, if you select Day-And-Time-Restrictions, you'll be prompted to configure the days and times to which this policy should apply.

8. Click Next when you've finished configuring connection policy conditions.

9. On the Profile screen, click Edit Profile to modify any additional settings that should apply to this policy.

10. Click OK when you've configured the connection request profile.

11. Click Next to continue.

12. Click Finish to create the new policy.

13. If there are multiple policies configured for the IAS server, right-click the policy and select Move Up or Move Down as necessary to place it in the correct processing order.

How It Works

In IAS, connection request policies contain a set of conditions and profile settings that determine how incoming RADIUS messages are handled by the IAS server. As with remote access policies, you can create multiple connection request policies so that certain RADIUS requests are processed locally, such as when IAS is being used as a RADIUS server, and other requests are forwarded to another RADIUS server. The latter configuration utilizes IAS as a *RADIUS proxy*.

You can determine whether an incoming connection should be handled locally or forwarded to a remote server based on the time of day and day of the week, the realm name being used in the request, the IP address of the requesting client, and any number of other conditions. Allowing a single IAS server to serve in both a local and proxy capacity allows you to deploy IAS to fit a number of RADIUS scenarios.

See Also

- Recipe 6-10 for configuring RADIUS server groups

- Microsoft TechNet: "Connection Request Policies" (http://www.microsoft.com/technet/prodtechnol/windowsserver2003/library/ServerHelp/32ac0173-a684-452c-af39-6fb903114103.mspx)

- Microsoft TechNet: "Processing a Connection Request" (http://www.microsoft.com/technet/prodtechnol/windowsserver2003/library/ServerHelp/e7ada3db-db30-4bf2-8efb-f128c18d47dd.mspx)

6-10. Managing RADIUS Server Groups

Problem

You want to create and manage a group of remote RADIUS servers, typically to specify a group of servers to forward client requests for processing.

Solution

Configuring a Typical RADIUS Server Group

To configure a typical RADIUS server group consisting of one primary server and one backup server, do the following:

1. Open the IAS MMC snap-in.

2. Expand the Connection Request Processing node in the left pane.

3. Right-click Remote RADIUS Server Groups and select New Remote RADIUS Server Group.

4. Click Next on the wizard's initial Welcome screen.

5. On the Group Configuration Method screen, select the Typical (one primary server and one backup server) radio button. Enter a descriptive name for the group in the Group Name text box. Then click Next.

6. In the Primary Server text box, enter the FQDN or IP address of the primary remote RADIUS server. Click Verify to make sure that the IAS server can access the remote host.

7. To configure a backup server, place a check mark next to Set Up a Backup Server for This Group, and enter the FQDN or IP address in the Backup Server text box. Click Verify to make sure that the IAS server can access the remote host.

8. Optionally, if you want to specify the shared secret to be used by this server group, enter it in the Shared Secret text box, and then reenter it in the Confirm Shared Secret text box.

9. Click Next to continue.

10. Click Finish to create the group. By default, there is a check mark next to Start the New Connection Request Policy Wizard when this wizard closes.

Configuring a Custom RADIUS Server Group

To configure a custom RADIUS server group, do the following:

1. Open the IAS MMC snap-in.

2. Expand the Connection Request Processing node in the left pane.

3. Right-click Remote RADIUS Server Groups and select New Remote RADIUS Server Group.

4. Click Next on the wizard's initial Welcome screen.

5. On the Group Configuration Method screen, select the Custom radio button. Enter a descriptive name for the group in the Group Name text box. Then click Next.

6. On the Add Servers screen, click Add to configure a new server as a member of this server group. The Add RADIUS Server dialog box will appear.

7. On the Address tab, enter the FQDN or IP address of the remote RADIUS server in the Server text box. Click Verify to make sure that the IAS server can access the remote host.

8. On the Authentication/Accounting tab, you can modify any of the following settings:

   • Authentication port

   • Shared secret used for authentication

   • Accounting port

   • Shared secret used for accounting (or specify that the same shared secret should be used for both)

   • Forward network access server Start and Stop notifications to this server

9. On the Load Balancing tab, you can modify any of the following settings:

   • The Priority setting, which indicates the status of a RADIUS server (a primary server has a priority of 1)

   • The Weight setting, which calculates how often connection requests are sent to this server versus other servers in the same group

   • Number of seconds without response before a request is considered dropped (defaults to 3)

   • Maximum number of dropped requests before server is identified as unavailable (defaults to 5)

   • Number of seconds between requests when server is identified as unavailable (defaults to 30)

10. Click OK when you've finished configuring group settings.

11. To add an additional server, click Add again. Click Next when you've added all the necessary server entries.

Note In step 11, you can also delete a server from the server group by clicking Remove or change the settings of a server you've already added by clicking Properties.

---

12. Click Finish to complete the creation of this server group. By default, there is a check mark next to Start the New Connection Request Policy Wizard when this wizard closes.

How It Works

Before you can configure an IAS server as a RADIUS proxy, you need to specify the remote RADIUS servers to which connection requests should be forwarded. The wizard allows you to quickly configure a remote server group that adheres to the most typical RADIUS server configuration; that is, a primary RADIUS server with an additional server acting as a backup to provide service continuity in case the primary server fails. Using this option will configure both servers using all default values for items such as the UDP ports that are used for authentication and authorization traffic, as well as the priority and weight of each server.

When submitting traffic to a remote server group, RADIUS will use the priority setting of each group member to determine which server to use. A server with a lower priority number will be used before a server with a higher priority number. The weight of each group member will assist in load balancing, determining how often a particular server will be used if two servers have the same priority. By default, a server group in the typical configuration will have a primary server with a priority of 1 and a weight of 50, and a backup server with a priority of 2 and a weight of 50. If the default group configuration is not sufficient for your needs, you can manually configure all aspects of the group.

Remember that the Standard Edition of Windows Server 2003 allows for a maximum of *two* remote RADIUS server groups. If you need to configure more groups, you'll need to move to the Enterprise or Datacenter Edition of Windows Server 2003, which allows for unlimited server groups.

See Also

- Microsoft TechNet: "Remote RADIUS Server Groups" (http://www.microsoft.com/technet/prodtechnol/windowsserver2003/library/ServerHelp/cccd7ee3-aeaa-4fb7-a7ba-cf808e2e9980.mspx)

- Microsoft TechNet: "Configure the Authentication and Accounting Settings of a Group Member" (http://www.microsoft.com/technet/prodtechnol/windowsserver2003/library/ServerHelp/f36d46f8-22bf-4fc4-8348-834babf82386.mspx)

- Microsoft TechNet: "Configure the Load Balancing Properties of a Group Member" (http://www.microsoft.com/technet/prodtechnol/windowsserver2003/library/ServerHelp/1b40a8a1-54f0-461f-a8df-ca4b40901dfb.mspx)

6-11. Adding RADIUS Attributes to a Remote Access Policy

Problem

You want to add RADIUS-specific attributes to an existing remote access policy.

Solution

1. Open the IAS MMC snap-in.

2. Select the Remote Access Policies node in the left pane.

3. Right-click the policy that you want to modify and select Properties.

4. From the Settings tab, click Edit Profile.

5. From the Advanced tab, click Add. You will see a long list of attributes, some of which are RADIUS standards and some that are vendor-specific. The following are the RADIUS-standard attributes:

Acct-Interim-Interval	Login-LAT-Service
Callback-Number	Login-Service
Class	Login-TCP-Port
Filter-Id	NAS-Port-Id
Framed-AppleTalk-Link	Reply-Message
Framed-AppleTalk-Network	Service-Type
Framed-Compression	Termination-Action
Framed-IP-Netmask	Tunnel-Assignment-ID
Framed-IPX-Network	Tunnel-Client-Auth-ID
Framed-MTU	Tunnel-Client-Endpt
Framed-Pool	Tunnel-Medium-Type
Framed-Protocol	Tunnel-Password
Framed-Route	Tunnel-Preference
Framed-Routing	Tunnel-Pvt-Group-ID
Login-IP-Host	Tunnel-Server-Auth-ID
Login-LAT-Group	Tunnel-Server-Endpt
Login-LAT-Node	Tunnel-Type
Login-LAT-Port	

6. In the list of available RADIUS attributes, double-click the attribute that you want to add to the profile. For each attribute that you add, you will be prompted to configure the appropriate information for that attribute. For example, if you select Day-And-Time-Restrictions, you'll be prompted to configure the days and times to which this policy should apply. Click Add when you've finished configuring the attribute.

Note By default, two profile attributes are added to every remote access policy: Service-Type is set to Framed, and Framed-Protocol is set to PPP.

---

7. Click Close when you've finished adding RADIUS attributes to the policy.

8. Click OK twice to save your changes.

How It Works

When you create a remote access policy to process RADIUS client connections, you can capture a great deal of information about the connecting client that can be used by the RADIUS server to accept, reject, or otherwise control the connection attempt. This information can be captured by the Windows Server 2003 computer itself if IAS is functioning as a RADIUS server, or it can be passed to a remote RADIUS server group if IAS is configured as a RADIUS proxy.

The attributes that you can specify include a list of RADIUS-standard attributes and a number of vendor-specific attributes that may not be supported by the RADIUS RFCs, but that can be used by specific hardware and software manufacturers such as Cisco, Microsoft, and USRobotics.

See Also

- Recipe 6-12 for defining custom RADIUS attributes

- Microsoft TechNet: "Add RADIUS Attributes to a Remote Access Policy" (http://www.microsoft.com/technet/prodtechnol/windowsserver2003/library/ServerHelp/2a041150-42f9-4a60-ab18-6de8ab231ee7.mspx)

6-12. Configuring Vendor-Specific Attributes

Problem

You want to configure a new vendor-specific attribute to control RADIUS connections based on the manufacturer of the NAS device to which the user is connecting.

Solution

1. Open the IAS MMC snap-in.

2. Select the Remote Access Policies node in the left pane.

3. Right-click the policy that you want to modify and select Properties.

4. On the Settings tab, click Edit Profile.

5. On the Advanced tab, click Add. You will see a large list of attributes, some of which are RADIUS standards and some that are vendor-specific. First verify that the attribute you wish to add does not already exist, and then double-click the Vendor-Specific attribute listed under the RADIUS Standard vendor.

6. On the Multivalued Attribute Information screen, click Add to begin adding a new vendor-specific attribute.

7. On the Vendor-Specific Attribute Information screen, select the vendor of your NAS from the Select from List drop-down box. If the vendor is not listed, select the Enter Vendor Code radio button and manually enter the vendor code for your NAS device as supplied by the vendor or as listed in RFC 1007, "SMI Network Management Private Enterprise Codes."

8. Specify whether the attribute that you are adding conforms to the RADIUS RFC specification for vendor-specific attributes. Select either the Yes, It Conforms radio button or the No, It Does Not Conform radio button.

9. Click Configure Attribute to add the vendor-specific attribute. If you are adding an RFC-compliant attribute, you will be prompted for the following on the Configure VSA (RFC compliant) screen:

- **Vendor assigned attribute number:** The numeric representation of the attribute you're defining, provided by your NAS vendor

- **Attribute format:** This format can be String, Hexadecimal, Decimal, or InetAddr

- **Attribute value:** The actual value of the attribute that this policy should check for.

10. Click OK to configure the vendor-specific attribute.

11. If you have more attributes to configure or delete, click the Add or Remove button.

12. To change the order of the vendor-supplied attributes that you've configured, click Move Up or Move Down as necessary.

13. To save your changes, click OK, and then click Close.

14. Click OK twice to update the remote access policy with the new vendor-specific attribute.

How It Works

The IAS in Windows Server 2003 comes preconfigured with hundreds of RADIUS attributes that you can use to control incoming connections, either those being processed locally or those being forwarded to a remote RADIUS group. Many of these attributes are defined in the RADIUS RFCs as standard attributes, but there are also a number of preconfigured attributes that are specific to particular vendors, such as Microsoft, Cisco, USRobotics, and Ascend Communications.

If you need to define a vendor-specific attribute in addition to the preinstalled ones, you can use the Vendor-Specific option to create a new one from scratch. First, you need to select the vendor for which you are specifying the attribute. IAS comes preconfigured with the names of the most common hardware and software vendors, or you can supply a numeric value that has been supplied to you by the vendor. You can then configure the attribute by defining its format as a string, a hexadecimal, or a decimal number.

You can arrange multiple RADIUS attributes in the appropriate order on the Multivalued Attribute Information screen to make sure that they are processed in the correct order. For example, if you've defined an attribute that you are using to automatically disconnect users who do not meet certain criteria, you should make sure that this attribute appears at the top of the list of defined attributes. You can use the Move Up and Move Down buttons to arrange vendor-specific attributes in the correct order.

See Also

- Recipe 6-11 for configuring RADIUS attributes

- Microsoft TechNet: "Sample VSA for a Cisco NAS" (http://www.microsoft.com/technet/prodtechnol/windowsserver2003/library/ServerHelp/4041ed2b-5441-4844-bc54-4f8b9d60389b.mspx)

- Microsoft TechNet: " Sample VSA for a US Robotics NAS" (http://www.microsoft.com/
  technet/prodtechnol/windowsserver2003/library/ServerHelp/
  4f2719d3-0901-4e08-936f-f9cefae5dbb1.mspx)

- IANA, "Network Management Parameters," for SMI network management private
  enterprise codes (http://www.iana.org/assignments/smi-numbers)

6-13. Configuring Remote Access Account Lockout

Problem

You want to configure remote access account lockouts on a Windows Server 2003 computer.

Solution

Using the Registry

To configure an individual computer to lock out a user account after three invalid remote
access authentication attempts, modify the following Registry value:

```
[HKEY_LOCAL_MACHINE\SYSTEM\CurrentControlSet\Services\RemoteAccess\
  Parameters\AccountLockout]
"MaxDenials"=dword:3
```

Note Set this value to 0 to disable remote access account lockouts.

To configure an individual computer to lock out a user account for 30 minutes, modify the
following Registry value:

```
[HKEY_LOCAL_MACHINE\SYSTEM\CurrentControlSet\Services\RemoteAccess\
  Parameters\AccountLockout]
"ResetTime (mins)"=dword:30
```

Note By default, the Registry Editor displays this value in hexadecimal format. Click the Decimal radio
button to enter the value normally.

Using a Command-Line Interface

The following command configures the remote access account lockout threshold to five failed
remote authentication requests:

```
> reg add HKLM\System\CurrentControlSet\Services\RemoteAccess\Parameters\
    AccountLockout /v MaxDenials /t REG_DWORD /d 5 /f
```

The following command configures the remote access account lockout duration to 60 minutes:

```
> reg add HKLM\System\CurrentControlSet\Services\RemoteAccess\Parameters\
    AccountLockout /v "ResetTime (mins)" /t REG_DWORD /d 60 /f
```

Using VBScript

This script will configure the account lockout threshold and lockout duration for an IAS server:

```
' This code configures the account lockout threshold and
' lockout duration for an IAS server
' ------ SCRIPT CONFIGURATION ------
Const HKEY_LOCAL_MACHINE = &H80000002
strComputer = "."
strKeyPath =
"SYSTEM\CurrentControlSet\Services\RemoteAccess\Parameters\AccountLockout"
dValueName = "MaxDenials"
dValue = "3"
' ------ END CONFIGURATION ---------

Set oReg=GetObject("winmgmts:{impersonationLevel=impersonate}!\\" & _
    strComputer & "\root\default:StdRegProv")

oReg.SetStringValue HKEY_LOCAL_MACHINE,strKeyPath,dValueName,dValue

dValueName = "Reset Time(mins)"
dValue = 30
oReg.SetDWORDValue HKEY_LOCAL_MACHINE,strKeyPath,dValueName,dValue
WScript.Echo "Value set."
```

How It Works

You can use the remote access account lockout feature of Windows Server 2003 RAS and IAS to specify how many times an incoming remote access connection can provide invalid authentication credentials before the user is denied access to the RAS or IAS server. This is a particularly important security feature when you are securing Internet-facing servers such as those that are hosting VPN connections, since a malicious Internet user can use the VPN connection process to perpetrate a dictionary attack against a valid user account. If you enable the remote access account lockout, this dictionary attack would be shut down after a certain number of failed logon attempts.

Remote Access Account Lockout Considerations

Before configuring remote access account lockout, you need to determine the following two configuration items:

- How many invalid logon attempts should be permitted before the user's account is locked out? You need to strike a balance between improving security by locking out potential attackers without inconveniencing legitimate users by being too stringent.

- Once a user account has been locked, how long should it remain that way? You can configure the account lockout reset time to maintain the account lockout for up to two days.

Caution The remote access account lockout feature is separate from an account lockout policy configured for a domain, and is not affected by any changes you make to Group Policy.

The reg.exe Command-Line Utility

You can use the reg.exe command-line utility to read, add, modify, or delete information from the Windows Registry. You can get a full list of available command options by typing reg /? at the command line. Type reg add /? for a fuller syntax of each individual command option. In this case, you're using the reg add command with the following switches:

HKLM\System\CurrentControlSet\Services\RemoteAccess\Parameters\AccountLockout: The location where the key is being added or modified.

/v MaxDenials: The name of the Registry key being added or modified. (Note that you need to use quotes for ResetTime—"ResetTime (mins)"—because it contains a space.)

/t REG_DWORD: The data type of the key being added or modified, in this case a DWORD value.

/d 60: The actual data being stored in the new or modified key

/f: Prompts reg.exe to overwrite any existing information; necessary to modify an existing Registry key.

See Also

- Recipe 6-14 for managing remote access account lockouts

- Microsoft TechNet: "Registry," (http://www.microsoft.com/technet/scriptcenter/scripts/os/registry/default.mspx)

- Microsoft TechNet: "Remote Access Account Lockout" (http://www.microsoft.com/technet/prodtechnol/windowsserver2003/library/ServerHelp/c03f130b-ecc8-4f71-8bb2-cf447a438a18.mspx)

- Microsoft TechNet: "Backing Up and Restoring the Registry" (http://technet2.microsoft.com/WindowsServer/en/Library/7cf151b7-03f3-45e9-9edb-ece32ba6a75f1033.mspx?mfr=true)

6-14. Managing Remote Access Account Lockouts

Problem

You want to view user accounts that have been locked by your remote access or IAS policy, and to unlock one or all of these accounts.

Solution

Using the Registry

To view the list of users whose accounts have been locked by the remote access or IAS policy, view the entries in the following Registry subkey.

```
[HKEY_LOCAL_MACHINE\SYSTEM\CurrentControlSet\Services\RemoteAccess\
Parameters\AccountLockout]
```

All locked accounts will have an entry under this key, formatted as *DomainName:AccountName*.

To unlock a user account, navigate to the same Registry key and delete the appropriate *DomainName:AccountName* entry.

Using VBScript

This script will unlock a user account:

```
' This code will unlock the account of a user named "jsmith"
' remote access account lockout
' ------ SCRIPT CONFIGURATION ------
  strLockoutKey = " SYSTEM\CurrentControlSet\Services\RemoteAccess\" & _
    "Parameters\AccountLockout"
  strDomain = "COMPANY.COM"
  strUser = "jsmith"

' ------ END CONFIGURATION ---------
Set objShell = WScript.CreateObject("WScript.Shell")

objShell.RegDelete "HKLM\" & strLockoutKey & "\" & strDomain & ":" & strUser

WScript.Echo("Account " & strUser & " unlocked")
```

How It Works

Unlike domain account lockouts that can be unlocked through the Active Directory Users and Computer graphical user interface in addition to command-line and VBScript options, remote access account lockout information is stored in the Registry of the RAS or IAS server. If you need to unlock a user account before the default reset time has elapsed, you need to navigate to the ~\Services\RemoteAccess\Parameters\AccountLockout key and delete the Registry key that corresponds to the locked-out user account. (These entries will be deleted automatically by the operating system when the account lockout reset time has elapsed.)

If you find that you are repeatedly required to unlock remote access accounts that have been locked, you may need to rethink the values that you've configured for MaxDenials and the reset time on the local IAS server. While you may initially think that it's good for security to create a very low value for a maximum number of bad passwords before accounts are locked, you need to balance this against the possibility that you may be inadvertently creating a denial-of-service attack against your own network through overly harsh lockout settings.

See Also

- Recipe 6-13 for configuring remote access account lockouts

- Microsoft TechNet: "Configuring Remote Access Account Lockout for a VPN Solution" (http://www.microsoft.com/technet/prodtechnol/windowsserver2003/library/DepKit/ 2c9f964c-5fae-4109-bd70-8a6fb65c9c69.mspx)

6-15. Creating a Quarantine IP Filter

Problem

You want to configure a remote access policy to restrict remote access on a Windows Server 2003 network that is configured for Network Access Quarantine Control (NAQC).

Solution

1. Open the IAS MMC snap-in.

2. Select the Remote Access Policies node in the left pane.

3. Right-click the policy that you want to modify and select Properties.

4. On the Settings tab, click Edit Profile.

5. On the Advanced tab, click Add.

6. On the Add Attribute screen, select the MS-Quarantine-IPFilter attribute, and then click Add.

7. On the IP Filter Attribute Information screen, click Input Filters.

8. On the Inbound Filters screen, click New to create a new input filter.

9. On the Add IP Filter screen, set the following:

   - Place a check mark next to Destination Network.

   - Enter the IP address or network number of your quarantine servers in the IP Address text box.

   - Enter the appropriate subnet mask in the Subnet Mask text box.

- In the Protocol drop-down box, select TCP.

- Enter **7250** in both the Source Port and Destination Port text boxes.

10. Click OK to return to the Inbound Filters screen.

11. For the Filter Action setting, select the Permit Only the Packets Listed Below radio button, and then click OK to return to the Add Attribute screen.

12. To add a quarantine session timer, select the MS-Quarantine-Session-Timeout attribute and click Add.

13. In the Attribute Value text box, enter the number of seconds that represents the maximum amount of time that client computers can remain connected in quarantine mode, and then click OK.

14. Click Close.

15. Click OK twice to save your changes to the remote access policy.

16. Make sure that this policy is listed first in the processing order. Right-click the policy and select Move Up if necessary.

■**Note** Once you've configured the quarantine policy as the first policy in the processing order, configure a second policy that allows normal access to your RAS server and internal network.

How It Works

One of the most exciting advances in Windows Server 2003 is NAQC. This service allows you to create a temporary "staging area" for clients who are attempting to gain access to your network, where you can determine if the computer in question meets your company's requirements for antivirus protection and software patching (not to mention a lack of spyware or worm infections) before allowing the client to access internal network resources.

IAS acts as a port of an NAQC solution by placing the necessary quarantine restrictions on incoming clients, controlling which systems the quarantined client can and cannot access. For example, if an incoming client does not have the necessary antivirus definitions, you may want to allow it access to a server that can provide it with updates, rather than simply denying that client access to your network. Once a client computer is determined to pass any necessary "health checks," IAS can then remove these quarantine restrictions and allow normal access to your network resources. You can also enable a quarantine timer that will disconnect clients after a certain amount of time, rather than allowing them to remain on the quarantined network indefinitely.

Configuring NAQC requires a significant amount of legwork before you can deploy it on a production network. Before you implement a remote access policy with quarantine IP filters and session timers on your network, you must complete the following steps:

1. Create a script that will run on the incoming client to validate its configuration.

2. Create a notification component that will inform the remote access server whether the script succeeded or failed. Alternatively, you can use the rqc.exe executable that comes with the Windows Server 2003 Resource Kit.

3. Create a *listener component* that will run on the remote access server. Once this listener receives information from the notification component that the client has passed its health checks, the listener will remove the client from quarantine and allow normal access to the network.

4. Distribute a Connection Manager profile (created with the Connection Manager Administration Kit) that includes the script and the notification component to your clients.

By default, both the notification and listener components of NAQC use port 7250, which is why you need to configure an input filter in the quarantine policy to allow this port. Otherwise, the listener and notification components would not be able to let each other know the status of the client and its health checks.

Note NAQC will be greatly improved and streamlined in the next release of Windows Server, in which it will be called *Network Access Protection* (*NAP*).

See Also

- Microsoft TechNet: "IAS Network Access Quarantine Control" (http://www.microsoft.com/technet/prodtechnol/windowsserver2003/library/ServerHelp/dba3afac-f178-46bf-9a48-350bfe7ccad8.mspx)

- Microsoft TechNet: "Network Access Protection" (http://www.microsoft.com/technet/itsolutions/network/nap/default.mspx)

6-16. Configuring RADIUS Authentication and Accounting

Problem

You want to configure a remote access server to use RADIUS for its authentication and accounting information.

Solution

Using a Graphical User Interface

1. Open the Routing and Remote Access MMC snap-in.

2. Right-click the server name for which you want to configure RADIUS authentication and accounting and select Properties.

3. On the Security tab, select RADIUS Authentication from the Authentication Provider drop-down box, and then click Configure.

4. Click Add to configure a new RADIUS authentication server.

5. Enter the IP address or FQDN of the server in the Server Name text box. Modify the following as necessary:

   - **Server name:** The FQDN or IP address of the server.

   - **Secret:** Allows you to manually specify the shared secret used to encrypt the messages sent between the RRAS server and the RADIUS server. Both the RRAS server and the RADIUS server need to be configured with the same shared secret in order for communications to be successful.

   - **Time-out:** The amount of time (in seconds) that the RRAS server will attempt to contact this RADIUS server before moving on to another configured server (defaults to 5 seconds).

   - **Initial score:** RRAS will use a RADIUS server's score to determine to which server to send messages. A RADIUS server's score is calculated based on its initial score and adjusted for its current level of responsiveness. The RADIUS server with the highest current score is the one that will be used for each client request.

   - **Port:** The UDP port being used by the RADIUS server. By default, this is port 1812 for authentication requests and 1813 for accounting messages.

   - **Always use message authenticator:** Enabling the use of the Message Authenticator provides additional security for PAP, CHAP, MS-CHAP, and MS-CHAPv2 authentication. (EAP authentication uses the Message Authenticator by default.)

6. When you have finished configuring RADIUS authentication servers, click OK.

7. Select RADIUS Accounting from the Accounting Provider drop-down box.

8. Click Add to configure a new RADIUS accounting server.

9. Enter the IP address or FQDN of the server in the Server Name text box. Modify the shared secret, time-out, initial score, and port configuration if necessary (see step 5). Optionally, place a check mark next to the Send RADIUS Accounting On and Accounting Off Messages. (This will create log information whenever the RAS is restarted.)

10. When you've finished configuring RADIUS accounting servers, click OK.

11. Click OK to save your changes to the remote access server.

Using a Command-Line Interface

The following command will add a RADIUS authentication server named `server1.mycompany.com` to the local RRAS server, using TCP port 1669 and a 10-second unavailability time-out:

```
> netsh ras aaaa add authserver name = server1.mycompany.com
  port = 1669 timeout = 10
```

The following command will add a RADIUS accounting server named `server2.`
`mycompany.com` to the local RRAS server (note that in this example, we've omitted the
optional `name =` before the server name):

```
> netsh ras aaaa add acctserver server2.mycompany.com
```

How It Works

The Windows Server 2003 RAS can use Windows authentication, such as Active Directory or a
Windows NT domain, to authenticate remote users, or it can forward authentication requests
to a RADIUS server. You can also choose to log information about successful and failed
connection attempts using the Windows accounting provider (using local log files) or by
forwarding accounting messages to a RADIUS server. In a large, heterogeneous environment,
it can be useful to configure some or all of your Windows RRAS servers to use RADIUS for one
or both of these functions. You have a great deal of flexibility in this matter, however, as you
can configure different RRAS servers or groups of servers to use different authentication and
accounting providers.

When configuring a RADIUS authentication and accounting provider, you can customize
a number of configuration details about the servers you're using.

See Also

- The Cable Guy – April 2004, "Configuring Routing and Remote Access for RADIUS
  Authentication and Accounting" (`http://www.microsoft.com/technet/community/
  columns/cableguy/cg0404.mspx`)

- Microsoft TechNet: "Security Information for Remote Access" (`http://www.
  microsoft.com/technet/prodtechnol/windowsserver2003/library/ServerHelp/
  e352f061-e9a5-4ac0-b273-921be8b7d530.mspx`)

6-17. Migrating IAS Configuration to Another Server

Problem

You want to copy the configuration information from one IAS server to another. This is often
useful in large server farms containing many IAS servers that need to be configured identically,
since it allows a standard configuration to be deployed quickly and with reduced risk of error.

Solution

Using a Command-Line Interface

The following command exports the current server's IAS configuration to a file called `c:\ias.txt`:

```
> netsh aaaa show config > c:\ias.txt
```

The following command imports the settings contained in `c:\ias.txt` into the current
server's IAS configuration:

```
> netsh exec c:\ias.txt
```

Using VBScript

This script will export the configuration of an IAS server to a text file:

```
' This script will export the configuration of
' an IAS server to a text file

set objFSO = WScript.CreateObject("Scripting.FileSystemObject")

strOutputFolder = "c:\temp"
strFileName = "ias-export.txt"
strOutputFile = strOutputFolder & "\" & strFileName

' Now execute the netsh command
set wshShell = CreateObject("WScript.Shell")
set oExec = wshShell.Exec("netsh aaaa show config > " & strOutputFile)

' To import a file into the local computer, replace the previous line
' with the following:
' set oExec = wshShell.Exec("netsh exec " & strOutputFile)

' Sit in a loop while the command is running
Do While oExec.Status = 0
  WScript.Sleep 1000
Loop

WScript.Echo("Settings export complete!")
```

How It Works

If you have a number of IAS servers configured in a server farm, it's important that each server be configured identically so that your end users will have a consistent experience, regardless of the server to which they connect. The easiest way to create an identical IAS configuration across multiple servers is to use netsh to export the configuration settings of one server into a text-based script file, and then to use the netsh exec command on the additional servers to create their configuration based on that file. By using the pipe command (> filename.txt), you are creating a binary-formatted file that can be read by a remote server to fully configure the IAS service.

In addition to exporting the configuration information for a Windows Server 2003 IAS server, you can also export the following information using netsh:

netsh show clients: Exports a list of configured RADIUS client

netsh show connection_request_policies: Exports a list of configured connection request policies only

netsh show logging: Exports only the logging configuration of the local computer

netsh show remote_access_policies: Exports the remote access policies defined on the local computer `netsh show server_settings`: Exports the server description, logging settings for authentication and accounting events in the system log, the ports used by IAS, and the remote access account lockout Registry keys

`netsh show version`: Displays the version of the IAS database

The RAS and IAS do not have a WMI provider specifically, but you can execute `netsh` commands via the WSH `Exec()` method.

See Also

- Microsoft KB 317588: "Configure a Primary Internet Authentication Service Server on a Domain Controller"

- Microsoft TechNet: "Netsh Commands for AAAA" (`http://www.microsoft.com/technet/prodtechnol/windowsserver2003/library/ServerHelp/9ffd261c-62e4-4f41-aa35-2790bd253477.mspx`)

CHAPTER 7

■■■

Internet Protocol Security (IPSec)

Similar to the TCP/IP suite, which is composed of a number of individual protocols designed to enable network communication, Internet Protocol Security (IPSec) is a collection of protocols that operate on top of TCP/IP to allow for private, secure communications over IP networks. IPSec can provide data integrity by adding a mathematical checksum to a network packet before it is transmitted. The receiver of that packet can use this checksum to confirm that the packet was not tampered with during transit, and that the packet originated from the host that it claims as its originator. IPSec can also provide for data confidentiality by encrypting data before it is transmitted over a network. This feature is especially useful when information is being transmitted over a public network such as the Internet.

In addition to its integrity and encryption features, IPSec also allows *mutual authentication* between communicating hosts. This feature is designed to protect against a so-called *man-in-the-middle* attack, where a malicious user will impersonate a legitimate host (like a domain controller) and attempt to fool you into transmitting confidential information and logon credentials because you think that you are dealing with a trusted host. Microsoft's implementation of IPSec complies with IPSec standards created by the Internet Engineering Task Force (IETF) IPsec Working Group, and is supported by the following Windows operating systems:

- Windows 2000 Professional

- Windows 2000 Server

- Windows XP Professional

- Windows Server 2003

IPSec integrates directly with Active Directory, and you can assign IPSec configuration through Group Policy, which will allow you to configure IPSec settings at the domain, site, or organizational unit (OU) level. You can also configure IPSec settings through a local computer's security policy or use the netsh utility to create full-featured IPSec configurations.

Windows Server 2003 has made a number of improvements and enhancements to IPSec, including the following:

- The NAT-Traversal (NAT-T) feature, which allows IPSec-encrypted traffic to be transmitted to and from hosts that reside behind a network address translation (NAT)-enabled firewall or proxy server

- Support for network load balancing

- Persistent policies that will protect the local computer even if a Group Policy-based IPSec policy cannot be applied

- Changes to the default IPSec exemptions, which allow more types of traffic to be secured by IPSec out of the box

Using a Graphical User Interface

To create and manage an IPSec policy that will apply only to a single computer, you'll use the IP Security Policy Management MMC snap-in. To manage IPSec policies that are stored in Active Directory, you'll use the Group Policy Editor, which is accessible via either Active Directory Users and Computers or the Group Policy Management Console.

When configuring IPSec policies via Active Directory, you can configure a separate IPSec policy within each Group Policy object (GPO). For example, this would allow computers located in the Finance OU (or some other OU containing sensitive resources) to be configured with a more stringent IPSec policy than other containers in your Active Directory domain.

Using a Command-Line Interface

The primary tool that you'll use to administer IPSec from the command line is netsh. You can use netsh commands to configure individual items on the fly, or you can combine multiple commands into a batch file. In this way, you can create an entire IPSec policy through a netsh batch file, and then use this file to configure multiple computers on your network.

7-1. Creating an IPSec Policy

Problem

You want to create an IPSec policy on a Windows Server 2003 computer.

Solution

Using a Graphical User Interface

1. Open the Group Policy Management Console or the IP Security Policy Management MMC snap-in.

2. Navigate to Computer Configuration\Windows Settings\Security Settings.

3. Right-click IP Security Policies and select Create IP Security Policy.

4. Click Next on the initial Welcome screen.

5. Enter a name for the policy in the Name text box, and enter a description in the Description field. Click Next to continue.

6. By default, you will see a check mark next to Activate the Default Response Rule. If you want to disable the default response rule, remove the check mark. Click Next.

7. If you chose to enable the default response rule, choose the authentication method to be used by the default response rule. Select from the following, and then click Next to continue.

   • Active Directory default (Kerberos v5)

   • Use a certificate from this Certification Authority (CA); then click Browse to select the certificate

   • Use this string to protect the key exchange (pre-shared key); then enter the string in the text box below

8. To create rules and filter lists to associate with this policy now, leave the check mark next to Edit Properties and click Finish. You'll be taken to the Properties page of the IPSec policy, where you'll be able to create new IPSec rules (see Recipe 7-2). To populate the policy later, remove the check mark and select Finish.

Using a Command-Line Interface

The following command creates an IPSec policy called Default IPSec Policy with the default response rule activated:

```
> netsh ipsec static add policy name = "Default IPSec Policy"
    activatedefaultrule = yes
```

The following command will rename the Default IPSec Policy to Domain IPSec Policy and adds it to the Corporate Domain Policy GPO:

```
> netsh ipsec static set store location = domain
> netsh ipsec static set policy name = "Default IPSec Policy"
    newname = "Domain IPSec Policy" gponame = "Corporate Domain Policy"
```

The following command will delete the Domain IPSec Policy that you just created:

```
> netsh ipsec static delete policy name = "Domain IPSec Policy"
```

The following command will delete all configured IPSec policies:

```
> netsh ipsec static delete all
```

Caution If your IPSec policies are assigned using Active Directory, you should unassign an IPSec policy 24 hours before deleting it. This will allow the change in assigned policies to propagate throughout Active Directory before deleting the policy. If you delete a policy that is stored in Active Directory without following this procedure, computers on your network may continue to use a cached copy of the deleted policy.

How It Works

To enable IPSec for a Windows Server 2003 computer, you must configure an IPSec policy that will apply to an individual computer or an Active Directory container. You can configure as many IPSec policies as you wish, but only one policy can be applied to a computer at any given time. (The only exception to this is *persistent policies*; see Recipe 7-17.)

Each policy provides you with almost unlimited configuration options, since it can consist of any number of individual IPSec *rules*. An IPSec rule dictates how IPSec will process a particular type of traffic (see Recipes 7-2 and 7-3). For example, you might have one rule that will block all inbound traffic on port 1433, another rule that will allow traffic to port 80 on your internal web server, and a third rule that will use a particular IPSec security method to secure traffic sent between workstations and servers. You'll combine all three of these (very different) rules into a single IPSec policy that you can then apply to a Windows Server 2003 computer.

When you're working from the command line, by default, `netsh` commands will operate against policies that are stored locally on a Windows Server 2003 computer. To manage IPSec policies that are stored in Active Directory, you need to issue the `set store location = domain` command. This will allow you to manipulate domain-based IPSec policies from the command line.

See Also

- Recipe 7-2 for managing IPSec rules

- Recipe 7-9 for assigning IPSec policies

- Microsoft TechNet: "Using Netsh Scripts to Assign IPSec Policies" (`http://www.microsoft.com/technet/prodtechnol/windowsserver2003/library/DepKit/a42bead8-0627-4b7f-a075-988308b68f3d.mspx`)

7-2. Managing IPSec Rules

Problem

You want to configure an IPSec rule to determine how the local computer should respond to traffic as part of an IPSec policy.

Solution

Using a Graphical User Interface

1. Open the Group Policy Management Console or the IP Security Policy Management MMC snap-in.

2. Navigate to Computer Configuration\Windows Settings\Security Settings\IP Security Policies.

3. Right-click the policy for which you want to configure a new rule and select Properties.

4. In the IPSec Security Rules section, remove the check mark next to Use Add Wizard, and then click Add to create a new IPSec rule.

5. On the IP Filter List tab, select the filter list that this rule should use. Each rule can apply to only a single IPSec filter. If the filter list that you require isn't listed, you can click Add to create it here.

6. On the Filter Action tab, choose the action that this rule should apply to any traffic that meets the criteria of the filter you selected.

7. On the Authentication Methods tab, select the authentication method that this rule should use. You can select Add, Edit, or Remove to modify the defined methods, or click Move Up or Move Down to change the order in which the methods will be attempted.

8. On the Tunnel Setting tab, select the This Rule Does Not Specify an IP Tunnel option if this IPSec rule uses the local computer as its endpoint. If the rule is being tunneled through another host, select the The Tunnel Endpoint Is Specified by This IP Address option and enter the endpoint IP address.

9. On the Connection Type tab, select the type of connection to which this rule should apply. You can select any one of the following:

    - All network connections

    - Local area connection (LAN)

    - Remote access

10. Click OK to save the rule.

Using a Command-Line Interface

The following command creates an IPSec rule for the Web Server policy, which blocks all traffic defined by the Port 1433 filter list:

```
> netsh ipsec static add rule name = "Block Port 1433"
    policy = "Web Server" filterlist = "Port 1433" filteraction = "Blocker"
```

The following command deletes the Block Port 1433 rule from the Web Server policy:

```
> netsh ipsec static delete rule name = "Block Port 1433" policy = "Web Server"
```

How It Works

Each IPSec policy consists of one or more IPSec rules. As the name implies, an IPSec rule will determine the behavior of a Windows Server 2003 computer configured for IPSec. Each rule consists of the following configuration items:

IPSec filter list: This is composed of one or more IPSec filters and determines which traffic will be affected by the rule.

IPSec filter action: This determines the action that the local computer will take when it encounters traffic that meets the criteria of the filter list.

Authentication method: This determines how IPSec peer computers will negotiate authentication with one another.

Since an IPSec policy can consist of more than one rule and each rule can consist of more than one filter, you may encounter a situation where a particular piece of network traffic fits the criteria of more than one rule. When this happens, Windows will apply the most specific rule out of any that are configured. So if Rule A is configured to apply to an entire IP subnet, and Rule B is configured to apply to the specific IP address, Rule B will be applied, since it is the more specific of the two. Or, in the case of two rules that contain the same value for IP addresses, ports, and protocols, but with two different filter actions, Windows will apply the rule with the more restrictive filter action. So if Rule A is configured to allow traffic to port 80 on a specific IP address and Rule B is configured to block traffic to port 80 on the same IP address, IPSec will apply Rule B and block the traffic.

See Also

- Recipe 11-8 for configuring authentication methods

- Microsoft TechNet: "IPSec Policy Rules" (http://www.microsoft.com/ technet/prodtechnol/windowsserver2003/library/ServerHelp/ 3b25ba1b-5adb-49a6-96f1-6409c84ce82b.mspx)

- The Cable Guy – February 2005, "IPSec Filtering Ordering" (http://www.microsoft.com/ technet/community/columns/cableguy/cg0205.mspx)

7-3. Managing IPSec Filter Lists

Problem

You want to create, edit, or delete an IPSec filter list.

Solution

Using a Graphical User Interface

1. Open the Group Policy Management Console or the IP Security Policy Management MMC snap-in.

2. Navigate to Computer Configuration\Windows Settings\Security Settings.

3. Right-click the IP Security Policies node and select Manage IP Filter Lists and Filter Actions.

4. On the Manage IP Filter Lists tab, do one of the following:

   - To create a new filter list, click Add. Enter the name of the list in the Name text box, and enter a longer description in the Description text box. Then click OK.

   - To delete an existing IP filter list, select the name of the filter list and click Remove.

   - To modify an existing filter list, select the name of the filter list and click Edit.

Note To modify filter lists on the local computer, use the IP Security Policy Management MMC snap-in instead of the Group Policy Editor.

Using a Command-Line Interface

The following command creates an IPSec filter list called Web Server on the local Windows Server 2003 computer:

```
> netsh ipsec static add filterlist name = "Web Server"
    description = "Protecting local HTTP traffic."
```

To modify the existing Web Server filter list, use the following command:

```
> netsh ipsec static set filterlist name = "Web Server"
```

The following command renames the filter list Web Server to Internal Web Server:

```
> netsh set filterlist name = "Web Server" newname = "Internal Web Server"
```

The following command deletes the IPSec filter list called Web Server from the local Windows Server 2003 computer:

```
> netsh ipsec static delete filterlist name = "Web Server"
```

The following command deletes all IPSec filter lists configured on a local computer:

```
> netsh ipsec static delete filterlist all
```

Caution You will not be permitted to create an IPSec filter list with the name All, since this will interfere with the netsh ipsec static delete filterlist all command.

How It Works

IPSec rules are at the heart of an IPSec policy. A rule is made up of a combination of an IPSec filter list, a filter action, and one or more authentication methods. An IPSec filter list, as the name suggests, includes one or more IP filters that can be grouped together and handled as a single unit. As an example, if you need an IPSec rule that will block all traffic to two specific IP addresses, configure a filter list consisting of two single IP filters: one that applies to each IP address. Once you have an IPSec filter list in place, you can create one or more rules to build a complete policy.

In addition to creating filter lists using the graphical user interface instructions in this recipe, you can also create one on the fly when you create an IPSec rule. Rather than adding an existing filter list to a new rule that you're creating, you can simply select Add during rule creation to configure an appropriate filter list.

See Also

- Recipe 7-2 for configuring IPSec rules

- Recipe 7-4 for configuring individual IPSec filters

7-4. Managing IPSec Filters

Problem

You want to create, edit, or delete an IPSec filter within an existing IPSec filter list.

Solution

Using a Graphical User Interface

To create an IPSec filter, follow these steps:

1. Open the Group Policy Management Console or the IP Security Policy Management MMC snap-in.

2. Navigate to Computer Configuration\Windows Settings\Security Settings.

3. Right-click the IP Security Policies node and select Manage IP Filter Lists and Filter Actions.

4. On the Manage IP Filter Lists tab, select the filter list for which you want to create a new filter and click Edit.

5. On the IP Filter List screen, remove the check mark next to Use Add Wizard, and then click Add.

6. On the Addresses tab, choose one of the following options from the Source Address drop-down box:

   - **My IP Address:** This policy will apply to any traffic originating from the local computer. This option is particularly useful when applying IPSec policies through Group Policy, so that you don't need to configure a rule for each source IP address on your network.

   - **Any IP Address:** This policy will apply to traffic originating from any computer or other device.

   - **A Specific DNS Name:** This policy will apply to any traffic originating from the fully qualified domain name (FQDN) that you specify in the Host Name text box.

   - **A Specific IP Address:** This policy will apply to any traffic originating from the numeric IP address that you specify in the IP Address text box. (You'll notice that the Subnet Mask text box is configured as 255.255.255.255 and is grayed out. A 32-bit subnet mask signifies the IP address of a single device.)

- **A Specific IP Subnet**: This policy will apply to any traffic originating from the range of IP addresses that you specify. Enter the network address in the IP Address text box, and the subnet mask of the network in the Subnet Mask text box.

- **DNS Servers <Dynamic>:** This policy will apply to any traffic originating from the Domain Name Service (DNS) servers configured for the local computer. This list of IP addresses is dynamically assigned based on the TCP/IP configuration of the computer in question.

- **WINS Servers <Dynamic>:** This policy will apply to any traffic originating from the Windows Internet Name Service (WINS) servers configured for the local computer. This list of IP addresses is dynamically assigned based on the TCP/IP configuration of the computer in question.

- **DHCP Server <Dynamic>:** This policy will apply to any traffic originating from the Dynamic Host Configuration Protocol (DHCP) server configured for the local computer. This IP address is dynamically assigned based on the TCP/IP configuration of the computer in question.

- **Default Gateway <Dynamic>:** This policy will apply to any traffic originating from the default gateway configured for the local computer. This IP address is dynamically assigned based on the TCP/IP configuration of the computer in question.

7. In the Destination Address drop-down box, select the destination IP address to which this rule should apply. You have the same configuration choices for the destination IP address as described in step 6.

8. To automatically configure the filter to apply in the opposite direction, place a check mark next to Mirrored. Match Packets with the Exact Opposite Source and Destination Addresses.

9. On the Protocol tab, select the protocol type from one of the following:

   - EGP

   - HMP

   - ICMP

   - Other

   - RAW

   - RDP

   - RVD

   - TCP

   - XNS-IDP

   - UDP

   - Any

10. If you selected TCP or UDP in step 9, select one of the following for the source port:

    • **From Any Port:** This filter will apply to traffic originating from any port.

    • **From This Port:** This filter will apply only to traffic originating from the port you specify.

11. If you selected TCP or UDP in step 9, select one of the following for the destination port:

    • **To Any Port:** This filter will apply to traffic being sent to any port.

    • **To This Port:** This filter will apply only to traffic being sent to the port you specify.

12. Click OK to save the new filter.

To edit or delete an existing filter, follow these steps:

1. Open the Group Policy Management Console or the IP Security Policy Management MMC snap-in.

2. Navigate to Computer Configuration\Windows Settings\Security Settings.

3. Right-click the IP Security Policies node and select Manage IP Filter Lists and Filter Actions.

4. Do one of the following:

    • To edit an existing filter, select the filter and click Edit.

    • To delete an existing filter, select the filter and click Remove.

Using a Command-Line Interface

The following command creates a new IP filter for the Web Server filter list, with a source IP address of my IP address (ME), a destination IP of any IP address, and a destination port of TCP 80:

```
> netsh ipsec static add filter filterlist = "Web Server" srcaddr = ME
    dstaddr = ANY protocol = TCP description = "Controlling web server traffic"
    mirrored = yes dstport = 80
```

The following command deletes the IP filter created in the previous example:

```
> netsh ipsec static delete filter filterlist = "Web Server" srcaddr = ME
    dstaddr = ANY protocol = TCP description = "Controlling web server traffic"
    mirrored = yes dstport = 80
```

Note There is not a `netsh` command syntax to modify an existing filter list.

How It Works

The IPSec filter is probably the most important component of an IPSec policy, since configuring filters correctly will mean the difference between a correctly functioning policy and one that can cripple the functionality of a network.

Configuring IPSec Filters

IPSec filters consist of the following configuration information:

- A source address (this can consist of a subnet or all IP addresses, as well as just a single IP address)

- A source port

- A destination address (this can consist of a subnet or all IP addresses, as well as just a single IP address)

- A destination port

To ease administration, you should configure IPSec filters to indicate the largest group of addresses to which they are applicable. For example, if you need to configure security for an entire network, create a filter that consists of the entire IP subnet rather than individual filters for each IP. This will allow you to add new devices to a subnet without needing to create a new filter each time.

Using the Command-Line Interface

Using the command-line interface, the `netsh ipsec static delete filter` command requires the following three parameters:

- `filterlist`

- `srcaddr`

- `dstaddr`

If you specify only the required parameters, and more than one filter meets those criteria, the `delete filter` command will delete *all* filters that meet those criteria. This is because IPSec filters, unlike filter lists, are not configured with easily identifiable name strings. You can specify one or more optional criteria to specify a particular filter more precisely.

See Also

- Recipe 7-3 for configuring IPSec filter lists

- Microsoft TechNet: "Add, Edit, or Remove IPSec Filters" (http://www.microsoft.com/ technet/prodtechnol/windowsserver2003/library/ServerHelp/ 207e34c8-f715-4aa8-8f26-e06bd1eca808.mspx)

7-5. Managing Filter Actions

Problem

You want to configure a filter action to control what the IPSec policy should do when it encounters traffic that meets the criteria of a configured IP filter.

Solution

Using a Graphical User Interface

1. Open the Group Policy Management Console or the IP Security Policy Management MMC snap-in.

2. Navigate to Computer Configuration\Windows Settings\Security Settings.

3. Right-click the IP Security Policies node and select Manage IP Filter Lists and Filter Actions.

4. On the Manage Filter Actions tab, remove the check mark next to Use Add Wizard, and then click Add.

5. On the General tab, enter a name for the action in the Name text box, and enter a description in the Description box.

6. On the Security Methods tab, select one of the following actions:

   - **Permit**: Traffic will be allowed.

   - **Block**: Traffic will be blocked.

   - **Negotiate Security**: Traffic will be secured using the methods you configure.

7. To accept unsecured incoming traffic while ensuring that all outgoing communications are secured, place a check mark next to Accept Unsecured Communication, But Always Respond Using IPSec.

8. To enable communication with other computers that do not support IPSec by allowing communications to continue if there is no response to a request for IPSec negotiation, place a check mark next to Allow Unsecured Communication with Non-IPSec-Aware Computers. Click Yes once you've read the warning message concerning the security risks inherent in allowing unsecured communications.

Note If the local computer is unable to negotiate IPSec traffic, it will attempt to renegotiate at five-minute intervals.

---

9. To configure IPSec to generate a new master key whenever a new session key is needed, place a check mark next to Use Session Key Perfect Forward Secrecy (PFS).

10. Click OK to save the filter action settings.

Using a Command-Line Interface

The following command creates a filter action called Blocker that will drop any traffic that meets the criteria specified by a filter list:

```
> netsh ipsec static add filteraction name = "Blocker"
    description = "Blocks all traffic" action = block
```

The following command creates a filter action called Fall Back to Clear that will secure traffic whenever possible, but will accept unsecured communication if necessary:

```
> netsh ipsec static add filteraction name = "Fall Back to Clear"
    action = negotiate soft = yes
```

The following command deletes the filter action called Blocker:

```
> netsh ipsec static delete filteraction name = "Blocker"
```

How It Works

Once an IPSec rule encounters traffic that meets the criteria of a particular filter within a filter list, the rule will check its configured filter action to determine what to do with the traffic in question. The following default filter actions are available in Windows Server 2003:

- Permit, which permits all traffic

- Request Security (Optional), which attempts to secure all traffic while still accepting traffic unsecured traffic

- Require Security, which will not communicate with untrusted computers

The only required configuration item for a new filter action is its name. But to make the filter list more functional, you can use the following optional parameters to configure the filter action at the command line:

description =: Configures the filter action description string.

qmpfs =[yes | no]: Dictates whether session key perfect forward secrecy is enabled. If you do not specify this option, it defaults to no.

inpass = [yes | no]: Configures the computer to accept incoming traffic that is unsecured, but to reply using IPSec-secured communications.

soft = [yes | no]: Configures the computer to fall back to unsecured communications when communicating with a device that doesn't support IPSec.

action = [permit | block | negotiate]: Configures the filter action.

qmsecmethods =: Configures the security method to be used by the negotiate filter action (see Recipe 7-6).

See Also

- Recipe 7-6 for configuring IPSec security methods

- Microsoft TechNet: "Filter Action" (http://www.microsoft.com/technet/prodtechnol/windowsserver2003/library/ServerHelp/efb378ae-8702-4ffb-b832-65641dc1d305.mspx)

7-6. Managing IPSec Security Methods

Problem

You want to configure security methods for an IPSec policy, to control how IPSec-enabled hosts will encrypt and authenticate communications with one another.

Solution

Using a Graphical User Interface

1. Open the Group Policy Management Console or the IP Security Policy Management MMC snap-in.

2. Navigate to Computer Configuration\Windows Settings\Security Settings.

3. Right-click the IP Security Policies node and select Manage IP Filter Lists and Filter Actions.

4. On the Manage Filter Actions tab, remove the check mark next to Use Add Wizard, and then click Add.

5. On the General tab, enter a name for the new security method.

6. On the Security Methods tab, select Negotiate Security.

7. In the Security Method Preference Order section, select Add to create a new security method.

8. From the New Security Method screen, choose one of the following:

   - **Integrity and encryption:** This will configure the 3DES ESP confidentiality algorithm and the SHA1 ESP integrity algorithm (no AH integrity algorithm).

   - **Integrity only:** This will configure the SHA1 ESP integrity algorithm (no AH integrity algorithm or ESP confidentiality algorithm).

   - **Custom:** This will configure the AH and ESP algorithms that you specify.

9. If you selected a Custom method in the previous step, you'll see the Custom Security Methods Settings screen. From here, configure the following settings:

   • To enable AH, place a check mark next to Data and Address Integrity Without Encryption (AH). Choose MD5 or SHA1 in the Integrity algorithm drop-down box.

   • To enable ESP, place a check mark next to Data Integrity and Encryption (ESP). Choose MD5 or SHA1 in the Integrity algorithm drop-down box, and DES or 3DES in the Encryption algorithm drop-down box.

   • In the Session key settings section, place a check mark next to either or both of the options: Generate a New Key Every *XXX* Kilobytes and Generate a New Key Every *XXX* Seconds.

10. Click OK to create the new security method.

11. Use the Move Up or Move Down buttons to change the order in which the security methods are attempted. IPSec will try to negotiate security using each defined method, starting at the top of the list and working to the bottom, until IPSec is able to successfully negotiate security.

Note Click Edit or Remove to modify or delete a security method that has already been defined.

---

12. Click OK to save your settings.

Using a Command-Line Interface

The following command creates an IPSec filter action called Custom Security that uses MD5 for ESP integrity and 3DES for ESP encryption:

```
> netsh ipsec static add filteraction name = "Custom Security" action = negotiate
    qmsecmethods = ESP[3DES,MD5]
```

How It Works

IPSec is composed of two separate protocols: the IPSec Authentication Header (AH) protocol, and the IPSec Encapsulating Security Payload (ESP) protocol. AH is used to provide authentication between hosts that are communicating with IPSec. ESP is used to provide encryption in addition to authentication.

Configuring AH and ESP

When you configure IPSec to secure information using AH, IPSec will create an *integrity check value* (ICV) on each packet before it is transmitted. The receiving computer can use this ICV to ensure that the packet has not been tampered with during transmission. (This ensures the integrity of the data being transmitted.) You can use one of two protocols to generate this ICV: Secure Hash Algorithm (SHA1) or Message Digest algorithm 5 (MD5).

You can also configure ESP to encrypt and authenticate the payload. Like AH, ESP can use SHA1 or MD5 as its integrity algorithm, and it will also use either Data Encryption Standard (DES) or Triple DES (3DES) as an encryption algorithm. The difference between AH and ESP is that AH will ensure the integrity of the entire packet for transmission, including its headers. ESP will protect only the integrity of the ESP headers and the packet payload; the rest of the headers remain unprotected.

Using the Command-Line Interface

Using the command-line interface, the `qmsecmethods` = switch requires a seemingly daunting syntax to add custom security methods, but it's quite logical once you break it into its component parts. To create a custom security method, you use one of the following three string formats:

`ESP[`*ConfAlg*`,`*AuthAlg*`]:`*k*`/`*s*: Specifies an ESP encryption and integrity algorithm, but no AH integrity algorithm. *ConfAlg* refers to the ESP encryption algorithm, and can be either DES or 3DES. *AuthAlg* refers to the ESP integrity algorithm, and can be either MD5 or SHA1. *k* refers to the kilobytes that corresponds to the Generate a New Key Every *XXX* Kilobytes Setting, and s refers to the number of seconds that correspond to the Generate a New Key Every *XXX* Seconds setting.

`AH[`*HashAlg*`]:`*k*`/`*s*: Specifies an AH integrity algorithm, but no ESP settings. *HashAlg* refers to the AH integrity algorithm, and can be either MD5 or SHA1. *k* refers to the kilobytes that correspond to the Generate a New Key Every *XXX* Kilobytes setting, and s refers to the number of seconds that correspond to the Generate a New Key Every *XXX* Seconds setting.

`AH[`*HashAlg*`+`*ESPConfAlg*`,`*AuthAlg*`]:`*k*`/`*s*: Specifies both an AH and ESP configuration. *HashAlg* refers to the AH integrity algorithm, and can be either MD5 or SHA1. *ConfAlg* refers to the ESP encryption algorithm, and can be either DES or 3DES. *AuthAlg* refers to the ESP integrity algorithm, and can be either MD5 or SHA1. *k* refers to the kilobytes that corresponds to the Generate a New Key Every *XXX* Kilobytes Setting, and s refers to the number of seconds that correspond to the Generate a New Key Every *XXX* Seconds setting.

You can specify multiple security methods in one command by separating them with spaces. Here is an example:

```
> netsh ipsec static add filteraction name = "Custom Security" action = negotiate
    qmsecmethods = ESP[3DES,SHA1] AH[MD5+ESP3DES,SHA1]
```

See Also

- Microsoft TechNet: "Security Information for IPSec" (http://www.microsoft.com/ technet/prodtechnol/windowsserver2003/library/ServerHelp/ e9ee44d6-4ac8-4626-8012-7b46a4258c05.mspx)

- Microsoft TechNet: "IPSec Architecture" (http://www.microsoft.com/technet/ itsolutions/network/security/ipsecarc.mspx)

7-7. Managing Key Exchange Settings

Problem

You want to configure key exchange settings for an IPSec policy, to define how cryptographic keys are handled during IPSec communications.

Solution

Using a Graphical User Interface

1. Open the Group Policy Management Console or the IP Security Policy Management MMC snap-in.

2. Navigate to Computer Configuration\Windows Settings\IP Security Settings.

3. Right-click the policy for which you want to configure key exchange settings and select Properties.

4. On the General tab, click Settings under the Perform Key Exchange Using Additional Settings section.

5. Place a check mark next to Master Key Perfect Forward Secrecy (PFS) to force IPSec to generate a new master key whenever it creates a new session.

6. To change the default values that define how often IPSec generates a new key, place a new value in one or both of the following text boxes:

   • Authenticate and generate a new key after every *XXX* minutes

   • Authenticate and generate a new key after every *XXX* sessions

7. To customize the security methods used by IPSec for key exchange, click the Methods button to create new security methods or modify existing methods. Click Add to create a new Internet Key Exchange method. You'll need to configure the following three settings:

   • **Integrity Algorithm:** Choose from MD5 or SHA1

   • **Encryption Algorithm:** Select DES or 3DES

   • **Diffie-Hellman Group:** Select Low (1), Medium (2), or High (2048)

8. Click OK to save your settings.

Using a Command-Line Interface

The following command creates an IPSec policy called Custom Security Policy that uses master key perfect forward secrecy:

```
> netsh ipsec static add policy name = "Custom Security Policy" mmpfs = yes
```

The following command creates an IPSec policy called Custom Security Policy that creates a new master key every 240 minutes:

```
> netsh ipsec static add policy name = "Custom Security Policy" mmlifetime = 240
```

The following command modifies an IPSec policy called Custom Security Policy to use a custom security method that uses 3DES for encryption, MD5 for integrity, and the High (2048) Diffie-Hellman group:

```
> netsh ipsec static set policy name = "Custom Security Policy"
    mmsecmethods = 3DES-MD5-3
```

How It Works

IPSec uses the Internet Key Exchange (IKE) protocol to define how computers will use IPSec to communicate with one another. This relationship is known as an IPSec *security association*, or SA. Creating an SA is a two-step process:

- In the first phase of the SA creation process, IKE creates a secure channel between the computers called an *IKE SA*, as well as generating a Diffie-Hellman key agreement. Phase 1 is also the point where the computers will authenticate with one another, using the authentication methods supported by Windows Server 2003: Kerberos, a digital certificate, or a preshared key.

Note The Diffie-Hellman key agreement protocol was developed in 1976 as a way to allow users or computers to exchange a secret key over an insecure medium such as the Internet.

- In phase 2, IKE will negotiate the SA itself, as well as generate any required security keys for IPSec and a second Diffie-Hellman key agreement.

Configuring Key Exchange Settings

In Windows Server 2003, you can specify key exchange settings for each IPSec policy, configuring a number of settings. Master key perfect forward secrecy will force IPSec to generate a new master key whenever it creates a new session. Beyond this, you can configure how often IPSec will generate a new master key based on the amount of time (in minutes) that has elapsed since the last key was created, as well as the number of sessions that the master key has generated.

Finally, you can specify the security methods that IKE will use. Similar to configuring an IPSec security method, you need to configure the encryption algorithm (DES or 3DES) and integrity algorithm (MD5 or SHA1) that IKE will use. In addition, you'll also need to configure the *Diffie-Hellman group* to be used. A Diffie-Hellman group establishes the length of the base numbers that are used during the key exchange process. Because the cryptographic strength of any key partially depends on this length, you'll use Diffie-Hellman groups to fine-tune the strength of keys you create.

Using the Command-Line Interface

The mmsecmethods = switch requires a specific syntax to specify custom security methods, but it's quite logical once you break it into its component parts. You can specify multiple security methods at the same time, each one separated by spaces:

```
> mmsecmethods = SecMethod1 SecMethod2 SecMethod3
```

The syntax to specify each method is as follows:

```
EncryptionAlgorithm IntegrityAlgorithm GroupNumber
```

The *EncryptionAlgorithm* setting can be either DES or 3DES. The *IntegrityAlgorithm* can be either MD5 or SHA1. The *GroupNumber* setting can be one of the following:

- 1 specifies a 768-bit key length (low)

- 2 specifies a 1024-bit key length (medium)

- 3 specifies a 2048-bit key length (high)

For example, the following snippet specifies two security methods: the 3DES encryption algorithm with the SHA integrity algorithm, using group number 1, and the 3DES encryption algorithm with the MD5 integrity algorithm, using group number 2.

```
> mmsecmethods = "3DES-SHA1-1 3DES-MD5-2"
```

See Also

- Recipe 7-6 for configuring IPSec security methods

- Cisco Press, "IPSec Overview Part Four, Internet Key Exchange" (http://www.ciscopress.com/articles/article.asp?p=25474&rl=1)

- RSA Security, "What is Diffie-Hellman?" (http://www.rsasecurity.com/rsalabs/node.asp?id=2248)

- Microsoft TechNet: "Define IPSec Key Exchange Settings" (http://www.microsoft.com/technet/prodtechnol/windowsserver2003/library/ServerHelp/acf4a4e2-687d-4b3e-8446-8a56731d879a.mspx)

7-8. Managing Authentication Methods

Problem

You want to configure the authentication method that is used by an IPSec rule.

Solution

Using a Graphical User Interface

1. Open the Group Policy Management Console or the IP Security Policy Management MMC snap-in.

2. Navigate to Computer Configuration\Windows Settings\IP Security Settings.

3. Right-click the policy for which you want to configure the authentication method and select Properties.

4. Select the rule that you want to modify and click Edit.

5. On the Authentication Methods tab, click Add to configure a new authentication method. You can select from one of the following:

   - **Active Directory default (Kerberos v5 protocol):** This will use Kerberos authentication between IPSec hosts.

   - **Use a certificate from this Certification Authority (CA):** This will use a public key certificate. Click Browse to select the certificate that should be used.

Note To prevent the name of the CA from being sent along with the certificate request, place a check mark next to Exclude the CA Name from the Certificate Request. Place a check mark next to Certificate to Account Mapping to enable account mapping for your certificates.

   - **Use this string (pre-shared key):** This will allow you to specify a string to be used for authentication.

Caution Preshared keys are the weakest form of IPSec authentication because the master key is less secure than when using other methods, and the key itself is stored in plain text. This method of authentication should be used only when absolutely necessary.

Using a Command-Line Interface

The following command creates an IPSec rule for the Web Server policy, which blocks all traffic defined by the Port 1433 filter list. It will use a preshared key for authentication.

```
> netsh ipsec static add rule name = "Block Port 1433"
    policy = "Web Server" filterlist = "Port 1433" filteraction = "Blocker"
    psk = 5243ab59c835d106583dfa358235
```

How It Works

The IKE protocol supports a wide variety of authentication methods for IPSec rules. The following are the supported authentication methods for Windows Server 2003:

Kerberos v5: This is the default authentication method used by Active Directory, which will authenticate computers using IPSec based on their Active Directory computer accounts.

Public key certificates: You can use a public key infrastructure (PKI) certificate from a commercial provider or from a certificate authority (CA) within your corporate network. This authentication method will rely on these PKI certificates to authenticate IPSec-enabled computers with one another.

Preshared key: In this authentication method, you manually supply a preconfigured string for each computer that is communicating using IPSec. IPSec will authenticate computers based on a master key generated using this string.

You can configure multiple authentication methods for each IPSec rule. IPSec will attempt to use each configured method in order until it is able to authenticate. If you are applying IPSec rule to computers that are authenticated by a Windows 2000 or Windows Server 2003 Active Directory domain, select the Kerberos v5 option. You should use the preshared key option only if it is absolutely necessary, since it is the weakest of the three methods—the keys generated by this method are weak, and the key string itself is stored in plain text.

See Also

- Microsoft TechNet: "Define IPSec Authentication Methods" (http://www.microsoft.com/technet/prodtechnol/windowsserver2003/library/ServerHelp/d3e4d311-32eb-4954-9cd8-6d03e4d63e53.mspx)

- Microsoft KB 323342: "How to Install a Certificate for Use with IP Security"

7-9. Assigning an IPSec Policy

Problem

You want to assign an IPSec policy to an Active Directory container so that the settings of that policy will apply to the computers in the container.

Solution

Using a Graphical User Interface

1. Open the Group Policy Management Console or the IP Security Policy Management MMC snap-in.

2. Navigate to Computer Configuration\Windows Settings\Security Settings\ IP Security Policies.

3. Right-click the security policy that you want to assign to the container and select Assign.

Using a Command-Line Interface

The following command assigns an IPSec policy called Default IPSec Policy:

```
> netsh ipsec static set policy name = "Default IPSec Policy" assign = yes
```

How It Works

Although you can define any number of IPSec policies on a local Windows Server 2003 computer or within Active Directory, you can apply the settings of only a single policy to a single computer at any given time. This process is known as *assigning* an IPSec policy. By assigning an IPSec policy to a computer or group of computers, you are indicating that the settings contained within that policy should apply to those computers.

■Note If you assign an IPSec policy when one is already assigned, the old policy will be unassigned in favor of the new one.

See Also

- Recipe 7-10 for unassigning an IPSec policy

- Microsoft TechNet: "Assign IPSec Policy" (http://www.microsoft.com/technet/ prodtechnol/windowsserver2003/library/ServerHelp/ 08231c39-157f-409c-b7d3-0c94acf09d53.mspx)

- Daniel Petri, "How Can I Configure an IPSec Policy Through GPO?" (http://www.petri.co.il/configuring_ipsec_policies_through_gpo.htm)

7-10. Removing IPSec Configuration Information

Problem

You want to remove (unassign) IPSec configuration information to troubleshoot network connectivity or return to a different configuration.

Using a Graphical User Interface

1. Open the Group Policy Management Console or the IP Security Policy Management MMC snap-in.

2. Navigate to Computer Configuration\Windows Settings\Security Settings\ IP Security Policies.

3. Right-click the security policy that you want to remove from the container and select Un-Assign.

Using a Command-Line Interface

The following command unassigns an IPSec policy called Default IPSec Policy:

```
> netsh ipsec static set policy name = "Default IPSec Policy" assign = no
```

How It Works

If you need to "turn off" the IPSec settings contained within a particular policy, you will unassign that policy. If you have assigned IPSec policies through group policy, you will need to wait for Group Policy to refresh before any changes will be reflected on the local computer. To apply changes immediately, go to the command prompt and type gpudate /force, and reboot if prompted to do so.

  If you wish to actually delete an IPSec policy that is stored in Active Directory, you should unassign the policy 24 hours before deleting it. This will allow the change in assigned policies to propagate throughout Active Directory before deleting the policy. If you delete a policy that is stored in Active Directory without following this procedure, computers on your network may continue to use a cached copy of the deleted policy.

See Also

- Microsoft TechNet: "Assign or Unassign IPSec Policy in Group Policy" (http://www.microsoft.com/technet/prodtechnol/windowsserver2003/library/ServerHelp/52b69518-ba98-4c7e-aa1d-4591ad74903a.mspx)

- Microsoft TechNet: "Assign or Unassign IPSec Policy on a Computer" (http://www.microsoft.com/technet/prodtechnol/windowsserver2003/library/ServerHelp/9e555f14-1bfa-4eba-ae93-d4d761d9d0f4.mspx)

- Microsoft TechNet: "Delete an IPSec Policy" (http://www.microsoft.com/technet/prodtechnol/windowsserver2003/library/ServerHelp/443a03ab-a870-4e1d-bc57-b80947f221ca.mspx)

7-11. Exporting an IPSec Policy

Problem

You want to export the IPSec configuration of a Windows Server 2003 computer. You can do this before making changes to save the current policy configuration to enable quick rollback, or to configure another computer with the same policy configuration.

Solution

Using a Graphical User Interface

1. Open the Group Policy Management Console or the IP Security Policy Management MMC snap-in.

2. Navigate to Computer Configuration\Windows Settings\Security Settings.

3. Right-click IP Security Policies, select All Tasks, and then select Export Policies.

4. Enter a name and a location for the export file, and then click Save.

Using a Command-Line Interface

The following command exports the current IPSec configuration to c:\temp\config.ipsec:

```
> netsh ipsec static exportpolicy c:\temp\config.ipsec
```

Note If you will be using this exported file to configure Windows 2000 computers, limit the length of the filename to 60 characters, including the path.

How It Works

In cases where you cannot use Group Policy to enforce a consistent IPSec configuration on multiple computers, you can use a single computer to create the configuration that you want, and then use the export function to create an .ipsec file based on that configuration. You can then import that file using netsh or the graphical user interface to create a consistent configuration on multiple computers.

Caution If you are using preshared keys for IPSec authentication, exporting your IPSec policies to a file might reveal the plain text of the key if the file is viewed by an unauthorized individual. This vulnerability doesn't exist if you're using Kerberos or digital certificates for IPSec authentication.

See Also

- Recipe 7-12 for importing IPSec policies

- Microsoft TechNet: "Export IPSec Policies" (http://www.microsoft.com/technet/prodtechnol/windowsserver2003/library/ServerHelp/38dcee43-6829-4331-8fce-3b9fee963e49.mspx)

7-12. Importing an IPSec Policy

Problem

You want to import a preconfigured IPSec configuration to a Windows Server 2003 computer.

Solution

Using a Graphical User Interface

1. Open the Group Policy Management Console or the IP Security Policy Management MMC snap-in.

2. Navigate to Computer Configuration\Windows Settings\Security Settings.

3. Right-click IP Security Policies, select All Tasks, and then select Import Policies.

4. Browse to the location of the .ipsec file and click Open.

Using a Command-Line Interface

The following command imports the current IPSec configuration to c:\temp\config.ipsec:

```
> netsh ipsec static importpolicy c:\temp\config.ipsec
```

How It Works

In a network environment that does not use Group Policy, you can use .ipsec files to import IPSec security policies that were configured on another computer. This feature allows you to deploy the same IPSec configuration to multiple Windows Server 2003 computers that do not use Group Policy, as well as to quickly roll back IPSec to a previous configuration.

■**Note** When you import IPSec policies, the import process will overwrite any policies configured on the local computer that have the same name as one being imported. Policies with unique names will be unaffected.

See Also

- Recipe 7-11 for exporting IPSec policies

- Microsoft TechNet: "Import IPSec Policies" (http://technet2. microsoft.com/WindowsServer/en/Library/ 38dcee43-6829-4331-8fce-3b9fee963e491033.mspx?mfr=true)

7-13. Configuring the Default Response Rule

Problem

You want to enable or disable the default response rule in an IPSec policy. The default response rule ensures that a computer will respond securely to any traffic to which no other IPSec rules apply.

Solution

Using a Graphical User Interface

1. Open the Group Policy Management Console or the IP Security Policy Management MMC snap-in.

2. Navigate to Computer Configuration\Windows Settings\Security Settings\ IP Security Policies.

3. Right-click the security policy for which you want to configure the default response rule and select Properties.

4. Do one of the following:

   - To enable the default response rule, place a check mark next to <Dynamic> IP Filter List.

   - To disable the default response rule, remove this check mark next to <Dynamic> IP Filter List.

Note If you are creating a new IPSec policy, you'll be prompted to enable or disable the default response rule during policy creation.

   - To edit the security methods or authentication methods used by the default response rule, highlight the rule and select Edit.

5. Click OK to save your changes.

Caution You cannot delete the default response rule; you can merely deactivate it. Additionally, you cannot change any properties of the rule except for the security methods and authentication methods it uses.

Using a Command-Line Interface

The following command enables the default response rule for an existing IPSec policy called Domain IPSec Policy:

```
> netsh ipsec static set policy name = "Domain IPSec Policy" activatedefaultrule = yes
```

The following command creates a new policy called Web Server Policy with the default response rule disabled:

```
> netsh ipsec static add policy name = "Web Server Policy" activatedefaultrule = no
```

Note If you do not specify a value for `activatedefaultrule` when creating a new IPSec policy, the default value is `yes`.

How It Works

When configuring an IPSec policy, you use the default response rule to ensure that a Windows Server 2003 computer will respond to all requests for secure communication, even if the request does not match any other configured IPSec rules. If the active IPSec policy does not have a rule defined for a particular computer that is requesting secure communication, the default response rule will be applied to negotiate security. So if Computer A makes a request to communicate securely with Computer B, and Computer B does not have any IPSec rules defined that match the IP address of Computer A, then Computer B will invoke the default response rule when responding to Computer A.

When configuring an IPSec policy, you cannot delete the default response rule; however, you can disable it if you do not want it to take effect. Additionally, you cannot modify the filter action defined for the default response rule; it will always use the Negotiate Security action. You can modify only two configuration items for the default response rule:

Security method: You can configure the same security methods here that you would for a custom filter action, including SHA1 or MD5 for data integrity and DES or 3DES for data encryption.

Authentication methods: You can configure the default response rule to use Kerberos v5, public key certificates, or a preshared key.

See Also

- Recipe 7-6 for configuring security methods

- Recipe 7-8 for managing authentication methods

- Microsoft TechNet: "IPSec Policy Rules" (`http://www.microsoft.com/technet/prodtechnol/windowsserver2003/library/ServerHelp/3b25ba1b-5adb-49a6-96f1-6409c84ce82b.mspx`)

7-14. Configuring IPSec Exemptions

Problem

You want to configure the types of traffic that are exempt from processing by IPSec.

Solution

Using a Command-Line Interface

The following command will configure IPSec to ignore multicast, broadcast, and Internet Security Association and Key Management Protocol (ISAKMP) traffic, but to continue to process Kerberos and Resource Reservation Protocol (RSVP) traffic:

```
> netsh ipsec dynamic set config ipsecexempt value = 1
```

Note You must reboot the computer for this change to take effect.

Using the Registry

To configure a computer to hold only ISAKMP exempt from IPSec filtering, create the following Registry value and reboot the computer:

```
[HKEY_LOCAL_MACHINE\SYSTEM\CurrentControlSet\Services\IPSec\]
"NoDefaultExempt"=dword:3
```

Using VBScript

The following script exempts multicast, broadcast, RSVP, Kerberos, and ISAKMP traffic from IPSec filtering:

```
' This code specifies that multicast, broadcast, RSVP, Kerberos,
' and ISAKMP traffic are exempt from IPSec filtering
' (This is the default configuration of Windows 2000 and Windows XP)

' ------ SCRIPT CONFIGURATION ------
  const HKEY_LOCAL_MACHINE = &H80000002
  strComputer = "."

  exemptions = 3 ' Can be set to 0, 1, 2, or 3. See How It Works for
                           ' an explanation of each setting
' ------ END CONFIGURATION ---------

Set oReg=GetObject("winmgmts:{impersonationLevel=impersonate}!\\" &_
strComputer & "\root\default:StdRegProv")

KeyPath = "SYSTEM\CurrentControlSet\Services\IPSec"
dwValue = NoDefaultExempt
oReg.SetDWORDValue HKEY_LOCAL_MACHINE,KeyPath,exemptions,dwValue
```

How It Works

When IPSec was first introduced in Windows 2000, it was not designed as a full-featured host-based firewall. Rather, it was intended to provide basic filtering functionality using source and host addresses, protocol information, and port information. IPSec in Windows 2000 created a number of traffic exemptions to enable Kerberos and quality of service (QoS) traffic, as well as exempting broadcast and multicast traffic from IPSec processing. Because some administrators were not aware of these exemptions, they often created policies that did not provide protection against attacks that use the default exemptions.

Because of this, Microsoft has removed most of these default exemptions for Windows Server 2003. You can now configure four levels of exemptions that correspond to the numeric value used in the Registry key and netsh command included in this recipe. If you need to configure your IPSec policies to coexist with ones created for Windows 2000, you may need to alter the default exemption behavior of Windows Server 2003. You can use the following four exemption configuration levels:

0: This exemption level specifies that multicast, broadcast, RSVP, Kerberos, and ISAKMP traffic are exempt from IPSec filtering. This setting was the default filtering behavior for Windows 2000 and Windows XP, and should be used only if you need to provide compatibility for computers running either of these operating systems.

1: This exemption level specifies that Kerberos and RSVP traffic are not exempt from IPSec filtering, but that multicast, broadcast, and ISAKMP traffic *are* exempt.

2: This exemption level specifies that multicast and broadcast traffic are not exempt from IPSec filtering, but RSVP, Kerberos, and ISAKMP traffic are not processed by IPSec.

3: This exemption level specifies that only ISAKMP traffic—the protocol necessary to initially negotiate an IPSec connection—will be exempt from IPSec filtering. This is the default setting for Windows Server 2003.

See Also

- Microsoft KB 810207: "IPSec Default Exemptions Are Removed in Windows Server 2003"

- Microsoft KB 811832: "IPSec Default Exemptions Can Be Used to Bypass IPSec Protection in Some Scenarios"

- Microsoft KB 253169: "Traffic That Can—and Cannot—Be Secured by IPSec"

7-15. Configuring Startup Protection

Problem

You want to configure startup protection for a Windows Server 2003 computer to protect network communications after the computer boots but before the IPSec Policy Agent starts.

Solution

Using a Graphical User Interface

1. Open the Services MMC snap-in.

2. Double-click the IPSec Services entry.

3. Choose one of the following startup types:

   • **Disabled**: The IPSec Policy Agent will not filter any incoming traffic.

   • **Manual**: The IPSec Policy Agent will not filter any incoming traffic.

   • **Automatic**: The IPSec Policy Agent will enter stateful mode, where it will permit inbound traffic in response to outbound connections initiated by the local computer.

4. Click OK to save your settings.

Using a Command-Line Interface

The following command will configure stateful protection during computer startup:

```
> netsh ipsec dynamic set config bootmode value = stateful
```

The following command will configure IPSec to block all incoming traffic during computer startup:

```
> netsh ipsec dynamic set config bootmode value = block
```

Using the Registry

To configure a computer to block traffic until an IPSec policy is applied, configure the following Registry key:

```
[HKEY_LOCAL_MACHINE\SYSTEM\CurrentControlSet\Services\IPSec\]
"OperationMode"=dword:1
```

Set this value to 0 to permit all traffic, or to 3 to configure stateful protection.

Using VBScript

The following script configures a computer to use stateful protection until an IPSec policy is applied:

```
' This code configures stateful protection on startup
' ------ SCRIPT CONFIGURATION ------
  const HKEY_LOCAL_MACHINE = &H80000002
  strComputer = "."

  bootMode = 3 ' set to 0 for permit, 1 for block.
                        ' 2 is a reserved value, 3 sets startup mode to stateful
' ------ END CONFIGURATION ---------
```

```
Set oReg=GetObject("winmgmts:{impersonationLevel=impersonate}!\\" &_
strComputer & "\root\default:StdRegProv")

KeyPath = "SYSTEM\CurrentControlSet\Services\IPSec"
ValueName = "OperationMode"
dwValue = bootMode
oReg.SetDWORDValue HKEY_LOCAL_MACHINE,KeyPath,ValueName,dwValue
```

How It Works

To understand the importance of configuring startup protection, it's necessary to understand the behavior of IPSec when a Windows Server 2003 computer boots up. This behavior can be broken down into two separate stages:

- When the computer first powers on, network access will be unavailable until both the TCP/IP driver and the IPSec driver are started and operational. This is a security enhancement in Windows Server 2003 since no network communication can take place until IPSec is "armed and ready."

- After the IPSec driver has started, the IPSec Policy Agent (listed as IPSec Services in the Services applet) will start and apply any local or GPO-enabled IPSec policies that have been configured for the local computer. However, TCP/IP traffic can be sent and received during the time period, however short, between the IPSec driver starting and the IPSec Policy Agent enabling an IPSec policy.

You set the IPSec startup mode to configure IPSec to protect the local computer until the IPSec Policy Agent is able to both start and successfully apply an IPSec policy. You can configure the IPSec Policy Agent in one of three startup modes:

Block: Drops all incoming packets until a local or domain-based IPSec policy is applied. This mode cannot be configured via the graphical user interface. You must use netsh or edit the Registry to set block mode.

Permit: Does not perform any IPSec filtering, and allows all traffic to pass unimpeded until an IPSec policy is applied. This behavior is configured by setting the IPSec Services startup mode to Disabled or Manual.

Stateful: Allows incoming traffic in response to any outgoing traffic initiated by the client. This behavior occurs when you assign an IPSec policy to the local computer and set the IPSec Services startup mode to Automatic.

■**Note** If no IPSec policy is configured for the local computer, the IPSec Policy Agent will load in permit mode, even if the service is set to Automatic startup.

IPSec will remain in startup mode until the IPSec Policy Agent is successfully loaded, at which point it enters *operational mode*. At this point, any configurations that apply to startup mode will be discarded. IPSec will then assume whatever configuration has been set through a local- or domain-configured IPSec policy or through a persistent IPSec policy configured via `netsh` (see Recipe 7-17).

See Also

- Recipe 7-16 for configuring boot mode exemptions

- Recipe 7-17 for configuring a persistent IPSec policy

- Microsoft TechNet: "Creating, Modifying, and Assigning IPSec Policies" (http://www.microsoft.com/technet/prodtechnol/windowsserver2003/library/ServerHelp/4f05f853-2eed-4ff8-b16f-e6228c050a6b.mspx)

7-16. Configuring Boot Mode Exemptions

Problem

You want to configure exemptions for IPSec startup protection. If you've configured the IPSec driver to start up using blocking mode, this will still allow access to administrative or other troubleshooting utilities.

Solution

The following command will configure the IPSec startup mode to blocking, and will configure an exception for inbound connections on TCP port 3389 for remote administration through Remote Desktop:

```
> netsh ipsec dynamic set config bootmode value = block
> netsh ipsec dynamic set config bootexemptions value=TCP:0:3389:Inbound
```

How It Works

If you configure the IPSec startup mode to block (see Recipe 7-15), all IP traffic will be dropped by the local computer until an IPSec policy is applied. This provides for a high level of security, but if an issue arises with the policy being applied, you can inadvertently cut off all communications with the computer in question. To guard against this, you can configure exemptions to the computer's startup protection using `netsh`.

The format for boot mode exemptions is as follows:

ProtocolType:SourcePort:DestinationPort:TrafficDirection

Use 0 to indicate a source or destination port of "all." So to configure a boot mode exemption that allows inbound connections to port 3389, use the following:

```
> netsh ipsec dynamic set config bootexemptions value=tcp:0:3389:inbound
```

For a boot mode exemption to allow outbound connections to TCP port 1433, use the following:

```
> netsh ipsec dynamic set config bootexemptions value=tcp:0:1433:outbound
```

See Also

- Recipe 7-15 for configuring startup protection

- Recipe 7-17 for creating a persistent IPSec policy

- Microsoft TechNet: "Understanding IPSec Driver Startup Modes" (http://
  www.microsoft.com/technet/prodtechnol/windowsserver2003/library/DepKit/
  b0b6adaa-6b38-4952-b055-14559f46e561.mspx)

7-17. Creating a Persistent Policy

Problem

You want to configure a persistent IPSec policy for a Windows Server 2003 computer. This will ensure that an IPSec policy is applied even if a Group Policy-based IPSec policy cannot be loaded.

Solution

The following command assigns a policy called Failsafe Policy and configures it as a persistent policy:

```
> netsh ipsec static set policy name = "Failsafe Policy" assign = yes
> netsh ipsec static set store location = persistent
```

How It Works

Persistent IPSec policies are a new feature in Windows Server 2003. Unlike Group Policy-assigned IPSec policies, which are stored in Active Directory, persistent polices are maintained in a Windows Server 2003 computer's local Registry and are in effect whether or not another IPSec policy can load successfully.

You can use a persistent policy to provide a unique protection configuration for one or two specific computers within an Active Directory container that has a Group Policy-based policy applied to it, as well as to provide a consistent IPSec configuration even when Group Policy or a local policy is not in use, or cannot be applied due to some error. If a persistent policy is configured for a computer that also has a local or Group Policy-based policy assigned, the persistent policy will override Group Policy to take effect. (This is the only instance where you can have more than one IPSec policy assigned to a single computer at a time.)

Caution If the persistent policy configured for a computer cannot be applied for any reason, the IPSec Policy Agent will revert to a blocking mode, where no network communication will be permitted.

See Also

Microsoft TechNet: "New Features for IPSec" (http://www.microsoft.com/
technet/prodtechnol/windowsserver2003/library/ServerHelp/
c30640b7-19e4-4750-82f6-61ca16e727d8.mspx)

7-18. Managing IPSec Hardware Acceleration

Problem

You want to enable or disable IPSec hardware acceleration on a network interface card (NIC). If you have hardware acceleration enabled on an NIC, you may wish to temporarily disable it as a troubleshooting measure.

Solution

Using a Command-Line Interface

The following command will disable IPSec hardware acceleration on a Windows Server 2003 computer:

```
> reg add HKLM\system\currentcontrolset\services\ipsec /v EnableOffload
    /t REG_DWORD /d 0 /f
```

Using the Registry

To disable IPSec hardware acceleration on a Windows Server 2003 computer, configure the following Registry key and reboot the target computer:

```
[HKEY_LOCAL_MACHINE\SYSTEM\CurrentControlSet\Services\IPSec\]
"EnableOffload"=dword:0
```

Set this value to 1 to reenable hardware acceleration.

Using VBScript

The following script disables hardware acceleration on a Windows Server 2003 computer:

```
' This code disables IPSec hardware acceleration on the local computer
' ------ SCRIPT CONFIGURATION ------
  const HKEY_LOCAL_MACHINE = &H80000002
  strComputer = "."

  accelerationEnabled = 0 ' set to 1 to enable
' ------ END CONFIGURATION ---------

Set oReg=GetObject("winmgmts:{impersonationLevel=impersonate}!\\" &_
strComputer & "\root\default:StdRegProv")

KeyPath = "SYSTEM\CurrentControlSet\Services\IPSec"
ValueName = "EnableOffload"
dwValue = accelerationEnabled
oReg.SetDWORDValue HKEY_LOCAL_MACHINE,KeyPath,ValueName,dwValue
```

How It Works

If there is a disadvantage to using IPSec, it is that the addition of integrity and encryption to each network packet can increase the processor usage on an IPSec-enabled computer. You can combat this by using network adapters that are capable of performing some of the "heavy lifting" involved with IPSec on the NIC itself (similar to the SSL acceleration feature available on other cards), rather than shunting the work off to the processor of the local computer. This feature is known as *hardware acceleration*, and consists of a few components:

- Offloading the calculation of IPSec cryptographic functions (*IPSec offload*)

- Calculating TCP checksums (*checksum offload*)

- Processing large TCP segments for very fast transmission (*large-send offload*)

If a Plug-and-Play NIC is capable of performing hardware offload, the card's driver will advertise this capability to TCP/IP and IPSec when its driver initializes. TCP/IP and IPSec will then automatically offload tasks to the NIC as needed.

For the most part, hardware acceleration is a useful process that does not require administrative intervention. However, if you are having network communication difficulties, you may wish to temporarily disable this feature to eliminate it as a source of the trouble. You can disable TCP/IP and IPSec hardware acceleration, IPSec hardware acceleration only, or all hardware offload functions enabled by the NIC driver. In the latter two cases, you'll need to reboot the target computer for the change to take effect. (You can disable TCP/IP and IPSec hardware acceleration without a reboot.)

See Also

- Microsoft TechNet: "IPSec Troubleshooting Tools" (http://www.microsoft.com/ technet/prodtechnol/windowsserver2003/library/ServerHelp/ ebcbc96d-b236-401d-a98b-91c965a3d18f.mspx)

- Microsoft TechNet: "How IPSec Works" (http://www.microsoft.com/ technet/prodtechnol/windowsserver2003/library/TechRef/ 8fbd7659-ca23-4320-a350-6890049086bc.mspx)

7-19. Restoring the Default IPSec Configuration

Problem

You want to restore the IPSec configuration of a Windows Server 2003 computer to the default values.

Solution

The following command restores the Windows Server 2003 policy examples for the local computer:

```
> netsh ipsec static restorepolicyexamples release = Win2003
```

■**Caution** You can restore only the default policy examples for a local computer. This procedure will not work for IPSec policies stored in Group Policy.

How It Works

If you've configured a number of IPSec policies on a Windows Server 2003 computer, it might be necessary to "wipe the slate clean" if that computer is being moved into another physical location on the network or is being migrated to serve a different logical role in your network infrastructure. By using the `restorepolicyexamples` command, you revert to the three IPSec policies that are installed by default on a Windows Server 2003 computer: Permit, Request Security (Optional), and Require Security. Any changes that you've made to these policies will be overwritten by this process.

The only drawback to this technique is that it is applicable to only IPSec policies that are stored locally. You cannot use this command to affect IPSec policies that are stored in Active Directory. For this reason, it is best not to directly edit the three default IPSec policies in Active Directory; rather, create new IPSec policies to meet your needs. This way, if you need to "start over" with your Active Directory policies for any reason, you have the three default policies in a pristine and unaltered state that you can restore at any time.

See Also

- Recipe 7-1 for creating an IPSec policy

- Microsoft TechNet: "Restore Default IPSec Policies" (http://www.microsoft.com/technet/prodtechnol/windowsserver2003/library/ServerHelp/1063886e-afca-4ea5-969d-2436946bc421.mspx)

7-20. Displaying IPSec Information

Problem

You want to view details of the current IPSec configuration that has been applied to a Windows Server 2003 computer. This should be your first step when troubleshooting network communication issues that you suspect are related to an IPSec policy.

Solution

Using a Graphical User Interface

1. Open the IP Security Monitor MMC snap-in,

2. Navigate to IP Security Monitor\\<*ServerName*>\\Active Policy. In the right pane, you'll see the following information:

   - Policy name

   - Policy description

- Policy last modified

- Policy store, which specifies whether the policy is being stored in Active Directory or in the Local Security Policy

- Policy Path, which specifies the file system or Active Directory path in which the active policy resides

- Organizational Unit, which specifies the OU in which the computer resides, if applicable

- Group Policy Object Name

3. For additional information on IPSec filters that are in place, navigate to Quick Mode\ Generic Filters. Double-click an individual filter to see the details of the filter definition.

4. For additional information and statistics on the security negotiation process, click the Quick Mode\Negotiation Policies node.

5. For IPSec performance statistics, click the Quick Mode\Statistics node.

Using a Command-Line Interface

The following command creates a file named display.txt that contains a detailed description of the current IPSec configuration:

```
> netsh ipsec static show all > display.txt
```

The following command will display debugging information and statistics about the IPSec negotiation process:

```
> netsh ipsec dynamic show all
```

How It Works

When troubleshooting communication issues on a network that has been configured for IPSec, you need to determine if IPSec itself is the cause of the failure, or if the failure occurs at another point in the network stack. The quickest way to determine if your IPSec configuration is the cause of a network failure is to temporarily disable the active IPSec policy to see if it corrects the issue, although this obviously has the negative side effect of removing IPSec security protection from your network.

If you've determined that IPSec is creating communications difficulties on your network, further troubleshooting will be aided by obtaining as much information about your current IPSec configuration as possible. You can use the tools listed in this recipe to obtain configuration and performance information about the IPSec policy of a computer running Windows Server 2003.

Using a Graphical User Interface

The IP Security Monitor is an MMC snap-in that is installed by default on Windows Server 2003 computers. It provides a graphical view of IPSec statistics, including the name and description of the active IPSec policy, the GPO that IPSec has been configured through, and the configuration details of specific filters that are in place.

■**Note** You can also use the built-in Network Monitor utility to obtain a capture of all traffic being sent to and from a local Windows Server 2003 computer. You can view this captured information through the Network Monitor, or save it to a text file for further analysis.

Using a Command-Line Interface

Regardless of the technology that you're working with, an important troubleshooting step is obtaining an accurate snapshot of your computer's current configuration. The netsh ipsec static show all and netsh ipsec dynamic show all commands will display information similar to the following:

```
FilterAction Details
--------------------


FilterAction Name        : NONE
Description              : NONE
Store                    : Local Store <OREILLY1>
AllowUnsecure(Fallback): NO
Inbound Passthrough      : NO
QMPFS                    : NO
Last Modified            : 7/31/2005 10:24:41 AM
GUID                     : {50B5FC20-0F4B-4852-BF6C-C192134F66E7}
Security Methods
   AH          ESP                         Seconds       kBytes
   ---         ---                         -------       ------
[NONE]    [SHA1 , 3DES]                       0            0
[NONE]    [MD5  , 3DES]                       0            0
[NONE]    [SHA1 , DES]                        0            0
[NONE]    [MD5  , DES]                        0            0
[SHA1]    [NONE , NONE]                       0            0
[MD5 ]    [NONE , NONE]                       0            0

Policy Name              : Server (Request Security)
Description              : For all IP traffic, always request security using K...
Store                    : Local Store <OREILLY1>
Last Modified            : 7/21/2005 11:11:30 AM
GUID                     : {72385230-70FA-11D1-864C-14A300000000}
Assigned                 : NO
Polling Interval         : 180 minutes
MainMode LifeTime        : 480 minutes / 0 Quick Mode sessions
Master PFS               : NO
```

```
Main Mode Security Method Order
   Encryption     Integrity     DH Group
   ----------     ---------     --------
     3DES           SHA1         Medium(2)
     3DES           MD5          Medium(2)
     DES            SHA1         Low(1)
     DES            MD5          Low(1)
```

See Also

- Microsoft TechNet: "IPSec Troubleshooting" (http://www.microsoft.com/technet/prodtechnol/windowsserver2003/library/ServerHelp/b0b726fc-c6b7-426a-964f-9c7b1c8ef3a8.mspx)

- Microsoft TechNet: "IPSec Troubleshooting Tools" (http://www.microsoft.com/technet/prodtechnol/windowsserver2003/library/ServerHelp/ebcbc96d-b236-401d-a98b-91c965a3d18f.mspx)

CHAPTER 8

■ ■ ■

Network Printing

For the sake of clarity, we need to provide some working definitions for the components of network printing. This is because the terms are very similar in construct, yet have important functional differences. The following terms will be used throughout this chapter:

Print device: This is the hardware that prints the electronic data onto paper or other printable media. Examples of print devices include laser, inkjet, and dot-matrix printers.

Print server: This is the system to which the print device is attached. It is accessible from other devices on the network and provides the functionality (services) needed to convert documents into printed paper. The print server can include an operating system, such as Windows 2003 Server, or it can be a hardware device such as a Hewlett-Packard (HP) JetDirect device that has its own embedded operating system.

Print driver: This is the software that provides the interaction between the print device and either the print server or the system requesting print services. Print drivers are typically available at the device manufacturer's website, or may be included with the print server operating system. Print drivers are typically available for the most common Windows operating systems, including Windows 95 and later.

Print spooler: This is the operating system service that stores and processes print jobs.

Printer: This is the overall, logical concept of the print device and its print driver that attaches it to a print server. Local printers are attached directly to your print server or are otherwise referenced through a local port, such as LPT1. Network printers are mapped to print devices attached to some form of network server and are most commonly referenced through network shares, such as *ServerName**ShareName*, or through TCP/IP ports, such as IP_192.168.0.2.

So now that we've provided a description of basic printing concepts, we still need to provide a working definition of *network printing*. For the purposes of this chapter, we will define network printing as the ability to print from a workstation to any nonlocal (remote) printer. The remote printer may be attached directly to the network, or it may be attached to a system functioning as a print server. In either case, sharing the printer from a print server allows you to take advantage of Windows security. Network printing will ideally support multiple platforms, including the latest versions of Windows, UNIX, Macintosh, and NetWare.

Printers shared on the network are preferable to local printers in small- to large-sized businesses, since you can centrally administer and configure them. Print processing occurs relatively quickly when sending a job directly to a printer, and the location of the print device is independent of its proximity to a server or workstation. The only requirement is a connection to the network, either wired or wireless.

Active Directory provides Group Policy support for network printing, and printers can be configured for or by members of a particular security group. In addition, the printers can be registered, or published, in Active Directory, providing a convenient method for end users to locate print devices that meet their needs.

Using a Graphical User Interface

All recipes that involve network printer management using a graphical user interface will refer to functionality accessible from the Printers and Faxes Control Panel applet. Most network print functionality can be accessed through the graphical user interface.

Using a Command-Line Interface

Network printing is typically managed from the command line using `printui.dll`, a component that is installed with Windows Server 2003. You invoke `printui.dll` by running the `rundll32` command, following the basic, case-sensitive syntax:

```
> rundll32 printui.dll, PrintUIEntry /parameters
```

To view the complete documentation of `PrintUI`, type the following:

```
> rundll32 printui.dll, PrintUIEntry /?
```

You can also access the online user's guide and reference at `http://www.microsoft.com/windowsserver2003/techinfo/overview/printuidll.mspx`.

Using the Registry

A number of entries in the Registry allow you to modify parameters needed to configure printers and related settings. All entries to which we will refer are located at the following key:

```
HKEY_LOCAL_MACHINE\SYSTEM\CurrentControlSet\Control\Print
```

We provide the usual warning when editing the Registry: Do so with care. Changing a value or key incorrectly can leave your system in an unusable state.

Using VBScript

Microsoft provides a number of scripts to manage network printing. These scripts are located in `%systemroot%\system32`. The following scripts are provided:

- `Prndrvr.vbs`, for administering printer drivers

- `Prnjobs.vbs`, for controlling print jobs

- `Prncnfg.vbs`, for reading or setting printer configuration

- `Prnqctl.vbs`, for printing a test page, pausing/resuming a printer, and managing print queues

- Prnmngr.vbs, for adding and deleting printers, listing printers and connections, and reading and setting the default printer

- Prnport.vbs, for reading and managing standard TCP/IP ports

- PrnAdmin.vbs, for calling other scripts to manage local and remote printers, including managing the following:

  - Printer connections

  - Forms

  - Ports

  - Drivers

  - Print jobs

  - General configuration

Note The PrnAdmin.vbs script is not installed by default. It is available in the Windows 2000 or 2003 Resource Kit.

8-1. Configuring the Server Spool Directory

Problem

You want to set or move the folder used by the Print Spooler service.

Solution

Using a Graphical User Interface

1. Open the Printers and Faxes administrative window.

2. Select File ➤ Server Properties.

3. Select the Advanced tab.

4. Enter the path of the folder that you want to use for the spool, such as e:\printspool.

5. Click OK to save your settings.

6. Restart the Print Spooler service (see Recipe 8-8).

Using the Registry

You can set or move the folder used by the Print Spooler service by modifying the following Registry value:

```
[HKEY_Local_Machine\System\CurrentControlSet\Control\Print\Printers\]
"DefaultSpoolDirectory"="<YourSpoolDirectory>"
```

Replace *<YourSpoolDirectory>* with the path to the directory, such as e:\printspool. Restart the Print Spooler service after you've made the change (see Recipe 8-8).

How It Works

Always set the print spooler directory on a drive that has ample free space to accommodate the jobs that are sent by users to the print device.

In addition to configuring the print spooler directory on a global basis, you can configure a printer-specific spool directory from the Registry by creating a SpoolDirectory value within the following key:

```
HKEY_LOCAL_MACHINE\SYSTEM\CurrentControlSet\Control\Print\Printers\<Printer-Name>\
```

For example, set the following value to configure the spool directory for your HP LaserJet 1300 printer at e:\spools\LaserJet1300Spool:

```
[HKEY_LOCAL_MACHINE\SYSTEM\CurrentControlSet\Control\Print\Printers\LaserJet1300\]
"SpoolDirectory"="e:\spools\LaserJet1300Spool"
```

Similar to its global counterpart, SpoolDirectory should be a string value and contain the path to the actual directory.

See Also

- Microsoft KB 137503: "Default Windows Spool Directory and Permissions." This article describes the permissions necessary on the spool folder.

- Microsoft KB 123747: "Moving the Windows Default Paging and Spool File." This article is about the process as it relates to earlier versions of Windows.

8-2. Creating and Configuring TCP/IP Printer Ports

Problem

You want to create a TCP/IP port or configure an existing one for your network printer.

Solution

Using a Graphical User Interface

To create a TCP/IP printer port, do the following:

1. Open the Printers and Faxes administrative window.

2. Select File ➤ Server Properties.

3. Select the Ports tab.

4. Click the Add Port button.

5. Select Standard TCP/IP Port.

6. Click the New Port button to start the Add Standard TCP/IP Printer Port Wizard.

7. Click the Next button.

8. Enter the IP address or the name of the printer. If you enter a valid IP address, the wizard will automatically name the port using the format IP_<Address>, such as IP_192.168.0.20. You can also enter a more meaningful name if desired.

9. Click the Next button. The wizard will attempt to locate the printer that you specified. If the printer is found, proceed to step 12.

10. If the device is not found, you will have the option of selecting the device type. You can select from a drop-down list of preconfigured devices, such as HP JetDirect, and then proceed to step 12. Alternatively, you can customize the type by selecting the Custom option and clicking the Settings button.

11. If you selected the option to customize the device type in the preceding step, follow these steps:

    a. Select the TCP protocol that you want to use. If you select RAW, provide the port number. The default value is 9100, which appears in the Port field. If you select LPR, provide a queue name and indicate whether you want to enable LPR byte counting.

    b. Select the option to enable Simple Network Management Protocol (SNMP), if desired, providing a community name and a device index.

    c. Click OK.

12. Click the Next button, and then click Finish.

To configure an existing TCP/IP printer port, do the following:

1. Open the Printers and Faxes administrative window.

2. Select File ➤ Server Properties.

3. Select the Ports tab.

4. Select the port that you want to configure.

5. Click the Configure Port button.

6. Configure the desired options, as described in step 11 in the preceding instructions.

Using the Registry

You can create a TCP/IP printer port by creating a new Registry subkey. Create a subkey with the desired name of your printer port. Create the subkey at the following key:

```
[HKEY_LOCAL_MACHINE\SYSTEM\CurrentControlSet\Control\Print\Monitors\
Standard TCP/IP Port\Ports\<YourNewPrinterPortName>]
```

Create the following values under the new subkey:

```
"IPAddress"="<YourPortIPAddress>"
"Protocol"=dword:<PortValue>
"SNMP Community"="<YourSNMPCommunityName>"
"SNMP Enabled"=dword:<EnabledFlag>
"SNMP Index"=dword:<YourSNMPIndex>
"Queue"="<QueueName>"
"PortNumber"=dword:<YourPortNumber>
"Double Spool"=dword:<DoubleSpoolEnabledFlag>
```

Protocol may take a value of either 1 (RAW port) or 2 (LPR port). SNMP Enabled may take a value of either 0 (disabled) or 1 (enabled). SNMP Index is required only if this port is SNMP-enabled. Double Spool may take a value of 0 (disabled) or 1 (enabled).

For example, to create a TCP/IP RAW port named IP_192.168.2.10 with an IP address of 192.168.2.10, enter the following information into the Registry. The port number will be the default value of 9100 (0000238c in hexadecimal notation), and SNMP will be disabled on this port.

```
Registry Editor Version 5.00
[HKEY_LOCAL_MACHINE\SYSTEM\CurrentControlSet\Control\...
    ...Print\Monitors\Standard TCP/IP Port\Ports\IP_192.168.2.10]
"IPAddress"="192.168.2.10"
"PortNumber"=dword:0000238c
"Protocol"=dword:00000001
"SNMP Community"="public"
"SNMP Enabled"=dword:00000000
"SNMP Index"=dword:00000001
```

To configure an existing port, modify the existing value/data pairs in the port's subkey as necessary.

Using VBScript

You can create a TCP/IP port or modify an existing one by executing prnport.vbs, located in the %systemroot%\system32 directory. Use the following syntax:

```
> cscript prnport.vbs {-a | -t} -r <PortName> [-s <RemoteComputer>] -h <IPAddress>
    [-u <UserName> -w <Password>] [-o {raw -n <PortNumber>| lpr}] [-q <QueueName>]
    [-m{e | d}] [-I <IndexName>] [-y <CommunityName>] [-2{e | d}] [-t]
```

Here is a description of the parameters:

-a | -t: Required parameter that tells the script that you intend to create or modify a standard TCP/IP printer port. Use -a to create a new port; use -t to configure an existing one.

-r PortName: Required parameter that specifies the port to which the printer is connected.

-s *RemoteComputer*: Optional parameter that specifies the name of a remote computer to which you want to add the port. If this parameter is omitted, the port will be added to the local print server.

-h *IPAddress*: Required parameter that indicates the IP address that you want to assign to the port.

-u *UserName*: Optional parameter that provides a username with permissions to create the port on a host. If you use this parameter, you must also specify the -w *Password* parameter.

-w *Password*: Optional parameter that provides a password to be used in conjunction with the -u *UserName* parameter.

-o {raw –n *PortNumber*| lpr}: Optional parameter that indicates whether you want to use the TCP RAW or the TCP LPR protocol. If you select TCP RAW, you must also specify a port number. The default port number is 9100.

-q *QueueName*: Optional parameter that specifies the name that you want to assign to the TCP RAW port.

-m {e | d}: Optional parameter that specifies whether SNMP is enabled. A value of e indicates that SNMP is enabled; a value of d indicates it is disabled.

-I *IndexName*: Optional parameter that specifies the SNMP index name.

-y *CommunityName*: Optional parameter that specifies the SNMP community name.

-2 {e | d}: Optional parameter that specifies whether a double spool is enabled for a TCP LPR port. A value of e indicates that double spooling is enabled; a value of d indicates it is disabled.

For example, the following script creates a TCP/IP printer port named IP_192.168.0.10 with an IP address of 192.168.0.10. The port is created using the Administrator account for credentials. The port type will be TCP RAW at port 9100, and the port will have a queue named MyQueue. Double spooling will be disabled.

```
> cscript prnport.vbs -a -r IP_192.168.0.10 -h 192.168.0.10 -u Administrator
    -w MyPassword -o {raw -n 9100} -q MyQueue –m d
```

How It Works

Although printers can be connected directly to Windows Server 2003 through LPT1 and then shared for network-wide access, most printers in business environments are attached directly to the network, using either a typical network interface card (NIC) or a non-Windows server, such as an HP JetDirect card. For nonlocal printers, the TCP/IP port provides the communication channel between the Windows server, the printer share, and the printer, or between the workstations and the printer (if the printer is mapped directly rather than through a server-based share).

The troubleshooting process for network printing frequently points to TCP/IP issues, and therefore a sound knowledge of basic networking is required to resolve any issues. A setting that is typically inadequately configured is that of the IP address on the printer. If a printer is configured to use Dynamic Host Configuration Protocol (DHCP) to acquire its address, then full loss of connectivity can occur if the address changes but the port is not updated to reflect this change. Therefore, it is recommended to either configure the printer with a static IP address or let it use DHCP but with a reservation created for that printer on the DHCP server. It is also helpful to define a company standard that states that all printers will have addresses within a certain range, such as between 192.168.0.10 and 192.168.0.20.

See Also

- Microsoft KB 814586: "The Standard Port Monitor for TCP/IP in Windows Server 2003." The article describes how to install the standard port monitor. The standard port monitor connects clients to network printers that use the TCP/IP protocol.

- Microsoft TechNet: "How Network Printing Works" (http://technet2.microsoft.com/ WindowsServer/f/?en/Library/d58ce7b9-49cf-4f5e-95e9-1ade005c13e01033.mspx). This article provides descriptions and explanations of terminology, architecture, protocols, and port assignments related to network printing.

- Microsoft TechNet: "Printer Connectivity Technical Overview" (http://www.microsoft. com/windowsserver2003/techinfo/overview/connectivity.mspx)

8-3. Deleting a TCP/IP Printer Port

Problem

You want to delete a TCP/IP port used by your network printer.

Solution

Using a Graphical User Interface

1. Open the Printers and Faxes administrative window.

2. Select File ➤ Server Properties.

3. Select the Ports tab.

4. Select the port that you want to delete.

5. Click the Delete button.

6. Click Yes when prompted for confirmation.

Using the Registry

You can delete a TCP/IP printer port by deleting the following key from the Registry:

```
HKEY_LOCAL_MACHINE\SYSTEM\CurrentControlSet\Control\Print\Monitors\
Standard TCP/IP Port\Ports\<YourPrinterPortToDelete>
```

For example, to delete a port named IP_10.0.0.20, locate and delete the key at the following:

```
HKEY_LOCAL_MACHINE\SYSTEM\CurrentControlSet\Control\Print\Monitors\
Standard TCP/IP Port\Ports\IP_10.0.0.20
```

Using VBScript

You can delete a TCP/IP port used by your network printer by executing prnport.vbs, located in the %systemroot%\system32 directory. Use the following syntax:

```
> cscript prnport.vbs -d -r <PortName> [-s <RemoteComputer>]
    -h <IPAddress> [-u <UserName> -w <Password>]
```

Here is a description of the parameters:

- d: Required parameter that tells the script that you intend to delete a standard TCP/IP printer port.

-r PortName: Required parameter that specifies the port to which the printer is connected.

-s RemoteComputer: Optional parameter that specifies the name of a remote computer from which you want to delete the port. If this parameter is omitted, the port will be deleted from the local print server.

-u UserName: Optional parameter that provides a username with permissions to delete the port from a host. If you use this parameter, you must also specify the -w Password parameter.

-w Password: Optional parameter that provides a password to be used in conjunction with the -u UserName parameter.

For example, to delete a TCP/IP printer port named IP_192.168.0.10 from the local host using the supplied Administrator credentials, run the following command:

```
> cscript prnport.vbs -d -r IP_192.168.0.10 -u Administrator -w MyPassword
```

How It Works

You will typically delete TCP/IP printer ports when you retire network printers from operation or when you make significant changes to their configuration and want to start with a new port and its default settings. Windows will not allow you to delete the port if it is in use. Therefore, if you want to delete the port but continue to use the printer, you must first assign a new port to the printer, and then delete the original port.

See Also

Microsoft TechNet: "How Network Printing Works" (http://technet2.microsoft.com/WindowsServer/f/?en/Library/d58ce7b9-49cf-4f5e-95e9-1ade005c13e01033.mspx). This article provides descriptions and explanations of terminology, architecture, protocols, and port assignments related to network printing.

8-4. Listing All TCP/IP Ports and Displaying Configuration Information

Problem

You want to list all TCP/IP ports on a print server and display configuration information regarding specific ports.

Solution

The graphical user interface and command-line interface solutions are limited, because you must select properties of each port individually. We recommend the VBScript solution described in this recipe, because it allows you to easily see all the configuration information.

Using a Graphical User Interface

1. Open the Printers and Faxes administrative window.

2. Select File ➤ Server Properties.

3. Select the Ports tab.

4. Select the desired TCP/IP port, and then click the Configure Port button to view its configuration information.

Using a Command-Line Interface

Open a command-prompt window by selecting Start ➤ Run and typing cmd in the dialog box. Then type the following code into the command-prompt window to invoke the Print Properties window with the Ports tab selected:

```
> rundll32 printui.dll,PrintUIEntry /s /t1 /n \\PrintServerName
```

The following are the parameters in the preceding command:

/s: Displays server properties.

/t#: Defines the interface page or tab on which to start. Replace the pound sign (#) with the appropriate integer.

/n: Provides the printer name, which immediately follows the parameter and should be formatted in UNC notation.

For example, to invoke the print server properties for a server named Print3, type the following:

```
> rundll32 printui.dll,PrintUIEntry /s /t1 /n \\Print3
```

Select the desired TCP/IP port, and then click the Configure Port button to view its configuration information.

Using VBScript

You can list all TCP/IP ports for your print server by executing prnport.vbs, located in the %systemroot%\system32 directory. Use the following syntax:

```
> cscript prnport.vbs -l [-s <RemoteComputer>][-u <UserName> -w <Password>]
```

Here is a description of the parameters:

-l: Required parameter that specifies that you want to generate a list of TCP/IP printer ports.

-s *Remote Computer*: Optional parameter that specifies the NetBIOS name of the remote printer whose ports you want to list. If this parameter is omitted, the local server will be displayed.

-u *UserName* -w *Password*: Optional parameters that provide credentials needed to perform the desired action.

For example, you can list all ports on the print server named Print2 by running the following command:

```
> cscript prnport.vbs -l -s Print2
```

If you do not want to list all the TCP/IP ports on your print server, you can display configuration information for a specific port by executing prnport.vbs:

```
> cscript prnport.vbs -g -r <PortName> [-s <RemoteComputer>]
    [-u <UserName> -w <Password>]
```

Here is a description of the parameters:

-g: Required parameter that specifies that you want to display the configuration information for a particular port.

-r *PortName*: Required parameter that specifies the name of the port whose configuration you want to display.

-s *RemoteComputer*: Optional parameter that specifies the NetBIOS name of the remote printer containing the port whose configuration you want to display. If this parameter is omitted, the local server will be assumed.

-u *UserName* -w *Password*: Optional parameters that provide credentials needed to perform the desired action.

For example, you can display configuration information for TCP/IP port IP_192.168.2.10 on the server named Print3 by executing prnport.vbs as follows:

```
> cscript prnport.vbs -g -r IP_192.168.2.10 -s Print3
```

How It Works

Create a list of all TCP/IP printer ports and their configuration when you need a comprehensive view of the network printing setup on a given device. You can easily generate reports on a per-machine or per-network basis by putting the results into a database or spreadsheet.

See Also

Microsoft TechNet: "How Network Printing Works" (http://technet2.microsoft.com/WindowsServer/f/?en/Library/d58ce7b9-49cf-4f5e-95e9-1ade005c13e01033.mspx). This article provides descriptions and explanations of terminology, architecture, protocols, and port assignments related to network printing.

8-5. Sharing and Publishing a Printer

Problem

You want to share a printer so that it is accessible over the network and publish it in Active Directory.

Solution

Using a Graphical User Interface

1. Open the Printers and Faxes administrative window.

2. Right-click the printer that you want to share and select Properties.

3. Select the Sharing tab.

4. Select the option to Share This Printer and provide a share name.

5. Select the option to List in Directory if you want to publish this printer in Active Directory.

6. Click Apply or OK to save your settings.

Using a Command-Line Interface

You can share and publish a printer from the command line using the following commands:

```
> rundll32 printui.dll,PrintUIEntry /Xs /n <PrinterName> Sharename <ShareName>
> rundll32 printui.dll,PrintUIEntry /Xs /n <PrinterName> Attributes shared
> rundll32 printui.dll,PrintUIEntry /Xs /n <PrinterName> Attributes published
```

The following are the parameters in the preceding command:

/Xs: Instructs the utility to set printer settings.

/n: Provides the printer name, which immediately follows the parameter and should be formatted in UNC notation.

For example, to share and publish a printer named HP LaserJet 1300 with the share name of HRPrinter, execute the following:

```
> rundll32 printui.dll,PrintUIEntry /Xs /n "HP LaserJet 1300" Sharename "HRPrinter"
> rundll32 printui.dll,PrintUIEntry /Xs /n "HP LaserJet 1300" Attributes shared
> rundll32 printui.dll,PrintUIEntry /Xs /n "HP LaserJet 1300" Attributes published
```

Using the Registry

You can share a printer by modifying the following Registry value:

```
[HKEY_LOCAL_MACHINE\SYSTEM\CurrentControlSet\Control\Print\Printers\<PrinterName>\]
"ShareName"="<YourShareName>"
```

Replace *<PrinterName>* with the name of your printer, and replace *<YourShareName>* with the desired share name.

Here is an example:

```
[HKEY_LOCAL_MACHINE\SYSTEM\CurrentControlSet\Control\Print\Printers\
HP LaserJet 1300\]
"ShareName"="Accounting Printer"
```

When you've finished, restart the Print Spooler service (see Recipe 8-8).

Using VBScript

You can share a network printer and publish it in Active Directory by executing the prncnfg.vbs script, located in your %systemroot%\system32 directory. Use the following syntax to create the share:

```
> cscript prncnfg.vbs -t -p <PrinterName> [-s <RemoteComputer>]
    [-u <UserName> -w <Password>] -h <ShareName> {+ | - }shared {+ | -}published
```

Here is a description of the parameters:

-t: Required parameter that indicates that you are going to configure the printer.

-p *PrinterName*: Required parameter that specifies the name of the printer that you are about to share. Enclose the printer name in quotation marks.

-s *RemoteComputer*: Optional parameter that specifies the name of the host if the share is on a remote system. Enclose the hostname in quotation marks.

-u *UserName* -w *Password*: Optional parameters that provide the credentials needed to take the action on the desired host. Enclose both the username and the password in quotation marks.

-h *ShareName*: Required parameter that specifies the share name. Enclose the share name in quotation marks.

+ | - shared: Parameter that specifies whether you plan to create or delete the share. The plus symbol (+) indicates that you will create the share. The parameter is optional in the overall syntax of prncnfg.vbs, but we will consider it required in this case, since part of the goal of this recipe is to share the printer.

+ | - published: Parameter that specifies whether the printer will be published in Active Directory. The plus symbol (+) indicates that you will publish the printer. The parameter is optional in the overall syntax of prncnfg.vbs, but we will consider it required in this case, since part of the goal of this recipe is to publish the printer.

For example, to share and publish a printer named HP LaserJet 1300 PCL 5e hosted on PrintServer2 using the share name HR Printer and using the Administrator credentials, run the following command:

```
> cscript prncnfg.vbs -t -p "HP LaserJet 1300 PCL 5e" -s "PrintServer2"
    -u "Administrator" -w "MyPassword" -h "HR Printer" +shared +published
```

How It Works

Although you can configure TCP/IP ports directly on workstations and let them print to devices through that channel, this offers no advantage in terms of centralized administration. Each user is equal in terms of access to the printer, and printing is completed on a first-come, first-served basis.

A more efficient solution for most organizations is to create a network share on a print server. You can then configure permissions on this share so that specific users or groups can manage the printer, while others can only print to it, or perhaps not even access it at all. In addition, you can manage its queue much more efficiently than you could if you had to visit each workstation.

Other advantages of sharing printers from a server include the ability to create multiple, logical printers for the same print device, each with a unique configuration. For example, you might create Printer1, which is accessible to members of the CorporateGuests groups only during business hours, and Printer2, which is accessible to CorporateManagement at all times of day.

In addition to sharing the printer, it is also convenient to publish it in Active Directory. This fairly straightforward technique allows users to quickly find the printer based on different criteria when conducting searches of the directory.

See Also

- Microsoft KB 234619: "Publishing a Printer in Windows Active Directory." This article describes how to publish printers in Active Directory, even when hosted on non-Windows 2000 or 2003 servers.

- Microsoft KB 303161: "How to Create a Container to List Printers in Active Directory." This article discusses a convenient method to create containers for printer objects in Active Directory. By doing this, users can either find the folder that contains the printers in My Network Places or add a network place to the folder that contains the printers.

- Microsoft TechNet: "Best Practices for Deploying Printer Location with Active Directory" (http://technet2.microsoft.com/WindowsServer/f/?en/Library/ f33624bc-7518-4c2d-8f73-8a3d4571dae91033.mspx)

8-6. Configuring General Printer Settings

Problem

You want to configure general printer settings, such as comment and location labels, separator text, and time periods during which the printer cannot be accessed.

Solution

Using a Graphical User Interface

1. Open the Printers and Faxes administrative window.

2. Right-click the printer that you want to configure and select Properties.

3. Select the General tab.

4. Enter descriptive text in the Location and Comment fields.

5. Select the Advanced tab.

6. Select options as follows:

   - Select an option to either make the printer always available or specify the time range during which the printer will be available.

   - Select the priority of the printer queue with regard to the spooler service.

   - Select an option to either print directly to the printer or to spool documents prior to printing. If you select the spooling option, further customize this option by selecting an option to either start printing after the last page is spooled or to start printing immediately.

   - Select the check box if you want to hold mismatched documents.

   - Select the check box if you want to print spooled documents before nonspooled ones.

   - Select the check box if you want to retain printed documents. If you select this option, be certain to pay close attention to available disk space.

7. Click the OK button to save your settings.

Using a Command-Line Interface

You can use the command line to configure printer settings. To do so, use the following command-line syntax:

```
> rundll32 printui.dll,PrintUIEntry /Xs /n <PrinterName> Comment <YourComment>
> rundll32 printui.dll,PrintUIEntry /Xs /n <PrinterName> Location <YourLocation>
> rundll32 printui.dll,PrintUIEntry /Xs /n <PrinterName> Priority <PriorityNumber>
> rundll32 printui.dll,PrintUIEntry /Xs /n <PrinterName> Attributes DoCompleteFirst
```

Here is a description of the parameters:

/Xs: Instructs the utility to set the printer settings.

/n *PrinterName*: Required parameter that specifies the name of the printer. Enclose the printer name in quotation marks.

Comment: Optional parameter that provides descriptive text for the general comment property of the printer.

Location: Optional parameter that provides descriptive text for the location property of the printer.

Priority: Optional parameter that specifies the priority of this printer with regard to the Print Spooler service.

Attributes DoCompleteFirst: Optional parameter that tells the system to spool the entire document before starting the print process.

Here is an example:

```
> rundll32 printui.dll,PrintUIEntry /Xs /n "HP LaserJet 1300"
    Comment "Human Resources Printer"
> rundll32 printui.dll,PrintUIEntry /Xs /n "HP LaserJet 1300"
    ·Location "Second Floor HR Office"
> rundll32 printui.dll,PrintUIEntry /Xs /n "HP LaserJet 1300" Priority 5
> rundll32 printui.dll,PrintUIEntry /Xs /n "HP LaserJet 1300"
    Attributes DoCompleteFirst
```

Using the Registry

You can configure printer-specific settings by modifying the following values in the Registry:

```
[HKEY_LOCAL_MACHINE\SYSTEM\CurrentControlSet\Control\
Print\Monitors\Printers\<PrinterName>\]
"Description"="<Descriptive comment text>"
"Location"="<Descriptive location text>"
"Priority"=dword:<PriorityNumber>
"Separator File"="<Path to separator file>"
"StartTime"=dword:<Start time of printer availability>
"UntilTime"=dword:<End time of printer availability>
```

The Description field should contain text for the general comment property of the printer. The Location field should contain text for the location property of the printer. Print queues with higher priority numbers receive their jobs before print queues with lower priority numbers. The path to the separator file should point to a text-formatted file containing the content to be printed on separator pages. The text file should have an .sep file extension, and the path should be in the format c:\SomeDirectory\separatorpage.sep.

Using VBScript

You can configure a network printer by executing the prncnfg.vbs script from your %systemroot%\system32 directory. This is the same script as used in the previous recipe, but you call it with different parameters. Use the following syntax:

```
> cscript prncnfg.vbs -t [-s <RemoteComputer>] -p <PrinterName>
    [-u <UserName> -w <Password>] [-r <PortName>] [-l <Location>]
    [-m <Comment>] [-f <SeparatorText>] [-st <StartTime>]
    [-ut <EndTime>] [-o <Priority>] [{+ | - }direct] [{+ | - }queued]
    [{+ | - }keepprintedjobs] [{+ | - }enabledevq]
```

Here is a description of the parameters:

-t: Required parameter that indicates that you are going to configure the printer.

-p *PrinterName*: Required parameter that specifies the name of the printer that you are configuring. Enclose the printer name in quotation marks.

-s *RemoteComputer*: Optional parameter that specifies the name of the host if the share is on a remote system. Enclose the hostname in quotation marks.

-u *UserName* -w *Password*: Optional parameters that provide the credentials needed to take the action on the desired host. Enclose both the username and the password in quotation marks.

-r *PortName*: Optional parameter that specifies the port to which the printer is connected, such as LPT1, COM1, or IP_<*IPAddress*>.

-l *Location*: Optional parameter that provides descriptive text for the location property of the printer. Enclose the text in quotation marks.

-m *Comment*: Optional parameter that provides descriptive text for the general comment property of the printer. Enclose the text in quotation marks.

-f *SeparatorText*: Optional parameter that points to a text-formatted file that contains the content to be printed on separator pages. The text file should have an .sep file extension. Enclose the text in quotation marks.

-st *StartTime* -ut *EndTime*: Optional parameters that specify the start and the end of the period during which the printer is available. Documents sent to the printer outside this interval will be held in the queue until the interval starts again. Enter the start and stop time in 24-hour format, such as 900 for 9:00 a.m. or 2100 for 9:00 p.m.

-o Priority: Optional parameter that specifies the priority of this printer with regard to the Print Spooler service. A print queue with a higher priority number receives its jobs before a print queue with a lower priority.

+ | - Direct: Optional parameter that specifies that documents should be sent directly to the printer without being spooled. Use the plus symbol (+) to enable this feature; use the minus symbol (-) to disable it.

+ | - Queued: Optional parameter that specifies that jobs should not be printed until the final page has been queued (spooled). Use the plus symbol (+) to enable this feature; use the minus symbol (-) to disable it.

+ | - KeepPrintedJobs: Optional parameter that specifies that the Print Spooler service should retain print jobs even after they have been printed. Use the plus symbol (+) to enable this feature; use the minus symbol (-) to disable it. If you configure the printer to retain jobs, be certain to pay close attention to available disk space.

+ | - EnableDevq: Optional parameter that specifies whether mismatched documents should be held in queue or printed. Use the plus symbol (+) to enable this feature; use the minus symbol (-) to disable it.

For example, to set some of the general configuration settings for a printer named HP LaserJet 1300 PCL 5e, run the following command:

```
> cscript prncnfg.vbs -t -p "HP LaserJet 1300 PCL 5e" -l "First Floor Hallway"
    -m "This printer is for HR only" -st 0800 -ut 1700 -Direct
    +Queued -KeepPrintedJobs
```

The printer will have a location field of First Floor Hallway, a general comment of "This printer is for HR only," and print availability only between the hours of 8 a.m. and 5 p.m. Documents will be spooled rather than going directly to the printer, held in queue until the final page has been spooled, and will not be retained once they are printed.

How It Works

You can configure a large number of settings for each printer. One of the more difficult chores in server management is re-creating printers and the appropriate settings if a print server is to be decommissioned or rebuilt. Microsoft has a convenient utility called the Print Migrator that will back up all printer-related settings to a CAB file and then allow you to restore these settings on a different machine from the same CAB file. As of this writing, the latest release of Print Migrator is version 3.1, which includes full support for Windows Server 2003 and previous versions of Windows, and includes a graphical user interface, as well as full command-line functionality.

See Also

Microsoft TechNet: "Microsoft Windows Server 2003 Print Migrator 3.1" (http://www.microsoft.com/WindowsServer2003/techinfo/overview/printmigrator3.1.mspx)

8-7. Listing, Installing, and Deleting Printer Drivers

Problem

You want to manage printer drivers on your system or on a remote system. In particular, you want to list all drivers that are in use, install a driver, or delete one or all unused drivers.

Solution

Using a Graphical User Interface

1. Open the Printers and Faxes administrative window.

2. Select File ➤ Server Properties.

3. Select the Drivers tab and click the Add button to start the wizard.

4. Click Next.

5. Select the manufacturer and model of the printer driver that you want to install. If the driver does not exist in the list, you can browse to its location in the file system by clicking the Have Disk button.

6. Click the Next button after you've selected the driver.

7. Select the processor and operating system of all computers that will be using this driver.

8. Click Next, and then click Finish to complete the wizard.

Using a Command-Line Interface

You can use `printui.dll` from the command line to manage printer drivers.

To add or delete a printer driver, run the following command:

```
> rundll32 printui.dll,PrintUIEntry [/ia | /dd] /c <MachineName> /m <DriverName>
    /h <Environment> /v <Version>
```

Here is a description of the parameters:

`/ia | /dd`: Required parameter that specifies that you will be installing or deleting a driver. Use `/ia` to install a driver; use `/dd` to delete the driver.

`/c` *MachineName*: Optional parameter that specifies the name of the machine to which you will be installing or from which you will be deleting the driver. If omitted, the local system will be assumed. Use UNC notation for this parameter.

`/m` *DriverName*: Optional parameter that specifies the name of the printer driver. This can either be an INF file or the friendly name that appears in the Browse list. Enclose the driver name in quotation marks.

`/h` *Environment*: Optional parameter that specifies the operating environment on the system on which the driver will be installed. Enclose the environment value in quotation marks. The environments and their corresponding versions (the `/v` switch) are as follows:

- `Windows NT x86` (supports versions 1, 2, and 3)

- `Windows NT Alpha_AXP` (supports versions 1 and 2)

- `Windows IA64` (supports version 3)

- `Windows NT R4000` (supports version 1)

- `Windows NT PowerPC` (supports version 1)

- `Windows 4.0` (supports version 0)

`/v` *Version*: Optional parameter that specifies the operating system version that will support this printer driver. A value of 0 corresponds to Windows 95, 98, or ME; a value of 1 corresponds to Windows NT 3.51; a value of 2 corresponds to Windows NT 4.0; and a value of 3 corresponds to Windows XP, 2000, or 2003. If omitted, the version of Windows on which the printer driver will be installed is used.

For example, to add the `AGFA-Accuset v52.3` printer driver to a machine named Voyager running Windows XP Professional in a Windows NT x86 environment, run the following command:

```
> rundll32 printui.dll,PrintUIEntry /ia /c \\Voyager /m "AGFA-AccuSet v52.3"
    /h "Windows NT x86" /v 3
```

Using VBScript

To manage printer drivers, use the prndrvr.vbs script in your %systemroot%/system32 directory.
You can list all drivers in use by invoking prndrvr.vbs with the -l switch:

```
> cscript prndrvr.vbs -l [-s <RemoteComputer>] [-u <UserName> -w <Password>]
```

Here is a description of the parameters:

-l: Required parameter that indicates that you want to generate a list of installed
printer drivers.

-s *RemoteComputer*: Optional parameter that specifies the NetBIOS name of the computer
whose drivers you want to list.

-u *UserName* -w *Password*: Optional parameters that provide credentials necessary to
perform the desired action.

For example, you can list the installed printer drivers on a server named PrintServer3 using
the Administrator credentials by running the following command:

```
> cscript prndrvr.vbs -l -s PrintServer3 -u Administrator -w MyPassword
```

The results will look like the following:

```
c:\> prndrvr.vbs -l -s PrintServer3 -u Administrator -w MyPassword

Microsoft (R) Windows Script Host Version 5.6
Copyright (C) Microsoft Corporation 1996-2001. All rights reserved.

Server name
Driver name hp LaserJet 1300 PCL 5e,3,Windows NT x86
Version 3
Environment Windows NT x86
Monitor name HP Master Monitor
Driver path C:\WINDOWS\system32\spool\DRIVERS\W32X86\3\UNIDRV.DLL
Data file C:\WINDOWS\system32\spool\DRIVERS\W32X86\3\HPC13005.GPD
Config file C:\WINDOWS\system32\spool\DRIVERS\W32X86\3\UNIDRVUI.DLL
Help file C:\WINDOWS\system32\spool\DRIVERS\W32X86\3\UNIDRV.HLP
Dependent files
 C:\WINDOWS\system32\spool\DRIVERS\W32X86\3\HPCUI05.DLL
 C:\WINDOWS\system32\spool\DRIVERS\W32X86\3\HPSMAC05.GPD
 C:\WINDOWS\system32\spool\DRIVERS\W32X86\3\HPCEVT05.DLL
```

You can install or delete a driver by invoking prndrvr.vbs with either the -a or -d switch:

```
> cscript prndrvr.vbs {-a | -d} -m <DriverName> [-v {0 | 1 | 2 | 3}]
    [-e <Environment>] [-s <RemoteComputer>] [-h <Path>]
    [-i <FileName.inf>] [-u <UserName> -w <Password>]
```

Here is a description of the parameters:

-a | -d: Required parameter that specifies whether you will install (-a) or delete (-d) the driver.

-m *DriverName*: Required parameter that specifies the name of the driver that you want to install. Driver names are frequently the same name as the printer, and should be provided in the printer documentation. Enclose the driver name in quotation marks.

-v {0 | 1 | 2 | 3}: Optional parameter that specifies the operating system version that will support this printer driver. A value of 0 corresponds to Windows 95, 98, or ME; a value of 1 corresponds to Windows NT 3.51; a value of 2 corresponds to Windows NT 4.0; and a value of 3 corresponds to Windows XP, 2000, or 2003. If omitted, the version of Windows on which the printer driver will be installed is used.

-e *Environment*: Optional parameter that specifies the operating environment on the system on which the driver will be installed. Enclose the environment value in quotation marks. The environments and their corresponding version (the -v switch) are as follows:

- Windows NT x86 (supports versions 1, 2, and 3)

- Windows NT Alpha_AXP (supports versions 1 and 2)

- Windows IA64 (supports version 3)

- Windows NT R4000 (supports version 1)

- Windows NT PowerPC (supports version 1)

- Windows 4.0 (supports version 0)

-s *RemoteComputer*: Optional parameter that specifies the NetBIOS name of the computer whose drivers you want to list. Enclose the computer name in quotation marks.

-h *Path*: Optional parameter that specifies the path to the driver file. If omitted, the path to the location from which Windows was installed will be used. This parameter is used only if you are installing the driver, not deleting it.

-i *FileName*.inf: Optional parameter that specifies the name of the driver file that will be used. If omitted, the selection will default to ntprint.inf. This parameter is used only if you are installing the driver, not deleting it.

-u *UserName* -w *Password*: Optional parameters that provide credentials necessary to perform the desired action.

For example, to add version 3 of the printer driver named Color Printer Driver 1 to the local computer running Windows XP Professional and which offers a Windows NT x86-based environment, type the following:

```
> cscript prndrvr.vbs -a -m "Color Printer Driver 1" -v 3 -e "Windows NT x86"
```

To delete the same driver, type the following:

```
> cscript prndrvr.vbs -d -m "Color Printer Driver 1" -v 3 -e "Windows NT x86"
```

How It Works

The most common issues related to network printing typically fall into the categories of connectivity or driver compatibility. Although this recipe has described different methods to list, install, and delete printer drivers, it is still necessary to take care when selecting the driver that you plan to use on your system.

You should routinely check or update printer drivers on your server, just as you do for any component that should be updated as part of routine maintenance. The printer manufacturer traditionally provides drivers on its website. If the manufacturer is trustworthy (a judgment call that only you can make), you can probably proceed to download and install the updated driver. However, if the manufacturer does not have a solid reputation, you should take caution and search the Internet for any reports of problems caused by the driver. Optionally, you can often download Microsoft-certified printer drivers directly from Microsoft via the Windows Update or Microsoft Update services.

See Also

- Microsoft KB 315285: "Windows 95, Windows 98, Windows 98 Second Edition, and Windows Me Print Drivers Are Removed If You Upgrade from Windows NT to Windows Server 2003, Standard Edition or Enterprise Edition." This article discusses driver-related issues that you may encounter if upgrading from Windows NT Server 4.0 to Windows Server 2003.

- Microsoft KB 888046: "You Receive an Error Message When You Try to Install a Shared Network Printer on a Windows Server 2003-Based or Windows XP SP1-Based Computer." This article addresses issues related to interactions between third-party printer drivers and shared printers.

- Microsoft TechNet: "Choosing the Right Printer Drivers" (`http://technet2.microsoft. com/WindowsServer/f/?en/Library/41249604-bd14-41a2-b3e1-67f3a7685e831033.mspx`). This article provides guidelines for the driver selection process.

8-8. Stopping and Starting the Print Spooler Service

Problem

You want to stop or start the Print Spooler service.

Solution

Using a Graphical User Interface

1. Start the Services Control Panel applet from the Administrative Tools folder in the Start menu.

2. Select the Print Spooler service.

3. Select the Action menu, and then select one of the following options:

- Stop to stop the Print Server service

- Start to start the Print Server service

- Restart to restart the Print Server service

Using a Command-Line Interface

To stop the Print Spooler service, type the following in the command window:

```
> net stop spooler
```

To start the Print Spooler service, type the following in the command window:

```
> net start spooler
```

Using VBScript

To stop the Print Spooler service on the local computer, put the following code into a VBS file:

```
'This code will stop the print spooler service
'---SCRIPT CONFIGURATION ---
strComputer = "."
'---END CONFIGURATION---
Set objWMIService = GetObject("winmgmts:" _
    & "{impersonationLevel=impersonate}!\\" & strComputer & "\root\cimv2")
Set colServiceList = objWMIService.ExecQuery _
        ("Select * from Win32_Service where Name='Spooler'")
For each objService in colServiceList
     errReturn = objService.StopService()
Next
WScript.Echo ("Script Complete")
```

To start the Print Spooler service on the local computer, use the following script:

```
'This code will start the print spooler service
'---SCRIPT CONFIGURATION---
strComputer = "."
'---END CONFIGURATION---
Set objWMIService = GetObject("winmgmts:" _
    & "{impersonationLevel=impersonate}!\\" & strComputer & "\root\cimv2")
Set colServiceList = objWMIService.ExecQuery _
        ("Select * from Win32_Service where Name='Spooler'")
Set colServiceList = objWMIService.ExecQuery _
    ("Select * from Win32_Service where Name='Spooler'")
For each objService in colServiceList
     errReturn = objService.StartService()
Next
WScript.Echo ("Script Complete")
```

To restart the Print Spooler service on the local computer, combine the previous two code segments into a single script, as follows:

```
'This code will start the print spooler service
'---SCRIPT CONFIGURATION---
strComputer = "."
'---END CONFIGURATION---
Set objWMIService = GetObject("winmgmts:" _
    & "{impersonationLevel=impersonate}!\\" & strComputer & "\root\cimv2")
Set colServiceList = objWMIService.ExecQuery _
        ("Select * from Win32_Service where Name='Spooler'")
For each objService in colServiceList
    errReturn = objService.StopService()
Next
Set colServiceList = objWMIService.ExecQuery _
    ("Select * from Win32_Service where Name='Spooler'")
For each objService in colServiceList
    errReturn = objService.StartService()
Next
WScript.Echo ("Script Complete")
```

Note that even though the preceding code sends the command to the local computer, you can perform this action on any computer to which you have access by modifying the value of strComputer. For example, if the remote computer is named Sales, modify the first line to read like this:

```
strComputer = "Sales"
```

How It Works

You may want to stop and start the Print Spooler service for the following reasons:

- You have made changes to network printers or to the server configuration and these changes are not visible to clients. Even though, ideally, most changes should not require that the service be restarted, the reality is that this is sometimes necessary.

- The printer queue is not despooling documents to the print device due to some technical problem. Restarting the Print Spooler service will typically clear documents from the queue so that you can start with a clear printer.

8-9. Pausing, Resuming, and Clearing Printer Queues

Problem

You want to manage the printer queue on your system or on a remote system. In particular, you want to pause or resume the printer, or clear all documents from its queue.

Solution

Using a Graphical User Interface

1. Open the Printers and Faxes administrative window.

2. Right-click the name of the printer that you want to manage and select one of the following:

   • To temporarily hold on documents in queue (pause the printer), select Pause Printing.

   • To resume printing, select Resume Printing.

   • To delete all documents in the queue, select Cancel All Documents.

Using VBScript

You can pause, resume, or clear a printer queue in VBScript by invoking the prnqctl.vbs script, located in the %systemroot%\system32 directory. Use the script with the following parameters:

```
> cscript prnqctl.vbs {-z | -m | -x} [-s <RemoteComputer>]
    -p <PrinterName> [-u <UserName> -w <Password>]
```

Here is a description of the parameters:

-z | -m | -x: Required parameter that specifies the action that you want to take. The -z parameter pauses the printer; the -m parameter resumes printing; and the -x parameter deletes all jobs from the queue.

-s *RemoteComputer*: Optional parameter that specifies the name of the server whose printer you want to manage. If omitted, the local server will be assumed. Enclose the server name in quotation marks.

-p *PrinterName*: Required parameter that specifies the name of the printer on which you want to take action. Enclose the printer name in quotation marks.

-u *UserName* -w *Password*: Optional parameters that provide the credentials needed to take the action on the desired host. Enclose both the username and the password in quotation marks.

For example, to pause printing on the HP LaserJet 1300 hosted on PrintServer3, run the following command:

```
> cscript prnqctl.vbs -z -s "PrintServer3" -p "HP LaserJet 1300"
```

How It Works

You may want to pause or clear printer queues for various reasons. For example, a user might decide that a document should not have been sent to the printer (perhaps it was too large), or the print device may be having hardware issues that need to be addressed.

To manage the queue on remote systems, it is necessary that you have the appropriate access rights on that system.

8-10. Printing Test Pages

Problem

You want to print a test page to a printer hosted on either a local or a remote server.

Solution

Using a Graphical User Interface

1. Open the Printers and Faxes administrative window.

2. Right-click the printer for which you want to print a test page (you can choose a local or remote computer) and select Properties.

3. Select the General tab if it is not already selected.

4. Click the Print Test Page button.

Using a Command-Line Interface

You can print a test page either locally or remotely using the following syntax:

```
> rundll32.exe printui.dll, PrintUIEntry /k /c <MachineName> /n <PrinterName>
```

Here is a description of the parameters:

/k: Required parameter that specifies that you want to print a test page.

/c *MachineName*: Optional parameter that specifies the name of the server or workstation from which you want to print the test page. If omitted, the local system will be assumed.

/n *PrinterName*: Required parameter that specifies the name of the printer for which you want to print a test page. Enclose the printer name in quotation marks.

As an example, to print a test page for the HP LaserJet 1300 PCL 5e printer hosted on server Printer4, run the following command:

```
> rundll32.exe printui.dll, PrintUIEntry /k /c Printer4 /n "HP LaserJet 1300 PCL 5e"
```

Using VBScript

You can print a test page using VBScript by executing the prnqctl.vbs script, located in the %systemroot%\system32 directory. Use the following syntax:

```
> cscript prnqctl.vbs -e [-s <RemoteComputer>]
    -p <PrinterName> [-u <UserName> -w <Password>]
```

Here is a description of the parameters:

-e: Required parameter that specifies that you want to print a test page.

-s *RemoteComputer*: Optional parameter that specifies the name of the server whose printer you want to manage. If omitted, the local server will be assumed. Enclose the computer name in quotation marks.

-p *PrinterName*: Required parameter that specifies the name of the printer on which you want to take action. Enclose the printer name in quotation marks.

-u *UserName* -w *Password*: Optional parameters that provide the credentials needed to take the action on the desired host. Enclose both the username and the password in quotation marks.

For example, you can print a test page on the HP LaserJet 1300 hosted on PrintServer3 by running the following command:

```
> cscript prnqctl.vbs -e -s "PrintServer3" -p "HP LaserJet 1300"
```

How It Works

It is always a best practice to print a test page from both the server and a typical workstation after making any sort of configuration change to print devices or printer settings. A failed test page is the first indication that there is a problem somewhere in the chain of network printing. The problem may have occurred with the printer driver or with the print device itself.

Administrators may configure and map printers and then print a test page from the server, but not do this test from a sample workstation. Later, they realize that a problem exists only because a frustrated user had to call the help desk.

Note You can use the Printer Troubleshooting Wizard to assist with the diagnosis of printer problems. Access the wizard by clicking the Troubleshoot button in the Print Test Page dialog box. The wizard will ask you a series of questions designed to pinpoint the source of the problem. Occasionally, it will be correct.

8-11. Listing, Pausing, Resuming, and Canceling Print Jobs

Problem

You want to manage print jobs. You want the ability to list, pause, resume, and/or cancel jobs on network printers.

Solution

Using a Graphical User Interface

1. Open the Printers and Faxes administrative window.

2. Double-click the printer that you want to manage.

3. View the print jobs that are in the printer queue in the default window.

4. From the Printer menu, select one of the following:

- Pause Printing to pause all jobs in the queue

- Pause Printing, which now has a check mark next to it, to resume the print jobs that you had previously paused

- Cancel All Documents to cancel all jobs in the queue

5. Confirm that you wish to take the selected action when prompted.

Note You can also pause, resume, or cancel individual jobs by right-clicking the particular job and selecting the appropriate action.

Using a Command-Line Interface

You can manage print jobs from the command line using the net print command. Before you can take action on a particular job, you must determine the job ID. To do this, run the following command:

```
> net print \\<ServerName>\<PrintShareName>
```

For example, the following command runs net print on a server named Voyager with a print share called LaserJet:

```
c:\>net print \\voyager\laserjet
```

You will receive results similar to the following:

```
Printers at \\voyager

Name                        Job #     Size        Status
------------------------------------------------------------------
laserjet Queue              2 jobs                *Printer Active*
      Administrator            7      5992        Waiting
      Administrator            8      7784        Waiting
The command completed successfully.
```

Notice that each job has an associated job number, or ID. You must determine which job corresponds to the one on which you want to take action. Once you know the ID, you can then run the following command:

```
> net print \\<ServerName> Job# [/HOLD | /RELEASE | /DELETE]
```

Here is a description of the parameters:

Job#: Required parameter that specifies the ID of the job on which you want to take action.

/HOLD | /RELEASE | /DELETE: Required parameter that specifies the action that you want to take on the particular job. The /HOLD parameter will pause the job; the /RELEASE parameter will resume the job; and the /DELETE parameter will cancel the job.

For example, to cancel the job with ID 7 from the printer queue on Voyager, run the following command:

```
>NET PRINT \\Voyager 7 /DELETE
```

Using VBScript

Use the prnjobs.vbs script in the %systemroot%\system32 directory to manage individual print jobs. Before you can take action on a particular job, you must determine the job ID. To do this, run the following command:

```
> cscript prnjobs.vbs -l
```

You will receive results similar to the following:

```
> c:\WINDOWS\system32>cscript prnjobs.vbs -l

Microsoft (R) Windows Script Host Version 5.6
Copyright (C) Microsoft Corporation 1996-2001. All rights reserved.

Job id 5
Printer hp LaserJet 1300 PCL 5e
Document Microsoft Word - My Speech.doc
Data type NT EMF 1.008
Driver name hp LaserJet 1300 PCL 5e
Description hp LaserJet 1300 PCL 5e, 5
Machine name \\VOYAGER
Notify Administrator
Owner Administrator
Pages printed 0
Parameters
Size 7784
Status
Time submitted 07/30/2005 15:29:15

Job id 6
Printer hp LaserJet 1300 PCL 5e
Document Microsoft Word - A Day to Remember.doc
Data type NT EMF 1.008
Driver name hp LaserJet 1300 PCL 5e
```

```
Description hp LaserJet 1300 PCL 5e, 6
Machine name \\VOYAGER
Notify Administrator
Owner Administrator
Pages printed 0
Parameters
Size 5992
Status
Time submitted 07/30/2005 15:32:23

Number of print jobs enumerated 2

c:\WINDOWS\system32>
```

After you have determined the job ID, you can take appropriate action.

To pause, resume, or cancel a print job, run the following command:

```
> cscript prnjobs.vbs -z|x|m [-s <RemoteComputer>]-p <PrinterName>
   -j <JobNumber> [-u <UserName> -w <Password>]
```

Here is a description of the parameters:

-z | x | m: Required parameter that specifies the action you will take. The -z parameter will pause the job; the -x parameter will cancel it; and the -m parameter will resume the paused job.

-s *RemoteComputer*: Optional parameter that specifies the name of the remote print server if the job is not local. Enclose the computer name in quotation marks.

-p *PrinterName*: Required parameter that specifies the name of the printer on which the job is queued. Enclose the printer name in quotation marks.

-j *JobNumber*: Required parameter that specifies the ID of the job on which you want to take action. This is the ID determined by executing the -l parameter.

-u UserName -w Password: Optional parameters that provide the credentials needed to take the action on the desired host. Enclose both the username and the password in quotation marks.

For example, to cancel a job with job ID 6 on a printer named HP LaserJet 1300 PCL 5e hosted on PrintServer2, run the following command:

```
> cscript prnjobs.vbs -x -s "PrintServer2" -p "HP LaserJet 1300 PCL 5e" -j 6
```

How It Works

Most network and system administrators have probably lost track of the number of times that users have had to call the help desk because their job is stuck in queue or the printer is jammed with paper. Driver incompatibilities may cause a simple 3-page document to print as 32 pages of bizarre symbols and fonts, none of which resemble the actual document.

Make sure that you use credentials that have rights to execute the scripts on the local or remote systems. Without these, the commands will fail.

8-12. Mapping Printers Using Group Policy

Problem

You want to use Group Policy to map network printers on workstations.

Solution

This problem does not have a straightforward solution using a graphical user interface, the command-line interface, or VBScript. This problem is somewhat unique in that regard. The solution requires knowledge of Group Policy configuration and is combined with a logon script that uses the `rundll32 printui.dll PrintUIEntry` syntax (used in previous recipes in this chapter).

1. Open Active Directory Users and Computers and navigate to the organizational unit (OU) that contains the computers to which this policy will apply. (If your computers still reside in the default Computers container, you should create a new OU and move the computers there.)

2. Right-click the OU and select Properties.

3. Select the Group Policy tab.

4. Open the Group Policy Editor. Create and link a Group Policy object to the desired OU. You can call it Map Printers or any other meaningful name.

5. Verify that the computers have permissions to both read and apply the Group Policy. You may want to use the Domain Computers security group, or you can use a group that you have created.

6. Right-click the policy and select the option to edit the policy.

7. Navigate in the left pane to Computer Configuration ➤ Windows Settings ➤ Scripts (Startup/Shutdown).

8. In the right pane, double-click Startup.

9. Click the Show Files button to open the scripts folder in Windows Explorer.

10. Create a text file in the scripts folder. Name it MapPrinters.bat, or use any other convenient filename as long as its file extension is .bat.

11. Edit the MapPrinters.bat logon script in Notepad.

12. Put the following code into the script file. Save it when complete and close the Windows Explorer window.

```
> rundll32 printui.dll,PrintUIEntry /ga /n \\<PrintServerName>
    \<PrinterShareName>/j "LanMan Print Services"
```

The parameters for the `rundll32 printui.dll,PrintUIEntry` command are as follows:

- `/ga`: Required parameter that specifies that you will be adding this printer to all profiles on the target computer.

- `/n`: Required parameter that specifies the server and share name to which you will map the printer.

- `/j "LanMan Print Services"`: Required parameter that specifies that you will be invoking LAN Manager print services.

For example, to globally add a printer connection that points to the printer at \\Voyager\LaserJet1300, enter the following command into your logon script:

```
> Rundll32 printui.dll,PrintUIEntry /ga /n \\Voyager
    \LaserJet1300/j "LanMan Print Services"
```

13. Click the Add button.

14. Click the Browse button next to the Script Name field, select the script that you just created, and click OK to accept the script.

15. Click OK to save your settings, and then close all Group Policy windows.

How It Works

Group Policy provides a great degree of control over the configuration of user and computer settings. Here are some key points to consider when implementing Group Policy to map printers through logon scripts:

- Create new policies rather than modifying the default (built-in) policy.

- Provide the Read and Apply Group Policy permissions in order for the computer to receive the policy. Provide these privileges to the Domain Computers group in order for all computers within the OU to receive the policy. You can refine this if you've created your own computer security groups.

- Use the wizard to place the batch file in the correct location. Do not just create a batch file and place it into the Netlogon share. The policy folder and the Netlogon share point to different locations on the file system.

- Verify that Group Policy settings above or below this OU do not interfere with implementation of the desired settings.

- Test the Group Policy settings. Verify that only the desired computers receive the printer mappings and that they function properly.

See Also

Active Directory Cookbook for Windows Server 2003 and Windows 2000 by Robbie Allen (O'Reilly Press, 2003). This book contains a number of recipes related to Group Policy implementation and configuration.

8-13. Enabling and Using Browser-Based Printing

Problem

You want to enable printing and printer management through a web browser.

Solution

To enable browser-based printing, you must first install the component if it is not already on your system, as follows:

1. Start the Add/Remove Programs Control Panel applet.

2. Select Add/Remove Windows Components.

3. Check the option to install Internet Printing from within Application Server ➤ Internet Information Services (IIS).

4. Click OK twice to return to the main screen.

5. Click Next to start the installation wizard.

Next, follow these steps to verify that Internet Printing is installed and enabled:

1. Start the Internet Information Services (IIS Manager) console from the Administrative Tools folder.

2. Expand *<ServerName>* ➤ Web Service Extensions in the left pane.

3. In the right pane, verify that Internet Printing is allowed. If it is not, right-click it and select Allow.

Now that you've installed and configured browser-based printing, you can access it either as an end user or as an administrator. To do so, go to any browser and navigate to http:// *<ServerName>*/Printers. Your browser will load a page with links to shared printers.

The following options are available in the View category:

- The Document List option shows a list of all documents queued for the given printer. Field names include document name, status, owner, pages, size, and time submitted.

- The Properties option shows a list of general properties of the printer, including print queue status, number of documents in queue, printer model, location, comments, network name (URL), number of documents in the queue, printer speed, color capabilities, printability on both sides of paper, and maximum resolution.

- The All Printers option shows a list of all network printers with hyperlinks to the printer. The list also includes the printer status, location, number of jobs pending, printer model, and comments.

The following options are available in the Printer Actions category:

- The Pause option puts the selected printer into pause mode so that documents will remain in the queue without being printed.

- The Resume option releases the printer from pause mode.

- The Cancel All Documents option deletes all documents from the queue.

The following options are available in the Document Actions category:

- The Pause option selects a document in the right pane. Click the Pause link to hold that document.

- The Resume option selects a document in the right pane. Click the Resume link to release that document for printing.

- The Cancel option selects a document in the right pane. Click the Cancel link to delete the document from queue.

How It Works

Browser-based printing is a convenient and often underutilized tool for both administrators and end users. However, in order to use it confidently, attention must be paid to the security environment.

In the early days of Windows 2000, a vulnerability was discovered that would allow an attacker to exploit the Internet Printing service and compromise the system (see Microsoft KB 815021 for details). Although Microsoft released a fix for this vulnerability, many administrators became concerned about the use of Internet Printing and were reluctant to deploy it.

Windows Server 2003 is much more secure than Windows 2000 "out of the box," yet it is not immune to attack, and vulnerabilities are frequently discovered. Therefore, administrators should take caution when exposing services to the Internet, or even to a trusted environment in which an insider threat may exist.

In either an intranet or Internet scenario, the administrator must address key issues, such as the following:

- Which users or groups should have rights to Internet Printing?

- What level of permissions should users have? Should they be administrators, operators, or end users?

- From where should users be able to access Internet Printing? Should they have access from all locations or from predefined IP addresses only?

- Over which channels should users have access? Should port 80 or an alternate port be opened on the firewall to allow direct, Internet-based access? Or should users be required to first establish an encrypted session, such as a virtual private network (VPN)?

See Also

- Microsoft TechNet: "Effectively Using IPP Printing" (`http://www.microsoft.com/windowsserver2003/techinfo/overview/internetprint.mspx`)

- Microsoft KB 323428: "How to Configure Internet Printing in Windows Server 2003." This article describes the security settings that can be configured for the Internet Printing feature.

CHAPTER 9

■ ■ ■

Network Troubleshooting

We'll wrap things up with a look at some of the tools and tricks involved in network troubleshooting. Troubleshooting is one of those tasks that is often an art as much as it is a science; you learn through trial and error to recognize common issues and their cures. In this chapter, we will give you an overview of some of the most common troubleshooting scenarios you'll encounter on a Windows Server 2003 network, and tools that you can use to correct them.

In the majority of cases, network troubleshooting boils down to one simple problem statement: "I can't reach Machine X to do Task Y." This makes a lot of sense when you think about it, since the entire purpose of network operating systems like Windows Server 2003 is to enable access to resources across some type of wired or wireless network connection. To begin troubleshooting network issues like these, it's best to begin at one end of the network "conversation," yourself, and work your way to the other end of the network until you can determine where and why the failure is occurring.

Using a Graphical User Interface

There are two particularly useful GUI tools that you can use for troubleshooting:

- PortQryUI: This is a GUI front end to the portqry command-line tool that enumerates listening ports on a local or remote computer. This tool is freely downloadable from the Microsoft website.

- Replmon: Available as part of the Windows Support Tools, Replmon provides a GUI front end to the powerful repadmin command-line utility. Replmon provides a graphical view of your Active Directory domain controllers and replication topology, and is useful in troubleshooting issues associated with sites, subnets, site links, and other elements of AD replication.

Using a Command-Line Interface

While there are a few GUI tools that you can use for network troubleshooting, the most valuable utilities will require you to do a bit of work at the command line. Some of these tools are built into the Windows operating system, while others are freely available as downloads from the Microsoft website or as a part of the Windows Support Tools.

The command-line tools that we will cover in this chapter include the following:

- **Ping:** Performs a basic connectivity check with a remote host.

- **Tracert:** Performs a more detailed connectivity check. Rather than simply reporting whether the remote host is reachable or not, tracert will display the path taken by the packets en route to the destination host and report the exact point along the path where any failure is occurring.

- **Pathping:** This utility is available for Windows 2000 and later, and combines the best aspects of ping and tracert. Pathping will first perform a tracert to the remote host, and will then send a series of pings to each hop in the route to give you a detailed view of network performance along the entire link between two hosts.

- **Netsh:** This is a command-line tool built into the Windows operating system that allows you to configure a number of different aspects of TCP/IP networking, including the Windows Firewall, basic TCP/IP configurations, DNS, DHCP, and more.

- **Netdiag:** Available as part of the Windows Support Tools, netdiag can perform a number of tests to diagnose DNS, WINS, and other TCP/IP services on your network. You can configure netdiag to run the entire battery of tests, or to only run one or two tests to zero in on a particular troubleshooting area.

- **Repadmin:** If you are an Active Directory administrator, this will be a tool that you turn to again and again. Like netdiag, it contains any number of subcommands that will allow you to troubleshoot and report on all aspects of your AD replication topology.

- **Portqry:** This tool is freely downloadable from the Microsoft website and provides a way to enumerate open ports on a local or remote computer.

- **Ipconfig:** This tool provides a detailed description of your computer's IP configuration and allows you to release or renew a DHCP-assigned IP address as well as display or flush your DNS cache.

- **Route:** This tool allows you to view and modify the contents of your local routing table, which controls how remote traffic is directed on your Windows Server 2003 computer.

9-1. Confirming TCP/IP Configuration

Problem

You want to confirm that your Windows Server 2003 computer is configured with the correct TCP/IP configuration.

Solution

Using a Graphical User Interface

To confirm that your computer is configured with a static IP address, do the following:

1. Open the Network Connections applet.

2. Right-click on the Local Area Connection icon and select Properties.

3. Click on Internet Protocol (TCP/IP), and select Properties.

4. Confirm that the radio button next to Use the Following IP Address is selected.

5. Confirm that the appropriate configuration information is present in the IP Address, Subnet Mask, and Default Gateway text boxes.

6. Click Close when you're finished.

To confirm that your computer is configured to receive its IP address from a DHCP server, do the following:

1. Open the Network Connections applet.

2. Double-click on the Local Area Connection icon.

3. Click on Internet Protocol (TCP/IP), and select Properties.

4. Confirm that the radio button next to Obtain an IP Address Automatically is selected.

5. Click on the Support tab. In the Connection Status section, confirm that the Address Type is listed as Assigned by DHCP. Confirm that the assigned IP Address, Subnet Mask, and Default Gateway are valid for the local network.

6. Click Close when you're finished.

Using a Command-Line Interface

The following command displays your current IP configuration:

```
> ipconfig /all
```

This command produces output like the following:

```
Windows IP Configuration

        Host Name . . . . . . . . . . . . : LAURAHOME
        Primary Dns Suffix  . . . . . . . :
        Node Type . . . . . . . . . . . . : Hybrid
        IP Routing Enabled. . . . . . . . : No
        WINS Proxy Enabled. . . . . . . . : No

Ethernet adapter LAN:

        Connection-specific DNS Suffix  . :
        Description . . . . . . . . . . . : Broadcom NetXtreme Gigabit Ethernet
        Physical Address. . . . . . . . . : 00-11-25-D2-41-5B
        Dhcp Enabled. . . . . . . . . . . : No
        IP Address. . . . . . . . . . . . : 10.0.0.83
        Subnet Mask . . . . . . . . . . . : 255.0.0.0
        Default Gateway . . . . . . . . . : 10.0.0.1
        DNS Servers . . . . . . . . . . . : 123.61.215.13
```

Using the Registry

To confirm the static IP address of your computer, examine the following registry keys:

```
[HKEY_LOCAL_MACHINE\SYSTEM\CurrentControlSet\Services\Tcpip\Parameters\
    Interfaces\{<Interface GUID>}]
"IPAddress"=REG_MULTI_SZ:"<IP Address>"

[HKEY_LOCAL_MACHINE\SYSTEM\CurrentControlSet\Services\Tcpip\Parameters\
    Interfaces\{<Interface GUID>}]
"SubnetMask"=REG_MULTI_SZ:"<Subnet Mask>"

[HKEY_LOCAL_MACHINE\SYSTEM\CurrentControlSet\Services\Tcpip\Parameters\
    Interfaces\{<Interface GUID>}]
"DefaultGateway"=REG_MULTI_SZ:"<Default Gateway>"
```

To confirm that your computer is receiving an IP address from a DHCP server, confirm that the following registry key is set to 1:

```
[HKEY_LOCAL_MACHINE\SYSTEM\CurrentControlSet\Services\Tcpip\Parameters\
    Interfaces\{<Interface GUID>}\]
"EnableDHCP"=dword:1
```

Using VBScript

This code displays the TCP/IP configuration for a computer.

```
' ------ SCRIPT CONFIGURATION ------
  strComputer = "."
' ------ END CONFIGURATION ---------

Set objWMIService = GetObject("winmgmts:" _
    & "{impersonationLevel=impersonate}!\\" & strComputer & "\root\cimv2")

Set nics = objWMIService.ExecQuery _
    ("SELECT * FROM Win32_NetworkAdapterConfiguration WHERE IPEnabled = True")

' set a counter to number the NICs, in case you need to display info
' for more than one.
n = 1
WScript.Echo

For Each nic in nics
   WScript.Echo "Network Interface Card: " & n
   WScript.Echo "=================="
   WScript.Echo "  Description: " & nic.Description

   WScript.Echo "  Physical (MAC) address: " & nic.MACAddress
   WScript.Echo "  Host name:              " & nic.DNSHostName
```

```
' display all IP addresses configured for this adapter
If Not IsNull(nic.IPAddress) Then
   For x = 0 To UBound(nic.IPAddress)
      WScript.Echo "  IP address:              " & nic.IPAddress(x)
   Next
End If


If Not IsNull(nic.IPSubnet) Then
   For x = 0 To UBound(nic.IPSubnet)
      WScript.Echo "  Subnet:                  " & nic.IPSubnet(x)
   Next
End If


If Not IsNull(nic.DefaultIPGateway) Then
   For x = 0 To UBound(nic.DefaultIPGateway)
      WScript.Echo "  Default gateway:         " & _
         nic.DefaultIPGateway(x)
   Next
End If


' now display DNS configuration information

WScript.Echo
WScript.Echo "  DNS Settings"
WScript.Echo "  ------------"
WScript.Echo "    DNS search order:"

If Not IsNull(nic.DNSServerSearchOrder) Then
   For x = 0 To UBound(nic.DNSServerSearchOrder)
      WScript.Echo "       " & nic.DNSServerSearchOrder(x)
   Next
End If

WScript.Echo "    DNS domain: " & nic.DNSDomain

If Not IsNull(nic.DNSDomainSuffixSearchOrder) Then
   For x = 0 To UBound(nic.DNSDomainSuffixSearchOrder)
      WScript.Echo "    DNS suffix search list: " & _
         nic.DNSDomainSuffixSearchOrder(x)
   Next
End If


' now display DHCP information

WScript.Echo
WScript.Echo "  DHCP Settings"
WScript.Echo "  -------------"
```

```
    WScript.Echo "    DHCP enabled:        " & nic.DHCPEnabled
    WScript.Echo "    DHCP server:         " & nic.DHCPServer

    If Not IsNull(nic.DHCPLeaseObtained) Then
       utcLeaseObtained = nic.DHCPLeaseObtained
       strLeaseObtained = WMIDateStringToDate(utcLeaseObtained)
    Else
       strLeaseObtained = ""
    End If

    WScript.Echo "    DHCP lease obtained: " & strLeaseObtained

    If Not IsNull(nic.DHCPLeaseExpires) Then
       utcLeaseExpires = nic.DHCPLeaseExpires
       strLeaseExpires = WMIDateStringToDate(utcLeaseExpires)
    Else
       strLeaseExpires = ""
    End If
    WScript.Echo "    DHCP lease expires:  " & strLeaseExpires

    ' now display WINS configuration information
    WScript.Echo
    WScript.Echo "  WINS settings"
    WScript.Echo "  -------------"
    WScript.Echo "    Primary WINS server:   " & nic.WINSPrimaryServer
    WScript.Echo "    Secondary WINS server: " & nic.WINSSecondaryServer
    WScript.Echo

    ' move to the next adapter, if applicable
    n = n + 1
Next

' takes a UTC date string and displays it in a friendlier format
Function WMIDateStringToDate(utcDate)
  WMIDateStringToDate = CDate(Mid(utcDate, 5, 2)  & "/" & _
    Mid(utcDate, 7, 2)  & "/" & _
    Left(utcDate, 4)    & " " & _
    Mid (utcDate, 9, 2) & ":" & _
    Mid(utcDate, 11, 2) & ":" & _
    Mid(utcDate, 13, 2))
End Function
```

How It Works

One of the first steps you should take when troubleshooting a network connectivity issue is to get a snapshot of your computer's TCP/IP configuration. Mistyping a default gateway or subnet mask can create errors that even the most seasoned network professionals can overlook if they skip this simple step. Earlier client operating systems like Windows 95 and Windows 98 offered winipcfg, a GUI utility that would provide a snapshot of the current IP configuration; in NT, 2000, and 2003, this has been mostly replaced by command-line tools and scripting solutions.

In addition to the options listed previously, both netsh and ipconfig can display a smaller subset of IP configuration information, and ipconfig can even be used to perform simple troubleshooting tasks. From the `netsh interface ip` prefix, you can issue the following `netsh` commands to display various IP addressing information:

`netsh interface ip show address`: Displays IP address configuration only; no DNS or WINS info

`netsh interface ip show dns`: Displays the configured DNS server addresses

`netsh interface ip show icmp`: Displays ICMP statistics on a RRAS server

`netsh interface ip show interface`: Displays IP interface statistics on an RRAS server

`netsh interface ip show ipstats`: Displays IP statistics on an RRAS server

`netsh interface ip show joins`: Displays multicast groups joined

`netsh interface ip show wins`: Displays the WINS server addresses

See Also

- Recipes 1-2 and 1-6 for more on configuring static and dynamic IP addressing

- Recipe 1-16 for more on displaying the current TCP/IP configuration of a Windows Server 2003 computer

9-2. Verifying That the TCP/IP Stack Is Functioning

Problem

You want to confirm that TCP/IP is installed and functioning correctly on your Windows Server 2003 computer.

Solution

Using a Graphical User Interface

1. Open the Enhanced Ping (eping) utility, a free download available from http://www. itoolpad.com/products/eping/.

2. Enter **127.0.0.1** or **localhost** and click Ping.

3. Confirm that localhost responds to the ping command with a time index of 0.

4. Click Quit to close the eping utility.

Using a Command-Line Interface

The following command confirms that the TCP/IP loopback interface is responding correctly:

```
> ping loopback
```

How It Works

In TCP/IP networking, the *loopback address* is a special IP address that is reserved for diagnostic testing. When you ping 127.0.0.1, you are essentially saying to your Windows Server 2003 computer, "Verify that my network interface card is functioning, that TCP/IP is installed correctly, and that I've been assigned a valid IP address."

It's important to note, however, that there is a difference between a *valid* IP address and a *correct* one. You can configure a computer with an IP address that should not be in use on your network—one that is in the incorrect subnet, for example—but as long as it is a valid IP address, you will still be able to ping the loopback address on the local computer. For this reason, pinging the loopback IP address is only the first step in troubleshooting connectivity issues; successfully pinging the loopback address eliminates corruption of the TCP/IP stack or a hardware failure on the local NIC as a cause of network failure. If you can successfully ping the loopback address but are still having communications issues, you'll know that the problem lies elsewhere in your computer's network configuration, or the configuration of the remote host to which you are trying to connect.

While it is usually easiest to issue the ping command from the command line, you may want to perform this task through a GUI as well. The Extended Ping (eping) utility is a free download available from http://www.itoolpad.com/products/eping/.

See Also

- iToolPad: Extended Ping utility (http://www.itoolpad.com/products/eping/).

- Wikipedia: "Loopback" (http://en.wikipedia.org/wiki/Loopback). This article discusses the loopback address.

- Microsoft TechNet: "IP Addressing" (http://www.microsoft.com/technet/itsolutions/network/evaluate/technol/tcpipfund/tcpipfund_ch03.mspx).

9-3. Verifying the Path to a Remote Host

Problem

You want to verify that there is a valid network connection to a remote host, either on the same subnet or a remote network.

Solution

Using a Graphical User Interface

1. Open the Enhanced Ping (eping) utility.

2. Enter the Fully Qualified Domain Name (FQDN) or the numeric IP address of the remote host and click Ping.

3. Confirm that the remote host responds to the ping command.

4. Click Quit to close the eping utility.

Using a Command-Line Interface

The following command confirms that a remote host with an IP address of 192.168.1.103 is responding:

```
> ping 192.168.1.103
```

■ **Note** Using the -a switch with the ping command will attempt to perform a DNS name lookup against the specified IP address in addition to attempting to determine if the host is online and responding.

How It Works

In TCP/IP networking, the Packet INternet Groper (Ping) utility is used to verify low-level connectivity between two TCP/IP-based hosts. Ping relies on the Internet Control Message Protocol (ICMP) echo function, which is detailed in RFC 792 for ICMPv4 and RFC 2463 for ICMPv6.

The Ping utility transmits an ICMP packet through the network to a destination DNS name or IP address. The computer that sent the initial ping will then wait for a return packet. If there is a valid network connection with the target host, if the target is online and functioning correctly, and if there is no firewall or other type of filtering device suppressing PING responses between you and the target computer, the target computer will send a response.

In addition to testing basic network connectivity, you can also use Ping as a basic test of name resolution. If you are able to ping a remote host by IP address but not by DNS or NetBIOS name, the issue is likely related to name resolution.

See Also

- iToolPad: Extended Ping utility (http://www.itoolpad.com/products/eping/)

- RFC 792: "Internet Control Message Protocol" (http://www.faqs.org/rfcs/rfc792.html)

- RFC 2463: "Internet Control Message Protocol (ICMPv6) for the Internet Protocol Version 6 (IPv6) Specification" (http://www.faqs.org/rfcs/rfc2463.html)

- Microsoft KB 325487: "How to Troubleshoot Network Connectivity Problems"

9-4. Resetting the TCP/IP Stack

Problem

You want to reset the TCP/IP stack to its default state. (This step is often necessary during trouble-shooting if the TCP/IP stack has become corrupt or if you are unable to resolve communications issues any other way.)

Solution

The following command will reset the TCP/IP stack to its default factory settings, using `c:\logfile.txt` to record information pertaining to the reset:

```
> netsh interface ip reset "c:\logfile.txt"
```

How It Works

In older versions of the Windows operating system, you had the ability to completely uninstall the TCP/IP protocol and reinstall it if you needed to start from scratch with your TCP/IP configuration. Beginning with Windows 2000, it was no longer possible to do this, since TCP/IP is the default protocol of the Windows 2000, XP, and 2003 operating systems. But nonetheless, it sometimes proves necessary; this is particularly common in disaster recovery situations when you've restored the system state of a Windows computer onto new hardware.

In Windows 2000, particularly on a domain controller, the procedure to reset the TCP/IP stack involved several pages of manual Registry edits, and then never really worked in most cases anyway. In Windows Server 2003, this procedure has become much simpler and has been reduced to a single `netsh` command.

When you reset the TCP/IP stack from the command line, you must enter the name of a log file that `netsh` can use to record the actions that it takes as it resets TCP/IP. The contents of this log file will vary depending on the unique hardware configuration of each computer; you can see a sample of this file here:

```
reset SYSTEM\CurrentControlSet\Services\Dhcp\
Parameters\Options\15\RegLocation

old REG_MULTI_SZ =
SYSTEM\CurrentControlSet\Services\Tcpip\
Parameters\Interfaces\?\DhcpDomain
SYSTEM\CurrentControlSet\Services\TcpIp\Parameters\DhcpDomain

added SYSTEM\CurrentControlSet\Services\Netbt\Parameters\
Interfaces\Tcpip_{2DDD011E-B1B6-4886-87AC-B4E72693D10C}\
NetbiosOptions

added SYSTEM\CurrentControlSet\Services\Netbt\Parameters\
Interfaces\Tcpip_{BAA9D128-54BB-43F6-8922-313D537BE03E}\
NetbiosOptions
```

```
reset SYSTEM\CurrentControlSet\Services\Netbt\Parameters\
Interfaces\Tcpip_{BD2859BA-B26A-4E2B-A3FE-3D246F90A81A}\
NameServerList

old REG_MULTI_SZ = 10.1.1.3
```

See Also

- Microsoft KB 317518: "How to Reset 'Internet Protocol (TCP/IP)' in Windows Server 2003"

- Microsoft KB 325356: "How to Remove and Reinstall TCP/IP on a Window Server 2003 Domain Controller"

- Microsoft KB 299451: "How to Remove and Reinstall TCP/IP on a Windows 2000 Domain Controller"

9-5. Troubleshooting Windows Sockets Corruption

Problem

You want to troubleshoot and repair Windows Sockets (Winsock) corruption on a Windows Server 2003 computer.

Solution

The following command will determine if there is Winsock corruption on a Windows Server 2003 computer:

```
> netdiag /test:winsock /v
```

The following command will reset the Winsock catalog on a Windows Server 2003 computer:

```
> netsh winsock reset
```

Note After resetting Winsock, you will need to reboot the local computer. This `netsh` option is new with Windows Server 2003 Service Pack 1.

How It Works

The combination of an IP address and a TCP or UDP port number is referred to as a *socket*. In the Windows implementation of TCP/IP, the software driver that manages connections between sockets is referred to as *Winsock* (or *Winsock2* for the latest version of the driver.)

When troubleshooting TCP/IP connections on a Windows computer, you may encounter unusual errors when using various programs and utilities that may indicate corruption of the Winsock driver. For instance, you may receive one of the following error messages when attempting to renew a DHCP lease using the `ipconfig /renew` command:

- An error occurred while renewing interface local area connection: an operation was attempted on something that is not a socket. Unable to contact driver Error code 2.

- The operation failed since no adapter is in the state permissible for this operation.

- The attempted operation is not supported for the type of object referenced.

- An error occurred while renewing interface "Internet": An operation was attempted on something that is not a socket.

When these occur, you can use `netdiag` from the Windows Support Tools to confirm Winsock's integrity by using the `/test:winsock /v` switches. (`/v` will produce more complete debugging output than running the command with only the `/test:` switch.)

Once you've confirmed that you are experiencing Winsock corruption, you can use `netsh` to reset it. Be aware, however, that certain applications such as antivirus scanners, third-party firewalls, and proxy clients may begin to malfunction after performing this reset. If this occurs, simply reinstall the third-party application from its installation media to return it to working order.

See Also

- Microsoft KB 811259: "How to Determine and Recover from Winsock2 Corruption"

- Microsoft TechNet: "Netdiag Overview" (`http://technet2.microsoft.com/ WindowsServer/en/Library/cf4926db-87ea-4f7a-9806-0b54e1c00a771033.mspx`)

9-6. Repairing a Network Connection

Problem

You want to repair a Windows Server 2003 network connection as part of the network trouble-shooting process.

Solution

Using a Graphical User Interface

1. Open the Network Connections applet.

2. Double-click on the Local Area Connection icon.

3. Click on Internet Protocol (TCP/IP), and select Properties.

4. Click on the Support tab, and select Repair.

5. Click Close when you're done.

Using a Command-Line Interface

The following commands will repair a Windows Server 2003 network connection. The first command releases and renews your IP address with a DHCP server:

```
> ipconfig /renew
> arp -d *
> nbtstat -R
> nbtstat -RR
> ipconfig /flushdns
> ipconfig /registerdns
```

We'll discuss each of these commands in the following section.

How It Works

Beginning with Windows Server 2003 and Windows XP, the Network Connections GUI has provided a quick shortcut to help you troubleshoot a misbehaving network connection. When you select the Repair button, the local computer automatically performs the following tasks:

- Releases the currently leased IP address, and then contacts the DHCP server to obtain a new lease (`ipconfig /renew`).

- Deletes the contents of the local Address Resolution Protocol (ARP) cache. Each local computer maintains a cache of IP address to MAC address mappings of remote computers that have recently been contacted; deleting this cache allows the local computer to start fresh (`arp -d *`).

- Deletes the contents of the local NetBIOS cache (`nbtstat -R`).

- Sends a release notification to the WINS server, and then reregisters the local NetBIOS name in WINS (`nbtstat -RR`).

- Deletes the contents of the local DNS cache (`ipconfig /flushdns`).

- Refreshes the DHCP lease one more time, and reregisters its DNS name with the locally configured DNS server (`ipconfig /registerdns`).

- Restarts the 802.1X Authentication service.

See Also

- Recipe 1-12 for more on managing dynamic DNS configuration

- Microsoft KB 314850: "The Syntax and Options for Using the IPConfig Diagnostic Utility for Network Connections"

9-7. Troubleshooting NetBIOS Name Resolution

Problem

You want to troubleshoot NetBIOS name resolution on your Windows Server 2003 network.

Solution

Using a Graphical User Interface

To confirm your computer's WINS configuration (used by many networks to streamline NetBIOS name resolution), do the following:

1. Open the Network Connections applet.

2. Double-click on the Local Area Connection icon.

3. Click on Internet Protocol (TCP/IP), and select Properties.

4. In the Internet Protocol (TCP/IP) Properties dialog box, click Advanced.

5. In the Advanced TCP/IP Settings dialog box, click the WINS tab and verify the following:

   - IP address of one or more WINS servers on your network. If WINS is in use on your network, verify that the correct server IP address or addresses are listed here.

   - Whether Lmhosts lookup is enabled. If you rely on Lmhosts files for NetBIOS name resolution on your network, and this check box is not enabled, it may prevent your clients from correctly resolving NetBIOS resources.

   - Whether NetBIOS over TCP/IP is enabled, disabled, or receiving its setting from the DHCP server. If you are using applications on your network that require NetBIOS to communicate, disabling NetBIOS can cause connectivity issues for those applications.

■**Note**   You should also verify the contents of the Lmhosts file on your Windows Server 2003 computer to confirm that any entries are correctly typed and up to date.

---

6. Click OK when you're done.

Using a Command-Line Interface

The following command will display the WINS servers configured for the local computer:

```
> netsh interface ip show wins
```

The following command will confirm that you can create a NetBIOS session with a remote computer called COMPUTER1:

```
> net view \\COMPUTER1
```

The following command will verify that the NetBIOS names on the local computer have been registered with a WINS server:

```
> nbtstat -n
```

The following command will list the NetBIOS names registered for a remote computer called COMPUTER2:

```
> nbtstat -a COMPUTER2
```

Note To use this command based on the IP address of a remote computer, use the -A *IPAddress* switch instead.

How It Works

Despite the fact that Windows 2000, 2003, and XP use DNS as their default name resolution scheme, you may still need to support (and therefore troubleshoot) NetBIOS name resolution when accessing certain business applications, as well as interacting with down-level clients and servers on your network.

Probably the most ubiquitous NetBIOS error occurs when you encounter the dreaded "System error 53 has occurred: The network path was not found" while attempting to access a remote resource using net use or the *Computername* syntax. The cause of this error typically boils down to one of two things:

- NetBIOS name resolution

- NetBIOS session issues

To rule out name resolution as the cause of the error, simply ping the remote host using its NetBIOS name. If the ping is successful, NetBIOS name resolution is functioning correctly and the issue lies in establishing a NetBIOS session with the remote host. If you are unable to ping the remote computer's NetBIOS name but you *are* able to ping its IP address, you should begin your troubleshooting steps with NetBIOS name resolution.

Probably the most useful command-line utility for troubleshooting NetBIOS issues is nbtstat. This tool has a number of switches, each of which performs a different task:

-a *<NetBIOS name>*: Returns the NetBIOS name table and MAC address of the computer name specified

-A *<IP address>*: Provides the same information as the -a switch based on the remote host's IP address

-c: Lists the contents of the local NetBIOS name cache

-n: Displays the locally registered NetBIOS names for the local computer

-r: Displays a count of all NetBIOS names resolved by the local computer, sorted by those resolved by broadcast versus those resolved using a WINS server

-R: Purges the name cache and reloads all entries in the Lmhosts file that are designated with the #PRE (preload) tag

-RR: Releases and reregisters all NetBIOS names with the configured WINS server

-s: Lists all active NetBIOS sessions, converting destination IP addresses to computer NetBIOS names

-S: Lists the current NetBIOS sessions and their status, displaying the remote IP address instead of the NetBIOS name

In addition to nbtstat, you can use netdiag (from the Support Tools) to run the following NetBIOS-related tests:

- NetBTTransports lists all active NetBIOS (NetBT) transports configured on the local computer.

- NbtNM provides similar data to the `nbtstat -n` command.

- WINS will send a name resolution query to all WINS servers configured on the local computer.

See Also

- Recipes 1-13, 1-14, and 1-15 for more on configuring WINS and NetBIOS on the local computer

- Microsoft TechNet: "NetBIOS Name Resolution: (`http://technet2.microsoft.com/WindowsServer/en/Library/4fbaebbb-6334-4b26-8118-cb36a261978a1033.mspx`)

- Microsoft TechNet: "Windows Server 2003 TCP/IP Troubleshooting" (`http://www.microsoft.com/technet/prodtechnol/windowsserver2003/operations/system/tcpiptrb.mspx`)

- Microsoft KB 172218: "Microsoft TCP/IP Host Name Resolution Order"

9-8. Troubleshooting DNS Name Resolution

Problem

You want to troubleshoot the DNS name resolution process on a Windows Server 2003 computer.

Solution

Using a Graphical User Interface

To confirm your computer's DNS configuration, do the following:

1. Open the Network Connections applet.

2. Double-click on the Local Area Connection icon.

3. Click on Internet Protocol (TCP/IP), and select Properties.

4. In the Internet Protocol (TCP/IP) Properties dialog box, click Advanced.

5. In the Advanced TCP/IP Settings dialog box, click the DNS tab and verify that the following are set correctly:

   • IP address of one or more DNS servers on your network

   • The configured DNS suffixes

   • Whether the host should update its information dynamically with the DNS server

6. Click OK when you're done.

Using a Command-Line Interface

The following command will confirm that you can connect to a remote host called www.mycompany.com by using its fully qualified domain name (FQDN):

```
> ping www.mycompany.com
```

The following command will send a query to the default DNS server configured for the local computer:

```
> nslookup www.mycompany.com
```

The following command will send a query to the DNS server with the IP address of 10.0.0.130:

```
> nslookup www.mycompany.com 10.0.0.130
```

How It Works

As when troubleshooting NetBIOS name resolution, you can confirm whether or not DNS is functioning correctly on a Windows Server 2003 computer by pinging or otherwise connecting to a remote host using its fully qualified domain name (FQDN). If the ping is successful, DNS name resolution is functioning correctly and the issue lies somewhere else: perhaps the file or service to which you are trying to connect on the remote server is unavailable. If you are unable to ping the remote computer's DNS name but you *are* able to ping its IP address, you should begin your troubleshooting steps at DNS name resolution. You may also run into a situation where DNS is incorrectly configured, where you may be pinging a DNS name that is resolving to an incorrect IP address. It's important to ensure that both pieces of the puzzle are correct when troubleshooting using ping.

To troubleshoot the accuracy of DNS records hosted on a local or remote DNS server, you can use the nslookup and netdiag command-line utilities. Like netsh, nslookup has a number of subcommands that you can use to customize the information you're looking for, including querying for a specific type of record (A, CNAME, or MX, for example), and to customize which DNS servers you are using to perform a query. The netdiag utility from the Windows Support Tools also includes a DNS component as part of its battery of tests. The netdiag /test:dns command will check whether the DNS cache service is running and whether the local computer's DNS records are registered correctly on its configured DNS servers. If the local computer is an Active Directory domain controller, the DNS test will also verify that any DNS entries in the netlogon.dns file are registered on the DNS server.

See Also

- Recipes 1-9 through 1-12 for more on DNS client configuration

- Microsoft TechNet: "Netdiag Syntax" (http://technet2.microsoft.com/WindowsServer/
en/Library/4907fb78-1808-41b2-9cef-c9dc3824eda81033.mspx)

- Microsoft KB 200525: "Using Nslookup.exe"

9-9. Troubleshooting IP-to-MAC Address Resolution

Problem

You want to verify the functionality of the Address Resolution Protocol (ARP) on your network. ARP handles the mapping of IP addresses to MAC addresses and is critical in accessing any type of resource on a LAN or WAN.

Solution

The following command displays the ARP cache of the local computer:

```
> arp -a
```

The following command will add a static ARP entry that maps IP address 192.168.1.140 to a MAC address of 00-0f-66-50-b6-93:

```
> arp -s 192.168.1.140 00-0f-66-50-b6-93
```

The following command will delete the static ARP entry associated with IP address 10.0.0.130:

```
> arp -d 10.0.0.130
```

How It Works

Each network interface card (NIC) comes preconfigured from its manufacturer with a media access control (MAC) address. This 64-byte number is burned into the read-only memory (ROM) of the card, and remains the same regardless of the IP address with which the NIC is configured. When you attempt to access a resource on a remote computer, you not only need to resolve the IP address of the remote computer, but the TCP/IP protocol needs to work in the background to resolve the IP address to the MAC address of the remote computer's NIC. Luckily, this process is handled by TCP/IP and with minimal administrator intervention.

In the rare instance when you need to troubleshoot the ARP resolution process, you can use the arp utility that comes preloaded on any TCP/IP-enabled computer. You can use this utility to do any of the following:

- View the local cache of MAC addresses that the local computer has resolved. These cached entries are maintained in memory for two minutes by default.

- Create a static ARP entry that will manually map an IP address to a MAC address; this static entry will persist when the computer is rebooted.

- Delete a static or dynamically cached ARP entry. There is no global command to delete all ARP entries at once; you'll need to delete the entries one at a time.

See Also

- Microsoft TechNet: "Address Resolution Protocol (ARP)"
  (http://technet2.microsoft.com/WindowsServer/en/Library/
  7b77bb1b-5c57-408f-907f-8b474203a5331033.mspx)

- Microsoft TechNet: "ARP" (http://technet2.microsoft.com/WindowsServer/en/
  Library/385c9661-4ad5-4743-9231-a991e5b4a8091033.mspx)

- Microsoft TechNet: "View the Address Resolution Protocol (ARP) Cache"
  (http://technet2.microsoft.com/WindowsServer/en/Library/
  cae0e239-267b-45df-88a8-f6f1303830471033.mspx)

- Microsoft TechNet: "Add a Static ARP Cache Entry" (http://technet2.microsoft.com/
  WindowsServer/en/Library/93dfda8f-bc47-4fae-b8d6-d9a14de8d9731033.mspx)

9-10. Troubleshooting IP Routing

Problem

You want to verify the functionality of IP routing on your Windows Server 2003 network. IP routing is necessary to ensure that you can access resources on local and remote computers.

Solution

The following command displays the routing table on the local computer:

```
> route print
```

The route print statement will produce output similar to the following:

```
===========================================================================
Active Routes:
Network Destination        Netmask          Gateway       Interface  Metric
          0.0.0.0          0.0.0.0         10.0.0.1       10.0.0.83     30
        127.0.0.0        255.0.0.0        127.0.0.1       127.0.0.1      1
         10.0.0.0        255.0.0.0        10.0.0.83       10.0.0.83     30
        10.0.0.83  255.255.255.255        127.0.0.1       127.0.0.1     30
   10.255.255.255  255.255.255.255        10.0.0.83       10.0.0.83     30
        224.0.0.0        240.0.0.0        10.0.0.83       10.0.0.83     30
  255.255.255.255  255.255.255.255        10.0.0.83               4      1
  255.255.255.255  255.255.255.255        10.0.0.83       10.0.0.83      1
Default Gateway:         10.0.0.1
===========================================================================
Persistent Routes:
  None
```

The following command will clear the contents of the routing table on the local computer, which is useful if a manually created route is incorrect or out of date:

```
> route -f
```

If you need to manually create a route to address a connectivity issue, the following command will specify that traffic to a remote network with the network address of 192.168.2.0 should be sent through the gateway with an IP address of 10.0.0.145, and will mark the route as persistent:

```
> route -p add 192.168.2.0 255.255.255.0 10.0.0.145
```

Note If you use the -f switch before adding or editing a routing table entry, the routing table will be cleared before the new entry is added or modified.

Likewise, the following command will remove the routing entry associated with the 157.0.0.0 remote network:

```
> route delete 157.0.0.0
```

How It Works

In order to transmit traffic to computers located on remote networks, all TCP/IP-enabled computers will maintain a routing table in memory. This table serves as a kind of "traffic officer" to determine how the local computer will transmit network packets based on its destination IP address. A TCP/IP-enabled computer will route all IP packets on the basis of the *next-hop address*. If the destination host is on the same network as the source, the next-hop address will be that of the destination computer. If the destination is on a remote network, the next-hop address will be a router or gateway on the local network; once the packet reaches the router, it will determine the subsequent next-hop address, and this process will repeat until the packet is routed to its ultimate destination.

In most cases, all remote traffic will be routed to a single default gateway; the routing table will be created and maintained automatically. In more complex routing environments, you may need to use the route utility to manually create, manage, and delete routing table entries to specify the path that particular remote traffic should traverse.

See Also

- Microsoft TechNet: "The Cable Guy—December 2001, IP Routing" (http://www.microsoft.com/technet/community/columns/cableguy/cg1201.mspx)

- Recipes 5-2 and 5-3 for more on configuring a Windows Server 2003 computer as a router

- Recipe 5-7 for more on configuring a static route

9-11. Determining the Reliability of a Link

Problem

You want to determine the reliability of a link between two TCP/IP networks. This is a useful troubleshooting step if you are experiencing intermittent connectivity failures between a local and a remote network.

Solution

The following command will determine whether the remote host with an IP address of 192.168.1.157 is reachable, and which hop is the point of failure if it is not:

```
> tracert 192.168.1.157
```

The following command will determine whether the remote host with an IP address of 192.168.1.157 is reachable, and which hop is the point of failure if it is not. It will not attempt to resolve the hostnames of any intermediate hosts:

```
> tracert -d 192.168.1.157
```

The following command will test the reliability of the network path between the local computer and 192.168.1.157:

```
> pathping 192.168.1.157
```

The following command will test the reliability of the network path between the local computer and 192.168.1.157 over a maximum of 15 hops:

```
> pathping -h 15 192.168.1.157
```

The following command will test the reliability of the network path between the local computer and computer1.mycompany.com. It will not attempt to resolve the hostnames of any intermediate hosts:

```
> pathping -n computer1.mycompany.com
```

How It Works

When you are attempting to troubleshoot slow response times between two networks, it is critical to understand how each hop along the path is performing rather than just monitoring the performance of the local network. The tracert utility extends the functionality of ping; rather than simply reporting whether a remote host is reachable or not, tracert will display the hostname or IP address of each host along the route.

Beginning in Windows 2000, Microsoft's TCP/IP implementation has included the pathping utility to assist with this. This command combines the features of ping and tracert into a single command, sending packets to each router on the path to the remote computer and displaying performance statistics for both the router and the links. This command will help you determine which routers or links are creating network issues by illustrating the degree of packet loss at each step.

■**Note** It's important to keep in mind that all three of these utilities depend on the Internet Control Message Protocol (ICMP) to function; if ICMP is being blocked by any firewall or router between you and the remote host, these tools can fail even if the host and the route to that host are functioning perfectly.

See Also

- Microsoft TechNet: "Using the Pathping Command" (http://technet2.microsoft.com/ WindowsServer/en/Library/dd7640ac-d923-470d-87c9-0927eb43b7cb1033.mspx)

- Wikipedia: "Pathping" (http://en.wikipedia.org/wiki/Pathping)

- Microsoft TechNet: "Using the Tracert Command" (http://technet2.microsoft.com/ WindowsServer/en/Library/66633f9d-a0fa-4548-9506-604539757c011033.mspx)

9-12. Verifying Services on the Local or Remote Computer

Problem

You want to determine the operational status of a network service that is running on a local or remote Windows Server 2003 computer.

Solution

Using a Graphical User Interface

To confirm that a service is running on the local computer, follow these steps:

1. Open the Services MMC snap-in.

2. Scroll to the entry for the World Wide Web Publishing Service, or the name of the service whose status you are attempting to verify.

3. If the Status column does not read Started, right-click on the service and click on Start.

■**Note** We have used the World Wide Web (WWW) service as an example here, but you can follow these steps to confirm the operation of any service on your local or remote Windows Server 2003 computer.

To confirm that a service is running on a remote computer called computer1.mycompany.com, follow these steps:

1. Open the Services MMC snap-in.

2. Right-click on the Services node in the left pane and select Connect to Another Computer.

3. From the Select Computer screen, make sure that the Another Computer radio button is selected.

4. Enter `computer1.mycompany.com` in the accompanying text box and click OK.

5. Scroll to the entry for the World Wide Web Publishing Service, or the name of the service whose status you are attempting to verify.

6. If the Status column does not read Started, right-click on the service and click on Start.

Note You will need to have administrative access to the remote computer to view and manage its services.

Using a Command-Line Interface

The following command will list all listening processes on a Windows Server 2003 computer and display the process ID (PID) associated with each listening port:

```
> netstat -ano
```

The output from this utility looks like the following:

```
C:\Documents and Settings\lhunter>netstat -ano
```

```
Active Connections

  Proto  Local Address          Foreign Address        State         PID
  TCP    0.0.0.0:135            0.0.0.0:0              LISTENING     1740
  TCP    0.0.0.0:445            0.0.0.0:0              LISTENING     4
  TCP    0.0.0.0:3389           0.0.0.0:0              LISTENING     1672
  TCP    0.0.0.0:3689           0.0.0.0:0              LISTENING     3932
  TCP    127.0.0.1:1029         0.0.0.0:0              LISTENING     2640
  TCP    127.0.0.1:5180         0.0.0.0:0              LISTENING     2464
  TCP    127.0.0.1:5335         0.0.0.0:0              LISTENING     1536
  TCP    10.0.0.83:139          0.0.0.0:0              LISTENING     4
  TCP    10.0.0.83:1387         64.12.25.41:5190       ESTABLISHED   2464
  TCP    10.0.0.83:1393         205.188.248.173:5190   ESTABLISHED   2464
  TCP    10.0.0.83:1406         207.46.6.26:1863       ESTABLISHED   4012
  TCP    10.0.0.83:1415         128.91.2.38:993        ESTABLISHED   3444
  TCP    10.0.0.83:2371         64.233.179.19:80       ESTABLISHED   684
  TCP    10.0.0.83:2389         128.91.2.38:993        ESTABLISHED   3444
```

In this output, the Local Address column details the IP address (0.0.0.0 for localhost) and the port number that the computer is listening on. The Destination Address column indicates the IP address of any computer that is connected (0.0.0.0 for no active connection). The State column indicates the current status of a connection, and the PID column indicates the process ID of the connection. You can use this information to track and manage individual connections on your Windows Server 2003 computer.

The following command will detail which ports are in a listening state on a remote computer called www.mycompany.com:

```
> portqry -n www.mycompany.com
```

Here is some sample output from this command, indicating that a remote computer is listening on port 80:

```
C:\PortQryV2>portqry -n www.mycompany.com
```

```
Querying target system called:
 www.mycompany.com
Attempting to resolve name to IP address...
Name resolved to 10.0.0.143
querying...
TCP port 80 (http service): LISTENING
```

How It Works

When a service is running on the local or a remote computer, it is said to be *listening* on a particular port or range of ports. This means that the service is waiting to accept unsolicited incoming connections from clients that want to connect to a particular resource on the local computer.

If clients are unable to connect to a service on the local computer, you should verify that the service or application is running. You can do this using the Services MMC snap-in, or by using the netstat utility to create a list of all listening ports on the local computer.

If clients are unable to connect to a service on a remote computer, you should similarly verify that the service or application is running by using the Services MMC snap-in, or by using the portqry utility to create a list of all listening ports on the local computer. Portqry is a freely downloadable tool available from the Microsoft website that will allow you to enumerate listening ports on a remote computer. (For those of you familiar with Unix/Linux tools, this is similar to netcat.) Portqry is available as a command-line utility, and PortqryUI provides the same functionality through a graphical user interface.

If you have confirmed that the service is running on the local or remote computer but clients still cannot connect to it, you should confirm that there is no firewall or IPSec configuration on either the local or remote computer that is preventing clients from connecting to this service.

See Also

- Recipe 3-18 for more on configuring inbound connectivity

- Recipe 7-1 for more on creating IPSec rules

- Microsoft TechNet: "Netstat" (http://technet2.microsoft.com/WindowsServer/en/Library/7b3ae3c0-4b95-4cb7-a290-57b22824194b1033.mspx)

- Microsoft KB 832919: "New Features and Functionality in PortQry Version 2.0"

- Microsoft TechNet: "PortQryUI—User Interface for the PortQry Command Line Port Scanner" (`http://www.microsoft.com/downloads/details.aspx?FamilyID=8355e537-1ea6-4569-aabb-f248f4bd91d0&DisplayLang=en`)

9-13. Troubleshooting IPSec

You want to view details of the current IPSec configuration that's been applied to a Windows Server 2003 computer. This should be your first step when troubleshooting network communication issues that you suspect are related to an IPSec policy.

Solution

Using a Graphical User Interface

1. Open the IPSec Monitor MMC snap-in.

2. Navigate to IP Security Monitor ➤ *<ServerName>* ➤ Active Policy

3. In the right pane, you'll see the following information:

   - Policy name.

   - Policy description.

   - Policy last modified.

   - Policy store. This specifies whether the policy is being stored in Active Directory or in the Local Security Policy.

   - Policy path. This specifies the file system or Active Directory path that the active policy resides in.

   - Organizational unit. This specifies the organizational unit that the computer resides in, if applicable.

   - Group Policy object name.

4. For additional information on IPSec filters that are in place, navigate to Quick Mode ➤ Generic Filters. Double-click on an individual filter to see the details of the filter definition.

5. For additional information and statistics on the security negotiation process, click on the Quick Mode ➤ Negotiation Policies node.

6. For IPSec performance statistics, click on the Quick Mode ➤ Statistics node.

Using a Command-Line Interface

The following command creates a file called `display.txt` that contains a detailed description of the current IPSec configuration:

```
> netsh ipsec static show all > display.txt
```

The following command will display debugging information and statistics about the IPSec negotiation process:

```
> netsh ipsec dynamic show all
```

How It Works

When troubleshooting communication issues on a network that's been configured for IPSec, you need to determine whether IPSec itself is the cause of the failure, or whether the failure occurs at another point in the network stack. The quickest way to determine whether your IPSec configuration is the cause of a network failure is to temporarily disable the active IPSec policy to see if it corrects the issue, though this obviously has the negative side effect of removing IPSec security protections from your network.

If you've determined that IPSec is the source of the communications failure on your network, further troubleshooting will be aided by obtaining as much information about your current IPSec configuration as possible. You can use the tools listed in this recipe to obtain configuration and performance information about the IPSec policy of a computer running Windows Server 2003.

Using a Graphical User Interface

The IPSec Monitor is an MMC snap-in that is installed by default on Windows Server 2003 computers. It provides a graphical view of IPSec statistics, including the name and description of the active IPSec policy, the Group Policy object through which IPSec has been configured, and the configuration details of specific filters that are in place.

Note You can also use the built-in Network Monitor utility to obtain a capture of all traffic being sent to and from a local Windows Server 2003 computer. You can view this captured information through the Network Monitor GUI, or save it to a text file for further analysis.

Using a Command-Line Interface

Regardless of the technology with which you are working, an important troubleshooting step is to always obtain an accurate snapshot of your computer's current configuration. The netsh commands listed in this recipe will display information similar to the following:

```
FilterAction Details
--------------------

FilterAction Name     : NONE
Description           : NONE
Store                 : Local Store <OREILLY1>
AllowUnsecure(Fallback): NO
Inbound Passthrough   : NO
```

```
QMPFS                 : NO
Last Modified         : 7/31/2005 10:24:41 AM
GUID                  : {50B5FC20-0F4B-4852-BF6C-C192134F66E7}
Security Methods
   AH        ESP          Seconds        kBytes
   --        ---          -------        ------
[NONE]    [SHA1 , 3DES]      0             0
[NONE]    [MD5  , 3DES]      0             0
[NONE]    [SHA1 , DES ]      0             0
[NONE]    [MD5  , DES ]      0             0
[SHA1]    [NONE , NONE]      0             0
[MD5 ]    [NONE , NONE]      0             0


Policy Name           : Server (Request Security)
Description           : For all IP traffic, always request security using K...
Store                 : Local Store <OREILLY1>
Last Modified         : 7/21/2005 11:11:30 AM
GUID                  : {72385230-70FA-11D1-864C-14A300000000}
Assigned              : NO
Polling Interval      : 180 minutes
MainMode LifeTime     : 480 minutes / 0 Quick Mode sessions
Master PFS            : NO
Main Mode Security Method Order
   Encryption     Integrity      DH Group
   ----------     ---------      --------
     3DES           SHA1         Medium(2)
     3DES           MD5          Medium(2)
     DES            SHA1         Low(1)
     DES            MD5          Low(1)
```

See Also

- Microsoft TechNet: "IPSec Troubleshooting" (http://technet2.microsoft.com/
  WindowsServer/en/Library/b0b726fc-c6b7-426a-964f-9c7b1c8ef3a81033.mspx)

- Microsoft TechNet: "IPSec Troubleshooting Tools" (http://technet2.microsoft.com/
  WindowsServer/en/Library/ebcbc96d-b236-401d-a98b-91c965a3d18f1033.mspx)

9-14. Troubleshooting DHCP Addressing

Problem

You want to troubleshoot the receipt of IP addresses from a DHCP server on a Windows
Server 2003 computer.

Solution

Using a Graphical User Interface

To confirm that your computer is configured to receive its IP address from a DHCP server, do the following:

1. Open the Network Connections applet.

2. Double-click on the Local Area Connection icon.

3. Click on Internet Protocol (TCP/IP), and select Properties.

4. Confirm that the radio button next to Obtain an IP Address Automatically is selected.

5. Click on the Support tab. In the Connection Status section, confirm that the Address Type is listed as Assigned by DHCP. Confirm that the assigned IP Address, Subnet Mask, and Default Gateway are valid for the local network.

6. Click Close when you're finished.

To release and renew the IP address lease of a DHCP-enabled computer, follow these steps:

1. Open the Network Connections applet.

2. Double-click on the Local Area Connection icon.

3. Click on Internet Protocol (TCP/IP), and select Properties.

4. Click on the Support tab and select Repair.

5. Click Close when you're done.

Using a Command-Line Interface

The following command will release the currently held IP address and request a new lease from the DHCP server.

```
> ipconfig /renew
```

Note You can perform this in two separate steps by first issuing an `ipconfig /release` command, followed by `ipconfig /renew`.

Using the Registry

To disable Automatic Private IP Addressing (APIPA) for a particular adapter, create the following Registry value:

```
[HKEY_LOCAL_MACHINE\SYSTEM\CurrentControlSet\Services\
Tcpip\Parameters\Interfaces\{<Interface GUID>}]
"IPAutoConfigurationEnabled"=dword:0
```

To disable APIPA for all adapters installed in a particular computer, create the following Registry value—no reboot is necessary:

```
[HKEY_LOCAL_MACHINE\SYSTEM\CurrentControlSet\Services\Tcpip\Parameters]
"IPAutoConfigurationEnabled"=dword:0
```

■ **Note** If either of these Registry entries is not present, the operating system assumes a default value of 1. This means that APIPA is turned on and enabled on all Windows Server 2003 servers by default.

How It Works

If you are unable to obtain an IP address from a DHCP server, you should first double-check your TCP/IP configuration to confirm that the Windows Server 2003 computer is configured to obtain its IP address automatically. If your TCP/IP configuration is correctly configured and you haven't received a valid IP address for your subnet, you can use the ipconfig utility to release your current DHCP lease and request a new one.

See Also

- Recipe 1-7 for more on configuring an alternate IP configuration

- Microsoft KB 220874: "How to Use Automatic TCP/IP Addressing Without a DHCP Server"

9-15. Troubleshooting Remote Administration

Problem

You want to troubleshoot the use of remote administration tools such as the Computer Management MMC snap-in on a remote Windows Server 2003 network.

Solution

Using a Command-Line Interface

The following command will verify whether the remote administration exception is configured on the local computer:

```
> netsh firewall show service
```

The following command verifies that a remote computer called computer1.mycomputer.com is able to receive connections on TCP port 445:

```
> portqry -n www.mycompany.com -o 445
```

Using Group Policy

Tables 9-1 and 9-2 contain the Group Policy settings that enable remote administration through the Windows Firewall in the domain and standard policies respectively.

Table 9-1. *Configure Remote Administration Exception—Domain Profile*

Path	Computer Configuration\Administrative Templates\Network\ Network Connections\Windows Firewall\Domain Profile
Policy name	Windows Firewall: Allow remote administration exception
Value	Enabled to allow remote administration through the Windows Firewall in the Domain Profile. Disabled to disallow it.

Table 9-2. *Configure Remote Administration Exception—Standard Profile*

Path	Computer Configuration\Administrative Templates\Network\ Network Connections\Windows Firewall\Standard Profile
Policy name	Windows Firewall: Allow remote administration exception
Value	Enabled to allow remote administration through the Windows Firewall in the Standard Profile. Disabled to disallow it.

How It Works

In a domain environment, you'll often want to remotely administer servers and workstations using tools such as the Computer Management MMC and Windows Management Instrumentation (WMI). This is because most of the administration tools you'll use need to make unsolicited connections to the computer that you're trying to administer, using TCP port 445 and the svchost.exe and lsass.exe executables.

Caution The ports and executables used by the remote administration exception are well-known attack vectors. Be sure to only permit this exception on trusted hosts.

In order to troubleshoot remote administration on a Windows Server 2003 computer or domain, you'll need to verify that the appropriate settings in Group Policy, the Windows Registry, or VBScript have been enabled; you cannot make this change in the Windows Firewall Control Panel applet.

In addition to verifying that the remote administration exception has been enabled, you need to verify that the correct *scope* has been configured. The *scope* of an exception refers to the IP addresses that are permitted to make remote administration connections. As with other Windows Firewall Group Policy settings, you can use LocalSubnet to specify the local subnet, * to specify all hosts, or a custom list of IPv4 addresses. For IPv6 addresses, you can only specify LocalSubnet or *; you can't create a custom exception list.

See Also

- Recipes 4-4, 4-5, and 4-9 for more on enabling the remote administration exception

- Microsoft TechNet: "Windows Firewall Settings: Remote Administration Tools" (`http://technet2.microsoft.com/WindowsServer/en/Library/ 62d661cc-8267-4440-aacc-55358c602a081033.mspx`)

9-16. Troubleshooting Remote Assistance and Remote Desktop

Problem

You want to troubleshoot access to Remote Assistance and Remote Desktop on a Windows Server 2003 computer.

Solution

To confirm that a Windows Server 2003 computer is configured to allow Remote Assistance requests, do the following:

1. Open the Network Connections applet.

2. Double-click on the Local Area Connection icon.

3. From the Advanced tab, click Settings. This will launch the Windows Firewall Control Panel applet.

4. From the Exceptions tab, verify that there is a check mark next to Remote Assistance.

5. To view or modify the scope of the exception, click on Edit, followed by Change Scope, and select from one of the following three options:

   - Any computer (including those on the Internet).

   - My network (local subnet).

   - Custom list. For this option, enter a single IP address using the syntax 192.168.1.151, or enter a range of addresses using the network ID of the range followed by its subnet mask, such as 192.168.1.1/255.255.255.0. Separate multiple entries using a comma.

6. Click OK when you're finished.

   To confirm that your Windows Server 2003 computer is configured to allow Remote Desktop connections, perform steps 1-6 again, but ensure that the remote desktop exception is enabled in step 4.

Using a Command-Line Interface

The following command enables Remote Assistance and Remote Desktop to pass through the Windows Firewall:

```
> netsh firewall set service type = remotedesktop mode = ENABLE
```

The following command verifies that a remote computer called `computer1.mycomputer.com` is able to receive connections on TCP port 3389:

```
> portqry -n www.mycompany.com -o 3389
```

Using Group Policy

Tables 9-3 and 9-4 show the settings that control the remote assistance exception within the Windows Firewall in the domain and standard profiles respectively.

Table 9-3. *Configure Remote Assistance Exception—Domain Profile*

Path	`Computer Configuration\Administrative Templates\Network\` `Network Connections\Windows Firewall\Domain Profile`
Policy name	Windows Firewall: Allow remote desktop exception
Value	`Enabled`

Table 9-4. *Configure Remote Assistance Exception—Standard Profile*

Path	`Computer Configuration\Administrative Templates\Network\` `Network Connections\Windows Firewall\Standard Profile`
Policy name	Windows Firewall: Allow remote desktop exception
Value	`Enabled`

■ **Note** You'll use the remote desktop exception in `netsh` and Group Policy to configure both Remote Assistance and Remote Desktop functionality.

How It Works

In Windows Server 2003, the Remote Desktop connection has replaced Terminal Services for administration in Windows 2000. Remote Desktop allows up to two administrators to run virtual sessions on a Windows Server 2003 server to perform administrative tasks. Remote Assistance, by contrast, is a feature in Windows XP and Windows Server 2003 that lets you share control of your computer with a remote user. Unlike a Terminal Services or Remote Desktop session, which provides a virtual, unique session, Remote Assistance allows you to simply view a user's desktop to offer them assistance, or else take control of their desktop. Creating a Remote Assistance connection requires the permission of the user that is currently logged onto the remote computer.

To enable Remote Assistance connections prior to Service Pack 1, you needed to manually configure the following program exceptions:

- `%WINDIR%\PCHealth\HelpCtr\Binaries\Helpsvc.exe`

- `%WINDIR%\PCHealth\HelpCtr\Binaries\Helpctr.exe`

- `%WINDIR%\SYSTEM32\Sessmgr.exe`

Additionally, you needed to enable access to TCP port 135.

On Windows Server 2003 computers with Service Pack 1 installed, you simply need to verify that the preconfigured Allow Remote Desktop Exception setting has been enabled through the Windows Firewall Control Panel applet, the Registry, or Group Policy. As with other Windows Firewall exceptions, you should restrict the scope of the remote assistance exception to protect your systems against attacks targeted at the well-known RPC port, TCP 135.

See Also

- Recipes 4-4, 4-5, and 4-11 for more on configuring the remote assistance exception

- Microsoft TechNet: "Configuring System Service Exceptions" (http://technet2.microsoft.com/WindowsServer/en/Library/ 9a29df7b-235a-42fd-9c25-13f6be94ad9a1033.mspx)

9-17. Troubleshooting Active Directory Replication

Problem

You want to troubleshoot Active Directory replication on a Windows Server 2003 computer.

Solution

Using a Graphical User Interface

To select one or more Active Directory domain controllers to view, do the following:

1. Open the Replmon Support Tools utility.

2. Right-click on the Monitored Servers node in the left pane, and select Add Monitored Server.

3. Select the Add the Server Explicitly by Name radio button, and click Next. Enter the Fully Qualified Domain Name (FQDN) of the server that you wish to monitor.

4. To specify a different set of credentials, place a check mark next to Use Alternate Credentials, and click Change. Enter an administrative username in the format *DomainName\UserName* in the Username text box. Enter the password in the Password text box, and click OK.

5. Click Finish.

6. Repeat steps 2–5 for any additional servers that you wish to monitor.

7. To view your current replication topology, right-click on a domain controller in the left pane and select Show Replication Topologies.

Using a Command-Line Interface

The following command will display all configured replication partners for a server named `computer1.mycompany.com`:

```
> repadmin /showreps computer1.mycompany.com
```

The following command will force replication to occur between two servers named `computer1` and `computer2`:

```
> repadmin /replicate computer1.mycompany.com computer2.mycompany.com
```

The following command will display all connection objects configured for `computer1.mycompany.com`:

```
> repadmin /showconn computer1.mycompany.com
```

How It Works

When troubleshooting Active Directory replication, the repadmin tool from the Windows Support Tools is one of the most powerful utilities available in your administrative arsenal. This single tool encompasses a wide range of functions using different command-line parameters. Some of the operations that you can perform with repadmin include the following:

`Bind`: Connects to a partition on a particular domain controller

`Bridgeheads`: Lists bridgehead servers for a site

`Checkprop`: Compares different domain controllers to see if they are up to date with one another

`Dsaguid`: Returns the server name associated with a particular globally unique identifier (GUID)

`Failcache`: Displays a list of failed replication events

`Istg`: Returns the name of the Inter-Site Topology Generator (ISTG) for a given site

`Kcc`: Forces the Knowledge Consistency Checker (KCC) to recalculate the replication topology for a particular domain controller

`Latency`: Returns the amount of time between replications

If you are more comfortable working with a graphical interface, you can use the Replmon tool (also in the Windows Support Tools) to approximate most of the features exposed by repadmin; however, you will probably find the command-line tool to be far more flexible and powerful, and well worth the effort to become familiar with.

See Also

- Microsoft TechNet: "Repadmin Examples" (http://technet2.microsoft.com/
  WindowsServer/en/Library/a103036b-5d82-4d99-8e61-23d434a8e6eb1033.mspx)

- Microsoft TechNet: "Repadmin Overview" (http://technet2.microsoft.com/
  WindowsServer/en/Library/24d8a2dd-2596-46cb-9b0f-179f977d434a1033.mspx)

Index

D

X

Find it faster at http://superindex.apress.com

You Need the Companion eBook

Your purchase of this book entitles you to its companion eBook for only $10.

We believe this Apress title will prove so indispensable that you'll want to carry it with you everywhere, which is why we are offering the companion eBook for $10 to customers who purchase this book now. Convenient and fully searchable, the eBook version of any content-rich, page-heavy Apress book makes a valuable addition to your programming library. You can easily find, copy, and apply code—and then perform examples by quickly toggling between instructions and the application. Even simultaneously tackling a donut, diet soda, and complex code becomes simplified with hands-free eBooks!

Once you purchase this book, getting the $10 companion eBook is simple:

❶ Visit **www.apress.com/promo/tendollars/**.

❷ Complete a basic registration form to receive a randomly generated question about this title.

❸ Answer the question correctly in 60 seconds and you will receive a promotional code to redeem for the $10 eBook.

2560 Ninth Street • Suite 219 • Berkeley, CA 94710

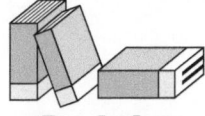

eBookshop

Offer valid through 1/07.

FIND IT FAST
with the Apress *SuperIndex*™

Quickly Find Out What the Experts Know

Leading by innovation, Apress now offers you its *SuperIndex*™, a turbocharged companion to the fine index in this book. The Apress *SuperIndex*™ is a keyword and phrase-enabled search tool that lets you search through the entire Apress library. Powered by dtSearch™, it delivers results instantly.

Instead of paging through a book or a PDF, you can electronically access the topic of your choice from a vast array of Apress titles. The Apress *SuperIndex*™ is the perfect tool to find critical snippets of code or an obscure reference. The Apress *SuperIndex*™ enables all users to harness essential information and data from the best minds in technology.

No registration is required, and the Apress *SuperIndex*™ is free to use.

❶ Thorough and comprehensive searches of over 300 titles

❷ No registration required

❸ Instantaneous results

❹ A single destination to find what you need

❺ Engineered for speed and accuracy

❻ Will spare your time, application, and anxiety level

Search now: *http://superindex.apress.com*